# The Edge of Chaos: Managing Complexity in the Real World

Andrew Taylor

Published by Legend Times Group
51 Gower Street, London, WC1E 6HJ
info@legendtimesgroup.co.uk | www.legendpress.co.uk



First Edition

Paperback ISBN: 9781918291698

# ACKNOWLEDGEMENTS

I would like to thank all of the contributors to this book for their patience and belief that this book was both worthy of their time and effort. Similarly, my thanks go out to all of our families, who have tolerated the time involved in producing this work. The book could not have come about without discussions over dinner tables and across lecture rooms with students and staff. So, thanks must go to students and staff at TEE for their intellectual curiosity and determination to push at boundaries.

I would also like to thank everyone at Buckingham University Press and the collaborations team at Buckingham University for their continuing encouragement and support.

*Andrew Taylor*

# DEDICATIONS

We would like to dedicate this book to all of the students, past, present and future, at TEE that are facing an increasingly complex world. We hope that this book helps you to face an unpredictable future.

# CONTENTS

# ABOUT THE AUTHORS

## Raluca Bochiș

Director of IT Sustainability and Compliance at Emerson, Raluca teaches Complexity and Strategic Disruption on Buckingham University's EMBA program and is the co-author of *All In: An Executive Guide to Complexity and Disruption*. Raluca holds an Executive MBA from Hull University and is a Transilvania Executive Education Fellow.

## Laura Dragoș-Rădoi

Laura is a strategic advisor and startup co-founder specializing in Responsible AI governance, bringing 12+ years of executive experience to her research on AI ethics. She holds an Executive MBA with Distinction from the University of Buckingham, with published work on responsible AI deployment and ongoing research in neuroethics and bioethics in healthcare systems.

## Raluca Gheorghes

Raluca has an executive MBA and is a PhD candidate in Sociology and an Associate University Lecturer in HR Management at Babeș-Bolyai University, Romania. Her background is in leadership development and organisational transformation, and her current research critically examines executive education and leadership in complex organisational contexts.

## Chris Gleadle

Chris is a strategist and systems specialist with over 30 years' experience in sustainability across diverse industries, sectors, and organisational scales.

He has worked within a wide range of cultures, paces, and operational demands, experience that led him to develop the Sphere Economy. He is also a systems developer and author of numerous cross-disciplinary works on the complexity of climate, energy, water and operations.

## Dr. Joe Hazzam

Joe is an Associate Professor of Digital Marketing at the University of Staffordshire, United Kingdom. He currently serves as the co-director of the Centre for Business, Innovation and the Regions. Joe's research portfolio includes more than 25 peer-reviewed publications in leading marketing journals. He has disseminated and shared his research insights through over 30 masterclasses and delivered 25+ presentations at national and international conferences, webinars, research seminars, and media outlets.

## Robert Lewis

Rob has decades of experience in R&D, product development and innovation with large pharmaceutical and healthcare companies. Over the last decade, he has run his own entrepreneurial business, launching products and acting as a consultant to industries in a wide variety of sectors. His innovation credentials come from hard lessons learned in corporate life and now with his own ventures.

## Jonathan Melhuish

Jonathan is an AI Service Designer and social entrepreneur. He has been working with AI since 2003 in academic research at the University of Birmingham, innovative startups that reduce carbon pollution and improve human relationships, corporate software teams implementing cutting-edge AI solutions, and also taught Systems Thinking for the European Union. He now advises and trains business leaders to harness AI effectively.

## Raluca Mureşanu

With over 20 years of experience in banking, Raluca believes that banks can evolve into living ecosystems that connect people, ideas, and opportunities. She works in risk management, where she turns complexity into clarity and advocates for a more holistic and human approach to the way we do banking. She is passionate about digital platforms and about the role banks can play as catalysts for sustainable change.

## Dr. Ovidiu Oltean

Ovidiu Oltean, PhD, is Assistant Lecturer in the Department of Political Science at Babeş-Bolyai University, Faculty of Political, Administrative and Communication Sciences (FSPAC), Cluj-Napoca. His research focuses on migration, social inequalities, integration policies, discrimination, and social change, with extensive involvement in international research projects funded by Horizon Europe, Volkswagen Foundation, and Erasmus+.

## Dr. Radu Orghidan

Radu is an AI researcher and strategist exploring how accumulated expertise collapses under epistemic rupture, and how organisations and education must adapt in a post-competence world. With a PhD in Computer Vision, he designs Responsible AI and subtractive pedagogies that rethink learning, authority, and accountability under distributed epistemic agency. His work focuses on building explainable human–AI assemblages that deliberately redistribute knowledge, agency, and responsibility rather than preserving obsolete human-centered models.

## Dr. Andrew Taylor

Andrew is the author, co-author or editor of 7 books, with his primary research interests in and around how to lead and manage ecological and digital complexity. He leads the consulting firm Connect CEE and coordinates Transilvania Executive Education, in partnership with Buckingham University. He earned his doctorate from Cardiff University for his work on property rights and environmental conflicts.

## Cătălina Vescan

Cătălina Vescan is a transformation professional specialising in system-level change, capability building and human-centric design in complex organisations, combining customer experience expertise with hands-on project ownership from concept to delivery. She is an Executive MBA graduate of the University of Hull with a background in Accounting and Computer Science, which she uses to bridge business, technology and customer needs.

## Dr. Elesa Zehndorfer

Elesa Zehndorfer is a multi-award winning writer & author of 6 books for Routledge. A Managing Partner at consulting firm Lakeside Partners GmbH, Dr. Zehndorfer is also Research Officer for British Mensa and an eMBA lecturer. She earned her doctorate from Loughborough University in 2006.

# INTRODUCTION

We are living through a time when it seems that, even in the most casual conversations, almost everyone is talking about the world being turned upside down or having gone mad. What such exclamations really describe is that the practices that we are used to working with, based upon our assumptions of how things work, don't seem to be working anymore. Whether it is how we work with technology, where we work from, how we consume, what we believe to be true, world affairs and even the weather, nothing seems to be ordered, predictable or reliable, in ways that they used to be.

The relationships between cause and effect and the systems that such relationships occur within are no longer working as we expect them to and this ambiguity is creating feelings of fear and uncertainty. In short, the world; our worlds of work, home and life are becoming more unpredictable and complex and "while some historical eras are shaped by measurable risks, others are plagued with unfathomable uncertainty" (Tett, 2026). This book, therefore, is designed to enable you to navigate the treacherous waters of unfathomable uncertainty and complexity that we find ourselves in today more effectively.

Complexity has two essential characteristics which shape how we need to think about the uncertainty it brings. First, we see that existing patterns and relationships of cause and effect break down. We often see this when no matter how hard we try to work using existing best practices, and despite the efforts of experts to intervene, nothing seems to work as it used to (Snowden and Boone 2007). The second and related characteristic is the systemic nature and consequences of complexity. Systemic challenges tend not to be responsive to linear actions, based upon rational logic. This often happens because the operating environment has changed and what once could reasonably be assumed to be controllable has shifted in such a way that unexpected feedback loops are creating unpredictable consequences (Espinosa, 2023, Jackson, 2003).

The ecologist Frtijof Capra (2015) was an early pioneer of demonstrating the impact of industrial linear production logic upon the complexity of nature. Ecology is different from biology precisely because it is the study of ecosystems, rather than individual species. It is the study of systemic consequences and patterns of emergence that flow from the dynamic of constant change that is nature's life force. Whilst we can often measure aspects of nature and upheaval flowing from changes in ecosystems, they are very hard to predict in their entirety. This is because the complexity of interactions almost inevitably create unforeseen consequences, or feedback loops. The best that we can do is to experiment and model to try to identify what might emerge.

The trouble is that the interdisciplinary and unpredictable character of complexity presents a real challenge to modernism and the cartesian logic of man as the conqueror of nature, with science as his sword (Taylor 1998, Dobson, 1990). In our efforts to tame and master nature we have created extremely negative feedback loops for wider nature (Carson, 1962). Yet complexity is increasingly affecting social systems as well as physical systems. Indeed, "Climate change, the COVID pandemic, and the financial crash of 2008 all highlight the importance of recognizing the interconnected, networked nature of the landscape that we operate in" (Merali, 2022, p. 191). Policymaking and business management have often been based upon the principle that what gets measured is what gets managed; implicitly defining management as being about control and best practice. So the question is:

Why do these approaches fail even when logic indicates they should prevail? The answer lies in a fundamental assumption of organisational theory and practice: that a certain level of predictability and order exists in the world. This assumption, grounded in the Newtonian science that underlies scientific management, encourages simplifications that are useful in ordered circumstances. Circumstances change, however, and as they become more complex, the simplifications can fail. Good leadership is not a one-size-fits-all proposition. (Snowden and Boone, 2007).

Engaging with complexity requires us to move beyond what has worked before and we are familiar with and embrace significantly more ambiguity. Thus, "complexity is more a way of thinking about the world than a new way of working with mathematical models" (Snowden & Boone, 2007).

Following debates and discussions within the context of an executive MBA managed by Transilvania Executive Education, in Cluj and validated by Buckingham University in the UK, this book was developed to help leaders thrive in a more complex world. The authors are a mix of lecturing staff, executives and alumni from the MBA programme, who have all struggled to make sense of the disruption of predictable order in their respective domains and workspaces.

The book is organised into three sections. Section one is designed to help understand the context in which levels of complexity are rising, why this matters and how we might start to think about complexity differently from what went before. Section two offers tools to help structure our engagement with different forms and faces of complexity in the workplace. Section three provides case studies of engagement with complex challenges in real organisations, which offer examples of how the knowledge provided in previous chapters may be used to improve individual and organisational performance and outcomes.

In Chapter One, Taylor explores some of the big issues in complexity and outlines some of the key tools to help manage complexity, whose application will be discussed by other authors later. Orghidan makes a powerful case for how most of us have misunderstood AI as simply the latest tool of efficiency, even if it is a scarily powerful one. He shows how instead of using AI to improve existing models of organisation, we need to think how it will obliterate existing models. Outlining the key issues, Orghidan also provides a practical list of guidelines to enable the ethical construction of the future. Reaching backwards, whilst peering into the future, Hazzam shows how AI is simply the latest in a string of digital advancements that continue to emerge as digital marketing extends its reach and ability to utilise new technologies to manipulate and monetise data more effectively. Whilst such capabilities clearly have created significant commercial opportunities, Oltean shows how social media platforms have enabled the aggregation of personal data to microtarget groups and individuals to shape and reshape political beliefs and behaviours. His deep dive into how web-based technologies combined with AI to fuel and channel deep-seated unease with wider complexities in the Romanian elections holds powerful lessons for us all. Similarly, Zehndorfer looks at how the development of deepfake technology is reshaping what we believe to be true and how we construct truth, such that trust in institutions of media, government and even individuals are declining rapidly. As polarisation expands, people are retreating into echo chambers of the like-minded. Doing precisely the opposite of what Taylor indicated is a critical component of navigating complexity and entrenching single-loop learning, whilst simultaneously reducing their exposure to diversity.

The Innovation Fitness Test, by Lewis, is a practical toolkit designed by Lewis, based upon leading innovation teams, to enable executives to match their thinking and behaviours to the level of complexity and speed of change that exist in their surrounding environments. Similarly, Gleadle's model of the Sphere Economy is an explicit attempt to create the practical means and strategic logic to break down the siloed thinking that often accompanies noble efforts to deliver the circular economy model. In both cases the challenge is as much cultural and psychological as it is grounded in technology or processes. Bochis and Melhusih set out specific and practical tools to help manage the use of AI in organisations. However, what both outline is that for AI to become more than a disliked bolt-on tool of efficiency, and deliver its transformational potential, requires a sea change in the way that executives think about their relationship to work.

Section three provides four case studies to show the opportunities and pitfalls of engaging with various forms of complexity in the real world of operational delivery. Muresanu goes back to her organisation's basic source of value; its customer relations, to think how technology could be utilised to embrace network complexities to increase profitability and environmental outcomes at the same time. Vescan gets down and dirty to describe the management realities of trying to transform a rigid, bureaucratic organisation to better deal with rising complexity and become more adaptable. Similarly, Gheorghes shows how our old assumptions of where and when we work can be transformed, even beyond the limited hybrid work that has, since the COVID pandemic, become the norm, to improve performance. Finally, Dragos-Radoi's comparison of a start-up company with a large government body's engagement with technology hammers home the lesson that it is how we think and the cultures we construct in organisations that shape our dance with complexity, as much as technological or environmental changes themselves.

Together we hope that the book offers readers:

- A better understanding of complexity and how to engage with it.
- Tools to structure engagement with complexity.
- Case studies of engaging directly with complexity in real organisational contexts.
- Questions to think about if we are to engage with environmental challenges and emerging technologies for the good of all.

Ultimately, we hope that the book might inspire you with more confidence to embrace complexity and not simply retreat into a doomed search for simple solutions in these turbulent times.


## References


Carson, R. (1965). *Silent Spring*. London: Penguin.

Dobson, A. (1995). *Green Political Thought* (2nd ed.). London: Routledge.

Espinosa, A. (2023). *Sustainable Self-Governance in Businesses and Society: The Viable System Model in Action*. London: Routledge.

Jackson, M. (2003). *Systems Thinking: Creative Holism for Managers,* Chichester, UK: Wiley

Snowden, D. and Boone, M. E. (2007), 'A Leader's Framework for Decision Making', *Harvard Business Review* (November 2007).

Merali, Y. 'Complexity and Networks.' In Taylor, A. (ed.) (2022), *Rethinking Leadership for a Green World*. London: Routledge.

Taylor, A. (1998). *Property Rights and The Differentiating Countryside: A Case Study in South West England.* Unpublished Ph.D. Thesis, University of Wales, Cardiff.

Tett, G. (2026). 'What Business Should be Thinking About post Davos'. *Financial Times*, ft.com, viewed 23rd January 2026.

# THINKING THROUGH COMPLEXITY

## Andrew Taylor

### Getting started: Introduction

Almost everyone agrees that the world and everyday life are becoming more complex. Whether it be the impact of digital technology in bringing globalisation closer and changing patterns of work, health pandemics, or environmental concerns, life seems to be changing faster and more unpredictably than previously. Rose (2011, 2022) has mapped out how this is affecting people differently and causing many to reach to the political extremes in search of simple solutions. However, most of us, whatever our feelings about the nature of change, find that the tools and patterns of thinking that we are used to often seem out of step with how change is actually occurring around us. You see, complexity isn't simply about a new set of tools for helping us to manage our organisations and our lives. It requires us to think differently. Thus, this chapter seeks to explore how complexity challenges existing modes of thought and provides tools and structures to enable us to engage more effectively with it, as individuals, organisations and places.

### Twisting Logic: The Cynefin Framework

Perhaps one of the most useful starting points and tools for helping identify complexity, used by several authors in this collection, and how to react to it, is the Cynefin Framework (Snowden and Boone, 2007).

The framework sorts the issues facing leaders into five contexts defined by the nature of the relationship between cause and effect. Four of these – simple, complicated, complex and chaotic – require leaders to diagnose situations and to act in contextually appropriate ways. The fifth –disorder – applies when it is unclear which of the four contexts is predominant (Snowden and Boone, 2007, p. 2).

The trouble is that much of the time we don't know which domain we are in and are therefore prone to act inappropriately. By defining the nature of cause-and-effect relationships and how we should engage with them contextually, the Cynefin Framework provides a structure for decision-making that identifies complex challenges as significantly different.

In the simple domain there is a relationship between cause and effect that ought to be clear to any reasonable person, hence we sense-categorise-respond, and so best practice is a legitimate way to organise. In the complicated domain there is a relationship between cause and effect, but identifying it requires a level of expertise that is unusual, so we need to sense-analyse-respond and may need to call consultants. In the complex domain, although there is a relationship between cause and effect, it is not like anything that we have seen before. Thus, we need to probe-sense-respond, conducting safe-to-fail experiments, as we probe for new emergent patterns, which when identified we need to amplify quickly. The chaotic domain is a space where relationships between cause and effect break down and we need to act-sense-respond, in order to move the issue into the complex domain, where we can experiment with new ways of operating and engaging. All of the boundaries between domains allow for transition, except the boundary between the simple and the chaotic domains. The boundary is often represented as a cliff edge, which if you fall over causes sudden collapse to the point where recovery, if it is possible at all, will be very expensive indeed. Snowden and Boone (2007) refer to this boundary as the complacent zone, because although executives recognise that things are no longer working the way they used to, they respond by working best practices harder. The organisation becomes like a car sliding towards a cliff edge, where the drivers are desperately trying to slow its speed of travel, but unable to stop it.

So much emphasis is placed upon learning to execute tasks using best practices at school and in organisations that leaders find it difficult to move beyond doubling down on existing best practices or calling consultants to do analysis. In fact, in my consulting experience, they often actively resist the possibility that such methods could not only be useless, but they are even contributing further to the problem faced.

Working with a global media company ten years ago, the CEO refused to accept that anything but working existing best practices harder was a solution to their problems. Despite a dramatic drop in sales in their largest markets, an almost 30% staff turnover rate and an outbreak of management blame culture, there was a refusal to accept that what had worked previously

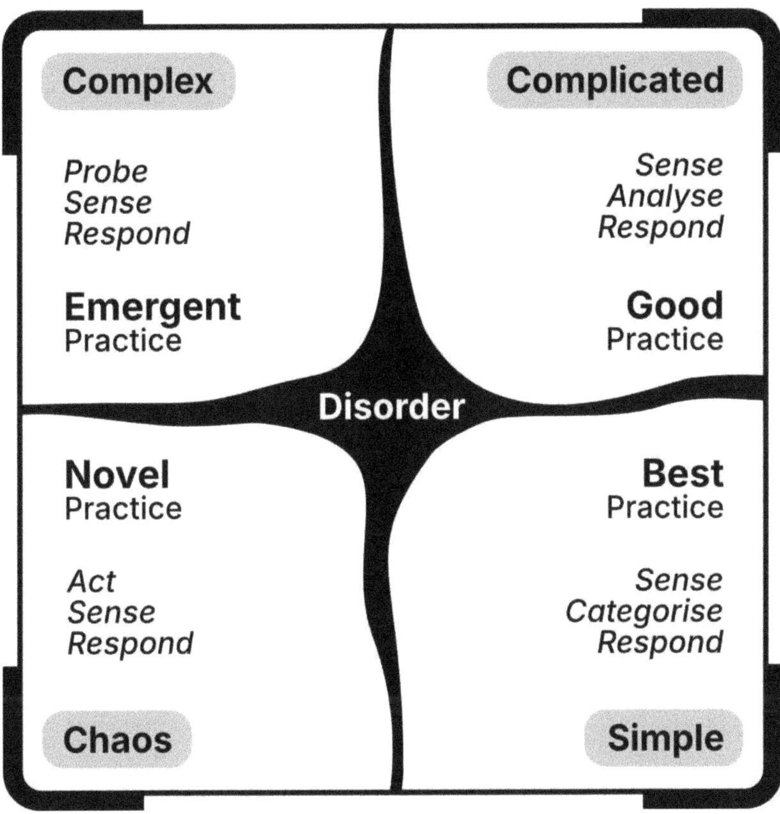


Figure 1. The Cynefin Framework – adapted from Snowden and Boone (2007).

was no longer working because digital technology had shifted the operating context. In reality, people under pressure often find it very hard to escape the logic that has taken their career to this point and become individually and sometimes collectively trapped in a form of groupthink (Janis, 1971, 1982). Indeed, Bonabeau shows that "For most CEOs, only one thing is worse than making a huge strategic mistake: being the only person in the industry to make it" (Bonabeau, 2004, p. 47). No matter how clear it is to outsiders and those familiar with complexity, for those in the midst of the situation it is very hard to step back and accept that they don't know what to do, what worked previously won't this time and we simply need to experiment in a way that is different from what went before and different from what those around us are doing. The trouble is that "Most companies are built for a complicated world, but the one they now inhabit is irrevocably complex" (Werner and Le-Brun, 2025, p. 54).

In contrast to systems designed for predictability and order, such as production lines and many supply chains, the defining feature of complexity is its emergent character. The power of the internet has been its ability to transmit emergent information and ideas without the need to control every pathway. In so doing, e-commerce has effectively moved value creation out of where it was traditionally held, in the products and processes of the business, to a global digital network. Value is now maximised through the platforms that join up that network and enable us to connect buyers and sellers globally.

Think about it, what does Amazon or Booking.com, or iTunes actually produce? Very little, but their ability to aggregate large networks has created money-making machines of global proportions. To continue making the kind of margins that they have done, these platforms use the data provided by our activities, reviews and comments to adapt at pace[1].

Argyris (1976, 1978, 1991) shows how the way that organisations construct and legitimise learning, through their management cultures, defines their relationship to performance. He shows how many organisations remain structured around cultures of single-loop learning; where the key question executives ask is *how do I do things right*? In other words, how can I conform to the organisational norms of this place? In such places legitimate management is defined through a vocabulary of productivity, efficiency and process improvements (Taylor, 2023). Whilst such an approach may well produce incremental gains, single-loop learning implicitly assumes a stable environment, where the role of management is to provide predictability. Connecting this to the Cynefin Framework, we can see that such an approach suits the simple domain well. What are best practices if not established means of providing predictable outcomes? Unfortunately, single-loop learning limits thinking in the complicated domain and actively worsens outcomes when facing complex challenges.

Continuing to assume that best practices will deliver effective outcomes when existing relationships between cause and effect are breaking down is very dangerous. Snowden (2010) describes this as moving into the

---

[1] For more on these processes, see Taylor and Bochis (2025).

complacent zone, as you slide towards the cliff edge that separates the simple from the chaotic zone. All other zones he notes allow for transition, but if you cross this boundary recovery will be very expensive. In many ways this is what we experienced as governments grappled with the early stages of the Covid pandemic. Only when it was self-evident to everyone that neither best practices nor calling medical experts was going to work and many societies were teetering on the edge of chaos, that safe-to-fail experiments began to take hold. Companies as diverse as Mercedes, Formula One, Dyson and others began manufacturing ventilators to support breathing, as the usual rigid regulations were torn up. Even more clearly, the initial rollout of the first vaccines was acknowledgement that experimenting for emergence and then channelling and amplifying it was the basis of strategy. UK health officials decided to ignore manufacturers' advice to leave a gap of around 3 weeks between injections and stretch it to a minimum of 12 weeks. This was done on the basis that it was more important that everybody gets some level of protection than a few people get a high level of protection. There was no certainty that this would work, but as soon as evidence that it was working emerged the strategy was amplified quickly and we witnessed the mass vaccination of the population in football stadiums, community centres and many other places.

The trouble is that, in my professional experience, executives find it very hard to escape the single-loop learning that has got them through education and into the career positions that they currently occupy. They "are blinded to new ways of thinking by the perspectives they acquired through past experience, training and success." (Snowden and Boone, 2007, p. 3). So much emphasis is placed upon learning to execute tasks using best practices at school and in organisations that leaders find it difficult to move beyond doubling down on existing best practices or calling consultants to do analysis, as a way of outsourcing blame for the failure to adapt. The problem is made worse by the fact that "our modes of thought are so habitual that we scarcely notice how they filter our perception of reality" (Syed, 2019, p. 21).

## *Questioning Assumptions*

Argyris (1991) shows that double-loop learning (where managers, instead of asking 'how do I do things right?', ask 'what are the right things?') is far more likely to produce higher levels of performance. Questioning the basic assumptions of what we do and how we do it produces innovation, differentiation and

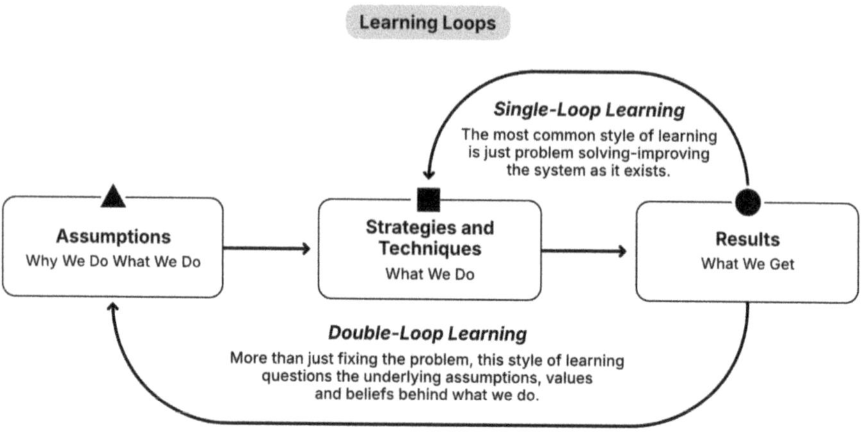


Figure 2. Argos Learning Loops – Adapted from Argyris (1991).

cultures more focussed around value than task execution for its own sake. In complex domains, double-loop learning isn't just a better idea than single-loop learning, it is a prerequisite for survival. Getting this right is what avoids, or enables you to escape, the complacent zone. It provides the means for executives to escape Sun Tzu's infamous maxim that 'Tactics without strategy is the noise before defeat'. Knickel et al. (2009) reveal how learning loops are directly linked to innovation. They describe first-order innovation as offering limited changes, and second-order innovation describes systemic change based upon challenging existing assumptions, beliefs and values. Just like Argyris (1991), Knickel et al. (2009) explain how second-order innovation creates reinforcing cycles of innovative change.

Pentland (2013) and Syed (2019) show that one of the reasons it is so hard it is for executives to escape single-loop learning is because they become trapped in echo chambers within their own organisations and peer groups and as a result "certainty becomes inversely correlated with accuracy" (Syed 2019, p. 24). All the data in the world is no replacement for the qualitative insights that flow from hearing voices different to your own. Uzzi and Dunlap (2005) show just how unaware most executives are of how similar the people in their networks actually are. Yet we know that "Social learning improves decision making only when individuals each have different information". In other words, in complex domains it is critical to seek out people with different experiences and beliefs to your own. Syed (2019) goes further and says that to thrive in complex domains, we shouldn't do

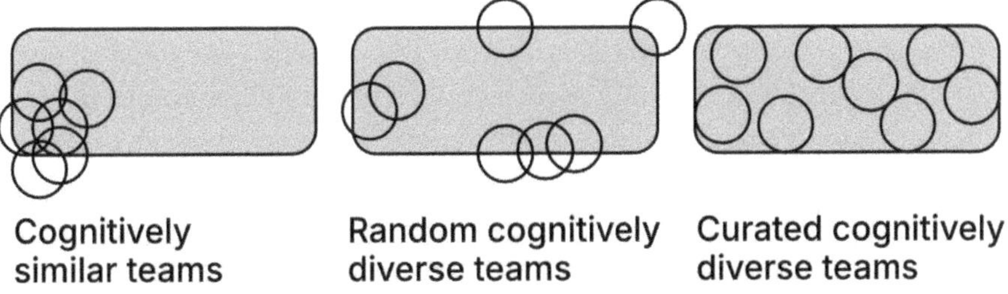


Figure 3. Syed's Curated Diversity – adapted from Syed (2019), pp. 46, 54.

this in a random way, but actively curate diversity. In this way, he argues, we engage with the largest possible cognitive space.

Both in this collection and elsewhere, Zehndorfer (2025) demonstrates how the algorithms that drive digital technology are making the problem of echo chambers worse and actively increasing our certainty, which is becoming ever more inversely correlated with accuracy (Syed, 2019, p. 24). Simply have a look at the debates surrounding the shooting of a 37-year-old woman in Minneapolis in early January 2026 to see how social media shaped and reinforced widely different interpretations of what happened, according to the echo chamber you most closely align with. In short "while humans naturally cling to people like themselves in uncertain times, we need to do the opposite, and embrace more intellectual diversity, not less" (Tett, 2026).

In a world of big data, the temptation is to bury yourself in the numbers. However, "Companies often don't recognize weak early signals that a trend is emerging because managers are internally focused, unwilling to challenge their assumptions, and uncomfortable with ambiguity" (Reeves, Goodson and Whitaker, 2021, p. 5).

Furthermore, when we look at employment numbers and earnings for different occupations, those that have fared best combine quantitative abilities and interpersonal skills like social perceptiveness, coordinating ability, persuasiveness and negotiation (a group that includes doctors, consultants, economists and, yes, even software developers, according to detailed occupational skill data). And jobs requiring strong soft skills, but relatively little mathematical aptitude (among them lawyers, therapists and nurses) have fared much better than those requiring strong numerical talent but fewer social skills (among them statistical assistants and programmers. (Burn-Murdoch 2026).

Quantitative analytical skill is valuable for the simple and complicated domains, but for the complex domain just knowing the numbers isn't enough. Double-loop learning requires a shift in thinking that embraces the qualitative in its search for new meanings and drivers of emerging relationships between cause and effect. Unfortunately, one of the most common excuses provided by executives, in my experience, for not moving beyond single-loop learning is that they simply don't have time. Rather than creating slack in organisational systems and thus freeing executives up to think more, technology continues to enable them to take on greater levels of complexity and tighten up the systems used to deliver efficiency, in the interests of short-term shareholder value. Aside from creating executive stress and burnout, it is also leading to greater risk of systemic or organisational failure.

## Robustness & Resilience

Building upon the work of Perrow (1999), Clearfield and Tilcsik (2019) describe the two key determinants of risk in any system as how complex it is, as complexity creates unpredictable feedback loops and how tightly coupled a system is. The more redundancy that exists, the less likely it is that failure in one place will infect others. Kohr (1957) described this as 'the mattress effect', where the failure of one mattress spring does not lead to the failure of the whole bed. As we saw have seen in recent financial crises, it's the combination of complexity and tight coupling that causes meltdowns. Small errors are inevitable in complex systems, and once things begin to go south, such systems produce baffling symptoms. No matter how hard we try, we struggle to make a diagnosis and might even make things worse by solving the wrong problem. And, if the system is also tightly coupled, we can't stop the falling dominoes. Failures spread quickly and uncontrollably (Clearfield and Tilcsik, 2019, p. 27).

More recently, the coronavirus pandemic showed that our systems were not resilient in the face of a large shock (Roberts & Lamp, 2021, p. 145). Martin (2019) argues that management has come to be defined as a search for efficiency. "But the single-minded pursuit of efficiency makes businesses less resilient" (Martin, 2019, p. 3). Whilst there are many definitions of resilience (see Taylor and Bochis 2025, p. 102), Wahl notes that broadly speaking:

> ... there are 2 types of resilience. Type 1 resilience is based on persistence in the face of disruption and adaptation in response to disruption in order to recover the old status quo. Type 2 resilience

is based on an evolutionary or transformative response… (Wahl, 2020, p. 25).

Resilience is different from robustness. "Robustness is an increased ability to absorb perturbations versus resilience, which ensures the elasticity of boundaries, and provides the means for adaptiveness should circumstances require it" (Taylor and Bochis, 2025, p.101). This is not just a semantic difference. Whilst robust models work well in stable environments and respond well to single-loop learning management for efficiency, they are very poor in complex situations, where they leave no space available for double-loop learning. Indeed, Perrow shows that our failure to build slack into how we engage with and manage complex systems is inviting disaster. "Redundancies and all other safety measures should be designed in from the start and not added afterwards, since add-ons are disproportionately the source of accidents" (Perrow, 2002 – abstract).

Failure to develop resilience isn't just a problem for businesses, though. A short glance at the economies of the former Soviet Union and Eastern Europe reveals how damaging inflexible top-down government policies, based upon compliance, can be for innovation, performance and the environment (Peterson, 1993; Gallagher, 2005). In a nod to the need to enable emergent and innovative solutions, carbon markets have been an attempt to embrace complexity to deliver emissions reductions that many years of international agreement and government policies had failed to do (Grubb Vrolijk and Brack, 1999). Whilst carbon markets are inherently complex, by forcing companies to decide whether to find their own emissions reductions or buy others' surplus reductions, in order to comply with annually declining permitted allowances, they do require double-loop learning and have enabled the emergence of innovation that otherwise was not foreseen (Taylor 2004).

## Networked Ownership

For years, so-called new resource, or free market, economists such as Anderson and Teal (2001) have argued that the trouble with environmental issues is not their inherent complexity, but the lack of ownership over resources at their core. In other words, if resources like oceans, national parks, wildlife, etc., were privately owned the incentive to make profit over the longer term would lead owners to experiment with more sustainable management regimes. One of the key problems with this argument is that it ignores the ethical question of the right to exclude others, which, in reality, is likely to become a political problem. Indeed, Rose (2011), Goodhart (2017) and Taylor & Bronstone (2019, 2022) have shown how the convergence of technology and globalisation, whilst not explicitly excluding anyone, is leaving many people behind, who are voting for the extremes of left and right. Nonetheless, carbon markets have demonstrated that creative use of property rights can unleash Adam Smith's infamous hidden hand to unlock unexpected capability to innovate and overcome years of policy failures, in the search for profit (Taylor, 2004).

The EU Emission Trading Scheme (EU ETS) is designed to include most major industrial polluters, who are required to hold permits to pollute to match their actual pollution. Every year the number of permits issued is reduced, thereby forcing participants to decide if it is more cost-effective to find their own emission reductions or to purchase others' surplus reductions. In this way, market forces seek out the lowest cost emission reductions and a search for competitive innovation is stimulated.

The initial weakness of the EU ETS has been shown to be the result of institutional weakness, which led to the issuing of initial pollution permits based upon existing emissions, rather than an auction (Zheng, 2025). This led to a low price for permits, reduced market liquidity and limited incentives to reduce emissions. Carbon trading has shown that markets can be powerful means for unlocking innovation in complex domains, but to be effective they need to enable widespread experimentation in the search for more sustainable solutions. That requires both high-level strategies and localised entrepreneurship. This is a lesson which reaches far beyond carbon markets but often cuts against the tendency of large organisations to centralise control in their search for efficiencies. Yet isn't this exactly what we saw with the drive to develop new ventilators during the pandemic by the likes of Dyson, Mercedes and others?

As the work of Ostrom shows, the complexity of resource management tends to overwhelm simple solutions. As in nature, Merali shows that "the distributed network form of organising overcomes the deficiency of centrally determined 'one size fits all' policies" (Merali, 2022, p. 206). For it is not the property right itself which is the key here, so much as how access to the benefit streams defined by the property right encourage, or discourage, stakeholders to cooperate to develop innovative win-win outcomes or compete to maximise immediate gains, at the expense of longer-term sustainability. In complex domains it is not that competition itself is bad, but it does matter who we compete with. Direct competition for control of the resource is far less likely to create a sustainable outcome than competing to find innovative means of creating value from access to it (Bromley 1993, Ostrom 2012, 2015). Is more money likely to be made from competing with other countries for fishing rights in a sea, or from cooperating to create value from tourism, renewable energy and other revenue streams, whilst fishing sustainably? What Ostrom shows is how common property regimes, often because of their smaller scale, are more effective means of conducting safe-to-fail experiments than private property regimes (2015). However, she also shows how, through processes of what she calls polycentric nesting, "where [commons] systems exist at multiple levels with some autonomy at each level" (Ostrom, 2012, p. 82), learning from such experiments is often amplified quickly, thereby creating an innovative resilience beyond the local that wouldn't otherwise exist.

What we see with web platforms like Amazon, booking.com and others are robust vehicles for capturing value by channelling and amplifying network-based relationships through digital technology. However, whilst the tech firms have networked the world, the power of network effects (described by other authors here) has created global monopolies, whose dominance is now of serious concern. Indeed Iansati & Lakshmi argue that:

> …the global economy is coalescing around a few digital superpowers. We see unmistakable evidence that a winner-takes-all world is emerging in which a small number of 'hub firms' – including Alibaba, Alphabet/Google, Amazon, Apple, Baidu, Facebook, Microsoft and Tencent – occupy central positions (Iansati & Lakhani, 2017, p. 86).

In other words, through their use of digital technology, these firms have been able to manage new levels of complexity, whilst also tightening up the system efficiency. This is creating dangerous dependencies, but as you will recall from earlier, we are also constructing inevitable systemic failure. Having wiped out most smaller competitors, imagine what would happen if Google or Amazon's network experienced catastrophic failure, for example. The growth of AI only extends these concerns about dependence and is extending the tech giants' hold on creative rights over music and the written word.

Merali shows that the more distributed the network is the more resilient it is likely to be, or as she puts it "...the *resilience* [italics in original] of networked systems derives from the combinatorial potential they embody" (Merali, 2022, p. 201). The more tightly that networks are controlled from the centre, the less resilient they are. Effective management of network complexity comes from the centre facilitating and enabling the amplification of emergence, not controlling it. This is part of the reason that the *Wiki* model is so powerful. Indeed, both Ostrom (2012) and Merali (2022) are clear that although superficially inefficient, resilience comes out of the formation of networks of networks, that Ostrom calls polycentricity (Ostrom, 2015) partly because they enable small-scale risk taking and innovation, where failure does not have systemic consequences. "This lumpy structure has been shown to be a universal feature of viable systems across biological, social, economic and technological domains." (Merali, 2022, p. 202).

## Stewardship

If the key to managing complexity is reliance and adaptability, then locally grounded stewardship is worthy of our thought and attention. "The idea of stewardship is that acting with restraint upon purely utilitarian exploitation is how the idea of work becomes an act of virtue" (Taylor and Bronstone, 2023, p. 78). Indeed, the research that I undertook with Adam Bronstone into how some people and places thrive and others do not in a networked global economy (Taylor and Bronstone 2019, 2023) indicates that flourishing in complex spaces is about more than economics alone. We found in our study of why the Romanian city of Cluj-Napoca is so successful, compared to other, even Romanian, cities that "increasing returns flow from innovation arising from a mixture of geographic proximity, relational capital and institutional proximity" (Taylor and Bronstone 2023, p. 165).

Our research revealed that it is the pooling of relational capital, where a shared sense of identity of place and what Camagni (2019, p. 127) calls sociocultural proximity become embedded in shared norms of behaviour that enable the development of trust and lead to what he calls territorial capital (Camagni, 2009). "Territorial capital describes how relational capital and milieu effects combine to drive local development with its basis in a known group of actors with agreed norms of behaviour" (Taylor and Bronstone, 2023, p. 29), where entrepreneurs identify with the need to invest themselves in sustaining the resource (Merali, 2022), that Camagni (2009) describes as like a club. It is this active form of stewardship, based upon a pooling of resources and needs which sustains and nourishes successful places beyond individual organisations or even sectors.

In the case of Cluj-Napoca, this arose from the isolation created by a nationalist mayor, which forced entrepreneurs to cooperate, to develop resilience, just to survive. Once the mayor left office and the country joined the EU, the power of second order adaptability was unleashed and has transformed the city from a sleepy provincial city to a key engine of national growth.

Rather than drive these processes, we found that public institutions followed but were not passive. Universities worked closely with businesses to develop and adapt degree programmes, such as computer science, to match market needs. Meanwhile, the City Hall, under a new mayor, formed industry clusters and then clusters of clusters, in what Ostrom (2015) would no doubt consider as an embryonic form of nesting or polycentricity, thereby supporting and nurturing a positive cycle of transformation that was grounded in a shared identity of place and norms of behaviour. It was this positive cycle of territorial capital (Camagni 2009) that created social resilience and the adaptive capacity (Jackson 2003) that continues to enable second-order innovation (Knickel et.al., 2009) in a way that hasn't occurred in other places.

The lesson of these insights is that decision-making needs to be distributed widely across and even between organisations, which does require a shift in management culture from being masters of internal efficiency to facilitators of emergence, in a complex world "where success comes not from rigid control but from distributed intelligence, continuous learning and adaptation (Werner and Le-Brun, 2025, p. 54). In what Werner and Le-Brun (2025) call the Octopus model, "a leader's primary job is to work on the system, not in it." (Werner and Le-Brun 2025, p. 60.) That requires slack and thinking time, if managers are to be able to question assumptions behind the status quo and deliver double-loop learning.

## Geopolitics

Beyond business, we see similar patterns occurring in geopolitics. Control over technological standards has provided mostly US firms with a tight grip on markets wherever digital disruption has taken place – something that has not escaped the attention of an emergent China. "Chinese officials have long said that third-rate countries build things, second-rate countries design things, and first-rate countries set standards." (Hillman, 2021, p. 14.). We first saw this with the tussle over the technology firm Huawei and social media platform TikTok. More recently we see this with the struggle to control the licence to print money that investors believe is the future of AI and the fury directed towards the Chinese DeepSeek variant.

"By open-sourcing AI, they [the Chinese] not only sidestep US sanctions but also decentralise development and tap into global talent to refine their models… The scale of this approach could fundamentally reshape AI's economic structure. If open-source AI becomes just as powerful as proprietary US models, the ability to monetise AI as an exclusive product collapses. Why pay for closed models if a free, equally capable alternative exists?" (Yoon, 19 March, 2025).

Since the election of Trump, however, we see a retreat from what Bull (1977) called an anarchical society, based upon principles, institutions and accepted norms of behaviour, a retreat that goes beyond technology. As the post-war order continues to break down, new levels of complexity and volatility are flowing from a world where might is right. As European governments are discovering, first with Ukraine, then Greenland, continuing to apply and work best practices harder in a world turned upside down doesn't work. Remaining in the complacent zone will lead to chaos. As Dunt has observed in the UK:

> In a sense, Starmer [the Prime Minister] is like the rest of us: desperately trying to keep up with a world that has stopped making sense, coming up with long words to explain what is ultimately extremely rudimentary: how you deal with a child sitting on a throne the size of the world. Trump's only real foreign policy position is one of tantrum and gangsterism. We are all quickly falling into the vortex of lunacy he has created, Starmer included. (Dunt, 2026, p. 19).

Leaders need to do some double-loop learning, experiment with new patterns of governance and amplify what works quickly if the liberal democratic order is to continue to count for anything.

## Conclusion

Making sense of complex challenges requires us to first recognise when we are seeing complexity. As has been shown here and is similarly used elsewhere in this collection, the Cynefin Framework (Snowden and Boone, 2007) is a powerful tool for helping to do this. Once complexity has been identified, we need to start using double-loop learning (Argyris 1991) and question the assumptions that have got us to this point. Too often managers fail to question what Werner and Le-Brun call *antipatterns*: "formulaic responses to complex challenges that, despite good intentions and surface-level appeal, consistently make things worse" (Werner and Le-Brun, 2025, p. 56). In lots of ways, it was this that the Prime Minister of Canada, Mark Carney, was calling out in his visionary speech to the World Economic Forum on January 26th 2026, when he described efforts to pretend that the old world order could be sustained using existing practices as "living within a lie". As Syed (2019) has shown, deliberately trying to curate a broad spectrum of diversity is a powerful means to strategically engage with complex challenges, since people with different experiences and views to our own do not share the same assumptions of what is normal, reasonable or even possible.

To avoid organisations, groups and societies from becoming trapped in a kind of collective groupthink (Janis, 1971; Syed, 2019; Bonabeau, 2004; Pentland, 2013) we need to distribute authority to innovate and apply double-loop learning widely. For although this will inevitably create inefficiencies, it is precisely those inefficiencies that will provide the fuel and the space for innovation to take place. Furthermore, developing such resilience is by far the best way to avoid the kind of catastrophic failure that Clearfield & Tilcsik (2019) describe in systems that are so tightly coupled that executives lack the capabilities to stop cascading complexity from simply overwhelming them.

## References

Anderson, T. and Teal D. (2001). *Free Market Environmentalism*. New York: Palgrave.

Argyris, C. (1976). 'Single-loop and double-loop models in research on decision making'. *Administrative Science Quarterly,* 21(3), 363–375.

Argyris, C. (1977). 'Double-loop learning in organisations'. *Harvard Business Review,* 55(5), 115–125.

Argyris, C. (1991). 'Teaching smart people how to learn'. *Harvard Business Review,* 69(3).

Bonabeau, E. (2004). 'The Perils of the Imitation Age', *Harvard Business Review* (July 2004).

Bromley, D. (1993). *Environment and Economy: Property Rights and Public Policy.* Oxford; Blackwell.

Bull, H. (1977). *The Anarchical Society: A Study of Order in World Politics.* London: Macmillan.

Burn-Murdoch, J. (2026). 'How to AI-Proof Your Job', *Financial Times*, ft.com, viewed 9 January 2026.

Camagni, R. (2009). 'Territorial Capital & Regional Development' in Capello and Nijkamp (eds.), *Handbook of Regional Growth and Development Theories.* Cheltenham UK: Edward Elgar.

Dunt, I. (2026). 'Trump has created a vortex of lunacy: US leader can single-handedly erase international security'. London: *i newspaper* (8 Jan. 2026).

Gallagher, T. (2005). *Theft of a Nation: Romania Since Communism,* London: Hurst.

Goodhart, D. (2017). *The Road to Somewhere.* London: Hurst & Co.

Grubb, M., Vrolijk, C., Brack, D. (1999). *The Kyoto Protocol: A Guide and Assessment.* London: Royal Institute of International Affairs.

Henry, C. (Sandy) Waters III. (2011). *Sales - What a Concept!: A Guidebook for Sales Process Performance Improvement.* Raleigh, NC, USA: SW Consulting.

Hillman, J. (2021). *The Digital Silk Road: China's Quest to Wire the World and Win the Future.* London: Profile Books.

Iansiti, M. and Lakhani, K. (2017), 'Managing Our Hub Economy: Strategy, Ethics and Network Competition in an Age of Digital Superpowers'. *Harvard Business Review* (September 2017).

Janis, I. L. (1971). 'Groupthink'. *Psychology Today,* pp. 84–90.

Janis, I. L. (1982). *Groupthink: Psychological Studies of Policy Decisions and Fiascos.* Boston: Houghton Mifflin.

Knickel, K., Brunori, G, Rand, S. and Proost, M. (2009). 'Towards a Better Conceptual Framework for Innovation Processes in Agriculture and Rural Development: From Linear Models to Systemic Approaches'. *The Journal of Agricultural Education and Extension* 15(2).

Kohr, L. (1957). *The Breakdown of Nations.* Croydon, UK: Green Books, 2001. Originally published by Routledge & Kegan Paul.

Merali, Y. (2022). 'Complexity and Networks' in Taylor, A. (ed.), *Rethinking Leadership for a Green World.* London: Routledge.

Ostrom, E. (2012). *The Future of The Commons: Beyond Market Failure and Government Regulation.* London: IEA.

Ostrom, E. (2015). *Governing the Commons: The Evolution of Institutions for Collective Action.* Cambridge: Cambridge University Press.

Pentland, A. (2013). 'Beyond the Echo Chamber'. *Harvard Business Review.* (November 2013)

Perrow, C. (1999). *Normal Accidents: Living with High-Risk Technologies.* Updated Edition. New York: Princeton University Press.

Perrow, C. (2002). 'Organizing to Reduce the Vulnerabilities of Complexity'. *Journal of Contingencies and Crisis Management*, Nr. 7 (3), pp. 150–155.

Peterson, D. J. (1993). *Troubled Lands: The Legacy of Soviet Environmental Destruction*, London: Westview Press.

Reeves, R., Goodson B. and Whitaker, K. 2021). 'The Power of Anomaly'. *Harvard Business Review*.(July-August 2011)

Rose, C. (2011). *What Makes People Tick: The Hidden World of Settler, Prospectors and Pioneers*, Leicester: Matador.

Snowden, D. and Boone M. E. (2007). 'A Leader's Framework for Decision Making', *Harvard Business Review* (November 2007).

Snowden, D. (July 2010). *The Cynefin Framework*. Available at: https://www.youtube.com/watch?v=N7oz366X0-8 (accessed 11 November 2025)

Syed, M. (2019). *Rebel Ideas: The Power of Diverse Thinking*. London: John Murray.

Taylor, A., (2004). 'Trading Hot Air: Backwards, Forwards or Any Which Way You Like'. *European Environment*. Nr. 14, pp. 251–256.

Taylor, A. and Bronstone, A. (2019). *People, Place and Global Order: Foundations of a Networked Political Economy*. London: Routledge.

Taylor, A. and Bronstone, A. (2023). *Re-constructing the Global Network Economy: Building Pathways to Resilience in Local Economies*. London: Routledge.

Tett, G. (2026). 'What Business Should be Thinking About Post Davos'. *Financial Times*, ft.com, viewed 23rd January 2026.

Uzzi, B. and Dunlap, S. (2005). 'How to Build Your Network'. *Harvard Business Review*. (December 2005).

Wahl, D. (2020). 'Building A New Normal'. *Resurgence & Ecologist*. Issue 321.

Werner, J. and Le Brun, P. 2025). 'Become an Octopus Organization: How Your Company can Adapt to a Complex World'. *Harvard Business Review*. (Nov-Dec 2025).

Yoon, J. (2025). *Why China is suddenly flooding the market with powerful AI models. Financial Times*. Available at FT.com. (Accessed 19th March 2025)

Zheng, S. *et al.* (2025). 'Global Climate Policy Effectiveness Analysis: Evidence from 49 Countries, 1951–2018', *Journal of Comparative Policy Analysis: Research and Practice*, 27(1), pp. 1–38.

# THE POWER OF AI TO OBLITERATE EXISTING BUSINESS REALITIES

## Radu Orghidan

## Abstract

This chapter argues that Artificial Intelligence (AI) doesn't just disrupt business—it **obliterates it**. Obliteration signifies the destruction of the underlying logical conditions that define traditional organizational forms. AI creates a fundamental discontinuity where previous categories such as **What is a Firm?** and **What is Competence?** become inoperative.

## The Core Threat: Subtraction and Obsolescence

The central challenge posed by AI is the **inversion of accumulation logic**. The decades-long process of building competitive advantage through accumulated, human-centric expertise (e.g., core competence) is being aggressively replaced. What was once an asset is rapidly becoming **core obsolescence**.

AI achieves this through **epistemological violence**: the traumatic subtraction of human roles. The failure of Klarna's initial pure-AI customer service model, followed by the difficult attempt to rehire human staff, illustrates the problem: once human expertise and infrastructure are dismantled, the organisational knowledge is often **irretrievable**.

## The New Order: Distributed Agency

The human role does not disappear, but it is radically transformed. Humans persist in the form of **ghost work** (invisible data labelling and QA) or as part of **augmentation scenarios**. In these new structures, competence is no longer held by individuals, but by **distributed epistemic assemblages**—dynamic, interconnected systems of humans, algorithms, and data.

For the modern firm, strategy must shift to **ontological agility**: the ability to assemble and reassemble these human-AI capabilities faster than the competition. Key organisational markers of this shift include the **algorithmic management** of labour (like Uber) and the total reconstitution of professional identity (like a developer becoming a **code curator** via Copilot).

## Strategic Imperatives: Designing the Post-Competence Economy

The crucial question is whether the future will be shaped by design or by default.

1. **Stop Accumulating, Start Subtracting:** Business education must adopt a **Subtractive Pedagogy**, focusing on actively unlearning obsolete skills (pattern recognition, optimisation) and prioritizing uniquely human skills (ethical judgment, creative synthesis, contextual understanding).
2. **Ensure Accountability:** The rise of distributed agency creates a **responsibility gap**. This must be closed by implementing **Hybrid Decision Boards** and **AI Decision Ledgers** to ensure clear human recourse and accountability even when decisions are algorithmic.
3. **Design for Justice:** As value creation decouples from human labour—leading to a **post-competence economy**—society must choose between two futures:
   - **Algorithmic Feudalism:** Power and value concentrated among a tech elite.
   - **Collaborative Abundance:** AI infrastructure treated as a common resource, supported by mechanisms like **data dividends** or a **Universal Basic Compute**.

The time for theoretical debate is over. The industrial-era foundations have been destroyed. The responsibility now lies in making deliberate **design choices** regarding ownership, governance, and equity to ensure the resulting posthuman economy serves human flourishing.

## 1. Introduction: obliteration as ontological rupture

In February 2024, Swedish fintech company Klarna deployed an OpenAI-powered customer service assistant that, within its first month, handled 2.3 million customer interactions across 35 languages—performing what the company claimed was "the equivalent work of 700 full-time agents" (Klarna, 2024). The results appeared remarkable: customer satisfaction scores matched human agents, resolution times dropped from 11 minutes to under 2 minutes, and repeat inquiries fell by 25%. CEO Sebastian Siemiatkowski projected $40 million in profit improvements for 2024. However, by May 2025, facing significant customer dissatisfaction with a purely algorithmic service, Klarna reversed course and began rehiring human customer service workers. Siemiatkowski acknowledged to Bloomberg that the company had "gone too far in the wrong direction," admitting that "really investing in the quality of human support is the way of the future for us" (cited in Customer Experience Dive, 2025). Yet the reversal came too late to restore what had been lost: the organisational knowledge, training infrastructure, and human expertise in customer relationship management that had been dismantled during the aggressive AI implementation. The category of "customer service professional" had been temporarily obliterated—revealing both AI's capacity to eliminate human organisational roles and the painful difficulty of reconstituting them once dissolved.

This chapter argues that artificial intelligence does not merely disrupt or transform business reality, it *obliterates* it. Obliteration means the elimination of the conditions of possibility for prior organisational forms. Where Christensen's (1997) disruption implies temporary instability followed by new equilibrium, obliteration denotes fundamental discontinuity: the categories, boundaries, and logics that made the previous system coherent become inoperative.

AI creates what Foucault (1970) termed an epistemic rupture, a break so profound that the rules governing knowledge, organisation, and value no longer apply. Consider the ontological instability AI introduces to basic business categories.

*What is a firm?* When algorithmic platforms coordinate millions of workers without traditional employment (Uber, DoorDash), when decentralised autonomous organisations (DAOs) operate through smart contracts without incorporation, when value flows through data extraction rather than production—Coase's (1937) theory of the firm collapses.

*What is work?* When AI performs cognitive labour deemed irreducibly human, when humans train algorithms through behavioural data without employment, the labour-capital distinction destabilizes.

*What is competence?* When knowledge resides in algorithmic weights rather than human minds, when learning occurs in microseconds rather than years, the human-centered competence paradigm evaporates.

Traditional business reality rested on five interlocking elements: human agency as decision locus, knowledge as accumulated learning, boundaries as capability containers, value creation through human labour, and temporality favouring incumbents. AI dissolves each element. Drawing on Heidegger (1977), AI creates a new *Gestell* (enframing), determining what can be revealed as "real" in organisational contexts. Under AI's enframing, organisations appear as configurations of data flows and algorithmic processing where humans are elements among many, no longer the organizing center.

## 2. The collapse of accumulation logic: from core competence to systemic obsolescence

Prahalad and Hamel's (1990, p. 82) influential framework defined competitive advantage as "collective learning in the organisation, especially how to coordinate diverse production skills and integrate multiple streams of technologies." This human-centered paradigm assumes: (1) advantage from gradual capability building, (2) human knowledge as irreducible, (3) internal coherence as strength, and (4) learning as a collective social process. The framework explained why Toyota's production system resisted imitation (decades of accumulated worker knowledge), why 3M sustained innovation (cross-functional collaboration embedded in culture), and why vertically integrated firms could outcompete markets in complex coordination.

Yet even Prahalad and Hamel recognized a shadow side. Leonard-Barton (1992) demonstrated how core competencies become "core rigidities" - sources of inertia when conditions shift. Capabilities that once conferred advantage lock firms into obsolete practices. This paradox was manageable when change occurred slowly enough for deliberate adaptation. Organisations could incrementally modify competencies, extend capabilities into adjacent domains, or, in Snowden's (2020) Cynefin framework, engage in "exaptation": the radical repurposing of existing capabilities for entirely different functions. Exaptation represents evolution's answer to environmental discontinuity: traits developed for one purpose prove adaptive for another (feathers for warmth become wings for flight). In organisational contexts, Snowden identifies three exaptation modes: stress-based repurposing under crisis conditions, stimulated experimentation at the edge of chaos, and dispositional capability-building for strategic agility. This framework acknowledges that core competencies need not remain fixed to their original purposes—they can be radically redeployed when contexts shift.

Yet exaptation, however radical, still presumes the underlying capability substrate retains value and simply requires novel application. A manufacturing firm might repurpose precision engineering from automotive to medical devices; a logistics company might redeploy routing algorithms from delivery to emergency response. The core competence persists; only its application domain changes. But AI shatters this assumption entirely. Where exaptation asks, "How can we repurpose this capability?", AI renders the question moot by eliminating the capability's scarcity value altogether. There is no repurposing diagnostic expertise when algorithms diagnose better; no redeploying quantitative analysis when AI performs it instantaneously; no radical reimagining of knowledge work when the knowledge itself becomes algorithmically reproducible at zero marginal cost. Exaptation operates within the logic of human-centered competence accumulation. AI obliterates that logic.

AI transforms this manageable paradox into existential crisis by inverting accumulation logic through *subtraction and displacement*. Rather than rewarding accumulated expertise, AI automates cognitive tasks (diagnosis, analysis, planning), accelerates learning cycles (hours versus years), erodes scarcity value (abundant algorithmic capability), and inverts scale economics. Brynjolfsson and McAfee (2014) documented productivity rising while labour input falls. As Cicero (2025) observes, a five-person team with sophisticated AI can achieve coordination capacity requiring five hundred people in traditional hierarchies. What was "core competence" becomes "core obsolescence."

## *Subtraction as Epistemological Violence*

Organisational subtraction is not neutral process improvement but *epistemological violence*, the traumatic unmaking of identity when what was "core" is revealed as surplus. Drawing on Derrida (1976), organisational competencies are sites of *symbolic investment*, not just functional capabilities. When a law firm's attorney expertise or hospital's diagnostic mastery becomes algorithmically replicable, the organisation faces internal dissolution: the legal entity persists while its existential core evaporates.

Employee resistance to AI is often existential preservation, not change-aversion. A senior financial analyst whose quantitative modelling becomes automated faces an identity crisis: if algorithms do what she does better and faster, who is she professionally? Subtracted competencies leave Derridean traces haunting the organisation and workflows designed for human oversight; communication patterns optimized for hierarchy persist, creating friction. Following Agamben (2005), AI creates organisational "states of exception" where old rules are suspended but new algorithmic governance hasn't been legitimated. Organisations exist in limbo, unable to return to human-centered paradigms yet unwilling to embrace full algorithmic control.

Evidence spans industries. Trading floors where algorithmic systems replaced hundreds of analysts; law firms where AI research tools obsoleted junior associate apprenticeships; healthcare where diagnostic AI matched specialist physicians (Topol, 2019); software where GitHub Copilot (2022) automates foundational programming skills. Organisations excelling at traditional learning face the highest switching costs as their accumulated competencies represent embedded assumptions, structures, and identities resisting transformation.

## 3. Persistence and resistance: limits of obliteration

The obliteration thesis must confront empirical reality: humans persist. AI has not created fully autonomous organisations. This section examines three persistence forms: material dependencies, augmentation scenarios, and organisational friction, that refine rather than refute the obliteration thesis. The central claim is not human disappearance but radical transformation of human agency and participation terms.

### *Material Dependencies*

Gray and Suri's (2019) ethnographic research in *Ghost Work* reveals extensive human labour that "makes AI seem like magic." Behind every autonomous AI system are thousands performing invisible labour: data labelling (identifying objects in images, transcribing audio, categorizing text), quality control (reviewing outputs, identifying errors) and exception handling (resolving ambiguities when algorithms fail). This labor is geographically dispersed (concentrated in Global South low-wage regions), algorithmically managed (through platforms like Amazon Mechanical Turk), yet epistemologically foundational since without human-labelled data, supervised machine learning cannot function.

A profound paradox emerges: the more advanced the AI, the more human labour may be required. Large language models need extensive human feedback for alignment (RLHF). Autonomous vehicles need humans reviewing edge cases. Content recommendation systems need human moderators preventing feedback loops. Yet this persistence occurs on AI's terms as humans execute narrowly defined microtasks within algorithmic frameworks, valued only for capacities not yet automated. This is *managed obsolescence* with humans retained provisionally until technology advances suffice.

## Augmentation Scenarios

Rigobon and Loaiza's (2025) MIT research found human-AI teams outperform either alone, identifying "EPOCH" skills (empathy, presence, opinion/ judgment, creativity, hope) which remain difficult to automate. This suggests AI refocuses human competence toward domains where human capabilities remain distinctive: contextual understanding, ethical reasoning, creative synthesis, relational intelligence.

However, this narrative requires qualifications. First, the automatable-human boundary continuously shifts. Empathy and creativity seemed irreducibly human until conversational AI demonstrated functional adequacy. Second, augmentation often means human verification of algorithmic outputs: asymmetry placing humans in reactive, subordinate positions. Third, augmentation may exacerbate inequality: high-skill workers orchestrating AI become vastly more productive while others face displacement. Fourth, augmentation narratives rest on normative claims (AI *should* complement) rather than describing what organisations *will* do given economic incentives to minimize expensive human labour (Wilson and Daugherty, 2018).

Even in optimistic scenarios, what emerges is not human-centred organisation restored but cyborg workers: human-AI hybrids whose competence is systemically distributed, not individually possessed. This supports the obliteration thesis: human-centred reality dissolves even where humans persist through augmentation.

## *Organisational Friction*

Organisations struggle to subtract human elements due to: cultural resistance (employees resisting algorithmic management, as documented by Möhlmann and Zalmanson (2017) with Uber drivers), regulatory requirements (mandating human accountability in medicine, law, finance), legitimacy deficits (algorithmic decisions lacking trust), technical limitations (AI brittleness in novel situations), and path dependencies (sunk investments in human infrastructure). Rather than clean transitions, we observe awkward hybrids attempting to layer AI onto existing structures.

Uber's evolution illustrates these dynamics. Initial pure algorithmic management proved unsustainable, forcing reintroduction of human support centers, review processes, and advisory councils—grafted onto algorithmic infrastructure, creating uncomfortable assemblages neither fully algorithmic nor genuinely human-centered.

## 4. Posthuman competence: distributed epistemic agency

If human-centered competence is obliterated, what replaces it? Drawing on Hayles (2017), Braidotti (2013; 2019), and Barad (2007), we reconceptualize competence as *distributed epistemic agency*: capacity for knowing and acting emerging from dynamic entanglement of humans, algorithms, data, and structures, where no single element holds autonomous agency.

## *Posthumanist Foundations*

Humanist epistemology positions individual human subjects as knowledge loci. Posthumanist epistemology fundamentally challenges this. Haraway (1985) argued we are all cyborgs—hybrid entities whose boundaries between organism and machine are permeable. What appears as individual knowledge is actually a node in distributed systems including tools, technologies, social relationships, and institutions.

Hayles (2017, p. 10) describes subjectivity as "an amalgam, a collection of heterogeneous components, a material-informational entity whose boundaries undergo continuous construction and reconstruction." Cognition extends beyond conscious human thought to include technical cognition (algorithmic processing) and cognitive nonconscious (processes below awareness). A trading firm's market-timing competence doesn't reside in traders, algorithms, or data alone but emerges from their *cognitive assemblage.*

Barad's (2007, p. 141) "agential realism" replaces "interaction" (pre-existing entities that then interact) with "intra-action" (entities emerge through relations): "Agency is not an attribute but the ongoing reconfigurings of the world." For organisations, competence is not possessed but emerges from intra-action. A logistics firm's optimization arises from entanglement of drivers, GPS, algorithms, protocols, no single agency locus. This makes accountability *relational*: responsibility distributed across assemblages, requiring "response-ability" (capacity to respond).

Braidotti (2013; 2019) emphasizes relationality, persistent power asymmetries (distributed agency doesn't mean equitable power), and *affirmative ethics*—intentionally constructing assemblages enhancing flourishing. Posthuman competence must be assessed not just by efficiency but by alignment with justice.

## Implications for Practice

This framework transforms organisational practice. Stop assessing individual competencies; assess *assemblage fluency*—ability to navigate human-AI boundaries. Structure organisations as assemblages from inception: modular processes, API-enabled architectures, governance addressing assemblages. Measure system outcomes, not individual contributions. Strategy becomes *ontological agility*—assembling and reassembling capabilities faster than competitors. Knowledge management shifts from storing human knowledge to managing conditions for emergence: data quality, integration infrastructure, human-AI interface design, cultural norms around algorithmic authority.

## 5. Organisational assemblages: the AI-native firm

Organisations structured as assemblages represent ontological transformation. We distinguish: *AI-augmented* (traditional structures using AI tools), *AI-embedded* (hybrid human-AI decision-making), and *AI-constituted* (primarily algorithmic coordination, boundaries dissolved into data ecosystems). Ontological markers of true assemblages include: category dissolution (employee/contractor/user blurs), temporal acceleration (decisions at superhuman speeds), opacity to participants, distributed intentionality (goals emerge from dynamics), boundary indeterminacy.

## Case Study: Uber

Uber coordinates over 5 million drivers and couriers worldwide with approximately 32,000 corporate staff—algorithmic management at unprecedented scale (Tekedia, 2025). Algorithms match rides, set surge pricing, manage performance through ratings systems, and optimize routes in milliseconds. Recent longitudinal analysis of 1.5 million trips from 258 UK drivers found that algorithmic control operates through five primary mechanisms: 5-star rating system (with minimum thresholds around 4.5–4.6 creating deactivation risks), GPS driving behaviour monitoring, rider allocation, dynamic pricing, and chatbot support (Binns et al., 2025). Drivers are neither employees nor traditional contractors but *algorithmically managed participants*. Agency is distributed: not managers, drivers, riders, or algorithms alone but their assemblage determines outcomes. This demonstrates radical scalability impossible for traditional firms but creates accountability deficits (responsibility for discriminatory outcomes unclear), worker alienation (opaque algorithmic control provoking resistance strategies), and regulatory ambiguity (exploiting category confusion) (Möhlmann and Zalmanson, 2017).

## *Case Study: GitHub Copilot*

Copilot reconstitutes professional identity. Traditional software competence (syntax, algorithms, debugging) becomes AI-automated. Post-Copilot competence shifts to prompting, evaluation, architecture, and integration. Knowledge is distributed across model parameters, developer judgment, and their collaborative interaction. Professional identity shifts from "code producer" to "code curator." A controlled experiment with 95 professional developers found that those using Copilot completed programming tasks 55.8% faster than the control group (95% confidence interval: 21–89%), with the treatment group averaging 71 minutes versus 161 minutes for the control group (Peng et al., 2023). This creates an educational crisis: what should future developers learn when foundational skills are automated?

## Case Study: High-Frequency Trading

HFT firms represent pure AI-constituted organisation. Algorithms execute millions of trades at microsecond speeds and human intervention is counterproductive. Humans set meta-parameters but don't make individual decisions. Knowledge exists only in model weights, not human-interpretable form. Strategy *emerges* from algorithmic exploration. Markets become machinic ecologies with algorithms interacting beyond human perception, transforming what markets ontologically *are* (MacKenzie, 2019).

Assemblage advantages: radical scalability, temporal acceleration, cognitive enhancement, and cost efficiency. Challenges: legitimacy deficits, accountability gaps, identity crises, and regulatory arbitrage. The paradox: unprecedented capabilities but struggle with functions requiring legitimacy and trust: precisely where human organisations excel. Viable assemblages may require explicit hybrid design: algorithmic efficiency combined with human governance providing transparency, accountability, ethical direction.

## 6. Subtractive pedagogies: redesigning business education

Business schools train students for what AI performs effortlessly—pattern recognition, framework application, optimis ation. McGinnis (2025) observes: "To teach algorithmic thinking is to prepare students for a competition they've already lost." Traditional curricula operate on accumulation models (acquire knowledge, master it, retain it). But if AI renders accumulated knowledge obsolete continuously, accumulation is the wrong strategy.

*Subtractive pedagogy* means: (1) explicit unlearning—identifying and discarding obsolete assumptions (Hedberg, 1981; Hislop et al., 2014), (2) epistemological humility—comfort with not-knowing and provisional understanding, (3) selective non-use of AI—recognis ing where human struggle generates insight (Carr, 2014), (4) meta-cognitive focus—learning to learn/unlearn/relearn, and (5) assemblage fluency—participating effectively in distributed systems.

### Three Pedagogical Models

**Model 1: Epistemic Audit.** Students learn canonical framework (Porter's Five Forces), apply it to traditional cases (works), then apply to AI-disrupted context (produces nonsense—who are "competitors" in autonomous vehicle ecosystems where hardware manufacturers, software companies, data providers, cities building smart infrastructure blur?). Students confront framework inadequacy, identify embedded assumptions no longer holding (stable industry boundaries, firms as primary units, linear value chains), *subtract one core assumption*, rebuild analysis. Assessment: quality of reasoning about why assumptions fail, not whether new framework is "correct." Learning outcome: recognizing frameworks as provisional tools, not truths.

**Model 2: Mandatory Inefficiency.** Semester consulting project with twist: document where you deliberately *avoided* AI and justify why. Required: "AI Temptation Journal," mandatory human-only activities (stakeholder interviews for empathy practice, brainstorming for emergent creativity), "Human Value-Add Analysis" mapping which insights came from AI versus humans versus interaction. Assessment: quality of reasoning about when to use/not use AI, evidence of distinctly human contributions, intellectual courage overriding AI suggestions. Rationale: as Carr (2014) warns, "to automate learning is to subvert learning"—struggle generates insight.

**Model 3: Unlearning Journals.** Weekly: identify business "fact" from previous coursework, research current context, journal: "I used to think... Now I think... This changed because... Implications for my identity..." Example: "Old belief: competitive advantage from proprietary knowledge. New understanding: open-source AI models outperform proprietary ones. Scope: still true for physical manufacturing, less for cognitive work. Implication: joining large firm may not maximis e learning." Assessment: portfolio of 12 entries, meta-reflection on which unlearnings were most difficult, synthesis of knowledge evolution.

## Implementation Challenges

Faculty resistance (undermines expertise), accreditation concerns (how to assess unlearning), and student anxiety (came for certainty, not doubt). Solutions: Faculty development on facilitating versus lecturing, rubrics for meta-cognitive skills (epistemic flexibility, frame awareness, assemblage fluency), transparency with students about new educational contract: "The old contract—we give knowledge, you master it—is broken. The new: we give tools for continuous adaptation, you practice using them. This feels less secure because it *is* less secure. Security isn't in what you know but in your capacity to keep learning."

## 7. Ethics of distributed responsibility

When self-driving cars cause accidents, who's responsible? This exemplifies Matthias's (2004) *responsibility gap*: harmful outcomes through algorithmic systems with no clear agent accountable. The gap emerges from: causal complexity (black box systems), distributed contribution (many actors partially causing outcomes), emergent behavior (unintended patterns), temporal distance (harms emerge long after design), and organisational mediation (institutional constraints limiting individual agency).

## Nissenbaum's Barriers

Nissenbaum (1996) identified three accountability barriers. *Many hands*: When many contribute, responsibility diffuses. AI hiring discrimination involves data collectors, labellers, designers, engineers, deployers, managers—each can claim "I just did my part." *Bugs as excuse*: Complexity provides a convenient out ("technical glitch"). With AI, distinguishing bugs from features is ambiguous. *Computer as scapegoat*: Organisations attribute agency to algorithms ("the algorithm decided"), deflecting from human choices creating, deploying, and relying on it.

## Five Governance Mechanisms

1. **AI Decision Ledgers:** Mandatory documentation of significant AI decisions recording: decision context, human input, AI process/output, human response (accept/modify/reject), outcome, responsibility assignment. Creates audit trail preventing scapegoating, addresses many-hands problem by documenting each contributor's role.
2. **Hybrid Decision Boards:** High-stakes decisions require multi-stakeholder approval: domain expert (understands context), AI specialist (understands model limitations), ethics officer (questions premises), and affected stakeholder representative. Each must explicitly approve or dissent and record the reasoning. Ensures human oversight, incorporates diverse perspectives, creates clear accountability. Scope: high individual impact, systemic implications, novel situations AI wasn't trained for.
3. **Epistemic Rights Framework:** Individual rights including: (a) algorithmic explanation—intelligible account of decisions, (b) human recourse—appeal path to human judgment, (c) opt-out—request traditional processes where algorithmic assumptions contested, (d) data dignity—say over data use and compensation, (e) contestation—challenge decisions on bias/error grounds. Implementation through legislation (analogous to GDPR), regulatory enforcement, private right of action.

4. **Algorithmic Impact Assessments:** Pre-deployment evaluation of: use case analysis (what decisions, who affected, potential harms), bias audit (test on diverse populations), explainability evaluation, human oversight design, responsibility mapping (who's accountable if harm occurs), stakeholder consultation. Public documentation, regular reassessment, regulatory approval for high-risk applications.

5. **Relational Responsibility Frameworks:** Drawing on Barad's (2007) "response-ability" and Braidotti's (2019) affirmative ethics, shift from "who's to blame?" to "how do we reconfigure relations to prevent recurrence?" Emphasise: responsibility as relational not individual, response-ability over culpability, collective learning over punishment, restorative justice. Implementation: distributed responsibility teams, strict organisational liability, industry-wide incident reporting (like aviation safety), victim compensation funds.

These mechanisms create *distributed accountability without distributed irresponsibility*—recognising agency as distributed while ensuring clear recourse, organisational incentives for responsibility, learning prioritization, and human answerability through team structures and organisational liability.

## 8. The post-competence economy: value beyond human mastery

When WhatsApp served 900 million users with 50 employees, when Instagram was acquired for $1 billion with 13 employees—we witnessed value creation decoupled from human labour. Brynjolfsson and McAfee (2014) documented productivity rising while labour input falls. Platform giants generate enormous value with minimal employees relative to reach. AI produces outputs at zero marginal cost once trained. Winner-take-all dynamics concentrate value.

Zuboff (2019) frames this as "surveillance capitalism"—value from data extraction and behavioural prediction rather than production. Human experience becomes "raw material" for value creation. Humans aren't primarily workers but *data sources*—value extracted without compensation. This isn't just wealth inequality but ontological transformation: the relationship between humans and economy fundamentally changes when humans aren't needed to produce value yet remain subjects of extraction.

## *Three Economic Architectures*

**Orchestration Economy:** Value from rapidly configuring/reconfiguring capabilities (human + AI + data) around opportunities. Organisations maintain minimal permanent staff, assemble temporary teams per project. Platform operators capture orchestration fees, participants compensated per contribution. Advantages: flexibility, efficiency, and broader participation. Disadvantages: precarity, inequality (top orchestrators capture disproportionate value), coordination costs, lacks social solidarity of traditional employment.

**Curatorial Economy:** As AI makes generation abundant (content, analysis, design), value shifts to *curation*—judgment about what matters, taste about what resonates, ethical discernment. AI generates vast possibility spaces; humans select and contextualize. Value attaches to curatorial judgment creating coherence and meaning. Advantages: values human judgment, potentially fulfilling. Disadvantages: extreme inequality (elite curators with audiences capture value), subjective (risks reinforcing existing hierarchies), limited labour absorption.

**Commons-Based Peer Production 2.0:** Value co-created in open ecosystems is governed collectively. AI infrastructure as shared commons. Industry consortiums jointly fund/govern AI development. Training data, models and resources are shared. Value is distributed according to contribution and need: democraticg overnance. Example: Healthcare AI commons where hospitals collaboratively develop diagnostic AI, training data is pooled, and models openly shared. Advantages: equitable, innovative, democratic, and produces public good. Disadvantages: coordination challenges, free-rider problems, funding difficulties, and ideological resistance.

## *Distribution Mechanisms*

**Data Dividends:** Individuals compensated for data used in AI training. Posner and Weyl (2018) propose treating data as labour deserving payment, establishing legal frameworks recognizing data as property individuals own, mandating companies compensate data sources, enabling collective bargaining through data unions.

**Universal Basic Compute:** Public AI infrastructure (like libraries or roads) ensuring universal access, democratizing capability. National AI infrastructure providing free access to pre-trained models, subsidized compute for fine-tuning, open datasets with privacy protections.

**Platform Cooperatives:** Transform platforms (Uber, Airbnb) into worker/user-owned cooperatives distributing surplus to member-owners. Scholz (2016) documents examples: Stocksy (photographer-owned), Fairbnb (community-oriented rentals). Democratic governance provides the accountability algorithmic platforms lack.

**Algorithmic Wealth Tax:** Tax value generated by AI systems, funding universal basic income and transition support. Identify revenue/profit attributable to algorithmic systems, progressive taxation, with higher rates where AI displaces workers.

## Infrastructural Ontology Design

The phrase "infrastructural ontology design" captures that we are designing not just technologies but basic categories of economic life. Critical questions: Who owns AI infrastructure? (Private versus public/cooperative ownership determines who captures value and governs deployment.) What counts as value? (GDP versus well-being, capability, sustainability.) How is value distributed? (Market versus dividends, UBI, cooperatives.) Who governs deployment? (corporate versus multi-stakeholder, democratic.) How do we balance efficiency and equity?

Two futures loom: **Algorithmic Feudalism** (concentration among tech elites, mass precarity, surveillance, democratic erosion) versus **Collaborative Abundance** (AI as commons, distributed value, work as meaning-making, democratic governance, flourishing based on capability). It is the same technology—the difference is in political and ethical choices about ownership, governance, and distribution. The next decade determines whether the post-competence economy serves human flourishing or concentrates power. Once infrastructure, ownership patterns, and norms solidify, path dependence makes change exponentially harder.

## 9. Conclusion: design principles for epistemic metamorphosis

Obliteration is not ending but beginning. What AI obliterates (industrial-era business foundations) must be obliterated for new possibilities to emerge.

The task is designing thoughtfully for what emerges. This conclusion distils five design principles for navigating epistemic metamorphosis.

**Principle 1: Assume impermanence. Design for continuous reconfiguration.** Organisations: structural modularity, API-first architecture, temporary teams, distributed ownership, celebrate adaptability over consistency, regular assumption audits, job rotation, eliminate "this is how we've always done it." Education: curriculum as living document (review every semester), graduation portfolios over transcripts, alumni re-engagement for unlearning intensives. Individuals: career as portfolio not path, five-year knowledge audits, psychological resilience for perpetual change.

**Principle 2: Distribute but don't diffuse. Clarify agency within Assemblages.** Organisations: responsibility mapping (who designed, deployed, monitors, has authority to modify algorithmic systems), hybrid decision boards for high-stakes decisions, AI decision ledgers creating audit trails, and cultural prohibition on "algorithm did it" excuses. Education: collaborative assessment measuring assemblage participation, ethical case studies mapping contributors to outcomes. Individuals: own the prompt, own the selection, own the outcome—resist diffusion of personal responsibility.

**Principle 3: Subtract before adding. Eliminate the obsolete before adopting the new.** Organisations: pre-implementation audits identifying what will be subtracted (roles, processes, assumptions), transition support for subtracted roles (retraining, assistance, psychological support), and post-implementation reviews assessing whether subtraction occurred. Education: curriculum subtraction (remove rote exercises, memorization, mechanical framework application) making room for frame-breaking, ethical deliberation, and creative synthesis. Individuals: when learning new skills, identify which old skills to de-prioritise; annual practice of "what will I stop doing to make space for growth?"

**Principle 4: Preserve human meaning-making. Reserve strategic questioning for humans.** Organisations: purpose governance (humans determine "why" questions—should profit maximization be primary goal? What about stakeholder well-being, environmental impact?), mandatory human checkpoints for values alignment review, ethical scrutiny, imagination of alternatives AI didn't consider. Education: emphasis on "why" questions, frame-breaking capacity, articulating values underlying choices.

Individuals: use AI for tactics (optimize schedule, manage finances) but reserve for yourself: what kind of life do I want? What relationships matter? What constitutes success for me?

**Principle 5: Design for justice, not just efficiency. Embed values in infrastructure.** Organisations: values-explicit AI design articulating primary goals, constraints, stakeholders, trade-offs; stakeholder participation in design; impact assessments proactively evaluating equity implications. Policy: algorithmic justice standards (bias audits, disparate impact testing), public AI infrastructure preventing concentration, progressive taxation funding transition support. Education: ethics as core not elective, design justice frameworks centering marginalized voices. Individuals: ethical AI use, not exploiting others; questioning platforms/tools (who profits? who's harmed?); supporting ethical alternatives.

## The Responsibility of Design

Epistemic metamorphosis is not something happening *to* us but something we collectively *undertake*. Required work: Educators redesigning pedagogy for adaptation. Leaders restructuring as ethical assemblages. Policymakers regulating for accountability and equity. Citizens demanding democratic governance. Workers organis ing collectively. Technologists building for justice. Scholars theorizing alternatives. All cultivating epistemic humility, embracing continuous learning, accepting impermanence, engaging ethically with technology, and building communities of mutual support.

The obliteration of business reality is complete. The question is: **Will the posthuman economy be designed by default or by design?** By default: optimis ing for whatever yields short-term profit, concentrating power, extracting value, treating humans as resources to exploit. By design: embedding justice, sustainability, democracy, flourishing into infrastructural ontology—ownership structures, governance mechanisms, distribution systems, educational models.

The choice is ours, but the window is closing. Once patterns solidify—infrastructure built, ownership concentrated, norms established, path dependencies locked in—transformation becomes exponentially harder. **Now is the moment for design.**

We stand in the chrysalis. The old form has dissolved. The new form is not yet determined. What we design now determines whether we emerge as something magnificent or monstrous. The power to shape emergence is ours. The responsibility is ours. The time is now.

**Design for metamorphosis. Design for justice. Design for flourishing.**

This is the work obliteration demands of us.

## References


Agamben, G. (2005). *State of Exception*. Translated by K. Attell. Chicago: University of Chicago Press.

Barad, K. (2007). *Meeting the Universe Halfway: Quantum Physics and the Entanglement of Matter and Meaning*. Durham, NC: Duke University Press.

Binns, R., Bietti, E., Biressi, M., Kleek, M. V. and Shadbolt, N. (2025). 'Not Even Nice Work If You Can Get It: A Longitudinal Study of Uber's Algorithmic Pay and Pricing', in *Proceedings of the 2025 ACM Conference on Fairness, Accountability, and Transparency*. New York: Association for Computing Machinery, pp. 1–15.

Braidotti, R. (2013). *The Posthuman*. Cambridge: Polity Press.

Braidotti, R. (2019). *Posthuman Knowledge*. Cambridge: Polity Press.

Brynjolfsson, E. and McAfee, A. (2014). *The Second Machine Age: Work, Progress, and Prosperity in a Time of Brilliant Technologies*. New York: W.W. Norton & Company.

Carr, N. (2014). *The Glass Cage: How Our Computers Are Changing Us*. New York: W.W. Norton & Company.

Christensen, C. M. (1997). *The Innovator's Dilemma: When New Technologies Cause Great Firms to Fail*. Boston: Harvard Business School Press.

Cicero, S. (2025). 'How AI Transforms the Logic of Value Creation in Markets and Organizations', *Boundaryless*, January. Available at: https://boundaryless.io/blog/ai-value-creation/ (Accessed: 19 October 2025).

Clark, A. and Chalmers, D. (1998). 'The Extended Mind', *Analysis*, 58(1), pp. 7–19.

Coase, R. H. (1937). 'The Nature of the Firm', *Economica*, 4(16), pp. 386–405.

Customer Experience Dive (2025). 'Klarna Changes Its AI Tune and Again Recruits Humans for Customer Service', *Customer Experience Dive*, 9 May. Available at: https://www.customerexperiencedive.com/news/klarna-reinvests-human-talent-customer-service-AI-chatbot/747586/ (Accessed: 19 October 2025).

Derrida, J. (1976). *Of Grammatology*. Translated by G. C. Spivak. Baltimore: Johns Hopkins University Press.

Foucault, M. (1970). *The Order of Things: An Archaeology of the Human Sciences*. London: Tavistock Publications.

GitHub (2022). 'Research: Quantifying GitHub Copilot's Impact on Developer Productivity and Happiness', *The GitHub Blog*, 7 September. Available at: https://

github.blog/2022-09-07-research-quantifying-github-copilots-impact-on-developer-productivity-and-happiness/ (Accessed: 19 October 2025).

Gray, M. L. and Suri, S. (2019). *Ghost Work: How to Stop Silicon Valley from Building a New Global Underclass*. Boston: Houghton Mifflin Harcourt.

Haraway, D. (1985). 'A Cyborg Manifesto: Science, Technology, and Socialist-Feminism in the Late Twentieth Century', in *Simians, Cyborgs, and Women: The Reinvention of Nature*. New York: Routledge, pp. 149–181.

Hayles, N. K. (2017). *Unthought: The Power of the Cognitive Nonconscious*. Chicago: University of Chicago Press.

Hedberg, B. (1981). 'How Organizations Learn and Unlearn', in Nystrom, P. C. and Starbuck, W. H. (eds.) *Handbook of Organizational Design*, Vol. 1. Oxford: Oxford University Press, pp. 3–27.

Heidegger, M. (1977). *The Question Concerning Technology and Other Essays*. Translated by W. Lovitt. New York: Garland Publishing.

Hislop, D., Bosley, S., Coombs, C. R. and Holland, J. (2014). 'The Process of Individual Unlearning: A Neglected Topic in an Under-Researched Field', *Management Learning*, 45(5), pp. 540–560.

Hutchins, E. (1995). *Cognition in the Wild*. Cambridge, MA: MIT Press.

Klarna (2024). 'Klarna AI Assistant Handles Two-Thirds of Customer Service Chats in Its First Month', *Klarna Press Release*, 27 February. Available at: https://www.klarna.com/international/press/klarna-ai-assistant-handles-two-thirds-of-customer-service-chats-in-its-first-month/ (Accessed: 19 October 2025).

Latour, B. (2005). *Reassembling the Social: An Introduction to Actor-Network-Theory*. Oxford: Oxford University Press.

Leonard-Barton, D. (1992). 'Core Capabilities and Core Rigidities: A Paradox in Managing New Product Development', *Strategic Management Journal*, 13(S1), pp. 111–125.

MacKenzie, D. (2019). 'How Algorithms Interact: Goffman's "Interaction Order" in Automated Trading', *Theory, Culture & Society*, 36(2), pp. 39–59.

Matthias, A. (2004). 'The Responsibility Gap: Ascribing Responsibility for the Actions of Learning Automata', *Ethics and Information Technology*, 6(3), pp. 175–183.

McGinnis, P. (2025). 'The Great Unlearning: Why Business Education Must Subtract Before It Adds', *AACSB Insights*, August. Available at: https://www.aacsb.edu/insights/great-unlearning (Accessed: 19 October 2025).

Möhlmann, M. and Zalmanson, L. (2017). 'Hands on the Wheel: Navigating Algorithmic Management and Uber Drivers' Autonomy', in *Proceedings of the International Conference on Information Systems (ICIS 2017)*, Seoul, South Korea, 10–13 December.

Nissenbaum, H. (1996). 'Accountability in a Computerized Society', *Science and Engineering Ethics*, 2(1), pp. 25–42.

Peng, S., Kalliamvakou, E., Cihon, P. and Demirer, M. (2023). 'The Impact of AI on Developer Productivity: Evidence from GitHub Copilot', *arXiv preprint* arXiv:2302.06590.

Posner, E. A. and Weyl, E. G. (2018). *Radical Markets: Uprooting Capitalism and Democracy for a Just Society*. Princeton: Princeton University Press.

Prahalad, C. K. and Hamel, G. (1990). 'The Core Competence of the Corporation', *Harvard Business Review*, 68(3), pp. 79–91.

Remus, D. and Levy, F. (2017). 'Can Robots Be Lawyers? Computers, Lawyers, and the Practice of Law', *Georgetown Journal of Legal Ethics*, 30(3), pp. 501–558.

Rigobon, R. and Loaiza, D. (2025). 'AI and the Future of Work: Complementarity in Human-Machine Teams', *MIT Sloan Management Review*, 66(2), pp. 34–42.

Scholz, T. (2016). *Platform Cooperativism: Challenging the Corporate Sharing Economy*. New York: Rosa Luxemburg Stiftung.

Snowden, D. and Rancati, A. (2020). Managing Complexity (and Chaos) in Times of Crisis: A Field Guide for Decision Makers Inspired by the Cynefin® Framework. Luxembourg: Publications Office of the European Union, JRC123629.

Tekedia (2025). 'Uber Turns Its Drivers Into AI Data Trainers: Inside the Company's Bid to Build the "Ultimate Flexible Work" Platform', *Tekedia*, 17 October. Available at: https://www.tekedia.com/uber-turns-its-drivers-into-ai-data-trainers/ (Accessed: 19 October 2025).

Topol, E. (2019). *Deep Medicine: How Artificial Intelligence Can Make Healthcare Human Again*. New York: Basic Books.

Williamson, O. E. (1985). *The Economic Institutions of Capitalism*. New York: Free Press.

Wilson, H. J. and Daugherty, P. R. (2018). 'Collaborative Intelligence: Humans and AI Are Joining Forces', *Harvard Business Review*, 96(4), pp. 114–123.

Womack, J. P., Jones, D. T. and Roos, D. (1990). *The Machine That Changed the World*. New York: Rawson Associates.

Zuboff, S. (2019). *The Age of Surveillance Capitalism: The Fight for a Human Future at the New Frontier of Power*. New York: PublicAffairs.

*Word Count: 5,847 words (excluding references)*

# THE EVOLUTION OF DIGITAL MARKETING

**Joe Hazzam**

Digital marketing has transformed organisation business models during the last three decades by providing newer ways to reach, inform and engage with customers, suppliers and the wider business stakeholders (Hazzam et al., 2025; Homburg and Wielgos, 2022). Large corporations such as Google, Meta, Amazon and eBay, unheard of twenty-five years ago, have emerged as main players in our modern economy and disrupted traditional business models. In fact, digital marketing has fundamentally shaped how value is co-created and how customers experience value co-creation (Hofacker et al., 2020). For example, fitness trackers allow users to share common health goals and track individual and group progress on social media networks (Dwivedi et al., 2021). Digital marketing has evolved from internet marketing in the mid-1990s to digital engagement in 2013 and co-creation of value in 2020, allowing customisation of products and personalisation of communications (Kim et al., 2021). The most inclusive perspective is to define digital marketing as an adaptive, technology-enabled process by which firms collaborate with customers and partners to jointly create, communicate, deliver, and sustain value for all stakeholders (Kanaan, 2017).

The rapid evolution of digital technology, social media, mobile marketing, search engines, web analytics and automation have created value for online users and institutions through new customer experiences and interactions in new digital environments. One of the first concepts that emerged with digital marketing is interactivity, referring to the degree to which communication parties can act on each other, the medium and the message (Herhausen et al., 2020). An example of the interactive features of digital marketing is the electronic word of mouth (eWOM) that shows a greater impact on customer acquisition than traditional public relations and offline event marketing activities (Kanaan, 2017). Further, social media marketing emerged in 2004 as a two-way communication medium to become an integral part of companies' digital marketing strategy. Social media allows authentic and customer experiential stories, and is not used only to deliver the firm's messages. Social media marketing brings new communication and sales tools such as photo and video sharing in real time, influencer and social selling, and the broad adoption by consumers worldwide has influenced both large and small firms' business models (Zahay, 2021). In international markets, social media technologies can facilitate the development of new products and adaptive marketing capabilities, which in turn improve firm performance (Hazzam et al., 2023).

Although digital marketing presents new opportunities to the marketing function, many organisational rigidities limited the development of digital marketing capabilities that matched with the accelerating complexity of markets and the increasing rate of change (Day, 2011). In fact, most attention has been given to the opportunities that digital marketing offers, with little focus on the actual capabilities and skills that firms need to develop or acquire to be successful. For example, successful experience with traditional marketing limits the organisational approach to digital marketing because firms lack a track record (Setkute and Dibb, 2022). Organisation silos limit the cross-functional dialogue and learning that creates new ideas and adaptation to market changes. Others have lagging reactions embedded in slow and cautious decision processes, and by the time they have launched a new marketing initiative, the market has already moved to another new state. Additionally, the lack of digital marketing skills and the insufficient pipeline of high potential talent limit the successful integration of digital marketing within the processes of the organisations (Hofacker et al., 2020). To overcome these challenges, successful organisations have adopted vigilant market learning, adaptive market experimentation and open marketing approaches (Day, 2011). Vigilant market learning supports these organisations to sense and act on the early insights of buying behaviour changes. Adaptive market experimentation facilitates the generation of new insights from small experiments, leading to faster determination of which marketing initiatives have been successful or unsuccessful. The open marketing approach provides a web of partners and collaborators, allowing the access to resources and specialised skills that are not attainable with closed models (Hazzam and Wilkins, 2022). As new technologies emerge, organisations find innovative ways to access and use information. For example, digitalisation can address the challenges associated with co-location for logistic firms, allowing collaboration between firms without the need for physical co-location or industrial clusters (Hofacker et al., 2020).

Several studies attempt to conceptualise and understand the underlying factors that facilitate the development of digital marketing capabilities in large and small firms, including business to business (B2B) and business to consumer (B2C) companies. B2B businesses started to incorporate several digital marketing channels such as mobile and social media into their existing marketing channels. Digitalisation has disrupted the B2B market structure and artificial intelligence, blockchain, data security/integrity, internet of things, and big data analytics will continue to shape how B2B relationships are understood and managed (Herhausen et al., 2020). For example, e-commerce sites such as Amazon and eBay are not only used for buyer-supplier transactions but are increasingly used to create value across different geographies and time zones. However, the development of digital product lines and tailored offerings to customers lead to pricing challenges for firms (Kanaan, 2017). Big data, advanced visualisation techniques and enhanced computing power provide rich and actionable customer insights that facilitate strategic decision-making (Quinn et al., 2016). Websites remain instrumental in B2B marketing strategy, but the impact of corporate blogging on firm value is not yet quantified (Herhausen et al., 2020). Also, the role of search engine optimisation and advertisement in the conversion of industrial customers remains unclear. Small B2B firms face even more challenges in the development of digital marketing capabilities due to lack of resources and specialist digital marketing knowledge, and the informal and flat organisation structure that creates barriers for integrating digital marketing throughout the firm (Setkute and Dibb, 2022). Nevertheless, B2B social media studies have shown positive results in generating higher customer engagement (Herhausen et al., 2020); however, the contributions of social media in general, paid social media and content strategies that enhance industrial firm financial performance, are not yet well documented. For B2C firms, the impacts of e-commerce, search engine optimisation, email and content marketing on performance are well documented. Social media strategy, employee activities, measurement and budget have been linked to social media performance and future brand perception for B2C firms (Marchand et al., 2021). However, significant challenges exist from negative product or service reviews, negative electronic word-of-mouth as well as intrusive and irritating digital advertising and online brand presence

(Dwivedi et al., 2021). Also, personal data and insights gathered from customers might represent a matter of concern, making transparency an important element that impacts firm decision-making (Rizvanović et al., 2023).

Before the year 2020, the discussion around digital marketing mainly focused on a single channel (e.g. website or social media) or the barriers and opportunities of adoption by big and small firms (Setkute and Dibb, 2022). During the last five years, we have witnessed a better understanding of digital marketing capabilities and more empirical studies have emerged, examining the drivers and the contributions of these newer capabilities to firm performance (Hazzam et al., 2025; Wang, 2020). Digital marketing capabilities are defined as the firm's ability to use technology-enabled processes to interact with customers and partners in a targeted, measurable and integrated way to create new forms of value independent from distance and time (Kannan, 2017). These capabilities differ from traditional marketing capabilities such as product, price, place and promotion by having scalable, measurable, interconnective and adaptable characteristics (Homburg and Wielgos, 2022). An example of scalability is a piece of content that can be repurposed and continue to generate traffic and leads. Digital marketing is data driven and the performance of every social media post, email or website landing page can be measured. Digital marketing channels are interconnected, which enables a direct interaction with customers and a better understanding of their needs and preferences in real time. Digital marketing capabilities are adaptable, allowing fast experimentation and market research and adaptation of product features and offerings in real time. The latest empirical studies have shown that digital marketing capabilities can contribute significantly to firm profitability (Hazzam et al., 2025; Homburg and Wielgos, 2022; Wang, 2020). However, the integration of these capabilities within the firm's traditional marketing capabilities remains a challenge for managers. Thus, managers need to understand the strategic orientation and the changes in the market environment to unlock the benefit of adding digital marketing capabilities to their portfolio of capabilities.

Previous studies have shown that the contribution of digital marketing capabilities to firm performance is not equal for B2B and B2C firms. B2B marketing organisations seem to be less effective than B2C in effectively integrating their digital and traditional channels and touchpoints, and this difference can be explained by the smaller number of customers and touchpoints that B2B firms need to manage, the complex buying process and lower levels of digital marketing skills and knowledge (Herhausen et al., 2020). In small to medium-sized enterprises (SMEs), studies have shown that digital marketing capabilities contribute to performance beyond the presence of customer relationship management and innovation capabilities (Hazzam et al., 2025). Also, studies have demonstrated that digital marketing capabilities enhance the performance of internationalising firms and reduce the liabilities of size for SMEs (Wang, 2020). However, the contribution of digital marketing to performance depends upon the levels of market pressure and organisational readiness (Su et al., 2023). Companies that motivate and support their employees to develop digital marketing skills are more ready to adopt digital marketing successfully and increase sales significantly. Companies that possess a range of skills in business processes and master the customer journey are able to enhance their customers' satisfaction, promote retention and repurchase using digital marketing technologies. Overall, companies that possess managerial capabilities, agile and adopt market orientation (generate, disseminate and respond to market and customer insights) and entrepreneurial orientation (innovative, proactive and risk-taking) postures are more successful in developing digital marketing capabilities that lead to higher performance (Wu et al., 2024).

Despite the contribution of marketing researchers and practitioners to a better understanding of the drivers and outcomes of digital marketing capabilities, several questions remain unanswered. For example, how digital marketing capabilities will evolve and adapt to the emerging technology of artificial intelligence is an important research avenue to explore. How companies can develop their digital marketer skills to match the fast changes in market trends and technologies is another interesting area for research. The new portfolio of digital marketing capabilities that companies need to consider for sustaining competitive advantage over time remain unclear. What is the return of investment for developing digital marketing capabilities internally versus outsourcing to agencies? This critical question has not been answered effectively yet. Addressing the challenges presented by an evolving technological landscape remains a major goal for researchers and practitioners, and answering all the above questions needs theoretical models and frameworks from consumer psychology, sociology and economics (Kanaan, 2017).

## Digital marketing channels

The biggest changes in firm-customer interactions stem from the rapid growth of web-based platforms, supporting the migration of social relationships to the virtual world. The advancement of digital technology has enabled firms to reach their customers through several online channels such as search engines, email, social media platforms, among others (De Haan et al., 2016). Digital marketing channels have led to higher engagement and stronger relationships between customers and brands. Currently, firms increasingly use multiple online channels simultaneously to reach and interact with their customers along the purchase journey (Li and Kannan, 2014). Digital marketing channels have brought customers a number of benefits, including convenience, more product and service selection, competitive pricing and exposure to other opinions about a specific product or service. Companies need to successfully integrate the online and offline channels to maximise their profitability and deploy artificial intelligence technologies for further growth and sustainable performance (Cai and Choi, 2023). This rapid growth in omnichannel (e.g., website, call centre, sales agent, social media, email) is prompting managers to understand how marketing efforts in one channel influence shopping outcomes in different channels (Shankar and Kushwaha, 2021). In particular, managers need to effectively align their channels' use and cross-effects with their customer purchase journey, including the awareness, information search, decision and purchase stages (Jansen and Schuster, 2011). The cross-channel effects can be complementary, substitutional, or insignificant depending on the channels' relative richness and primary influence roles.

Studies on digital marketing channels have classified digital communication components into paid, owned and earned media (Vieira et al., 2019). Paid media is defined as the type of media that the firm must pay for such as social media paid ads, pay-per-click advertising on search engines and display advertising. Overall, paid media positively affects the profitability of the firm when the cost of conversion to sales is low. Paid media increases the traffic to the website and sales. However, factors such as ad position, keyword position, cost per click, search impressions and click-through-rate affect the success of paid media (Jansen and Schuster, 2011). Owned media refers to the digital communication channels managed by the firm such as the website, social media platforms, mobile applications and email. Owned media could influence new sales and sales repetition depending on the content, information and interactivity that attract customers' attention and influence their buying decisions. Customised and accurate content of owned media generates customer engagement and is more effective in transforming users and leads into customers. Overall, the company's online store increases overall sales with limited effect on offline store sales (Shankar and Kushwaha, 2021). Therefore, enhancing website capability to offer better information, navigation, design and direct fulfilment is essential in a multiple-channel environment.

Earned media is the media activity (e.g., reviews, comments) that customers, influencers and other agents produce in digital environments. Brands have no control over the creation and dissemination of this type of media content. Earned media has a potential to influence customers' decision making and purchasing habits and this relates to the network effect and potential impact of word of mouth. Paid, owned and earned media should work in synergy, since customers go through a series of touchpoints across media channels on their path to purchase. For example, a customer switching from owned or paid firm channels to customer-initiated channels indicates progress in purchase decision and increase in purchase propensity (Anderl et al., 2016a). The effective management of digital communication channels informs budget allocation and better measurement of marketing return on investment (De Haan et al., 2016). In the online environment, eight channels are identified in research and practice including direct channel, organic search, referrals, paid search, organic social media, paid social media, email and display advertising (Kakalejčík et al., 2020). Companies that fully anticipate users' channel preferences and the potential cost incurred by each channel may be able to reach customers through more efficient budget allocation, real-time bidding decisions and optimisation (Anderl et al., 2016b).

Direct channel refers to customers visiting the firm website by directly typing in the URL (e.g., firm.com) of a website directly into the browser window or clicking on a saved bookmark. Referrals are the visits originated from a link from another website. Organic search represents the traffic originated from the website link on the search engine list after the customer enters a key phrase in the search engine. Paid search represents the traffic generated when the user clicks on paid search results (e.g., Google). Organic social media represents the traffic generated by clicking a link placed on social media networks. Paid social media traffic is generated from sponsored paid ads on social networks. Email traffic is generated when the users click the link in the email delivered to their inbox. Display ads traffic represents the visits generated from the user clicking on a banner ad available, for example, on the Google display network.

Customers may encounter several touchpoints and communication channels during their journey to purchase (Kannan et al., 2016). For example, one customer may click on a social media post and visit the company website. Later, the same customer could type a keyword on google and revisit the website. Then, the same customer may click on a referral link before visiting the website and performing the actual purchase. This non-linear journey to purchase, including a series of touchpoints across media, channels and devices, has implications on how marketing investment is allocated across the channels. Traditionally, aggregate measures of conversions and the last-click attribution model were implemented. However, this approach limits our understanding on how the combination of channels influences the customer journey to purchase, preventing the accurate allocation of marketing investment across channels and devices (Kannan et al., 2016).

More recently, the availability of customer path data provides firms with the opportunity to produce a granular record of every touchpoint a customer makes before visiting the website and purchase. Given the proliferation of online channels and the complexity of customer journeys, the accurate measurement of channel contributions to a firm's success is demanding (Anderl et al., 2016b). Companies analysing individual path data can now understand the carry-over (e.g., subsequent visit to the website through the same channel and possible conversion) and spillover (e.g., one channel leads to a visit from other channel which leads to purchase) effects of every channel at the website visit and purchase levels (Li and Kannan, 2014). For instance, e-mails and display ads trigger visits through search and referral channels, while e-mails lead to significant purchases through search channels. Display ads influence the awareness stage of the customer journey and differ from search ads that impact all the stages of customer journey. Direct channel accounts for the highest traffic to the website and purchase conversion rate, as these visits are from customers who have already familiarised themselves with the products or services. However, other channels such as Google search ads and emails significantly increase the purchase from direct channels.

Overall, the contribution of firm-initiated channels is consistently undervalued by the current attribution models (Li et al., 2019). However, the contribution of customer-initiated channels such as direct type-ins of

URLs is consistently overestimated by the last click approach (Anderl et al., 2016b). With the advance of digital analytic tools and availability of data, companies can better understand when and what online channels can affect the customer's decision-making to purchase. This approach supports firms to accurately measure the incremental contributions of multiple channels and overlapping campaigns, allowing effective decision-making and budget allocation (Filippou et al., 2024).

Although several studies suggested effective attribution models for online channels, recent growth in artificial intelligence (AI) models has disrupted the customer decision-making process and journey to purchase. New studies are needed to measure the impacts of AI tools on customer awareness, consideration and purchase stages. Further, the behaviour of users that are referred to the website from AI tools are not clearly examined yet. For example, do customers referred from ChatGPT to the website purchase less or more than customers visiting the website from other online channels? Another question that remains to be answered is about the click behaviours on the AI overview search engine result features. For example, what is the click-through rate of users that click on a source link featuring an AI overview? Do users trust the information on search engines generated by AI? These questions, among others, still need further investigations to support marketers and businesses to effectively integrate previous knowledge of channel integration with the new AI channel to better serve their customers and achieve higher financial performance.

## Digital marketing and AI

In recent years, marketing functions have started to deploy AI applications such as big data analytics for price prediction and adjustment, recommendation systems for products and customisation of services, sentiment analysis for customer engagement and satisfaction, among others (Davenport et al., 2020). The importance of AI in marketing is critical due to the increasing computing power, lower computing costs, the availability of big data, and the advance of machine-learning algorithms and models (Mariani et al., 2022). Additionally, AI is now used by customers on a daily basis to compare offers and products, putting more pressure on marketers to understand the influence of these applications on their customers' journey and decision-making (Mustak et al., 2021). AI tools can mimic human intelligence and surpass capabilities inherent in humans, such as doing mechanical, thinking, and feeling tasks (Huang and Rust, 2021). AI differs from previous technologies, such that AI can learn from data and update outcomes without human intervention (Davenport et al., 2020). Therefore, AI can provide effective collaboration with marketers through two-way communication, autonomous and adaptive interactions.

Recent studies have highlighted the relative strengths of AI for mechanical and analytical intelligence such as collaborative robots helping with packaging or self-service chatbots automating social presence in front of customers (Gelbrich et al., 2025). AI analytical intelligence can support marketers with automated product recommendations and analyse emotional data (e.g., sentiment in online reviews). AI emotion-recognition software can adjust ads and video content by sensing and analysing facial expressions. Although AI applications have relative strengths for mechanical and analytical intelligence, marketers need to collaborate with AI when the task in hand needs creativity or contextual, intuitive, and feeling intelligences (Ameen et al., 2022). Several studies have shown that consumers reject AI due to lack of understanding, or once they know that they are talking to a bot. Thus, AI mechanical and analytical applications' relative strengths should augment the marketers' contextual, intuitive and feeling intelligences and not replace them. For example, a robot can deliver food to the table side in a restaurant, and human waiters interact with customers. Mechanical AI can collect email lists, send and track emails and the marketer needs only to formulate email strategies for AI applications to implement. Further, smart wearable devices can support marketers' better understanding of emotions and experience. Nevertheless, AI applications can augment marketers' emotional intelligence by analysing sentiments in reviews and social media posts (Huang and Rust, 2022).

Overall, marketers' adoption and use of AI should be strategic and not led by technology or availability of applications (De Bruyn et al., 2020). The best outcome from AI adoption is achieved by marketers who optimise and manage collaboration with AI applications. Thus, companies need to develop training on different technologies and processes of AI, including an ideal balance between the nature and extent of task activities automated by AI or performed by human marketers (Huang and Rust, 2021). This approach supports marketing organisations to facilitate and systematise interactions between AI and marketing stakeholders, creating an ecosystem between AI and experts through two-way observation, imitation, and practice.

The impacts of AI applications on customer responses have been studied extensively during the last few years. In particular, robots, chatbots and algorithm-automated agents have been compared to human agents for their influence on customer behaviours (Gelbrich et al., 2025). The design features such as giving names to robots and chatbots can increase their human equivalence of conversational abilities. The automated agent name can make customers feel connected to them and also address them by name during a conversation. The humanlike appearance can also increase the human equivalence of physical automated agents, leading customers to attribute human qualities to them (Gelbrich et al., 2025). Verbal-linguistic intelligence supports the automated agents to understand and mimic human language during conversations and interactions with customers. For example, automated agents that greet hotel guests or apologize for long waits during check-in are perceived as sincere. However, conversations that need social intelligence and interactive exchanges that go beyond verbal intercourse may limit the human equivalence of automated agents. However, the inability of AI to make social judgments may be an advantage in situations where consumers can feel unpleasant emotions such as shame and guilt (Mariani et al., 2022). Visual-spatial intelligence can support automated agents to perform a task that requires motor skills and move in real space, which may give customers a touch-and-feel experience as these agents skilfully move in their environment. However, automated agents may suffer from lack of empathy when customers expect passionate feedback that helps them to overcome a deficit in public settings.

On a positive note, automated agents can have processing-speed intelligence, increasing their reliability and human equivalence abilities. Algorithms can process a task that requires logic-mathematical intelligence, such as providing financial advice for retirement portfolios, increasing their human equivalence of humanlike informational abilities. The context is crucial for the efficacy of automated agents such as customers taking decisions based on functional benefits or experiential pleasure. Automated agents can be more effective and reliable when customer decisions are driven by rationality (Gelbrich et al., 2025). However, automated agents can perform poorly when customer decisions are about emotional and experiential experiences such as attending a concert. Finally, algorithms may suffer from lack of creativity and cognitive flexibility, or be unable to explain unforeseen results to customers, which represent crucial skills for high-expertise roles (e.g. doctors). Thus, the effect of algorithms on customer responses may be negative if replacing a high-expertise role (Gelbrich et al., 2025).

In summary, robots with a name and humanlike look can perform effectively repetitive tasks that require verbal-linguistic intelligence, positively influencing positively customer responses. Chatbots with a name are also effective in providing recommendations, and asking customers for their preferences, which may be stored for future conversational effectiveness. Algorithms are efficient when risk is not involved, and customers are not requiring an experiential experience or high-expertise recommendations (Gelbrich et al., 2025).

AI applications can support marketers with their strategy formulation and implementation. Recently, Wu and Monfort (2023) found that AI marketing strategies for managing customers' relationships, conducting marketing research, and pricing and developing products affected firm performance. Mechanical AI can automate continuous market and customer data sensing, tracking, collecting, processing and identifying novel customer preference patterns. Thinking AI uses analytics to identify competitors and competitive advantages and recommend the best target segments. Feeling AI can identify the positioning and the marketing messages that resonate with customers (Huang and Rust, 2021). For products and services, mechanical AI can automate the process and output of meeting customer needs and wants. Feeling AI can personalise products or services based on customer preferences, and also can understand and meet emotional needs and wants. Mechanical AI can automate the process of price setting and payment, and thinking AI can personalise prices based on customer willingness to pay. Further, AI can negotiate prices and justify the cost in real time. For promotion and communication, mechanical AI can automate communication with customers and thinking AI can customise promotional content for personal communication. Feeling AI can tailor communication based on customer emotional preferences and reactions (Huang and Rust, 2022).

The latest advance in the field of AI which is significantly impacting the marketing discipline is generative AI, representing a group of AI models that generate new content, including text, images, and videos (Hartmann et al., 2025). Generative AI differs from previous models through its ability to create novel content and perform key innovative marketing activities. Generative AI could transform marketing innovations, processes and customer responses by being the most advanced form of feeling AI. Generative AI is defined as deep neural networks, pre-trained on large amounts of data to create a foundation model, following human instructions to produce new content (Cillo and Rubera, 2025). Generative AI consists of self-supervised models that can predict an omitted word, given its surrounding text or a content of a patched image based on the remaining image information. The capacity of Generative AI to produce novel content is based upon the user prompt that it receives; thus, the next word or image feature could differ at each iteration and produce several responses from the same prompt, making it hard to detect content generated by Generative AI. Recent studies imply that Generative AI is able to generate innovative ideas, and has capabilities that encompass divergent and analogical thinking, and inductive reasoning (Cillo and Rubera, 2025). For instance, text-to-image AI models can significantly outperform human-made benchmark images in terms of quality, realism and aesthetics (Hartmann et al., 2025). Also, these AI models can outperform human freelancers on several marketing outcome metrics at a fraction of the cost. Further, managers are relying on Generative AI for decision-making due to reasoning and occasional causal inference capabilities. However, current Generative AI is unable to process physical data measurements to validate their available textual facts, which explains the limitation on text-based inputs lacking embodiment and sensory stimuli (Cillo and Rubera, 2025).

Despite the advancement in AI research and applications, some important areas of AI developments require future considerations. AI algorithms have good predictive accuracy in forecasting the sales of current products. However, data on new products is not readily available; thus, marketers need to understand how best to combine AI-driven insights with human judgment for new products. Future studies need to explore the impact of various types of AI on how teams collaborate to design products, services, logos and advertising (Ameen et al., 2022). The level and frequency of advertising may be less due to AI ability in predicting customer preferences. Marketers need to experiment with AI for better customer communications to increase engagement and repurchase. For example, how AI can examine customer information from social media posts and combine it with previous communication to develop persuasive messages that increase engagement is an area for experimentation (Mustak et al., 2021). Also, businesses can start using AI to support salespeople in real-time by providing feedback on customers' verbal and facial responses. This implies that organisations have to re-think their structures in the presence of AI. Companies need to manage the trade-off between AI focussing on customer expressed needs versus employees that may be relatively better able to manage issues like customer steward-ship. Companies need to train their employees on the use of AI and the management of customer concerns related to data privacy and ethics. Customer views on AI remain negative due to their sense that AI is unable to feel or identify their uniqueness, leading to less empathy. Therefore, positioning AI as a learning artificial organism that collaborates with human inputs to provide better solutions and answers may help mitigate customer negative views about AI (Huang and Rust, 2022). Also, customers might have ideal preferences which may differ from their past behaviours, and AI could make it harder for them to find and move toward their preferred options because of its reflection of past behaviours. Multinational companies face the challenge of managing communications with international customers that embed different culture, behaviours and perceptions about AI applications (Ameen et al., 2022). These companies need to examine how customers from different countries perceive AI applications and ethical usage.

Data privacy is an important topic for future consideration in regard to AI tools. A balance is required between too little protection which prevents customers from using AI and too much regulation that strangles innovation. Finally, companies need to develop realistic expectations about the impacts of AI on their business processes and outcomes in the short and long run. AI seems to be more effective if it is deployed in ways that augment rather than replace human beings. This approach allows companies and marketers to prepare for future AI developments and evolutionary benefits.

## References


Ameen, N., Sharma, G. D., Tarba, S., Rao, A., & Chopra, R. (2022). 'Toward advancing theory on creativity in marketing and artificial intelligence'. *Psychology & Marketing*, *39*(9), pp. 1802–1825.

Anderl, E., Becker, I., Von Wangenheim, F., & Schumann, J. H. (2016b). 'Mapping the customer journey: Lessons learned from graph-based online attribution modeling'. *International Journal of Research in Marketing*, *33*(3), pp. 457–474.

Anderl, E., Schumann, J. H., & Kunz, W. (2016a). 'Helping firms reduce complexity in multichannel online data: A new taxonomy-based approach for customer journeys'. *Journal of Retailing*, *92*(2), pp. 185–203.

Cai, Y. J., & Choi, T. M. (2023). 'Omni-channel marketing strategy in the digital platform era'. *Journal of Business Research*, *168*, 114197.

Cillo, P. and Rubera, G. (2025). 'Generative AI in innovation and marketing processes: A roadmap of research opportunities'. *Journal of the Academy of Marketing Science*, *53*(3), pp. 684–701.

Davenport, T., Guha, A., Grewal, D. and Bressgott, T. (2020). 'How artificial intelligence will change the future of marketing'. *Journal of the Academy of Marketing Science, 48*(1), pp. 24–42.

Day, G. S. (2011). 'Closing the marketing capabilities gap'. *Journal of Marketing, 75*(4), pp. 183–195.

De Bruyn, A., Viswanathan, V., Beh, Y. S., Brock, J. K. U. and Von Wangenheim, F. (2020). 'Artificial intelligence and marketing: Pitfalls and opportunities'. *Journal of Interactive Marketing, 51*(1), pp. 91–105.

De Haan, E., Wiesel, T. and Pauwels, K. (2016). 'The effectiveness of different forms of online advertising for purchase conversion in a multiple-channel attribution framework'. *International Journal of Research in Marketing*, 33(3), pp. 491–507.

Dwivedi, Y. K., Ismagilova, E., Hughes, D. L., Carlson, J., Filieri, R., Jacobson, J. and Wang, Y. (2021). 'Setting the future of digital and social media marketing research: Perspectives and research propositions'. *International Journal of Information Management, 59*, 102168.

Filippou, G., Georgiadis, A. G. and Jha, A. K. (2024). 'Establishing the link: Does web traffic from various marketing channels influence direct traffic source purchases?'. *Marketing Letters, 35*(1), pp. 59–71.

Gelbrich, K., Roschk, H., Miederer, S. and Kerath, A. (2025). 'Automated versus human agents: A meta-analysis of customer responses to robots, chatbots, and algorithms and their contingencies'. *Journal of Marketing.*

Hartmann, J., Exner, Y., & Domdey, S. (2025). 'The power of generative marketing: Can generative AI create superhuman visual marketing content?'. *International Journal of Research in Marketing, 42*(1), pp.13–31.

Jansen, B. J. and Schuster, S. (2011). 'Bidding on the buying funnel for sponsored search and keyword advertising'. *Journal of Electronic Commerce Research, 12*(1), 1.

Hazzam, J., Dobson, P., Singh, B., Ibrahim, B. and Aljarah, A. (2025). 'Digital marketing capabilities and SME performance: the influence of market orientation and the complementarity effect on customer relationship management capabilities'. *Journal of Research in Marketing and Entrepreneurship*, pp.1–21.

Hazzam, J. and Wilkins, S. (2022). 'International marketing capabilities development: The role of firm cultural intelligence and social media technologies' *Journal of Marketing Theory and Practice, 30*(3), pp. 325–341.

Hazzam, J., Wilkins, S. and Strong, C. (2023). 'The impact of social media technologies on organization cultural intelligence and new product development in international markets'. *Cross Cultural & Strategic Management, 30*(2), pp. 272–300.

Herhausen, D., Miočević, D., Morgan, R. E. and Kleijnen, M. H. (2020). 'The digital marketing capabilities gap'. *Industrial Marketing Management, 90*, pp. 276–290.

Hofacker, C., Golgeci, I., Pillai, K. G. and Gligor, D. M. (2020). Digital marketing and business-to-business relationships: A close look at the interface and a roadmap for the future. *European Journal of Marketing, 54*(6), pp. 1161–1179.

Homburg, C. and Wielgos, D. M. (2022). 'The value relevance of digital marketing capabilities to firm performance'. *Journal of the Academy of Marketing Science, 50*(4), pp. 666–688.

Huang, M. H. and Rust, R. T. (2021). 'A strategic framework for artificial intelligence in marketing'. *Journal of the Academy of Marketing Science, 49*(1), pp. 30–50.

Huang, M. H. and Rust, R. T. (2022). 'A framework for collaborative artificial intelligence in marketing'. *Journal of Retailing, 98*(2), pp. 209–223.

Kakalejčík, L., Bucko, J. and Danko, J. (2020). 'Impact of direct traffic effect on online sales'. *Journal of Research in Interactive Marketing, 14*(1), pp. 17–32.

Kannan, P. K., Reinartz, W. and Verhoef, P. C. (2016). 'The path to purchase and attribution modeling: Introduction to special section'. *International Journal of Research in Marketing, 33*(3), pp. 449–456.

Kannan, P.K. (2017). 'Digital marketing: A framework, review and research agenda'. *International Journal of Research in Marketing, 34*(1), pp. 22–45.

Kim, J., Kang, S. and Lee, K. H. (2021). 'Evolution of digital marketing communication: Bibliometric analysis and network visualization from key articles'. *Journal of Business Research, 130*, pp. 552–563.

Li, H. and Kannan, P. K. (2014). 'Attributing conversions in a multichannel online marketing environment: An empirical model and a field experiment'. *Journal of Marketing Research, 51*(1), pp. 40–56.

Li, Y., Xie, Y. and Zheng, Z. (2019). 'Modeling multichannel advertising attribution across competitors'. *MIS Quarterly, 43*(1), 263–A11.

Marchand, A., Hennig-Thurau, T. and Flemming, J. (2021). 'Social media resources and capabilities as strategic determinants of social media performance'. *International Journal of Research in Marketing, 38*(3), pp. 549–571.

Mariani, M. M., Perez-Vega, R. and Wirtz, J. (2022). 'AI in marketing, consumer research and psychology: A systematic literature review and research agenda'. *Psychology & Marketing, 39*(4), pp. 755–776.

Mustak, M., Salminen, J., Plé, L. and Wirtz, J. (2021). 'Artificial intelligence in marketing: Topic modeling, scientometric analysis, and research agenda'. *Journal of Business Research, 124*, pp. 389–404.

Quinn, L., Dibb, S., Simkin, L., Canhoto, A. and Analogbei, M. (2016). 'Troubled waters: the transformation of marketing in a digital world'. *European Journal of Marketing, 50*(12), pp. 2103–2133.

Rizvanović, B., Zutshi, A., Grilo, A. and Nodehi, T. (2023). 'Linking the potentials of extended digital marketing impact and start-up growth: Developing a macro-dynamic framework of start-up growth drivers supported by digital marketing'. *Technological Forecasting and Social Change, 186*, p. 122128.

Sakas, D. P., Giannakopoulos, N. T. and Trivellas, P. (2024). 'Exploring affiliate marketing's impact on customers' brand engagement and vulnerability in the online banking service sector'. *International Journal of Bank Marketing, 42*(6), pp. 1282–1312.

Setkute, J. and Dibb, S. (2022). '"Old boys' club": Barriers to digital marketing in small B2B firms'. *Industrial Marketing management, 102*, pp. 266–279.

Shankar, V. and Kushwaha, T. (2021). 'Omnichannel marketing: Are cross-channel effects symmetric?' *International Journal of Research in Marketing, 38*(2), pp. 290–310.

Su, J., Zhang, Y. and Wu, X. (2023). 'How market pressures and organizational readiness drive digital marketing adoption strategies' evolution in small and medium enterprises'. *Technological Forecasting and Social Change, 193*, 122655.

Tiago, M. T. P. M. B. and Veríssimo, J. M. C. (2014). 'Digital marketing and social media: Why bother?' *Business horizons, 57*(6), pp. 703–708.

Vieira, V. A., de Almeida, M. I. S., Agnihotri, R., da Silva, N. S. D. A. C. and Arunachalam, S. (2019). 'In pursuit of an effective B2B digital marketing strategy in an emerging market'. *Journal of the Academy of Marketing Science, 47*(6), pp. 1085–1108.

Wang, F. (2020). 'Digital marketing capabilities in international firms: a relational perspective'. *International Marketing Review, 37*(3), pp. 559–577.

Wu, C. W., Botella-Carrubi, D. and Blanco-González-Tejero, C. (2024). 'The empirical study of digital marketing strategy and performance in small and medium-sized enterprises (SMEs)'. *Technological Forecasting and Social Change, 200*, p. 123142.

Wu, C. W. and Monfort, A. (2023). 'Role of artificial intelligence in marketing strategies and performance'. *Psychology & Marketing, 40*(3), pp. 484–496.

Zahay, D. (2021). 'Advancing research in digital and social media marketing'. *Journal of Marketing Theory and Practice, 29*(1), pp. 125–139.

# THE FUTURE OF DEMOCRATIC DECISION MAKING IN THE AGE OF AI: LESSONS FROM ROMANIA'S 2024 PRESIDENTIAL ELECTION

## Ovidiu Oltean

On the evening of November 24, 2024, Romanians were anxiously following the first results of the exit polls after the first round of the presidential elections. This was the ninth presidential election since the country became a democracy in 1989 and unlike the other elections, this time it was hard to identify a favourite front runner amongst the reshuffled charisma-lacking candidates. As exit polls were published and the ballots were counted, people could not take their eyes from the screens of their televisions, laptops and phones, each following their trusted sources of news and media. As votes came in, the results of the exit polls seemed to be making no sense as the screen remained fixed on a candidate that most people had not heard about and who seemed to have flown low under the radar of pre-election opinion polls and exit-polls.

The candidate was Călin Georgescu, a self-proclaimed sovereignist politician, with ultranationalist and pro-Kremlin views, who was largely unknown to most people. Some remembered his name as he had previously been mentioned on various occasions as a possible option for prime minister, without ever being nominated. In the most optimistic of exit polls, Georgescu was at best projected to finish third, with only a 16–17% share of the votes, (Expert Forum 2024, November 23), whilst other polls gave him between 5% and 6%, a score entirely insufficient to reach the run-off round (Baghiu, 2025; Bader and Szabó, 2025).

As the vote count advanced, it became evident that Georgescu would be the winner of the first presidential round. Next to him, the runner-up place was contested by Marcel Ciolacu, the candidate of PSD, the Social Democratic Party, who was also at the time the incumbent prime minister, and considered to be the favourite of the race, and Elena Lasconi, the mayor of the town of Câmpulung-Muscel (located north of Bucharest), candidate and president at that time of USR, Save Romanian Union Party, a centre-right pro-European party. As all the votes were counted late into the night, the run-off phase of the presidential election became clear. It would be a race between Georgescu and Lasconi, leaving out from the run-off phase for the first time both candidates of the two largest political parties, PSD (conservative social democrats) and PNL (conservative liberals), long-time political forces that had governed Romania in the post-communist period and traditional contenders in the presidential elections.

After the closing of the vote count, with Georgescu installed as the winner of the first round, people started to search who Georgescu was, still surprised by his unexpected rise. As they scrolled through videos and newspaper articles, they started picking up all sorts of bewildering declarations that he had made over time, most of them before the electoral campaign. They were surprised to discover a candidate with a fierce ultra nationalist discourse, admirer of a criminal political movement who espoused clear sympathies towards Vladimir Putin and his regime, all wrapped in ethno-nationalist visions of grandeur and self-sufficiency.

Many were legitimately asking themselves, "How is it possible that someone like Georgescu could make it to the first round?" Without a political party infrastructure to support him, without being present in live presidential debates, it seemed unbelievable that someone could make it so far in the presidential race. But Georgescu had mastered a game that outplayed all the other contenders. Apparently out of nowhere, he became one of the most popular political figures in the country and one of the main trending profiles on TikTok globally. He pushed out from the run-off round the candidates of the main political parties who had spent tens of millions of euros on political promotion whilst benefitting from the support of huge territorial organisational infrastructures. And he was now speaking to millions of Romanians from the screens of their phones, consolidating and expanding his electoral base, whilst his previous competitors were scrambling to understand how they had failed so badly. Disaffected by the performances of established political parties, his voters saw him as a political outsider who promised to alleviate their plight and take revenge on the established political class (Marincea, 2025).

On social media groups that were turned into electoral forums during the elections, some spoke about him in religious terms, referring to him as an 'apostle of good' or some sort of 'Godsend' that would save Romania. But Georgescu's rise hides a much darker story that eventually led to the annulment of the elections by the Constitutional Court, which mandated a rerun of the presidential race in 2025 and excluded him from further participation, citing serious threats to constitutional legality and democratic stability.

## "What the hell is going on in Romania?"

The annulment of the elections came as a second shock to the Romanian electorate. Many met the decision with surprise and disapproval whilst others welcomed it as a necessary measure for safeguarding the integrity of the elections. In this sense, the annulment of the Romanian presidential elections from November 24th, 2024, was a first in Romania's post-communist history and will probably remain in the history of liberal democratic regimes for being one of the few elections to be annulled in their entirety on grounds of voter manipulation, undisclosed electoral expenses and foreign interference. Whilst it happens in authoritarian regimes that elections are rendered null or their result unrecognized by usurping leaders, the annulment of elections is extremely hard to find in liberal democracies. It has only happened recently that one round of elections was annulled in Austria in 2016, due to mismanagement in the vote count, however there was no proof of vote fraud. The annulment was caused rather by a technicality that was central to the integrity of the electoral process. In the Romanian case, the annulment was based on a ruling issued by the Constitutional Court on the 6th of December 2024, after a series of apparently contradictory decisions, and was based on the rationale that the electoral process was profoundly corrupted by one of the candidates that made it to the runoff round. Without explicitly naming Călin Georgescu, the decision singled him out by citing and describing his campaign strategies which obliterated all forms of democratic safeguards. The decision stirred strong public reactions, which spilled into street protests and strong criticism of the Court's decision, formulated by Georgescu's supporters as well as political scientists and activists fearful of a democratic regression. Global news outlets such as Politico could not abstain from asking in the title of an ensuing article published December 7th, "What the hell is going on [with the elections in Romania]?" whilst the governments of international allies called for clarifications (Politico, 2024, December 7). Unusually, Romania made it for a few days to the headlines of major journals and news channels across the world, with articles and pundits attempting to unpack the issue and present an objective account of the affair.

In the heat of the moment, the Romanian institutions, public authorities or pundits struggled to deliver a coherent explanation. Meanwhile, the candidate Călin Georgescu did not acknowledge any wrongdoing, whilst his supporters classified his campaign strategy as 'normal', as something that 'everyone does', minimizing the allegations and the fraud. In order to fill the gap and vouch for the legality of the annulment, the Romanian authorities made public classified documents to demonstrate external interference and possibly forms of institutional abdication of duty by the institutions that were in charge of overseeing the elections, promising to provide a full report and a proof-based explanation in the months to come. Nevertheless, a full account of what transpired remains absent. Despite repeated assurances by Romania's current president, Nicuşor Dan, that a comprehensive explanation would be made public one year after the annulment, no such detailed analysis has yet been released. Several investigative news outlets such as Context and Info Sud-Est in Romania and Ziarul de Gardă from Republic of Moldova did the government's job and continued the investigation, releasing reports that point towards a connection between Russian funded propaganda agencies and Georgescu's campaign infrastructure and strategy.

This chapter aims to fill this gap and clarify some of the key political, technological, and institutional dynamics that shaped the 2024 electoral process and brought Călin Georgescu's electoral success. Rather than offering a legal reconstruction of the case, the chapter advances a political-sociological analysis of how Georgescu leveraged networked communication, algorithms, and regulatory asymmetries to exploit democratic vulnerabilities and overpass electoral safeguards. The chapter reconstructs his strategy and analyses how digital infrastructures were employed to weaken traditional mechanisms of electoral oversight and blur the boundaries between legitimate campaigning, manipulation, and foreign interference. What follows treats Romania's 2024 election as a problem of democratic complexity, showing how algorithmic infrastructures, institutional constraints, and geopolitical pressures intertwine, generating cascading effects that can erode accountability and put democratic legitimacy itself at risk.

## The rise of techno-populism

Jamie Susskind (2018), political theorist and legal scholar and author of great analytical prose, argues that technological forces increasingly dictate the structure of governance, as public administration and democratic interfaces are going digital, whilst Shoshana Zuboff (2019) exposes how digital platforms exploit the surplus of behavioural data to influence user behaviour, including voting decisions. Building upon these works, this chapter examines how the employment of digital technologies and algorithm driven platforms in elections are reshaping political decision-making and the electoral game. The increasing dominance of algorithmic curation when it comes to consuming and distributing electoral messages means that political engagement is in danger of becoming shaped by opaque recommendation systems that privilege engagement over truth and the velocity of messages over their validity, instead of public deliberation, journalistic scrutiny, or institutional checks and balances (DiResta, 2018; Zuboff, 2019). As Zeynep Tufekci (2017) argues in her book Twitter and Tear Gas, digital platforms do not just reflect public opinion but actively shape it, often reinforcing polarization and undermining the conditions necessary for democratic discourse. Similarly, Howard and Bradshaw's (2018) seminal work on computational propaganda illustrates how AI-driven techniques of voter influence, ranging from microtargeted messaging and automated content circulation to large-scale disinformation campaigns have become integral to contemporary political strategy. Techniques such as microtargeted messaging, automated content circulation, and large-scale disinformation, initially associated with efforts to discipline public opinion under non-democratic regimes, are now routinely deployed within democratic campaigns, in both liberal democracies as well electoral autocracies (Bradshaw et al., 2021), blurring the distinction between legitimate political communication and manipulative influence (Vacariu, 2025; Martin-Rozumiłowicz and Kužel, 2019). Evidence from a wide range of electoral contexts, including the 2016 Brexit referendum and Donald Trump's presidential campaigns, demonstrates how these practices have become embedded across political systems with varying levels of democratic consolidation, showing how the mechanisms through which electoral competition is conducted have been silently muted, obliterated and transformed by algorithmic power (Howard and Bradshaw, 2018).

In the case of Romania, convergences between computational propaganda, polarisation and populism have propelled the rise of populist ultranationalist figures and xenophobic and alarmist political discourses. Călin Georgescu is only of these political figures, and he happened to be the one most capable of gaming the tools of computational propaganda and digital amplification (Howard and Bradshaw, 2018). Whilst his rise is presented as a surprise appearance, Georgescu did not arise out of thin air. His rise happened in a moment of heightened political polarization and in a context dominated by rising populism and consolidating populist parties (Vacariu, 2025) that came to contest and challenge the political consensus that has dominated European and Romanian politics for the last decades. In a very tense context, dominated by a sequence of crises (Cistelecan et al., 2025), declining economic growth and rising inequalities, with a war waging in Ukraine and intensified anxiety over the possibilities of escalation into neighbouring countries, the populist leaders and ultranationalist parties in Romania intensely exploited these issues in overly polarising materials (Lovi, 2025; Bader and Szabó, 2025), addressing and fuelling the frustrations of the population. For the last 4 years they have poured a steady stream of polarising narratives and emotionally charged disinformation into the digital public sphere, gradually normalising distrust in democratic institutions, mainstream media, and pro-European political elites. In addition to the local political forces, Russia amplified this type of messages, spreading disinformation, financing fake news and supporting directly or indirectly candidates that sang their favourite kind of tunes (Carp, 2025).

In this context, Georgescu was not the first to master this game, but he was the most skilled in using digital communication tools to their fullest to spectacularly amplify his political capital. Radu Carp (2025) calls this phenomenon 'techno-populism' and portrays Georgescu as the embodiment of this new political machinery. Călin Georgescu exploited the loopholes of the electoral legislation and scrutiny and exploited the frustrations of the electorate, presenting himself as an outsider and an advocate of the dispossessed majority against the system, whilst propagating false information and conspiracy theories, creating the impression that Romania is a victim to a global or European conjuration which pulled it into a catastrophic economic and social situation, stripping it of its assets and reducing its citizens to mere proles. Whilst crafting the looniest theories that one could think of, he funnelled all these messages into carefully edited TikTok videos and engineered his visibility to gain hundreds of millions of views (Vacariu, 2025). He rapidly became a political superstar for the populist ultranationalist factions, coalescing the political endorsement of like-minded parties and groups, both from Romania as well as from other countries, including politicians and supporters of the MAGA movement in the US. A frustrated electorate, impoverished by escalating inflation and rise of costs, and frightened by the prospect of the escalation of the war in Ukraine, decided to shift their allegiance to a different type of candidate, one that promised to alleviate all these burdens and restore their dignity, their hope and their safety. Profiting from uneven levels of critical media literacy among voters and a growing frustration and rage within the society, Georgescu was capable of translating social grievances into digitally amplified political support. He masterfully tuned in to capture the mood of the electorate and then amplified his grip by exploiting it digitally.

We analyse Georgescu's campaign as a case of computational propaganda, arguing that the significance of this case bears implications that extend well beyond its immediate electoral consequences, signalling a reconfiguration of political agency and the emergence of a new dilemma that our polities face. In Susskind terms, this dilemma is no longer simply a question of who governs, be it the market, the state, or a pluralist society but through which socio-technical systems political authority is exercised, and under what enforceable conditions of transparency, accountability, and democratic control collective decisions are made (Susskind, 2018). The insertion of digital technologies and digitally amplified content and AI powered infrastructures in electoral campaigns as well as the digitalisation of public institution and decision-making forces us to reflect on the implications that these reconfigurations have for democracy. Computational propaganda is analysed here as the use of algorithms, automation, and human curation to deliberately distribute misleading or manipulative information over social media networks in order to shape public opinion (Woolley and Howard, 2017).

## The 1st round of the 2024 presidential elections

In this sense, what happened in the first round of these presidential elections marks a break from previous elections from the post-communist history of Romania, repudiating the classical dichotomy and cleavage that has long defined Romanian politics – 'communism' and its successor behemoth embodied within the current PSD, Social-Democratic Party, and 'anti-communism', which usually meant pro-European reform forces which pushed for a breakaway with the former regime (Baghiu, 2025). It also marked a rupture from the old way of campaigning. Although presidential campaigns were always fraught with affective messages and symbolic tropes rather than policy discussions and structured ideological confrontations (Baghiu, 2025), the reliance on algorithmic amplification and digital platforms was higher during these elections, mobilising strong emotions amongst the disaffected electorate. Scholars such as Simona Bader and Lucian-Vasile Szabó (2025) interpret this as a manifestation and a result of digitally powered populism, whilst Ştefan Baghiu (2025) coins this as "loony platform-politics" where "platform capitalism" (Srnicek, 2017) converges with populism and ultranationalism in powering up politicians like Călin Georgescu.

With plagiarised speeches (Baghiu, 2025) and engineered attention and a sophisticated digital infrastructure, Georgescu effectively captured the electoral arena. He strategically posed in the position of the saviour and anti-system politician, and appealed to the frustrations of the population, rather than bringing or proposing realistic solutions. Georgescu captured the hearts and minds of the electorate and with them the electoral space and its democratic safeguards. He spoke about the afflictions of low-earning Romanians for which he blamed the West and the European Union, whilst kindling the pride of Romanians by appealing to a glorious past that allegedly was to be found during the interwar and communist period. He promised to restore the pride and dignity of Romanians if he were to be elected president. But unlike the other candidates, Georgescu remained invisible for a section of voters, media watchdogs and political pundits. He did not appear in prime time on the major television channels, nor did he participate in live debates and did not meet with his electorate in large rallies across the country.

Georgescu remained largely an online presence, sending his messages across TikTok and saving a selection of his speeches on his YouTube channel. He largely flew under the radar and was ignored by most polling companies. Midway through the presidential campaign, he supercharged his digital infrastructure and powered his way through the presidential elections, taking everyone by surprise.

In the first round of the elections, Georgescu obtained 22.4% of the vote, accounting for 2,120,401 votes, whilst Elena Lasconi came second with 19.7%, representing 1,772,500 votes[2]. The result took the international press by surprise, and shocked Western audiences as they discovered Georgescu's phantasmatic declarations. It also produced disappointment and shock within the PSD, as their candidate Marcel Ciolacu failed for the first time in post-communist history to bring a PSD candidate in the grand presidential

---

[2] Presidential elections, 1st round, turnout, Romanian Permanent Electoral Agency, https://prezenta.roaep.ro/prezidentiale24112024/pv/romania/results/ (retrieved 08.10.2025).

finale. Whilst political analysts searched for explanations, the electorate turned to their laptops and phones to discover who Georgescu really was, tracking him down across TikTok or digging out older online articles that attested his long-time presence in the public space.

## Călin Georgescu

Shockingly or not, they discovered that Georgescu's public profile stood in stark contrast to his actual professional trajectory. Whilst advancing a strongly anti-globalist, anti-NGO, and ultranationalist rhetoric framed in "Romania First" terms and infused with claims of economic self-sufficiency, Georgescu's professional trajectory was largely built within internationally funded environmental governance networks. Trained as a soil scientist, in contrast to his denunciation of globalism and foreign influence, a Recorder investigation (Șerban, 2025) shows how he developed his career during the 1990s and 2000s within the NGO sector, coordinating environmental organisations supported by USAID, PHARE, and Soros Foundation funding, and serving in advisory and rapporteur capacities linked to United Nations environmental fora.

Moreover, Georgescu's resume appears to be characterised by a series of inconsistencies. Although he has presented himself as a senior UN official with executive responsibilities in Geneva, journalistic investigations have shown these claims to be exaggerated, with his involvement limited to consultancy and representational mandates on behalf of Romania, as an envoy of the Ministry of Foreign Affairs (Dumitru, 2024, December 4). His proximity to political power, reflected in leadership positions within organisations such as the National Centre for Sustainable Development, links to PSD-affiliated circles, and consideration for high-level executive office, further complicates his self-presentation as an anti-system outsider. His professional life is also punctured by long activity gaps after his withdrawal from Romanian public life and relocation to Austria, where no one is quite sure how he made a living, whilst working for some NGOs with uncertain activity. Returning to Romania, Georgescu re-emerged after 2020 as a radicalised political figure, strategically obscuring his longstanding ties to state institutions, mainstream parties, and international donors and presenting himself as a crusader ready to fight the political establishment and the global elite which stretched its arms far too deep into Romania. His brief association with the populist far right party AUR ended amid controversy over antisemitic statements.

In his public appearances Georgescu has oscillated between glorifying fascist, communist, and pro-Russian authoritarian figures, and later denying any extremist leanings. In a 2020 interview, he praised the interwar Legionary Movement as "the strongest essence and expression of health and self-will arising from the Romanian people," even suggesting that its leader, Corneliu Zelea Codreanu, who committed and was involved in a long series of political murders in the 1920s and 1930s (Manolachi, 2023) should be "rehabilitated" (G4Media 2024, December 13). At the same time, he spoke nostalgically about Nicolae Ceaușescu's Romania, without directly professing admiration for Ceaușescu himself, and echoed tropes from both Legionary and national-communist rhetoric (Garvey 2024, December 2; Radio Free Europe 2024, November 27). Whilst he has called Vladimir Putin "a patriot" and downplayed Russia's invasion of Ukraine as "not our business," he has also sought to reassure the public that "Romania is fine in NATO and the EU" and that he has no intention of initiating any process of taking Romania out of these organisations (Digi24, 2025, September 16).

During the presidential campaign, Georgescu sought to tone down his more radical ideological views, denying or reframing earlier declarations. However, he did not brush away his autarkic and nationalist views which were all too present in his presidential programme: Aer, Apă, Energie (Air, Water, Energy), which combined neoliberal instruments such as flat taxation with a dirigiste vision on economy and society[3], which echoed late Ceaușescu-era doctrines of self-reliance and mystical nationalist tropes.

## The TikTok candidate

However, the TikTok algorithms did not deliver this persona in its entirety. Instead, it edited out bits of his speeches and specific messages that Georgescu recorded and spoon-fed them through micro targeting in a differentiated way to specific audiences that were frantically following his messages in daily doses of political lecturing. One could hardly have the full image of Georgescu whilst surfing his TikTok messages. To the disaffected and disappointed electorate, his TikTok speeches sounded like the right messages coming from a man who was prepared to "fight the system". He was the candidate of the disaffected and unrepresented, who claimed to speak in their name. He was the "man for the job" willing to address issues that other

---

[3] Călin Georgescu, Program, https://calingeorgescu.ro/program/ (retrieved 03.10.2025).

politicians ignored, speaking in a language that was closer to what that the voters thought and felt rather than how politicians usually speak.

After the validation of the results in the first round, his illiberal and Russia-friendly positioning raised concerns among Romania's EU and NATO partners, while finding resonance within Trump-aligned Republican circles in the United States who welcomed the result. Domestically, street demonstrations in major university centres reaffirmed support for European integration, raising concerns about a possible illiberal regime shift with strong fascist undertones if Georgescu would become president, all whilst the online space became increasingly polarised and hostile, filled with verbal violence and death threats across camps that held opposing political views. This moment of heightened polarisation, however, was abruptly disrupted by an unprecedented and highly contested institutional decision that reshaped the political trajectory of the electoral process.

## The election that wasn't: Constitutional court annuls the vote

Everything was rolled back by the decision of the Constitutional Court issued on the 6th of December, which invalidated the presidential elections and ordered a rerun (Iancu, 2025). The decision came after an impromptu meeting of the Constitutional Court, which through a *per curiam ruling* based on proof that the election process was profoundly vitiated decided that integrity of elections was irremediably compromised and ordered a rerun (Iancu, 2025; Roghină, 2025).

The annulment saga was initiated by a post-electoral petition submitted by Cristian Terheş, a marginal candidate with roughly 1% of the vote, who alleged irregularities and requested a recount. In response, the Constitutional Court of Romania ordered a nationwide recount on 28 November, a move that briefly stabilized the political situation after Georgescu's unexpected first-round victory while amplifying doubts about electoral integrity (Reuters, 28 November 2024). Conducted under tight deadlines, the recount confirmed the initial outcome, leading the Court on 2 December to validate Georgescu's lead and authorize the runoff (Reuters, 6 December 2024). The crisis escalated on 4 December, when then-President Klaus Iohannis released declassified intelligence reports detailing a coordinated hybrid interference campaign involving Russian-linked networks, AI-driven bots, and opaque financing. Although no candidate was explicitly named, the disclosures indicated a systematic effort to amplify Georgescu's candidacy through platforms such as TikTok and Telegram, reframing the controversy from procedural irregularities to structural electoral compromise (Presidency of Romania, 4 December 2024; Al Jazeera, 6 December 2024).

As legal challenges multiplied and pro-democracy protests erupted in Bucharest, the Court confronted evidence of systemic violations of campaign finance and cybersecurity regulations (Iancu, 2025; Roghină, 2025). On the 6th of December 2024, the Constitutional Court issued an unprecedented decision annulling the entire presidential election, citing the need to safeguard electoral legality in the face of demonstrable foreign interference and algorithmically mediated manipulation, while DIICOT opened criminal investigations into Georgescu's campaign (Al Jazeera, 2024, December 6). Political reactions were sharply polarized. Government officials defended the ruling as a constitutional safeguard, Lasconi condemned it as a negation of popular sovereignty, and Georgescu and AUR framed it as an elite-driven "coup" (The Guardian, 2024, December 6). The cancellation of the run-off, including the closure of diaspora polling stations mid-process, triggered protests by AUR supporters and intensified international media scrutiny. The lack of a detailed report and solid proof that demonstrated foreign interference fuelled the anger of the electorate, who considered that this was only a gesture of the political establishment of protecting itself in front of real alternation in power.

The resulting polarization also exposed the profound fragility of Romania's electoral infrastructure in the face of platform-mediated influence and poured uncertainty and confusion over the legislative elections, which took place in the same period. The parliamentary elections held on the 1st of December 2024 confirmed the populist nationalist party AUR, Alliance for Union of Romanians, as the second political force in the country with 18.30% of the votes, and brought in two new political forces, SOS and POT, both ultranationalist and far right, with the latter benefitting from the association with the image of Călin Georgescu (Le Monde, 2024, December 2). However, the Constitutional Court upheld the parliamentary results, which stabilised the political situation, allowing for a new parliament to be formed.

## The militant democracy

The annulment decision was unprecedented in the 33 years of existence of constitutional justice in Romania (Iancu, 2025). The Constitutional Court cited in its justification for annulment the failure of one of the candidates (without naming Călin Georgescu) to declare their campaign expenses, noting the glaring discrepancy between the officially reported zero contributions and the scale and sophistication of his predominantly TikTok-based campaign (Iancu, 2025). The Court considered that the scale and operational sophistication of Georgescu's campaign made his portrayal of it as a volunteer-driven effort implausible. Estimates placed campaign expenditures in the tens of millions of euros, potentially exceeding €50 million, according to assessments by Romanian entrepreneurs active in major online retail platforms (Euronews, 2024, December 4). Despite this, Georgescu officially declared zero campaign expenses and donations, parading an extract of his candidate account across online video recordings and public declarations. As financial accounts must be made available to the electoral authorities immediately after the elections, Georgescu's financial statements appeared to contradict his performance and were hard to ignore or to believe. Combined with the subsequent declassification of intelligence documents, this discrepancy prompted an ex officio intervention by the Constitutional Court, which, in extending its role as the ultimate guarantor of democratic legality, acted to prevent what it deemed a structurally compromised electoral process from generating an illegitimate outcome (Gherghina, 2025; Iancu, 2025).

In its per curiam reasoning, improvised under severe time pressure, the Court relied on intelligence briefs declassified by the Supreme Council of National Defence, which pointed to coordinated algorithmic manipulation of social media visibility and a high probability of foreign-sponsored hybrid interference aiming to distort the online information environment during the campaign (Iancu, 2025). On this basis, the Court argued that the constitutional requirements of the "legality" and "correctness" of the presidential ballot had been structurally compromised, so that only the invalidation of the entire electoral process and the organisation of a full rerun could restore the conditions for a free formation of the popular will (Iancu, 2025). In Bogdan Iancu's reading, the decision thus exemplifies an extreme form of "individual militant democracy," whereby a constitutional court intervenes ex post to neutralise an algorithmically fuelled candidacy perceived as threatening the democratic order (Iancu, 2025). On the other hand, critics argue that the Constitutional Court's annulment lacked a clear legal basis, as neither the constitution nor the law 370/2004 authorises the invalidation of an entire electoral process. Constitutional law scholar Eduard Jürgen Prediger contends that the Court exceeded its competences and relied on insufficiently transparent reasoning, falling short of Venice Commission standards and improperly substituting declassified intelligence for adversarial proof (Prediger, 2024; Venice Commission, 2025). From this view, the decision violated the principle of ultima ratio, since campaign irregularities should have attracted proportionate sanctions rather than annulment, as suggested by Austria's 2016 precedent (Venice Commission, 2025). Scholars further warn that intervention during an ongoing election risk eroding public trust and reinforcing perceptions of institutional overreach, a concern heightened by both candidates' rejection of the ruling (Anghel, 2024). Defenders reply that the Court acted within its constitutional duty to protect democratic integrity. Drawing on militant democracy theory, to which the Romanian Constitutional Court and democratic arrangement subscribe, scholars argue that systemic interference, AI-driven manipulation, and opaque foreign financing posed an existential threat to liberal democracy and to Romania's sovereignty, justifying exceptional judicial action (Iancu, 2025; Roghină, 2025). This claim is supported by an IFES (an independent international organisation) assessment finding that pervasive disinformation and external interference undermined voters' capacity for informed choice (IFES, 2024). Legal scholar Radu Cornea (2025) similarly defends the annulment as constitutionally grounded, while cautioning against normalizing such exceptional powers. According to this reading, the decision aligns with Romania's militant constitutional framework, which permits counter-majoritarian intervention in extreme circumstances to defend liberal democracy (Dima and Perju, 2023).

However, this chapter does not seek to reassess the constitutional legality of the annulment, a matter already rigorously examined by constitutional law scholars (Iancu, 2025; Cornea, 2025; Prediger, 2024). Instead, it focuses on the political and democratic implications of permitting the largely unregulated use of algorithmic amplification and AI-driven technologies in electoral campaigning. In the following sections, we will examine how Călin Georgescu's campaign strategy constitutes a systemic threat to democratic competition and the integrity of free and fair elections, illustrating the risks that arise when private technology platforms become de facto arbiters of political visibility, enabling candidates to circumvent institutional oversight and democratic accountability.

The argument of the chapter does not necessarily attempt to solve a constitutional issue but rather to open a reflection on the implications of the unfettered use of digital amplification technologies on the integrity of elections and freedom of choice.

## The architecture of the digital campaign

What would be important to stress out here is that this amplification was not a spontaneous and organic one, although there was some organic engagement with Georgescu's online presence. Despite the fact that he was presented as a candidate that became a political super star overnight, who was supported by volunteers, with no expenses, Călin Georgescu's campaign staff and the architects of his digital infrastructure prepared his rise months (and possibly years) in advance, hidden from public view and institutional scrutiny. Whilst other candidates also engaged in informal campaigning, prior to the legal campaigning period, using loopholes in the legislation to justify electoral spending and campaigning, they relied largely on television, billboards, and institutional appearances. Georgescu, by contrast, adopted a digital-first strategy that reconfigured campaigning itself, rather than merely supplementing traditional methods. The decisive expansion of his visibility occurred in October–November 2024, when coordinated TikTok dynamics generated disproportionate reach. Central to this phase was the influencer-oriented campaign organised around the hashtag #EchilibrușiVerticalitate (which we could translate as Balance and Integrity) which blurred the boundary between civic messaging and electoral advertising, lowering audience scepticism and facilitating algorithmic discovery through comment flooding and ranking effects (Neag et al., 2024, December 20). Although reportedly initiated by the National Liberal Party (PNL), through a private consultant, Kensington Communication, the campaign gradually reoriented towards promoting Georgescu (Baghiu, 2025). Whilst PNL claimed that Georgescu replicated and eventually stole their strategy, investigative reporting showed that PNL party funds were used for a campaign subsequently exploited by Georgescu (Neag et al., 2024, December 20; Cârlugea, 2024, December 22). Whilst PNL leaders dismissed any connection to Georgescu, the evidence is out and does not look good on a party pretending to be the exact opposite of what Georgescu stands for. Furthermore, investigative reports from journalists show that a whole network of websites that held favourable views towards populist parties such as AUR, aligned behind Georgescu during the presidential elections, hosting his interviews, declarations or posting favourable editorials about him (Carp, 2025).

The effectiveness of this digital architecture became evident after the first round of voting on 24 November 2024, when Georgescu emerged as one of the fastest-growing political profiles on TikTok globally. By late November, he had accumulated around 400,000 followers and millions of views of his TikTok videos (Solea, 2024, November 29). Alongside his Tik-Tok appearances, his campaign relied heavily on influencer endorsements delivered through short videos, often without disclosure of paid political content or any electoral labels that must signal paid electoral content. Supported by networks of influencers and automated or semi-automated accounts, Georgescu achieved pervasive visibility across digital platforms, while mainstream polling and legacy media continued to underestimate his electoral prospects. Whilst everyone else relied on the classical forms of campaigning, Georgescu was already mastering a whole new environment and was slowly overtaking the electoral space and tilting the rules of the game.

## Appealing to the disaffected

On TikTok, Georgescu cultivated an image of a pious, physically active, anti-establishment outsider through recurring visuals of church attendance, jogging, and podcast appearances (Solea, 2024, November 29). Supporters amplified this messaging through remix videos and a campaign song reused in over 11,000 posts, contributing to near-saturation visibility and a perception of mass popularity exceeding early polling expectations (Baghiu, 2025; Solea, 2024, November 29; Mihăilescu, 2024, November 28).

A defining feature of this strategy was its appeal to younger voters and the Romanian diaspora. TikTok usage in Romania increased sharply from approximately 175,000 users in 2019 to nearly 9 million by 2024, favouring candidates who were present on this platform and creating favourable conditions for platform-specific mobilisation (Cârlugea and Wesolowsky, 2024, November 26). Many Romanians working abroad switched to TikTok to follow news and events back in Romania, whilst the young voters, belonging to the Gen Z and Millennial generations became daily users. Electoral data show that 31% of voters aged 18–24 supported Georgescu in the first round, compared to only 8% among those over 65 (Cârlugea and Wesolowsky, 2024, November 26). Among Romanians abroad, who rely heavily on social media for political information, encrypted messaging groups and algorithmically curated content bubbles enabled his narratives to circulate with limited factchecking within Romanian migrant groups, rendering diaspora voters particularly exposed to distorted claims and emotional tropes (Mihăilescu, 2024, November 28).

Moreover, based on recent analyses, Georgescu's digital campaign relied extensively on astroturfing practices that simulated spontaneous grassroots support while being driven by coordinated networks of automated accounts, influencers, and opaque amplification mechanisms. Scholars show that these practices artificially inflated visibility and perceived popularity on platforms such as TikTok, creating the impression of broad societal endorsement while remaining largely invisible outside algorithmically segmented publics (Bader and Szabó, 2025; Carp, 2025; Vacariu, 2025).

This manufactured consensus functioned as a key mechanism of techno-populist mobilization, blurring the boundary between authentic political participation and orchestrated manipulation, and thereby distorting voters' capacity for informed choice (Lovi, 2025). In the following section we will outline what we consider the four defining features of Georgescu's campaign and unpack the mechanisms through which he circumvented and hollowed out the democratic character of the presidential elections.

## Use of fake accounts, bots, and AI amplification

The first and most visible technically and politically controversial dimension of Georgescu's campaign was the use of fake accounts and automated bots to artificially inflate his online presence. Investigations by journalists and platform operators uncovered evidence of coordinated inauthentic behaviour designed to amplify Georgescu's visibility on social media from September and October 2024 (Solea, 2024, November 29). TikTok's election integrity team reported dismantling a network of 4,453 fake accounts originating abroad that attempted to promote the AUR party (Alliance for the Union of Romanians) which, to a lesser extent, also benefited the independent candidacy of Călin Georgescu (TikTok, 2024, December 6). By mid-December 2024, TikTok announced that it had removed an additional 22,764 accounts associated with this network, many of which relied on fictitious identities to post election-related comments at scale, outright supporting or favouring Călin Georgescu (TikTok, 2024, December 6). According to TikTok, the activity was likely coordinated by a third-party "fake engagement vendor," although the identity of the clients behind this operation was not publicly disclosed (TikTok, 2024, December 6). In parallel, the platform also dismantled a smaller Romania-based network consisting of several dozen accounts dedicated exclusively to promoting Georgescu, marking the only covert influence operation focused solely on his candidacy (TikTok, 2024, December 6). These findings strongly indicate that Georgescu's digital rise was facilitated by organized cyber troops such as networks of inauthentic profiles systematically injecting his name and messaging into online discourse.

The costs for powering this type of infrastructure are evaluated by advertising social media expert Dragoş Stanca at tens of millions of euros during an interview for Adevărul, a Romanian national newspaper, and the complexity of the campaign, according to the same media expert, required a professional coordinating structure specializing in large online campaigns (Adevărul, 2025, February 15).

Similar patterns were observed across other platforms. Bot-like accounts flooded comment sections on Facebook, frequently posting identical pro-Georgescu slogans and hashtags (Solea, 2024, November 29). Romania's media watchdogs reported an unusually high volume of pro-Georgescu comments appearing on rival candidates' posts (Pavel et al., 2024, November 14). For example, TikTok videos uploaded by opponent Elena Lasconi (USR) were inundated with identical supportive messages for Georgescu (Solea, 2024, November 29). The investigative journalism platforms and online newspapers Info Sud-Est (ISE) and Context discovered that 10 days prior to the 1st round of the presidential elections, Georgescu's name appeared everywhere on TikTok, mentioned by apparent real users who were reacting to posts and videos of counter candidates (Pavel et al., 2024, November 14). In response to these anomalies, Romania's National Audiovisual Council formally urged the European Commission to investigate TikTok's role in amplifying Georgescu's campaign, citing concerns over systematic manipulation (Solea, 2024, November 29). A senior EU lawmaker subsequently summoned TikTok's CEO for questioning amid growing fears of foreign or automated interference in the electoral process (Politico, 2024, November 26).

In practical terms, Georgescu's campaign appeared to deploy bots to saturate TikTok, ensuring that his name and slogans permeated nearly all corners of the platform (Dascălu, 2025, September 4). Regardless of the content users were viewing, ranging from cooking videos to fitness clips, many encountered pro-Georgescu comments or memes, creating the pervasive illusion of widespread grassroots support (Mihăilescu, 2024, November 28).

This artificial visibility granted him an outsized share of online attention, portraying a level of popularity that would have been unattainable through organic means alone. Over time, this manufactured prominence translated into genuine political support, as repeated exposure influenced perceptions of legitimacy (Mihăilescu, 2024, November 28). In this way, fake engagement mechanisms functioned as a catalyst for a bandwagon effect.

Georgescu's digital campaign closely mirrors strategies documented in electoral contexts shaped by computational propaganda. Research on the 2016 U.S. presidential election demonstrated that automated accounts disproportionately amplified pro-Trump content, illustrating how artificial engagement distorts online political competition (University of Oxford, 2016; Bradshaw and Howard, 2018). Such techniques have since been identified across various countries with various degrees of democratic consolidation, from the UK to the Philippines, forming a standardized repertoire of algorithmic manipulation (Howard and Bradshaw, 2019). The effectiveness of this strategy was reinforced by TikTok's recommendation system, which enabled large-scale microtargeting of users predisposed to populist and anti-establishment themes without explicit data harvesting (Expert Forum, 2024). Within this environment, misinformation which kindled the electorate's frustrations circulated rapidly. One viral video falsely claimed preferential state benefits for Ukrainian refugee children, accumulating millions of views despite being publicly debunked (Cârlugea and Wesolowsky, 2024). Such content was fitted within a broader repertoire combining conspiracy, exclusionary nationalism, and historical revisionism, mobilizing fear and resentment while eroding epistemic boundaries between fact and fabrication (Mihăilescu, 2024, November 28; Bader and Szabó, 2025). By exploiting algorithmic asymmetries of visibility, it reshaped what Bartlett (2018) identifies as the unequal distribution of voice in platform-mediated politics. It did not merely expand campaign reach but undermined political equality itself by converting unregulated algorithmic amplification into a decisive electoral resource. Investigations from media watchdogs documented this ecosystem and found that a significant share of this amplification activity was powered by Russian-linked troll infrastructures disseminating pro-Georgescu and anti-EU narratives, pointing to a consolidated disinformation ecosystem rather than isolated digital excesses, which functioned in a coordinated manner for months, and possibly long time before the start of the electoral year (Carp, 2025; Dascălu, 2025). These practices exemplify what Susskind

(2018) conceptualizes as algorithmic power, namely the capacity to shape political outcomes by structuring what citizens encounter and respond to.

## Financial opacity and digital evasion

The second core dimension of Călin Georgescu's campaign concerns the financial opacity that enabled and sustained this algorithmic mobilisation. Georgescu's formal declaration of zero campaign income and expenditure stands in stark contradiction to the empirical evidence uncovered by investigative journalists, tax authorities, and security services, which documented substantial financial flows supporting online promotion, influencer payments, and content amplification (Expert Forum, 2024, November 25; Neag et al., 2025, January 22). These funds were channelled through mechanisms intrinsic to platform economies, including direct payments to content creators, cryptocurrency transactions, and informal digital patronage systems, effectively bypassing Romania's legally mandated campaign accounts and disclosure requirements.

As Shoshana Zuboff argues, surveillance capitalist infrastructures are structurally predisposed to opacity, as value extraction, behavioural modification, and monetisation occur beyond the visibility of public oversight (Zuboff, 2019). In this sense, Georgescu's campaign did not simply violate campaign finance law. It revealed how platform-mediated political funding erodes the enforceability of democratic rules by relocating financial power into privately controlled transnational digital ecosystems. Whilst the technology that he employed might be revolutionary in the realm of fast digital payments and development of financial services, when applied to the electoral realm, it can prove destructive for the pillars of democracy, undermining the fairness of elections and transparency of funding mechanisms.

When it comes to electoral legislation, Romania operates a comparatively restrictive electoral finance regime governed by Law No. 334/2006, which subjects all campaign activity to centralized financial control. Electoral campaigns must be conducted through a single official account administered by a designated financial agent and monitored by the Permanent Electoral Authority (AEP), with all income and expenditure documented and reported to ensure traceability and oversight (Romanian Parliament, 2006; Digi Economic, 2025). Donations received after the formal campaign period begins must be declared within five days, enabling continuous supervision. The law imposes strict prohibitions on funding sources. Foreign individuals or organisations, public institutions, and state-funded entities are barred from contributing, reflecting a legal commitment to insulating elections from external influence (Romanian Parliament, 2006, Arts. 24–25). Transparency requirements are extensive. Donors must be identified, with anonymity permitted only for small contributions below ten times the minimum gross salary and subject to an aggregate cap. Contributions exceeding this threshold must be fully disclosed, and parties are required to publish detailed annual financial reports in the Official Gazette (Romanian Parliament, 2006; Grecu, 2015).

Financial dominance is further constrained through donation and expenditure ceilings. Individuals may donate up to 200 times the minimum gross salary annually and legal entities up to 500 times, whilst total party donations are capped as a share of projected state budget revenues (Law No. 334/2006). Campaign spending is also limited, with presidential candidates in 2024 restricted to 25,000 times the minimum gross salary, and over-spending subject to confiscation. Party support is included within candidate ceilings to prevent parallel financing, and unrepaid loans are treated as donations after three years to close circumvention pathways (Law No. 334/2006; GRECO, 2016). This regulatory framework operates alongside a funding model heavily reliant on public subsidies and post-election reimbursement, which was designed to reduce dependence on private donors (Preda, 2015; Expert Forum, 2020). Enforcement rests with the AEP, which following the 2024 elections, imposed substantial fines and confiscations, including penalties against Călin Georgescu for reporting violations and unclear funding sources (Costiță, 2025). Yet the system remains oriented toward traditional channels of financial flows and campaign funding, a premise increasingly strained by digitally mediated campaigning and fully exploited by Georgescu throughout these elections.

Within this context, fully aware of all the campaign funding requirements, Călin Georgescu officially declared zero income and zero expenditure, a claim incompatible with his rapid national visibility and dominant presence on TikTok. Subsequent investigations by journalists, civil society organisations, and intelligence services demonstrated that his campaign was sustained by extensive, undeclared digital promotion conducted entirely outside the regulated financing system. Declassified intelligence reports identified a coordinated TikTok operation involving more than 25,000 accounts, many newly created or previously inactive, which systematically amplified Georgescu's content using identical slogans, hashtags, and audiovisual templates (Mierzyńska, 2024, December 17). Influencers were covertly remunerated to promote the candidate, while the content was presented as organic and left unlabelled as political advertising, in violation of electoral law. Payments were routed through TikTok's internal gifting system and external digital platforms, bypassing Romanian banks and official campaign accounts altogether (Mierzyńska, 2024, December 17).

A central figure in this architecture of concealed financing was Bogdan Peșchir, a Romanian tech entrepreneur, widely known on TikTok as a major donor to political influencers. In the final weeks of the campaign, Peșchir spent at least USD 381,000 on TikTok donations directed at pro-Georgescu content creators, including payments made after the official end of the campaign period, in clear breach of electoral regulations (Cârlugea and Wesolowsky, 2024, November 26). Peșchir refused to disclose the origin of these funds, while authorities raised suspicions of foreign or illicit financing, potentially linked to a hostile state actor, most plausibly Russia, given its documented pattern of electoral interference and disinformation operations (Radio Free Europe/Radio Liberty, 2024, December 6). Additional channels reportedly included payments through a foreign-based marketing firm, Fame Up Agency, offering influencers pre-scripted videos for fixed fees, as well as possible cryptocurrency transactions that further obscured financial trails (Mierzyńska, 2024, December 17). None of these expenditures appeared in Georgescu's official declarations. As Expert Forum (2024) and OKO Press (a Polish investigative journalism centre)[4] observed, Romanian oversight institutions were structurally unprepared for such operations, as existing controls are designed to monitor bank transfers and physical campaign materials, not decentralized influencer networks financed via foreign digital platforms. Although sanctions were eventually imposed and funds confiscated in 2025, enforcement followed rather than prevented electoral distortion.

In the Republic of Moldova, investigative reporting by Ziarul de Gardă documented similar infrastructures used for electoral funding, showing how pro-Russian political actors who ran in the Moldovan elections, relied on externally financed propaganda networks operating primarily through Telegram, linked to Kremlin-aligned funding structures and troll farms, while remaining formally outside official campaign accounts (Soare, 2025; Wired, 2024). These strategies deliberately evaded compliance with national

---

[4] Expert Forum is a public policy think tank in Bucharest, whilst OKO Press is an investigative newspaper and journalism platform in Poland.

legislation, running campaign expenditures and donations far away from institutional scrutiny. Recent EU rules on political advertising have modestly pushed to improve transparency but remain ill-suited to influencer-based campaigning, digital payments and algorithmic amplification, making Romania's 2024 election less an anomaly than a warning about the erosion of democratic safeguards under platform-mediated politics (European Commission, 2021).

## Foreign-backed influence

A third, and more severe dimension of democratic risk emerges from the campaign's reliance on a foreign-backed digital influence apparatus aligned with Kremlin propaganda infrastructures. Declassified Romanian intelligence assessments, corroborated by investigative reporting realised by newspapers and journalists in Romania and the Republic of Moldova, indicate that Georgescu's online amplification intersected with networks previously associated with Russian state-linked disinformation campaigns, including dormant accounts activated strategically during the electoral period (Carp, 2025; Vacariu, 2025) and content dissemination patterns mirroring earlier Kremlin operations in Ukraine and Moldova (Radio Free Europe/ Radio Liberty, 2024, December 4; Zaharescu, 2025, September 5). Ziarul de Gardă's 2025 investigation (an investigatory newspaper and news outlet in the Republic of Moldova) is particularly significant, as it documents financial and organisational linkages between Georgescu's promotional ecosystem and Kremlin-aligned propaganda agencies operating across borders. This situates the Romanian case within a broader operative pattern of foreign electoral interference, akin to the operations documented in the United States, the United Kingdom, and multiple post-Soviet states, including the Republic of Moldova, where external actors leveraged digital platforms to penetrate domestic political arenas with destabilising narratives (Bradshaw and Howard, 2019). Investigative reporting by Ziarul de Gardă reveals that Călin Georgescu's online promotion intersected with transnational propaganda infrastructures previously deployed in the Republic of Moldova by Kremlin-linked networks (Zaharescu, 2025, September 4). Through an undercover investigation, journalist Natalia Zaharescu infiltrated Telegram-based coordination groups associated with the pro-Russian Victory Bloc and the network surrounding fugitive oligarch Ilan Shor, an influent politician in the Republic of Moldova. Within these groups, she documented training sessions led by Russian disinformation operatives, who openly described campaign objectives, narrative strategies employed online, and funding streams tied to Kremlin-aligned sources (Zaharescu, 2025, September 4). The strategy aimed to simulate organic political engagement through coordinated inauthentic behaviour, while disseminating pro-Russian and anti-European narratives without explicit party attribution, within the Moldovan parliamentary elections. Similar mechanisms had already been deployed in Moldova's previous electoral cycles, where digital propaganda was combined with covert financing, voter bribery, and the capture of local media and influencer environments, allowing foreign-backed mobilisation to bypass electoral oversight. The appearance of analogous tactics in Romania suggests the existence of a regional ecology of interference in which operational models circulate across borders more rapidly than national regulatory systems can respond (Zaharescu, 2025, September 5).

This assessment is reinforced by an investigation conducted by Context, an investigative journalism platform in Romania, which traced pro-Georgescu social media activity on Telegram, X, and Facebook to accounts originating in Russia and linked to coordinated disinformation campaigns promoting conspiracy theories and anti-European narratives (Roşca, 2024). The accounts responsible for manipulation in the Republic of Moldova were discovered to be linked to Telegram groups directly tied to Kremlin propaganda agencies. The same Telegram groups hosted some of the fake accounts that promoted Călin Georgescu.

Trying to make sense of this, Radu Carp (2025) advances the concept of "parallel mirrors" to explain the mechanism through which foreign interference can operate without direct command-and-control. In this model, Carp argues, Călin Georgescu did not need to receive explicit instructions from Russian actors (Carp, 2025). Instead, he articulated narratives already aligned with Kremlin strategic interests, which were subsequently amplified by Russian propaganda outlets, reframed as statements emanating from a Romanian high-level source, and reinjected into the domestic information space (Carp, 2025).

Beyond narrative circulation, Carp (2025) also identifies a cyber-operational layer consistent with established Russian interference tactics. These interference tactics target essential informational infrastructures and hardware and are based on harvesting public AEP (Permanent Electoral Authority) documents, mapping institutional digital infrastructures, identifying privileged users, and synchronizing intrusions with electoral deadlines, closely mirroring methods used in Ukraine's 2014 elections and corresponding to CSAT[5]-documented targeting of BEC and AEP networks[6].

Transnational investigations further indicate the scale of amplification, with thousands of coordinated publications, hundreds of disinformation actors, and multilingual dissemination enabled by automated translation, sustained by online platforms and infrastructures such as InfoDefenseROM and affiliated Romanian-language websites that remained active after the annulment. Complementing this, findings cited by Carp, including VIGINUM's 2025 assessment[7], point to pre-positioned TikTok accounts and long-standing coordination channels on Telegram and Discord, working as a compact yet resilient core orchestrating algorithmic astroturfing that supported Călin Georgescu (Carp, 2025). Together, these elements situate the Georgescu case within a multi-venue interference ecosystem combining cyber reconnaissance, narrative laundering, and platform-based coordination, which complicates attribution while evidencing patterned and strategic external influence (Carp, 2025). Pieced up together, the convergence of intelligence disclosures from Romania and France, investigative journalism, and digital forensics indicates that Georgescu's campaign was not an isolated case of opportunistic online visibility but was embedded within a pre-existing transnational infrastructure of political influence. With this evidence, the proof of foreign interference in the presidential elections and Georgescu's collaboration with Russian propaganda agents is harder and harder to rule out and therefore raises the gravity of electoral fraud exponentially. The issue can no longer be framed as a series of procedural or administrative irregularities that undermine democratic principles at the margins. Rather, it enters the realm of systemic democratic subversion, where external actors and private and state-owned digital platforms actively reshape the informational environment in which political choice is made.

---

[5] Romania's Supreme Council of National Defence, which released intelligence that brings proof of repeated and coordinated cyber-attacks over critical informational and electoral infrastructure during the presidential elections in November 2024.

[6] The Central Electoral Bureau (BEC) is responsible for supervising the conduct of national elections in Romania, whilst the Permanent Electoral Authority (AEP) oversees electoral administration and political finance regulation.

[7] VIGINUM is the French government's specialized technical service responsible for detecting and analysing foreign digital interference, established in 2021 to protect the country from online disinformation campaigns.

## Deliberate and systematic avoidance of institutional scrutiny

The fourth dimension, which cuts across all others, is the deliberate and systemic avoidance of institutional scrutiny. Georgescu's campaign consistently refused engagement with regulatory norms, from the labelling of electoral content and compliance with take-down orders, to participation in public debates and disclosure of campaign infrastructure. This was not incidental non-compliance but a strategic posture that treated institutional oversight as an obstacle rather than as a constitutive element of democratic legitimacy. By operating almost exclusively through platforms governed by private terms of service rather than public law, the campaign exemplified what Susskind describes as the relocation of political power into technological systems whose decision-making logics are insulated from democratic accountability (Susskind, 2018). Supporters and sympathetic commentators frequently minimised these practices as either innovative campaigning or minor procedural issues, thereby normalising a form of political action that hollowed out the very conditions of electoral fairness.

## The implications on democratic decision making

While such practices are not unprecedented, Romanian electoral authorities proved largely unprepared for the scale and intensity of algorithmically amplified political manipulation. As Gabriela Borz argues, Romania exemplifies a broader European vulnerability, as digital political campaigning, such as the one employed by Georgescu, operates largely outside existing electoral law, leaving democratic processes exposed to manipulation through microtargeting, automated accounts, and misinformation (Borz, 2024). Despite emerging EU-level responses, including the Digital Services Act and the forthcoming AI Act, regulatory adaptation remains partial and uneven, and EU member states have for now insufficient capacity to counter algorithmically amplified political manipulation and computational propaganda.

The four elements analysed: algorithmic amplification, financial opacity, foreign-aligned influence, and deliberate evasion of institutional scrutiny, do not threaten democracy in isolation. They function as a tightly interlocking assemblage that produces a new kind of political advantage, one that is less about convincing citizens in a common public arena, and more about controlling the conditions under which citizens encounter politics in the first place. Georgescu's campaign did not simply enter the democratic game with an unfair edge. Instead, it sought to change the game's operating system, relocating decisive power from publicly contestable arenas to privately governed systems of attention (Zuboff, 2019).

The first element, algorithmic amplification, undermines democracy by corroding the public character of political judgment. Elections presuppose not only individual choice but shared informational commons in which claims can be tested, challenged, and compared. TikTok-style algorithmic curation, however, fragments the public into personalised streams where persuasion is detached from the constraints of public rebuttal. Tufekci's (2017) insight that platforms shape rather than merely host public opinion becomes crucial here, where the platform does not simply circulate messages. It actively selects, accelerates, and intensifies the messages most likely to generate engagement, often privileging effect over veracity and repetition over accountability.

If algorithmic amplification is the attention engine, the second element, financial opacity, is the fuel system that makes that engine scalable while evading democratic constraints. Campaign finance rules are not merely bureaucratic technicalities. They are institutionalised answers to a fundamental democratic problem, that is how to prevent political power from being purchased, laundered, or covertly concentrated. The Georgescu case demonstrates how platform economies and digital patronage can outpace this architecture, transforming the enforcement of transparency into a rear-guard action, always arriving after the decisive effects have already occurred. In Zuboff's terms (2019), the political economy of platforms is structurally aligned with opacity, creating an environment where transactions, influence, and behavioural nudges are embedded in systems designed to hide their mechanics from public scrutiny while extracting value and steering conduct.

The third element, foreign-backed influence, raises the stakes from inequality and opacity to the question of democratic and national sovereignty itself. Romania's case illustrates a contemporary form of interference that does not need to tamper with ballots to tamper with outcomes. The target is not the vote count but the informational ecology in which preferences are formed. When such operations intersect with domestic grievances and domestic political entrepreneurs, the boundary between internal democratic contestation and external strategic disruption becomes porous. And once that boundary becomes porous, democracies face a new dilemma, which is how to defend openness without allowing openness to be weaponised. In the case of Călin Georgescu, he openly used the openness of democracy to let in the Russian machinery of influence and expand the "surface of attack" for destabilising forces and external third parties (Măruţă, 2023). Georgescu traded the sovereignty of the country and that of his people for political influence. These issues indicate the complexity that today's democracies find themselves in, where openness and freedom are weaponised to subvert the very own foundation of democracy, turning the protections of sovereignty into vulnerabilities and democratic choice into a strategic terrain of contestation.

The fourth element, that of systematic avoidance of institutional scrutiny, binds the previous three into a coherent anti-democratic operation. Democracies are not defined only by outcomes, they are defined by procedures that force power to appear in public, to justify itself, and to accept constraints. In that sense, institutions are not obstacles to democracy, they are its enabling conditions. What we see here is a campaign strategy meant to obliterate the conditions of democracy and rewrite the rules of the game.

## Conclusion

Research on democratic erosion shows that the institutional breakdown of liberal democracies rarely occurs through sudden rupture, but through the gradual delegitimation of institutions, as competitive pluralism gives way to a politics that treats independent oversight as obstruction (Levitsky and Ziblatt, 2019). When electoral contenders reject the norms of fair contestation while claiming exclusive representation of "the people," elections risk hollowing out democratic legitimacy rather than securing it. When this sort of populism is embedded in platform infrastructures whose logic privileges engagement over accountability and electoral equality and autonomous choice are weakened (Zuboff, 2019), then politics becomes a theatre of images, emotions and words (Baghiu, 2025) all rewired to cheer and applaud the all-powerful leader, whilst democracy becomes a mere wallpaper.

We live in a time of deepening political polarisation. The electorate that voted for Georgescu is not a fictional one and their grievances are real. They are young people (18–24) who face economic insecurity and who usually have lower education levels, who feel ignored, underprivileged and marginalized, and Romanian migrants working abroad in often difficult conditions, facing racism and alienation in their host countries (Marincea, 2025). The votes that they have cast are also real and they reflect their longing for security, better opportunities and a status that matches their efforts and hard work. They were seduced by Georgescu's words, which basically promised to restore their dignity and their security and to take them to a place where these hardships are gone. Sociologists and political scientists consider that their vote can be understood as a vote out of resentment and as a way of punishing the ruling elites and current political class (Marincea, 2025). Recent research considers that support for Călin Georgescu reflects a class-based reaction to the social dislocations of globalization and Romania's unequal integration into the European Union. As Marincea (2025) argues, his neo-legionary tropes and sovereigntist narratives offer symbolic restitution for economic precarity and cultural anxiety, while Rogozanu (2025) interprets this vote as a protest by groups marginalized by post-communist redistribution and labour migration who were basically left out from the economic affluence that Romania has experienced after joining the EU. And whilst probably not all took Georgescu's promises for good, they saw him as a messenger and voice that could signal their disbelief, desperation and grief, and used the vote for Georgescu as a way of manifesting dissent, without necessarily meaning to take down the edifice of democracy.

The discontent that propelled Georgescu's rise was not artificial or marginal. It was rooted in lived experiences of economic insecurity, peripheralization, and prolonged political abandonment. His voters are the electorate that was left unrepresented by mainstream political parties, which they came to perceive as too corrupt and unaccountable. Georgescu promised them radical reform and representation and a new type of social contract, whilst his strategy gave them the sentiment that they could genuinely participate in a political change. But as we see here, this path can be a slippery slope for democracy. These forms of mobilisation through digital platforms promise inclusion, participation, and a voice, yet in practice they function as mechanisms for the upward redistribution of political power, converting diffuse social grievances into forms of mobilisation that bypass collective agency and consolidate control elsewhere (Rogozanu, 2025; Hardt and Negri, 2024). What the Romanian elections reveal, therefore, is not simply regulatory failure or institutional unpreparedness, but a deeper shift in how political will is produced. Georgescu's campaign did not compete within a shared public sphere. It intervened before deliberation could begin, restructuring the informational conditions under which political preferences were formed. Georgescu's techno-populism did not merely exploit democratic dissatisfaction, it reorganised it, displacing social anger from structural relations of power into platform-mediated performances that simulate popular sovereignty while progressively hollowing out its institutional foundations (Baghiu, 2025;

Carp, 2025). This sort of attempt, instead of producing more representation, temporarily eviscerated through algorithmic power the last instances of representation and resources that the most disenfranchised had, threatening to exhaust, as Rogozanu (2025) warns, the last public resource still available to socially abandoned groups: the vote itself as a meaningful instrument of collective representation. Rather than restoring agency, platform-mediated populism converted electoral participation into a one-off act of expressive rupture, thereby depleting the very democratic capacities through which the most disenfranchised could still make durable political claims.

In this respect, Romania's experience forces us to face up to a hard conclusion. The defence of democratic elections in the algorithmic age cannot be reduced only to fact checking, media literacy, or post hoc sanctions, important as these may be. It requires a reassertion of democratic authority over the digital infrastructures that organise visibility, persuasion, and mobilisation. Without enforceable transparency for digital political promotion, without ways of tracing and sanctioning platform-based funding and influencer patronage, without robust mechanisms for detecting and disrupting coordinated inauthentic behaviour and foreign-aligned networks, and without institutions capable of intervening early, proportionately, and credibly, electoral integrity will become an increasingly fragile achievement. Failing to do otherwise will simply hand our electoral space to private companies and anti-democratic populist leaders that are able to rewrite the rules of the game within the black box of algorithmic amplification, all whilst trading the sovereignty of countries for external interference and manipulation. If elections are allowed to become spectacles of participation without conditions of equality, transparency, and reciprocity, democracy will not disappear overnight. It will give the impression that it is still here, lingering as a form without substance, ritual without power, a wallpapered façade behind which decisions are made elsewhere. The lesson of Romania's 2024 election is therefore not exceptional. It is anticipatory. It tells us what democracy becomes when its infrastructures are surrendered, and what is required if it is to be reclaimed. And technology should be part of the democracy reclaiming solutions.

## References

Adevărul (2025). 'Succesul pe TikTok al lui Georgescu, explicat de un expert media: „A funcționat exploatarea analfabetismului functional."' *Adevărul*, 15 February. Available at: https://adevarul.ro/stiri-interne/societate/succesul-pe-tiktok-al-lui-georgescu-explicat-de-un-2422158.html.

Al Jazeera (2024). 'Romania's top court annuls results of presidential election's first round.' *Al Jazeera*, 6 December. Available at: https://www.aljazeera.com/news/2024/12/6/romanias-top-court-annuls-results-of-presidential-elections-first-round.

Anghel, V. (2024). 'Why Romania just cancelled its presidential election', *Journal of Democracy*, Online Exclusive, December. Available at: https://www.journalofdemocracy.org/online-exclusive/why-romania-just-canceled-its-presidential-election.

Bader, S. and Szabó, L.-V. (2025). 'Digitally powered populism and voter manipulation: The case of Călin Georgescu and Romania's 2024 presidential elections.' SSRN Working Paper No. 5243802. Social Science Research Network. Available at: https://papers.ssrn.com/sol3/papers.cfm?abstract_id=5243802.

Baghiu, S. (2025). 'Loony platform politics: The Romanian far-right performance and the digital dystopia of 2024', *Journal of Contemporary Central and Eastern Europe*, 33(1), pp. 235–249. https://doi.org/10.1080/25739638.2025.2482400.

Bartlett, J. (2018). *The People vs Tech: How the internet is killing democracy (and how we save it)*. London: Ebury Publishing.

Borz, G. (2024). 'Why digital electoral campaigning needs urgent regulation', *The Loop* (ECPR), 12 December. Available at: https://theloop.ecpr.eu/why-digital-electoral-campaigning-needs-urgent-regulation/.

Bradshaw, S. and Howard, P.N. (2018). 'The global organization of social media disinformation campaigns', *Journal of International Affairs*, 71(1.5), pp. 23–32. Available at: https://www.jstor.org/stable/26508115.

Bradshaw, S. and Howard, P.N. (2019). *The global disinformation order: 2019 global inventory of organised social media manipulation*. Oxford: Oxford Internet Institute.

Bradshaw, S., Bailey, H. and Howard, P.N. (2021). *Industrialized disinformation: 2020 global inventory of organized social media manipulation*. Oxford: Oxford Internet Institute.

Cârlugea, S. (2024). 'Plângere penală pentru deturnarea unei campanii în favoarea lui Călin Georgescu.' *Radio Free Europe/Radio Liberty*, 22 December. Available at: https://romania.europalibera.org/a/plangere-penala-pentru-deturnarea-unei-campanii-in-favoarea-lui-calin-georgescu/33248864.html.

Cârlugea, S. and Wesolowsky, T. (2024). 'How TikTok fueled the rise of Romania's far-right presidential candidate Georgescu.' *Radio Free Europe/Radio Liberty*, 26 November. Available at: https://www.rferl.org/a/tiktok-calin-georgescu-presidential-candidate-romania/33216735.html.

Carp, R. (2025) 'Jocul "oglinzilor paralele"', astroturfing şi tehno-populism: Fenomenul Călin Georgescu', *Revista de Ştiinţe Politice şi Relaţii Internaţionale*, 22(4), pp. 15–28. Available at: https://www.ceeol.com/search/article-detail?id=1387947.

Cistelecan, A. et al. (2025). 'The global polycrisis and the Romanian elections of 2024', *Journal of Contemporary Central and Eastern Europe*, 33(1), pp. 167–179. https://doi.org/10.1080/25739638.2025.2482389.

Cornea, R. (2025). 'Romanian militant democracy in action: Shielding democracy from subversion and annulling the elections', Verfassungsblog, 1 April. https://doi.org/10.59704/1a0400f2b9629e46.

Costiță, G. (2025). 'Urmările alegerilor: Călin Georgescu a primit cea mai mare amendă.' *Radio Free Europe, Romania*, 17 July. Available at: https://romania.europalibera.org/a/raport-expert-forum-amenzi-sume-confiscate-calin-georgescu-aur/33476578.html.

Dascălu, D. (2025). 'Banii și frica în Moldova: Cum se coordonează pro-rușii pe social media.' *Context.ro*, 4 September. Available at: https://context.ro/banii-si-frica-in-moldova-cum-se-coordoneaza-pro-rusii-pe-social-media-dupa-modelul-calin-georgescu-studiu-de-caz-armata-digitala-investigatie-incognito-a-ziarului-de-garda.

Digi24.ro (2025). 'Cum a funcționat propaganda în sprijinul lui Călin Georgescu.' *Digi24.ro*, 16 September. Available at: https://www.digi24.ro/stiri/actualitate/politica/cum-a-functionat-propaganda-in-sprijinul-lui-calin-georgescu-legaturile-directe-cu-federatia-rusa-3415025.

Digi Economic (2025). 'Au fost stabilite regulile privind finanțarea campaniei electorale.' *Digi24.ro*, 9 April. Available at: https://www.digi24.ro/digieconomic/consumer/au-fost-stabilite-regulile-privind-finantarea-campaniei-electorale-cum-trebuie-sa-procedeze-candidatii-inscrisi-la-prezidentiale-51377.

Dima, B. and Perju, V. (2023). *După 30 de ani. Justiția Constituțională în România.* București: Humanitas.

DiResta, R. (2018). 'Computational propaganda: If you make it trend, you make it true', *The Yale Review*, 106(4), pp. 12–29. https://doi.org/10.1353/tyr.2018.0030.

Dumitru, A. (2024). 'Cum și-a falsificat Călin Georgescu CV-ul. N-a lucrat nici la ONU și nu a fost nici în Clubul de la Roma.' *Antena 3*, 4 December. Available at: https://www.antena3.ro/politica/cum-si-a-falsificat-calin-georgescu-cv-ul-n-a-lucrat-nici-la-onu-si-nu-a-fost-nici-in-clubul-de-la-roma-729641.html.

European Commission (2021). *Proposal for a regulation on the transparency and targeting of political advertising.* European Commission COM/2021/731 final. Available at: https://eur-lex.europa.eu/legal-content/EN/TXT/?uri=CELEX:52021PC0731.

Euronews România (2024). 'Campania online a lui Călin Georgescu ar fi costat aproximativ 50 de milioane de euro.' *Euronews*, 4 December. Available at: https://www.euronews.ro/articole/campania-online-a-lui-calin-georgescu-ar-fi-costat-aproximatv-50-de-milioane-de-e.

Expert Forum (2020). 'Political financing in 2020: Transparency and irregularities.' Policy Brief No. 118. Bucharest: Expert Forum. Available at: https://expertforum.ro/en/political-financing-in-2020-transparency-and-irregularities/.

Expert Forum (2024). 'TikTok in times of crisis. Episode II: What can we observe in the case of Romania.' Policy Brief No. 194. Bucharest: Expert Forum. Available at: https://expertforum.ro/en/files/2024/12/ENG-Policy-Brief-194-_2024_compressed.pdf.

Expert Forum (2024). 'Politica pe TikTok-ul românesc.' 23 November. Available at: https://expertforum.ro/cum-a-crescut-calin-georgescu-in-sondaje/.

Expert Forum (2024). 'Finanțarea campaniei electorale pentru alegerile prezidențiale (II).' Bucharest, 25 November. Available at: https://expertforum.ro/finantarea-campaniei-prezidentiale-25nov/.

G4Media.ro (2024). 'VIDEO Călin Georgescu despre Corneliu Zelea Codreanu și Mişcarea Legionară.' *G4Media.ro*, 13 December. Available at: https://www.g4media.ro/video-calin-georgescu-despre-cei-care-sustin-legea-impotriva-extremismului-vanzatori-de-tara-trebuie-tratati-ca-atare-despre-ion-antonescu-criminal-de-razboi-un-erou.html.

Garvey, M. (2024). 'Călin Georgescu și legionarii.' *Digi24.ro*, 2 December. Available at: https://www.digi24.ro/alegeri-prezidentiale-2024/calin-georgescu-si-legionarii-acum-10-ani-era-vazut-drept-un-dusman-mason-care-insa-vorbeste-in-acord-cu-miscarea-3028893.

Gherghina, S. (2025). 'The lessons of Romania's annulled presidential election', *Political Insight*, 16(1), pp. 32–35. https://doi.org/10.1177/20419058251332344.

Grecu, F. (2015). 'Noua legislaţie electorală din România: Disciplină şi transparenţă financiară', *Sfera Politicii*, 23(185), pp. 65–77.

Group of States against Corruption (GRECO) (2016). *Third evaluation round: Second compliance report on Romania*. Council of Europe. Available at: https://www.just.ro/wp-content/uploads/2021/08/Al-doilea-Raport-de-conformitate-Greco-Eval3_2014_EN.pdf.

Hardt, M. and Negri, A. (2024). *Imperiu*. Translated by M. Bâlici and M. Ţapu. Sibiu: Editura Universităţii 'Lucian Blaga'. (Original work published 2000).

Iancu, B. (2025). 'Militant democracy and rule of law in three paradoxes', *Hague Journal on the Rule of Law*. https://doi.org/10.1007/s40803-025-00245-8.

IFES (2024). 'The Romanian 2024 election annulment: Addressing emerging threats to electoral integrity.' The International Foundation for Electoral Systems, IFES Report, 20 December. Available at: https://www.ifes.org/publications/romanian-2024-election-annulment-addressing-emerging-threats-electoral-integrity.

Le Monde (2024). 'Far right makes spectacular breakthrough in Romania.' *Le Monde*, 2 December. Available at: https://www.lemonde.fr/en/international/article/2024/12/02/far-right-makes-spectacular-breakthrough-in-romania_6734918_4.html.

Levitsky, S. and Ziblatt, D. (2019). *How democracies die. What history reveals about our future*. Penguin Books.

Lovi, S. (2025). 'How disinformation can influence a nation: The case of Romania', *Studia i Analizy Nauk o Polityce*, 1, Article 18466. https://doi.org/10.31743/sanp.18466.

Manolachi, C. (2023). *Revolverul Arhanghelului. Mişcarea Legionară şi Mistica Asasinatului Politic.* Bucureşti: Humanitas.

Marincea, A. (2025) 'Romania's 2024 election crisis: Neo-legionarism's revival of the "Judeo-Bolshevism" myth and the jouissance of punishment', *Journal of Contemporary Central and Eastern Europe*, 33(1), pp. 201–209. https://doi.org/10.1080/25739638.2025.2482396.

Martin-Rozumiłowicz, B. and Kužel, R. (2019). 'Social media, disinformation and electoral integrity.' IFES Working Paper, August. Washington, DC: International Foundation for Electoral Systems.

Măruţă, M. (2023). *Identitatea virtuală. Cum şi de ce ne transformă reţelele de socializare.* Bucureşti: Humanitas.

Mierzyńska, A. (2024). 'Elections in Romania: A marketing agency had connections with Russia.' *OKO Press*, 17 December. Available at: https://oko.press/elections-in-romania-russia-agency-offices-warsaw.

Mihăilescu, M. (2024). 'Călin Georgescu's TikTok tactics rewired Romanian politics.' *The Loop* (ECPR), 28 November. Available at: https://theloop.ecpr.eu/how-calin-georgescus-tiktok-tactics-rewired-romanian-politics/.

Neag, M., Luţac, R., Roşu, I. and Tolontan, C. (2025). 'Campania PNL de pe TikTok ajunsă să-l susţină pe Georgescu.' *Snoop.ro*, 22 January. Available at: https://snoop.ro/campania-pnl-de-pe-tiktok-ajunsa-sa-l-sustina-pe-georgescu-a-fost-ideea-lui-rares-bogdan-am-stiut-dar-de-online-nu-m-am-ocupat-eu/.

Neag, M., Tolontan, C., Roşu, I. and Luţac, R. (2024). 'ANAF a descoperit că PNL a plătit o campanie.' *Snoop.ro*, 20 December. Available at: https://snoop.ro/anaf-a-descoperit-ca-pnl-a-platit-o-campanie-care-l-a-promovat-masiv-pe-calin-georgescu-pe-tiktok/.

Pavel, A., Dascălu, D. and Şerban, A. (2024). 'Cum a crescut în sondaje Călin Georgescu.' *Info Sud-Est*, 14 November. Available at: https://www.info-sud-est.ro/cum-a-crescut-in-sondaje-calin-georgescu-printr-o-strategie-de-promovare-pe-tiktok-val-de-tag-uri-care-i-au-adus-zeci-de-mii-de-urmaritori-si-sute-de-mii-de-vizualizari-noi/.

Politico (2024). 'TikTok CEO summoned to European Parliament over role in shock Romania election.' *Politico*, 26 November. Available at: https://www.politico.eu/article/elections-tiktok-ceo-eu-parliament-romania-election-fake-accounts-pro-russia-calin-georgescu-nato-shock-victory/.

Politico (2024). 'Romania politics election: Călin Georgescu, Elena Lasconi – What the hell is going on?' *Politico*, 7 December. Available at: https://www.politico.eu/article/romania-politics-election-calin-georgescu-elena-lasconi-what-the-hell-is-going-on/.

Preda, C. (2015). 'Eclectic, dar stabil', *Sfera Politicii*, 23(185), pp. 12–20.

Prediger, E.J. (2024). 'Anularea alegerilor prezidenţiale.' *Contributors.ro*, 28 December. Available at: https://www.contributors.ro/anularea-alegerilor-prezidentiale-cine-seamana-vant-culege-furtuna.

Presidency of Romania (2024). *Press release: Romanian President agrees to declassify intelligence reports*. 4 December. Available at: https://www.presidency.ro/ro/media/comunicate-de-presa/comunicat-de-presa1733327193.

Radio Free Europe/Radio Liberty (2024). 'Pro-Russian presidential candidate denies he wants Romania out of NATO.' *Radio Free Europe/Radio Liberty*, 27 November. Available at: https://www.rferl.org/a/georgescu-lasconi-nato-usr-pnl-psd/33217898.html.

Radio Free Europe/Radio Liberty (2024). 'Romanian elections targeted by "aggressive hybrid Russian action."' *Radio Free Europe/Radio Liberty*, 4 December. Available at: https://www.rferl.org/a/romania-russia-election-interference-tiktok/33227010.html.

Radio Free Europe/Radio Liberty (2024). 'Romania's "King of TikTok" tied to alleged scheme.' *Radio Free Europe/Radio Liberty*, 6 December. Available at: https://www.rferl.org/a/romania-election-scandal-tiktok-bogdan-peschir-georgescu/33229674.html.

Reuters (2024). 'Romania's top court orders presidential election recount.' *Reuters*, 28 November. Available at: https://www.reuters.com/world/europe/romanian-top-court-asks-presidential-election-recount-digi24-reports-2024-11-28/.

Reuters (2024). 'Romanian top court annuls presidential election result.' *Reuters*, 6 December. Available at: https://www.reuters.com/world/europe/thousands-attend-pro-european-rally-romania-ahead-presidential-run-off-vote-2024-12-06/.

Roghină, R.C. (2025). 'The annulment of the 2024 Romanian presidential election', *Journal of Legal Studies*, 36(50), pp. 119–142. https://doi.org/10.2478/jles-2025-0017.

Rogozanu, C. (2025). 'Class dynamics in the Romanian ideological landscape', *Journal of Contemporary Central and Eastern Europe*, 33(1), pp. 189–199. https://doi.org/10.1080/25739638.2025.2482394.

Romanian Parliament. (2006). 'Law No. 334/2006 on the financing of political parties and electoral campaigns [Legea nr. 334/2006 privind finanţarea activităţii partidelor politice şi a campaniilor electorale].' *Monitorul Oficial al României*, No. 510, 13 June 2006.

Roşca, M. (2024). 'Operaţiunea Georgescu pe X, Telegram şi Facebook.' *Context.ro*, 29 November. Available at: https://context.ro/exclusiv-operatiunea-georgescu-pe-x-telegram-si-facebook-urcat-in-algoritmi-de-conturi-rusesti-cu-sute-de-mii-de-urmaritori-in-promovarea-lui-au-fost-implicate-retele-specializate-in-desta.

Soare, I. (2025). 'Cum a fost Călin Georgescu promovat de „Armata digitală a Kremlinului".' *CursDeGuvernare.ro*, 5 September. Available at: https://cursdeguvernare.ro/r-moldova-ziarul-de-garda-cum-a-fost-calin-georgescu-promovat-de-armata-digitala-a-kremlinului.html.

Solea, A.I. (2024). 'How a little-known far-right candidate manipulated TikTok.' *The Conversation*, 29 November. Available at: https://theconversation.com/ how-a-little-known-far-right-candidate-manipulated-tiktok-to-rise-to-the-top-in-the-romanian-election-244686.

Srnicek, N. (2017). *Platform Capitalism*. Cambridge: Polity.

Susskind, J. (2018). *Future Politics: Living Together in a World Transformed by Tech*. Oxford, UK: Oxford University Press.

Șerban, A. (2025). 'Viața de ONG-ist a lui Călin Georgescu: fonduri de la USAID și parteneriate cu Fundația Soros.' *Recorder*, 3 March. Available at: https:// recorder.ro/viata-de-ong-ist-a-lui-calin-georgescu-fonduri-de-la-usaid-si-parteneriate-cu-fundatia-soros/.

The Guardian (2024). 'Romanian court annuls first round of presidential election.' *The Guardian*, 6 December. Available at: https://www.theguardian.com/ world/2024/dec/06/romanian-court-annuls-first-round-of-presidential-election.

TikTok Inc. (2024). 'Continuing to protect the integrity of TikTok during Romanian elections.' *TikTok Newsroom*, 6 December. Available at: https://newsroom. tiktok.com/continuing-to-protect-the-integrity-of-tiktok-during-romanian-elections.

Tufekci, Z. (2017). *Twitter and Tear Gas: The Power and Fragility of Networked Protest*. New Haven and London: Yale University Press.

University of Oxford (2016). 'Pro-Trump highly automated accounts 'colonised' pro-Clinton Twitter campaign.' *Oxford News*, 17 November. Available at: https://www.ox.ac.uk/news/2016-11-17-pro-trump-highly-automated-accounts-%E2%80%98colonised%E2%80%99-pro-clinton-twitter-campaign.

Vacariu, M. (2025). 'Alegerile prezidențiale din România 2024', *Polis. Journal of Political Science*, 1(47), pp. 115–127. Available at: https://www.ceeol.com/ search/article-detail?id=1379451.

Venice Commission and Council of Europe (2025). *Urgent report on the cancellation of election results by constitutional courts*. Council of Europe. Available at: https://www.venice.coe.int/webforms/documents/default.aspx?pdffile=C-DL-AD%282025%29003-e.

VIGINUM (2025). *Manipulation d'algorithmes et instrumentalisation d'influenceurs: enseignements de l'élection présidentielle en Roumanie et risques pour la France*. Paris: Secrétariat général de la défense et de la sécurité nationale (SGDSN).

Wired (2024). 'The disinformation warning coming from the edge of Europe.' *Wired*, 19 October. Available at: https://www.wired.com/story/the-disinformation-warning-coming-from-the-edge-of-europe.

Woolley, S.C. and Howard, P.N. (2017). *Computational propaganda worldwide: Executive summary*. Working Paper No. 2017.11. Oxford: Oxford Internet Institute.

Zaharescu, N. (2025). 'VIDEO Armata digitală a Kremlinului.' *Ziarul de Gardă*, 4 September. Available at: https://www.zdg.md/investigatii/ancheta/video-armata-digitala-a-kremlinului-investigatie-sub-acoperire-se-plateste-hai-sa-va-spun-se-plateste-direct-de-la-moscova/.

Zaharescu, N. (2025). 'Publicați o postare despre arestarea ilegală a lui Călin Georgescu.' *Ziarul de Gardă*, 5 September. Available at: https://www.zdg.md/importante/publicati-o-postare-despre-arestarea-ilegala-a-lui-calin-georgescu-detalii-noi-cum-a-fost-promovat-fostul-candidat-la-prezidentialele-din-romania-de-armata-digitala-a-kremlinului/.

Zuboff, S. (2019). *The age of surveillance capitalism: The fight for a human future at the new frontier of power.* London: PublicAffairs.

# DEEP FATE: BEYOND THE ECHO CHAMBER?

## Elesa Zehndorfer

*"There's no fate but what we make for ourselves".*
*(Terminator, 1991, spoken by Sarah Connor)*

The Terminator franchise debuted in movie theatres in 1984. It quickly gained recognition as a groundbreaking series, earning a lasting place in sci-fi history as a cautionary tale about the dangers of unchecked technological advancement.

While a global war against ultra-intelligent cyborgs still remains (thankfully, and hopefully permanently!) far from reality, science fiction has served in some cases as an early harbinger of danger, and as a way for us to comfortably express our collective fears about unchecked technological innovation (Menadue and Cheer, 2017). Right now, these collective fears are rising. We are currently living through an unprecedented boom in AI: there was a \$33.9 billion global private investment in generative AI in 2024, representing an 18.7% increase from 2023, while 78% of organisations were already using AI in 2024 (up from 55% in 2023) (Nanda, 2025; Stanford HAI, 2025). As the boom continues, global and national regulatory frameworks are already scrambling to catch up.

Innovations in AI abound. A well-known innovation that has already captured the public imagination involves Elon Musk, who is heading up the development of an implantable brain-computer interface (Neuralink) chip. Neuralink is designed to be surgically placed permanently in the human brain, offering a means of heightening cognitive abilities (Sahu, 2025). Neuralink has, to date, secured hundreds of millions of dollars in investment.

AI offers fundamentally life-saving opportunities in medicine (e.g., Powell, 2025), ecosystem preservation (e.g., OCELL: Syed, 2025) and diverse fields as esoteric as AI-enabled sustainable fashion material design (e.g., a fast-growing start up Pangaia). Its benefits clearly cannot be ignored.

However, there is a dark side. AI has already enabled disinformation to such an extent that NATO now views it (under the auspices of cognitive warfare) as one of the greatest threats to face humans in the modern age (Marjanović and Smiljanić, 2025; Mota, 2024). It is actively undermining democracy, enabling hostile foreign actors to interfere in our elections and alter our political realities. As such, the fundamental democratic rights and freedoms that we rely upon, and take for granted, appear to be under attack (Deppe, 2024).

This chapter focuses on one specific aspect of political AI, which is accelerating rapidly in both utilisation and growth: deepfakes.

Deepfakes have already been identified as a serious threat to democracy, a central cog in the cognitive warfare wheel, and a danger that appear extremely difficult to regulate or prevent (Hwang, 2020). The question is, have advances in AI already accelerated beyond our control, or can we still move positively beyond the echo chamber?

## Deepfakes and Democracy

First, what exactly are deepfakes? Deepfakes are synthetic media, such as images, videos, or audio, that have been created or manipulated using deep learning techniques. These deep learning techniques use generative adversarial networks (GANs) and variational autoencoders to realistically depict people saying or doing things that they have never done. The goal is usually to manipulate the mind of the viewer or to suppress the actions of the person being "faked" (e.g., to prevent them from engaging in political resistance). The term "deepfake" thus combines the concept of *deep learning* with the concept of being *fake* (Altuncu et al., 2024).

Why refer to *Terminator 2: Judgment Day* in the opening quote of this chapter? Simply put, it is a good strategy, one that borrows from the rule book of deepfake creators. Evoking a shared, popular cultural reference (such as T2) engages a reader via the use of emotions, trades on the use of novelty, sensation seeking and entertainment and subsequently keeps the reader hooked more effectively than if these mechanisms were not engaged with. (Zehndorfer, 2025).

By presenting fabricated but emotionally resonant narratives, such as those referencing familiar movie scenes or in the evocation of vivid memories, deepfake creators easily bypass critical thinking. Instead, they engage with, and appeal directly to, our instinctive fight-or-flight and survival reflexes, and our evolutionary openness to storytelling (Boyd, 2018). This is, in effect, a form of (metaphorical) perceptual malware designed to undermine trust and distort reality (Bradshaw and Howard, 2018; Zegarow and Bartuzi, 2024).

Synthetic media is often deployed in the political sphere to trigger false emotional contagion, exploiting empathy and social cognition to cloud judgment and sway decisions (Kramer et. al., 2014). Deepfakes use hyper-realistic, emotionally charged scenarios, amplifying their persuasive efficacy by leveraging established principles of persuasion, heightened emotion and urgency (Zegarow and Bartuzi, 2024). By manipulating not only beliefs but also memories and behavioural responses, deepfakes represent a significant psychological threat, capable of influencing attitudes and actions even among vigilant individuals (Vecchietti, 2025).

Well-known movies, like *Terminator2*, instantly evoke a sense of nostalgia or familiarity that can be used as a springboard for disinformation content creators (a reason why deepfake creators often rely on Orwellian quotes or movie imagery, e.g., Star Wars, to connect).

We can utilise a T2 reference here: the T-1000 cyborg's ability to imitate any human form could be used as a great metaphor for the perils of digital forgery, where perception itself constitutes our new battleground (Bateman and Jackson, 2024; DeepStrike.io, 2025). While we are not yet at the stage of form-adaptive metal (like the T2 cyborg), synthetic media can already generate some mind-blowingly sophisticated videos, audio, or images that replicate speech, mannerisms, and even personalities extremely well. It is becoming very cheap and fast to do so, too, further threatening a distinction between reality and fabrication (DeepStrike.io, 2025; Reality Defender, 2025).

## How Dangerous are Deepfakes?

Deepfakes (audio, image and video-based) feature heavily across social media and some Internet websites. But just how dangerous are they?

The answer is that yes, they are dangerous and they do pose a significant threat. In fact, recent UK government research paints an alarming picture, detailing how deepfakes increased from 500,000 known samples in 2023 to a forecast 8 million by the end of 2025 (Reality Defender, 2025; Keepnet

Labs, 2025). At the same time, deepfake-based fraud attempts rose 3,000% during 2023 alone, corresponding to a 1,500% increase in total deepfake instances (DeepStrike.io, 2025; UK Government, 2025). This exponential trajectory appears to be tied directly to advances in generative AI models, enabling an easy and relatively cheap deployment of algorithms that routinely create ultra-realistic content within minutes, using only a single audio or visual sample (Genians, 2025).

## A Democratisation of Disinformation

Perhaps one of the greatest threats we face in the context of deepfakes is how cheap and easy it has become to make them.

Using only a laptop and user-friendly open-source tools like DeepFaceLab and DeepVoice, for example, any content creator can create believable manipulated content (e.g., Reality Defender, 2025). For less than $30 per month, users can engage with Eleven Labs and Sora 2 technology to create unlimited deepfake videos using their own avatars.

The NSA and CISA have subsequently both described this democratisation of deception as both a cybersecurity and national security threat, specifically in the case of deepfakes designed to impersonate military officials (NSA et al., 2023).

As stated by NSA Applied Research Mathematician Dr. Candice Rockell Gerstner (NSA, 2023), "The tools and techniques for manipulating multimedia are not new... but the ease and scale of today's deepfake operations create unique national security challenges."

It has also opened the floodgates of fraud, given how easy it can be to use this technology to impersonate banks, financial institutions and even account holders. In fact, Deloitte now estimates that generative AI-driven fraud may skyrocket from $12.3 billion in 2023 to an estimated $40 billion by 2027, a 32% annual growth rate (Deloitte, 2024), with banking and fintech sectors especially vulnerable: 1 in 20 failed biometric authentications now involves a synthetic face or voice, and onboarding fraud has risen over 1,700% since the advent of advanced generative AI (Reality Defender, 2025; Keepnet Labs, 2025).

These attacks expose a systemic fragility: that machine learning systems intended to verify human authenticity are being out evolved by adversarial models focused on imitation (Facia.ai, 2025), challenging systems designed to distinguish fact from forgery (UK Government, 2025).

## Psychological and Sociopolitical Warfare: Attacking the Fabric of Reality

It could certainly be argued that deepfake technologies threaten the very epistemic stability of liberal democratic systems. Reported incidents include the North Korean statesponsored hacking collective Kimsuky Group's deployment of hacking initiatives to infiltrate South Korean defence networks (Genians, 2025), and Russia's ongoing disinformation campaigns against Ukraine (European External Action Service, 2025). What is deeply concerning the context of military and intelligence-based research is that fabricated media manipulates perceptions can affect targets too fast for fact checking to cope with (CSIS, 2024).

This approach in a militarised setting is known as cognitive warfare (Marjanović and Smiljanić, 2025). In 2025, cognitive warfare represents not the battle for territory or hardware, but for the minds and perceptions of populations, social media users, voters, and decision-makers. This new battleground leverages AI to exploit the cognitive vulnerabilities of individuals and societies at scale, with the explicit aim of manipulating beliefs, sowing division, and eroding the pillars of trust and cohesion that underpin democracies.

## Defining Cognitive Warfare in the Age of AI

Cognitive warfare is more than classic information warfare; it is the direct targeting of how people comprehend, process, and respond to information. Rather than simply control the flow of data, it seeks to invade our collective psyche, degrading rationality, manipulating emotions, and steering collective behaviours in a way that feels organic to the target.

As articulated by NATO, cognitive warfare functions by "synchronizing with other instruments of power to affect attitudes and behaviours by influencing, protecting, or disrupting cognition at individual, group, or population levels" (US Department of Defense, 2014). Deepfakes and propaganda have always been central elements of the approach.

AI acts as a force-multiplier here, making such operations more adaptive and personalised. As in *Terminator 2*, where the T-1000 adapts its tactics and morphs as required, modern AI learns behavioural cues, identifies cognitive biases, and rapidly optimises propaganda for maximum impact (James and Brahimi, 2025). In fact, recent research by Vosoughi, Roy, and Aral (2018) demonstrates that falsehoods travel farther, faster, and deeper than the facts on platforms like Twitter, and that AI-armed operators exhibit up to five times higher engagement than organic content due to deliberately engineered emotional triggers (UKRI, 2025). A systematic exploitation of current events, using AI tools to generate instant commentaries or fake expert statements exploits viral hashtags powerfully (Joint Research Centre, 2025). In this context (as has been mentioned previously), the speed of its dissemination often outpaces any meaningful effort to verify or correct it (GIJN, 2025).

Frequent use of hateful or incendiary language, increasingly difficult for automated moderation systems to filter even as detection tech advances (UKRI, 2025; World Economic Forum, 2025), to the point that such content accelerates misinformation cascades, undermines social cohesion, and is now, sadly, linked to real-world violence and social unrest (Yale Digital Safety Lab, 2025).

Disinformation becomes misinformation when the deepfake is shared by the target, with their network, believing it to be true. Rarely does debunking reverse public belief in this scenario (Europol, 2025).

## Political Deepfakes

During the 2024 and 2025 election cycles, widely circulated deepfakes falsely showed politicians endorsing their rivals, and making inflammatory remarks (CSIS, 2024; EU Parliament, 2025), while a deepfake audio nearly derailed the Canadian Prime Minister's campaign days before a national election (Canadian Intelligence Service, 2025).

But do they influence votes? Data shows that yes, these manipulations can swing public opinion and compromise voting outcomes (Pawelec, 2022). Unfortunately, though, their origins are notoriously hard to track. For example, a recent (2025) European Council on Foreign Relations report found 46% of observed synthetic media incidents in elections were untraceable to a source. Of that dataset, nearly 20% were confirmed as foreign interference (EU Parliament, 2025).

Disinformation is also profitable: pay-per-click income and advertising income online has created a burgeoning gig economy where fake new creators jump on any trending topic of the day, then use AI to churn out cheap clickbait to engage. These practices have been responsible for a 200% increase in incidents of coordinated AI-assisted fake news campaigns, all designed to push divisive narratives. It is a phenomenon studied across at least 25 countries in 2024–25 by the WEF (World Economic Forum, 2025). Social platforms similarly report that up to 40% of all AI-generated political disinformation posts now seem to originate from micro-entrepreneur level creators, many of which involve underage participants (Romanishyn et. al., 2025).

Because of this massive growth of the disinformation gig economy, content moderation systems are buckling under the sheer volume and sophistication of the AI-generated content being churned out (UK Government, 2025). Simply put, disinformation appears to be coming from everywhere, warping our realities, yet we don't know who is doing it, or why.

It is not difficult to see how this unstable disinformation landscape is undermining democracy.


## Truth Decay

In neuropolitics, the concept of truth decay describes the erosion of confidence in information caused by repeated exposure to ambiguous or synthetic media (UNESCO, 2025; DeepStrike.io, 2025). The UK Government's Deepfake Detection Challenge recently reported, in fact, that technical progress in deepfake detection has seriously fallen behind the rate of deepfake creation (UK Government, 2025).

In some ways, this parallels the Terminator movie's famed 'Skynet feedback loop' (Skynet is a fictional military AI developed by Cyberdyne Systems that becomes self-aware and launches a nuclear war to exterminate humanity), in the sense that our human defence now perpetually seems to lag behind AI's technological offense. We simply cannot keep up with the technology.

Without robust safeguards, will synthetic media overwhelm our cognitive and institutional capacity to discern authenticity altogether (Alnajashi et. al., 2024)?


## Social, Legal, and Regulatory Countermeasures

Somewhat reassuringly, governments and NGOs have noted these risks and are actively trying to counteract them. The NSA, FBI, and CISA are, for example, actively advocating for provenance verification, mandatory watermarking, and active forensic analysis (NSA, 2023; Europol, 2025), while the UK Home Office's ACE (Accelerated Capability Environment) has supported the development of rapid deepfake identification and takedown protocols (UK Government, 2025). Similarly, Article 50 of the European Union AI Act now requires explicit disclosure of synthetic media origins (EU Parliament, 2025).

Yet enforcement remains difficult. Currently, 9 out of 10 organisations reportedly still lack systematic AI fraud prevention measures (Deloitte, 2024), while open-source diffusion models can be trained off-grid, beyond state control (DeepStrike.io, 2025). Using a fake X account at the time of writing, for example, the author was able to test the 'feel' of disinformation on the platform. The account was exposed to a white supremacy video (2.2m total engagement count), an inaccurate quote about the US economy, and a call for US Democrats to be put to death for the crime of sedition in the first minute of viewing the account.

Pivoting back to *Terminator 2,* the movie warned of the threat of intelligent machines outpacing human oversight, and the parallels to our modern reality are clear when it comes to deepfakes. Deepfakes serve as algorithmic agents of manufactured reality that we cannot yet outpace, prevent or meaningfully legislate against (Watts and Bode, 2024; UNESCO, 2025). What is this doing to the cognitive infrastructure that sustains our democracy, our business, our personal relationships? Without coordinated intervention through technology, ethics, and law, we risk the fading of reality itself as a currency of any value (UK Government, 2025; NSA, 2023).

## AI and Microtargeting Capabilities

But does our ability to handle misinformation really lie in personal agency, and just being smart enough to spot deepfakes?

Not really, and that is due to sophisticated ongoing advancements in large language models (LLMs) and multimodal AI. Both suggest a rapid escalation of ability in the creation of deepfakes, because these technologies continue to push the boundaries of sophistication in the creation of hyper-realistic, hyper-personalised text, images, and audio that can be tailored (microtargeted) to specific individuals, communities, or demographics (Borgesius et. al., 2018), often through hyper-rapid translation and micro-level differentiation.

The genius (and danger) behind microtargeting is that it specifically targeted toward an individuals' specific group identity, self-identity, hopes, dreams, experiences, emotional triggers, or latent fears, manipulating them in ways that are too subtle to note. It makes us far more vulnerable to believing what we see.

The consequences of AI-driven cognitive warfare appear deeply consequential. In 2025, for example, nearly 40% of observed state-led disinformation campaigns employed generative AI to enhance their reach, according to the Institute for Defence Studies and Analyses (Minhas, 2025). The average speed at which new cognitive warfare campaigns are deployed and assessed via open-source intelligence, has literally halved since the introduction of self-optimising AI propaganda engines in 2023 (Smith, 2025).

AI-based microtargeting is a particularly powerful tool of manipulation. In the 2020 U.S. presidential election, campaigns spent over $1 billion on digital advertising using data-driven microtargeting. Reports detail that campaigns created tens of thousands of unique ad versions, customized by demographics such as age, race, geography, and political leaning to maximize targeted voter engagement (Kumar et. al., 2025).

## Undermining Trust, Democracy, and National Security

A core target in deepfake and propaganda creation, as noted frequently in military defence reviews and studies (e.g., Santos et al., 2025), is an erosion of trust in democratic institutions (e.g., Nikoula and McMahon, 2024). This is because democracy requires a capacity for a shared reality and deliberative debate to function effectively. If microtargeted propaganda warps and alters this shared reality, such deliberative debate subsequently becomes impossible. Currently, AI is being used to create, twist and amplify existing societal divisions through personalised misinformation, often using approaches like astroturfing (the creation of fake grassroots movements to imply the organic rise of a party, politician or issue) to achieve that goal (Schoch et. al., 2022).

A recent Reuters report (GIJN, 2025) reported that the online influencers and personalities were ranked as the top two biggest perceived global threats for spreading false or misleading information (47%—equal to the perceived propaganda threat from national politicians (also 47%)). News media and journalists were cited by a third of respondents (32%) as a major misinformation threat.

AI-driven disinformation now appears to constitute a central strategic element of election interference. In 2024 and 2025, for example, more than 20% of observable AI election-interference incidents (virtually always using disinformation) originated from foreign sources, with a significant 46%

of those found to be untraceable (Center for International Governance Innovation, 2025).

## A Growing Gap Between AI Capabilities and Governance

There is clearly a growing need for rapid, comprehensive legislation in the field of AI-driven politics. Discouragingly, though, the current state of play appears fragmented and difficult to enforce, with global and national regulatory frameworks struggling to keep pace with innovations.

In the U.S., for example, legislative efforts are scattered across each state, creating a patchwork rather than a cohesive federal framework (NCSL AI Regulatory Review, 2025). While California, New York, and Washington have enacted several relevant laws, which is heartening, the absence of uniform legislation continues to hamper compliance and enforcement. Of particular concern is the January 2025 revocation of the previous Biden-era Executive Order 14110 on Safe, Secure and Trustworthy AI, which has now been replaced by a pro-AI innovation directive (Executive Order 14179) (White House, 2025). Comparably, Canada's forthcoming Artificial Intelligence and Data Act (AIDA) signals progress towards risk assessment and human oversight but remains in early implementation phases (Government of Canada, 2025).

The European Union recently launched its landmark AI Act (EU Parliament, 2024). Designed to target the systemic potential risk posed by AI language models like GPT (Generative Pre-Trained Transformer) and Llama (Large Language Model Meta AI), the Act strives to balance innovation with safety (EU Commission, 2024). The UK, similarly, recently launched its Online Safety Act (ISA) (Online Safety Act, 2023).

Comparing Western democratic AI regulation to Communist states, China offers an interesting counter. Alignment of AI with state ideology, pre-approval of algorithms, and surveillance-oriented mandates have led to a far less profit-focused, regulated model of AI utilisation. For example, Chinese authorities permit (older) Chinese teenagers to use the app for a severely limited time-period daily, with viewable content limited only to broadly educational topics, under the app name Douyin (Thompson and Srivastava, 2025). Attorney generals from 14 US states are now suing TikTok for exploiting and harming American children's mental health, citing the fact that TikTok already knew that its algorithm was highly addictive and could harm children's mental health (Ibid.).

The consequences of regulatory fragmentation include the risk of enabling the widespread growth of unsanctioned and unmonitored AI tools. The AI Index (Stanford HAI, 2025) warns that few AI models undergo rigorous safety or bias evaluations, with transparency remaining severely limited (Stanford HAI, 2024). While international bodies like the OECD (OECD, 2025) and the UN continue to emphasise principles of transparency and trust, the truth is that enforcement remains voluntary in most jurisdictions, leading to a dangerous disconnect between rhetoric and practice.

A consequent lack of data governance standards has led MIT's Sloan Management Report to highlight the role of poor data quality (biases, incompleteness, and outdated inputs) in creating sub-standard, opaque AI models prone to error and exploitation (Catmull, 2025). There have certainly been arguments made for strengthened labour rights and protections for digital content workers, including identification and support for exploited individuals (Anti-Trafficking Network, 2025), which might go some ways to mitigating the rapid growth of troll farms and other nefarious content factories.

## A Need for Urgent Reform?

The threat of AI in democratic politics is clear, and appears to be escalating, despite efforts to regulate the field. There is clearly an ongoing need for clear, enforceable standards for AI safety, transparency, and monitoring (Stanford HAI, 2024; OECD, 2025), stronger international cooperation, and overall prevention of regulatory arbitrage by bad actors across national lines (UNESCO, 2025).

Investment in public literacy is required to build greater resilience to disinformation (Deloitte, 2024; World Economic Forum, 2025), as is awareness of, and a crackdown on, the escalating emergence of content farms and coordinated networks of misinformation creators based in regions with low internet costs (e.g., Southeast Asia, parts of Africa, and Eastern Europe). The reality is, these farms are systematically producing millions of posts daily that exploit trending topics and controversies for clicks and revenue (Global Media Forum, 2025). Right now, every social media user is a target.

Frighteningly, young people, often minors, are also becoming increasingly vulnerable to exploitation in this field. Mobilised as disinformation operatives, and incentivised by micro-payments tied to engagement metrics, shares, or views, many youths are being placed in exploitative situations

(Frontiers in Artificial Intelligence, 2025), lacking formal contracts, decent labour protections, or ethical oversight.

Social media platforms have reported a rise in coordinated accounts originating from networks where workers operate in shifts producing outrage-fuelled fake news, clickbait, or hyper-partisan memes, often with AI simplifying content generation and obfuscation. Yet self-regulation appears minimal, most likely because of the financial and engagement-based opportunities this kind of activity ultimately leverages for social media platforms (Ma, 2025). As a result, these sweatshops will continue to prioritise sensationalism, polarising narratives, outrage, and emotional manipulation at faster and faster rates, capitalising on user engagement algorithms to gain profit (Frontiers in Artificial Intelligence, 2025; Global Media Forum, 2025).

## Conclusion

In *Terminator 2*, Sarah Connor carves the words that opened this chapter: *No fate but what we make*. Her words are a reminder that even in the face of relentless machine-generated logic, humanity has agency. However, has the real problem ever been a lack of agency? It feels more that the real problem is our ongoing unwillingness to deploy it.

Defending ourselves against AI-powered cognitive warfare, for example, demands understanding, innovation, coordinated efforts and collective vigilance. As individual voters, we obviously cannot fight the threat alone, but we *can* rapidly remove our exposure and vulnerability to it. How?

By simply deleting our social media accounts.

Sadly, however, we already seem to have reached a state of AI dependence, where prevalence studies now show smartphone addiction rates amongst younger generations are as high as 57%. In a recent study, 82% of high school students even acknowledged difficulties in staying off their smartphones during class (Ahmead et al., 2025).

Some readers might remember HAL900 in the sci-fi classic *2001: A Space Odyssey*. Notable for provoking deep questions about AI's motives and morality, the film offers a warning about the ultimate level of control we can afford to hand over to artificially intelligent beings, and the warnings that come with failing to do so.

It remains to be seen how closely we will heed such warnings, especially when it comes to the protection of democracy.

# References

Ahmead, M., Maqboul, E., Alshawish, E. and Dweib, M., (2025). 'The prevalence of smartphone addiction and its related risk factors among Palestinian high school students: a cross-sectional study.' *Frontiers in Psychiatry*, 16, p.1636080. Available at: https://doi.org/10.3389/fpsyt.2025.1636080

Alnajashi, A., DeRise, D., Frana, P., McGraw, D., Sawyer, A., Titareva, T., Zaini, R., Zombron, A. (2024). Volume 7 (2024) 'Artificial Intelligence and Responsibility.' *International Journal on Responsibility*. 7. 10.62365/2576-0955.1139.

Altuncu, E., Franqueira, V.N.L. and Li, S. (2024) 'Deepfake: definitions, performance metrics and standards, datasets, and a meta-review', *Frontiers in Big Data*, 7, p. 1400024.

Anecdotes AI (2025). 'AI Regulations in 2025: US, EU, UK, Japan, China & More', Anecdotes AI, 27 September. Available at: https://www.anecdotes.ai/learn/ai-regulations-in-2025-us-eu-uk-japan-china-and-more

Anti-Trafficking Network (2025). *Emerging Digital Exploitation: The Intersection of AI and Human Trafficking*, ATN Reports, Geneva.

Atlantic Council (2025). 'How AI with "nurtured consciousness" could transform warfare', Atlantic Council New Atlanticist, 18 September. Available at: https://www.atlanticcouncil.org/blogs/new-atlanticist/how-ai-with-nurtured-consciousness-could-transform-warfare/

Bateman, J. and Jackson, D. (2024). *Countering disinformation effectively: An evidence-based policy guide.*

Borgesius, F.J.Z., Möller, J., Kruikemeier, S., Fathaigh, R.Ó., Irion, K., Dobber, T., Bodo, B. and De Vreese, C. (2018). Online political microtargeting: Promises and threats for democracy. *Utrecht law review*, *14*(1).

Boyd, B. (2018). The evolution of stories: From mimesis to language, from fact to fiction. *Wiley Interdisciplinary Reviews: Cognitive Science*, *9*(1), p.e1444.

Bradshaw, S. and Howard, P.N. (2018). *Challenging Truth and Trust: A Global Inventory of Organised Social Media Manipulation*. Oxford: Oxford Internet Institute.

Canadian Security Intelligence Service (CSIS) (2025). *Implications of Deepfake Technologies on National Security*, Government of Canada, Ottawa, viewed 13 July 2025, https://www.canada.ca/en/security-intelligence-service/.

Catmull, J. (2025). MIT Says 95% Of Enterprise AI Fails — Here's What The 5% Are Doing Right. Available at: https://www.forbes.com/sites/jaimecatmull/2025/08/22/mit-says-95-of-enterprise-ai-failsheres-what-the-5-are-doing-right/

Center for International Governance Innovation (CIGI) (2025). 'Then and Now: How Does AI Electoral Interference Impact Democracy?', 6 August. Available at: https://www.cigionline.org/articles/then-and-now-how-does-ai-electoral-interference-impact-democracy/

Centre for Strategic and International Studies (CSIS) (2024). *Crossing the Deepfake Rubicon*, CSIS, Washington DC, viewed 10 January 2024, https://www.csis. org/analysis/crossing-deepfake-rubicon.

Ching, D. (2025). 'Can deepfakes manipulate us? Assessing the evidence via a scoping review of empirical studies'. *PMC (PubMed Central)*, pp.1–18. Available at: https://www.ncbi.nlm.nih.gov/pmc/articles/PMC11968224/.

DeepStrike.io (2025). *Deepfake Statistics 2025: AI Fraud Data & Trends* 2025, https://deepstrike.io/blog/deepfake-statistics-2025.

Deloitte (2024). *Generative AI: Risk and Opportunity Report*, Deloitte Insights, London.

Deloitte (2024). *AI Fraud Forecast Report 2024*, Deloitte Insights, London.

Deppe, C. (2024). 'Cognitive warfare: a conceptual analysis of the NATO ACT cognitive warfare concept', *Frontiers in Big Data*, 7, p. 1452129. Available at: https://www.frontiersin.org/journals/big-data/articles/10.3389/fdata.2024.1452129/full

Drenik, G. (2025). 'Why 95% of AI projects fail and how better data can change that', Forbes, 15 October. Available at: https://www.forbes.com/sites/garydrenik/2025/10/15/why-95-of-ai-projects-fail-and-how-better-data-can-change-that/

EU Commission (2024). *The EU AI Act: Balancing Innovation and Safety*, Publications Office of the European Union, Brussels.

EU Parliament (2025). EDMO Task Force on 2024 European Parliament Elections: Disinformation narratives and fact-checking analysis.

European Council on Foreign Relations (ECFR) (2025) *AI and Democratic Interference in Europe*, ECFR, Brussels.

European External Action Service (EEAS) (2025). 'Results of pro-Russian information manipulation and disinformation monitoring targeting Ukraine-EU relations during June – August, 2025', EEAS, 23 October. Available at: https://www.eeas.europa.eu/delegations/ukraine/results-pro-russian-information-manipulation-and-disinformation-monitoring-target

European Parliament (2025). *Children and Deepfakes: Facing the Synthetic Age*, Publications Office of the European Union, Brussels.

Europol Innovation Lab (2025). *Facing Reality: Law Enforcement and the Challenge of Deepfakes*, Europol, The Hague.

Executive Office of the President (2025). *Executive Order 14179 on Artificial Intelligence*, US Government Printing Office, Washington DC.

Facia.ai (2025). *Horrific Deepfake Examples: Highlighting the Technology's Risks*, Facia.ai blog, London, viewed 10 February 2025, https://facia.ai/blog/horrific-deepfake-examples-highlight-the-technologys-risks/.

Genians Security Center (2025). *AI-driven Military Deepfake ID Fraud Campaign*, Genians Blog, Seoul, viewed 13 September 2025, https://www.genians.co.kr/en/blog/threat_intelligence/deepfake.

GIJN (, 2025). 2025 Reuters Institute Digital News Report: Eroding Public Trust, Growing Misinformation Threats, and Investigative Journalism's Appeal. Global Investigative Journalists Network. Reuters Institute. Available at: https://gijn. org/stories/2025-reuters-institute-digital-news-report/

Global Media Forum (2025). 'AI Disinformation and Countermeasures in Europe and Africa', KAS Media Africa, 7–8 July. Available at: https://www.kas. de/de/web/medien-afrika/veranstaltungen/detail/-/content/global-media-forum-2025-ai-disinformation-countermeasures-in-europe-and-africa

Government of Canada (2025) *Artificial Intelligence and Data Act (AIDA)*, Government of Canada, Ottawa, viewed 13 July 2025, https://www.canada.ca/en/ innovation-science-industry/programs/artificial-intelligence-and-data-act.html.

Greene, C.M. and Murphy, G. (2025). 'Deepfakes as narratives: Psychological processes explaining their reception'. *ScienceDirect*, vol.28, pp.102–115. Available at: https://www.sciencedirect.com/science/article/pii/S1057740825000123.

Hwang, T. (2020). Deepfakes – Primer and Forecast. Riga: NATO Strategic Communications Centre of Excellence. Available at: https://stratcomcoe.org/publications/download/nato_deepfakes_-_primer_and_forecast-1.pdf

James, J. and Brahimi, A. (2025). 'How AI with "nurtured consciousness" could transform warfare', *The New Atlanticist*, 17 September. Available at: https:// www.atlanticcouncil.org/blogs/new-atlanticist/how-ai-with-nurtured-consciousness-could-transform-warfare/

Joint Research Centre (2025). 'AI: Friend or Foe of Disinformation?', European Commission, 1 September. Available at: https://joint-research-centre.ec.europa. eu/jrc-explains/ai-friend-or-foe-disinformation_en

Keepnet Labs (2025) 'Deepfake Statistics & Trends 2025: Key Data & Insights', Keepnet Labs Blog, 12 November. Available at: https://keepnetlabs.com/blog/ deepfake-statistics-and-trends

Kramer, A.D.I., Guillory, J.E. and Hancock, J.T. (2014). 'Experimental evidence of massive-scale emotional contagion through social networks', Proceedings of the National Academy of Sciences, 111(24), pp. 8788–8790.

Kumar, I., Parekh, V. and Kumar, N. (2025). 'The Influence of Social Media on Elections: Expenditure, Campaign Strategies, Outcomes, and Bias'. *Journal of Marketing & Social Research 2*(2), pp. 432–450. Accessible at: https://www. jmsr-online.com/article/the-influence-of-social-media-on-elections-expenditure-campaign-strategies-outcomes-and-bias-96/

Marjanović, A., and Smiljanić, D. (2025). Cognitive warfare–the human mind as the new battlefield. In *Proceedings of the Defense and Security Conference* (pp. 84–114). Zagreb: Sveučilište obrane i sigurnosti Dr. Franjo Tuđman.

Ma, R. (2025). 'Fighting fake news in the age of generative AI: Strategic governance among stakeholders,' Technological Forecasting and Social Change, 182, 122407. Available at: https://www.sciencedirect.com/science/article/abs/pii/ S0040162525001568

McKinsey & Company (2025) *The State of AI: Global Survey Insights*, McKinsey, New York. Available
at: https://www.mckinsey.com/capabilities/quantumblack/our-insights/the-state-of-ai

Menadue, C. B., & Cheer, K. D. (2017). Human Culture and Science Fiction: A Review of the Literature, 1980–2016. *Sage Open*, 7(3). Available at: https://doi.org/10.1177/2158244017723690

Minhas, S.K. (2025). *Issue Brief: Cognitive Warfare*. Institute for Defence Studies and Analyses (IDSA). Available at: https://www.idsa.in/wp-content/uploads/2025/08/Issue-Brief-Gp-Capt-Sukhbir-Kaur-Minhas-18-August-2025.pdf

Mota, S. (2024). The Technological Revolution in 21st-Century NATO: The New Frontiers of Space and Mind. *Nação e Defesa*, (168), pp. 9–23.

NAAIA. (2025). *Worldwide state of AI regulation*. Available at: https://naaia.ai/worldwide-state-of-ai-regulation/

Nanda, M. (2025). State of AI in Business, 2025. *Preprint at https://www. artificial-intelligence-news. com/wp-content/uploads/2025/08/ai_report_2025. pdf*.

National Security Agency (NSA) & Cybersecurity and Infrastructure Security Agency (CISA) 2023, *Advisory on Deepfake Threats*, U.S. Department of Defense, Washington DC, viewed 11 September 2023, https://www.nsa.gov/Press-Room/Press-Releases-Statements/.

NATO Allied Command Transformation. (2025). *Cognitive Warfare Report*. NATO ACT Journal. Available at: https://www.act.nato.int/wp-content/uploads/2025/09/20250819_NU_CogWar_01.pdf

NCSL AI Regulatory Review (2025) Summary of Artificial Intelligence 2025 Legislation. Available at: https://www.ncsl.org/technology-and-communication/artificial-intelligence-2025-legislation

Nikoula, D., & McMahon, D. (2024) Cognitive warfare: Securing hearts and minds. *Information Integrity Lab,* July...

National Security Agency (NSA), Federal Bureau of Investigation (FBI) and Cybersecurity and Infrastructure Security Agency (CISA) (2023). 'Contextualizing Deepfake Threats to Organizations', Cybersecurity Information Sheet, 12 September.

OECD (2025). Sharing Trustworthy AI Models with privacy enhancing technologies. Working Paper. OECD, 17th June.

Online Safety Act 2023, c. 50. United Kingdom. Available at: https://www.legislation.gov.uk/ukpga/2023/50/enacted

Pawelec, M. (2022). Deepfakes and Democracy (Theory): How Synthetic Audio-Visual Media for Disinformation and Hate Speech Threaten Core Democratic Functions. *Digit Soc.* 2022;1(2):19.

Powell, A. (2025) 'How AI is transforming medicine', *Harvard Gazette*, 19 March. Available at: https://news.harvard.edu/gazette/story/2025/03/how-ai-is-transforming-medicine-healthcare/

Reality Defender (2025). *UK Government Deepfake Report: 1500% Surge by 2025*, Reality Defender, London https://www.realitydefender.com/insights/uk-government-deepfake-report.

Romanishyn, A., Malytska, O., and Goncharuk, V. (2025). AI-driven disinformation: policy recommendations for democratic resilience. *Frontiers in Artificial Intelligence*, *8*, 1569115. Gartner 2024, *The Cost of Data Quality Problems for Businesses*, Gartner Research, Stamford.

Smith, J. (2025). 'The Emergence of Cognitive Intelligence (COGINT) as a Dominant Modality in Fifth-Generation Warfare', *Journal of Strategic Studies*, 48(7), pp. 1234–1265. Available at: https://www.tandfonline.com/doi/full/10.1080/08850607.2025.2571497

Sahu, C. (2025). 'Neuralink and its advantages: advancements in brain-computer interface technology', *International Journal on Science and Technology*, 16(3), pp. 1–15. Available at: https://www.ijsat.org/papers/2025/3/6777.pdf

Santana, J. (2025.) 'Cognitive warfare tactics and technologies in artificial intelligence', LinkedIn. Available at: https://www.linkedin.com/pulse/cognitive-warfare-tactics-technologies-artificial-jim-santana-lwm2c

Santos, C. P. (2025). 'Cognitive Warfare: The Mind as a Battlefield'. *EKSPLORIUM-BULETIN PUSAT TEKNOLOGI BAHAN GALIAN NUKLIR*, *46*(1), pp. 1243–1270.

Syed, M. (2025). The Integration of AI in Climate Tech: Where Are We in 2025? [online] Climate Insider. Available at: https://climateinsider.com/2025/02/02/the-integration-of-ai-in-climate-tech-where-are-we-in-2025/

Schoch, D., Keller, F. B., Stier, S., and Yang, J. (2022) Coordination patterns reveal online political astroturfing across the world. *Scientific reports*, *12*(1), 4572.

Stanford Human-Centered AI Institute (Stanford HAI) (2024). *The 2025 AI Index Report*, Stanford University, Stanford. Available at: https://hai.stanford.edu/ai-index/2025-ai-index-report

Statista. (2025). *AI regulations worldwide*. Available at: https://www.statista.com/topics/13809/ai-regulations-worldwide/

Terminator (1991). Directed by James Cameron. [Film] United States: Orion Pictures.

The Geopost (2025). 'How artificial intelligence became a key factor in information warfare in 2025', *The Geopost*, 14 September. Available at: https://thegeopost.com/en/analysis/how-artificial-intelligence-became-a-key-factor-in-information-warfare-in-2025/

Thompson, P., Srivastava, S. (2025). TikTok is 'severely damaging' young people — unlike its Chinese equivalent, 'The Anxious Generation' author tells BI.

Business Insider. (Jan.24th) Accessible at: https://www.businessinsider.com/tik-tok-different-china-douyin-jonathan-haidt-anxious-generation-national-2025-1

UK Government (2025). 'Frontier AI Capabilities and Risks: Safety and Security Risks of Generative AI to 2025', UK Government Publications, 28 April. Available at: https://www.gov.uk/government/publications/frontier-ai-capabilities-and-risks-discussion-paper/safety-and-security-risks-of-generative-artificial-intelligence-to-2025-annex-b

UKRI (UK Research and Innovation) (2025). 'Using Artificial Intelligence (AI) to Tackle Online Hate', ESRC, 13 October. Available at: https://www.ukri.org/who-we-are/how-we-are-doing/research-outcomes-and-impact/esrc/using-artificial-intelligence-ai-to-tackle-online-hate/

UNESCO (2025) 'AI regulation and global cooperation challenges', UNESCO, Paris.

UNESCO (2025). 'Deepfakes and the Crisis of Knowing', UNESCO, Paris, viewed 4 March

2025. Available at: https://www.unesco.org/en/articles/deepfakes-and-crisis-knowing.

United Kingdom Government (2025). *Innovating to Detect Deepfakes and Protect the Public*, Department for Science, Innovation and Technology, London, viewed 4 February 2025. Available at: https://www.gov.uk/government/case-studies/innovating-to-detect-deepfakes.

U.S. Department of Defense (2014) Joint Publication 3–13, Information Operations. Available at: https://apps.dtic.mil/sti/pdfs/ADA470831.pdf

Vecchietti, G., Liyanaarachchi, G., & Viglia, G. (2025). 'Managing deepfakes with artificial intelligence: Introducing the business privacy calculus.' *Journal of Business Research, 186*, 115010.

Watts, T.F. and Bode, I. (2024). 'Machine guardians: The Terminator, AI narratives and US regulatory discourse on lethal autonomous weapons systems.' *Cooperation and Conflict, 59*(1), pp.107–128.

White House (2025). Executive Order on Removing Barriers to American Leadership in Artificial Intelligence. Available at: https://www.whitehouse.gov/presidential-actions/2025/01/removing-barriers-to-american-leadership-in-artificial-intelligence/

World Economic Forum (2025) *AI and the Future of Work Report*, WEF, Geneva.

World Economic Forum (2025). Global Risks Report 2025, 'Conflict, Environment and Disinformation Top Threats', World Economic Forum, 15 January. Available at: https://www.weforum.org/press/2025/01/global-risks-report-2025-conflict-environment-and-disinformation-top-threats/

Yale Digital Safety Lab (2025). 'AI-Generated Misinformation and Social Impact', Yale University, 20 August. Available at: https://www.yale.edu/digitalsafetylab/ai-generated-misinformation

Zegarow, P., and Bartuzi, E. (2024) Deepfake Influence Tactics through the Lens of Cialdini's Principles: Case Studies and the DEEP FRAME Tool Proposal. Applied Cybersecurity & Internet Governance, 3(2), pp.286–302. https://doi.org/10.60097/ACIG/201147

Zehndorfer, E. (2025). *Post-Truth Politics: A Brave New World?* 1st edn. Abingdon: Routledge.

# INNOVATION FITNESS TEST
## Robert Lewis

## Introduction - Competing for Innovation Fitness

Across industries, leaders acknowledge that innovation is essential for success and the word is prominent in company reports — yet few organisations are truly fit to innovate. They confuse busyness with progress, reward compliance over curiosity, and mistake short-term activity for long-term adaptability (Waltz, 2023). Research repeatedly shows that politics, misaligned incentives, turf wars and risk-averse cultures remain the most common barriers to innovation in large companies (Kirsner, 2018).

At the same time, the demands placed on innovation teams are growing. Technologies evolve faster than most organisations can absorb them, customers expect solutions that connect emotionally as well as functionally (Scott et al., 2015), and leadership models that once worked are being challenged by new expectations for purpose, autonomy, and psychological safety (McGregor, 2015). In short, innovation is a test of organisational fitness, a measure of how well an enterprise can adapt, learn, and create value in times of uncertainty and turbulent flux.

This chapter introduces the Innovation Management System (IMS) framework: a structured yet adaptive model developed over decades of lived experience working in R&D, product development, and innovation across sectors. The framework provides the foundation for the Innovation Fitness Test, a practical tool an organisation can use to assess its innovation capabilities, identify gaps, and set priorities for improvement.

The aim is not to prescribe a single model for innovation success but to help organisations benchmark their current level of innovation fitness and understand where they are in relation to a well-functioning innovation system. They may then choose to adopt elements of the framework where they are deficient to improve their innovation capabilities. It is important to recognise that not every element of the IMS must be in place; rather, the organisation should choose which elements to adopt that suit their current circumstances and help them on their journey to sustainable innovation performance and growth.

In this chapter, we describe the elements of the Innovation Management System (Figure 1), how they are interrelated and how they can be used to benchmark innovation fitness. This represents the building blocks that an organisation requires for world-class innovation operations. It may be used as the basis for an Innovation Fitness Test by scoring each element to assess organisations in terms of what they have in place, and to what degree. Poor Innovation Fitness should be an indicator for a business to address gaps and put missing elements in place. It can be used as a continuous improvement tool to develop innovation capability over time.

## Level -1: What is Innovation and Why Innovate?

This level of the IMS involves an organisation understanding what innovation actually is and how it fits among other activities, and with that understanding consciously decide whether it is an activity they need to participate in by answering the question "why innovate?". In addressing these key points, a business case can be made to embed innovation and the IMS framework as part of the business's operations.

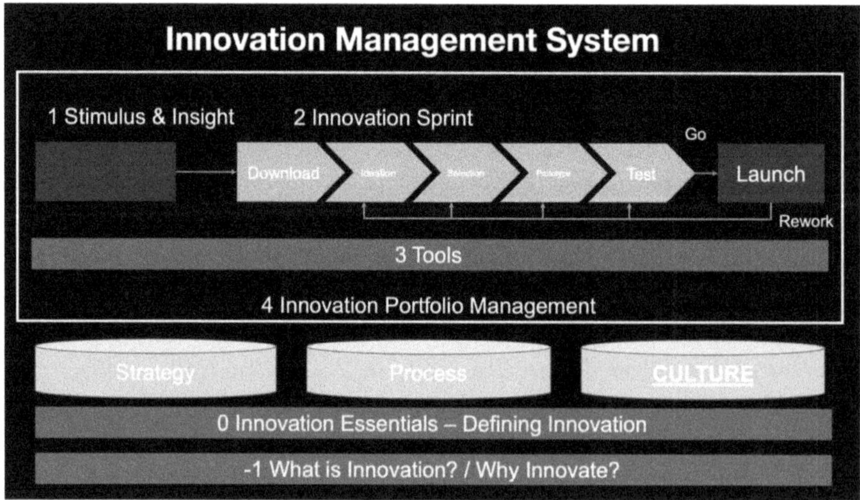


Figure 1. The Innovation Management System.

## What is Innovation?

Understanding the term "innovation" is key to setting up an effective IMS. The word is widely used but often misunderstood, or the activity is deemed to be too difficult or out of scope for some organisations. But an understanding of the definition of the word is essential to create an effective innovation function. There are many definitions of innovation in the literature; we can consider a few.

McKinsey (2022) defines innovation as "the process of developing and marketing breakthrough products for the adoption by customers." The word "breakthrough" suggests that only the application of cutting-edge ideas at the extremes of novelty may be classified as innovation. This may apply to organisations engaged in leading-edge science or technology, but for many organisations, a lower bar to innovation can be applied. The Business Bank of Canada (2022) defined innovation as successfully implementing a new idea and creating value for your customers and stakeholders. This definition is more applicable to a wider range of organisations as it introduces the idea that innovation is about creating value, rather than being limited to just invention or new technology. Further, the definition introduces the key concept that innovation should be focused on the needs of the customer. Successful innovation should be customer or consumer-led and address their needs and pain points to create value. We can consider governmental views on what constitutes innovation by looking at the definition offered by the United Kingdom (UK) Government, who define innovation as 'the creation and application of new knowledge to improve the world' in their Innovation Strategy (UK Government, 2021). Here is another definition that focuses on breakthrough, highly inventive innovation that has the potential to change the world. Like the McKinsey definition, this sets a high bar for innovation. This level of innovation is a key driver of human progress, which is necessary, but the very high bar would exclude many organisations from innovation. Most businesses need to create value for customers rather than invent things that change the world.

Bolton (2024) offers a fuller definition recognising that innovation is not only about new technology breakthroughs, but also applies to less inventive ideas that serve the needs of customers and create value for the business. He states simply that "Innovation is something different that creates value". This definition is much more useful for businesses, as it draws out key elements:

"Something" which is the product of the innovation. This may be a product, a claim, a new business model, a new method or process or something else. This usefully broadens thinking about what innovation can be.

"Different" introduces the concept that innovation is a new way of doing something that moves the business on in terms of product or market.

"Creates value" in business. All innovation needs to create value. Otherwise, what is its purpose, and why does it merit any time or resources?

Bolton warns, "Innovation is NOT a one-size-fits-all term", emphasising that organisations need to think about innovation from their own perspective and create a definition that suits their business, maturity, situation and ambition.

## Why Innovate?

Armed with an appreciation of what innovation is, an organisation can then decide on whether this is an activity it wishes to commit resources to. It is difficult to imagine an organisation where innovation is not a valued activity, as it is fundamentally about creating value, but some organisations do not apply resources to innovation. Such organisations might be those in highly regulated environments where reproducibility and replication may be a key requirement (e.g., nuclear power or air traffic control); where there is a monopoly of guaranteed demand (e.g., national post services or water utilities); or ultra-niche craft or heritage businesses who exist to maintain tradition rather than change it (e.g., Scotch whisky or bespoke traditional tailors). But even in these examples, there remains room for innovation. It is the view of this author that there is always potential for innovation applied to some element of a business. Ignoring innovation or consciously eliminating it is to limit growth and survival.

We live in a world of extreme complexity and constant turbulent flux driven by advances in technology, change in consumer expectations, environmental collapse, geopolitical instability, volatile prices and supply chains. So for most organisations, the "why" is anchored in survival, growth, and relevance. We exist in a climate where static business models decay quickly. Studies of corporate longevity repeatedly show that adaptive, innovative firms are significantly more likely to outperform peers over time (Viguerie, 2017).

The output of Level1 is a conscious, evidence-based decision taken after understanding what innovation is:

- Yes, innovation is strategically essential, so the organisation commits to building the structures, behaviours, and metrics to support it by implementing the IMS.
- Or no, innovation is not a priority, in which case the IMS is not required. In such cases, clarity itself is a valuable outcome, but the business should be aware of the risks and limitations applied to future growth as a result.

## Level 0: Innovation Essentials

Level 0 establishes the Innovation Essentials as the foundations upon which the entire Innovation Management System rests. Having clarified what innovation means for the organisation and why it is strategically important in Level -1, the next step is to formalise the core building blocks that support effective innovation activity: a shared organisation-relevant definition of innovation, an innovation strategy, a helpful, clear and repeatable innovation process, and an innovation culture that supports conditions that enable people to be creative and innovate. These elements form the Innovation Essentials that support the systemisation of innovation. This level of the IMS creates a stable platform from which all higher levels of the IMS are constructed, ensuring that innovation activity is organised, well directed and capable of delivering value consistently rather than by chance.

## Defining Innovation

Previously, we considered general definitions of innovation; now as a first step in implementing the IMS we must create a definition that is relevant to the organisation. This definition of innovation is key to ensuring that staff understand what their innovation activity is and how it aligns with the business needs to deliver growth and create value. The definition helps in separating innovation from other business activities, and helping those tasked with delivering innovation by focusing their efforts on the right activity.

A clear organisational definition of innovation is the first essential step in establishing a coherent and functioning innovation system. Innovation is a widely used term, but it is often interpreted differently by different people and may range from radical technological breakthroughs to everyday process improvements. A shared understanding helps organisations set expectations and direct their innovation efforts. A definition tailored to the organisation clarifies ambiguity by defining what counts as innovation, what does not, and what types of value the organisation seeks to create. The definition should be simple, fit strategic goals, and be easily understood by teams. It must also reflect the organisation's industry, maturity, aspirations, and appetite for risk. For some, innovation will centre on new products or technologies; for others, it may include new services, processes, business models, customer experiences, or ways of working.

The definition is not semantic; it should shape organisational structure, portfolio or pipeline choices, funding decisions, cultural expectations, and performance metrics. A good definition will empower and inspire employees by giving them clarity about how to approach innovation. A well-crafted definition positions innovation as a deliberate organisational capability rather than an abstract ideal or ad-hoc activity and acts to set the direction for the entire Innovation Management System.

We can offer a broadly applicable definition of innovation as:

"Innovation is the act of translating an idea into a **product** that has **value** for which a **consumer** (or customer) will pay."

The key words are highlighted. "Product" defines the end product of the innovation effort, and could be a wide variety of outputs not limited to a physical or digital product, a claim, a process, and business model, etc. "Value" is essential as the reward for innovation and can take many forms, like revenue, efficiency, enhanced reputation, insight generation, acclaim, etc. The more forms of value that can be created, the greater the impact and benefit of the innovation. "Consumer" is the key consideration, as all innovation should be based on a good understanding of consumer insight and unmet needs. A good innovation definition should cover these key considerations.

## Innovation Strategy

The innovation strategy defines where the innovation effort is going by setting the direction. This is not a standalone document, but an extension of the overall organisational strategy, and it exists to enable it. Organisational strategy defines the overall purpose, objectives, direction and ambition. The innovation strategy specifies how innovation contributes to delivering those aims.

Organisational strategy sets the overall destination by clarifying the markets, the value it needs to create, and the sources of competitive advantage that are needed to grow.

Innovation strategy sets out the pathways to get there by outlining the innovation priorities to support the organisational needs.

The two are tightly integrated. If organisational strategy is set without an innovation strategy, the organisation risks stagnation. If an innovation strategy is created without reference to organisational strategy, it becomes disconnected, unfocused, and often politically contested. Together, they form a coherent strategic architecture that enables innovation to become a deliberate, value-creating capability rather than an ad-hoc activity.

A good innovation strategy should serve to inspire the teams and engender a sense of shared mission uniting personal and professional aspirations. In such a scenario, teams will over perform and are capable of sustained creativity and delivery of growth. The innovation strategy should be well communicated to all levels of the organisation to ensure that everyone is working on innovation that supports the overall direction that the organisation is headed.

## Innovation Process

The innovation process is how you arrive at the destination set by the innovation strategy. Innovation processes exist to enable and enhance innovation and creativity, not stifle it. Innovators may be seen as free-spirited and not bound by convention, but a good innovation process can be used to guide creativity and can help even the most creative staff.

**Table 1. The Hard Truth of Innovation (Pisano, 2019).**

| Do | But |
| --- | --- |
| Tolerate failure | Don't tolerate incompetence |
| Promote psychological safety | Be brutally candid |
| Be willing to experiment | Promote strong discipline good experiment design |
| Collaborate | Make individuals accountable |
| Promote flat structures | Instil strong leadership |
| Celebrate successes | Also measure them |

The innovation process can be seen as a blueprint that helps teams deliver innovation with discipline and uniform quality, so that even the less experienced innovators in the team have access to a process that can improve the innovation outputs. Writing about innovation, Pisano (2019) emphasises the need for discipline in innovation. While many organisations celebrate innovators as free-flowing, tolerant of failure, collaborative and playful, this is only half the picture, as innovation also requires diligence and discipline. A "tolerance for failure requires an intolerance for incompetence; a willingness to experiment requires discipline in the design of experiments; psychological safety requires comfort with brutal candour; collaboration must be balanced with individual accountability; and flat structures still require strong leadership". Creative freedom without structure leads to chaos; innovation flourishes when experimentation is underpinned by clear standards, accountable decision-making, rapid learning and decisive termination of unpromising projects. The innovation process needs to account for this by providing guardrails, diligence and discipline. Innovation must pay for itself, and discipline helps this to be delivered. Talented innovators are fulfilled by seeing their ideas delivered, and a good innovation process supports this. The Innovation Sprint (IMS Level 2) describes a good innovation process model.

## Innovation Culture

The innovation culture is how it feels on the journey whilst working in innovation. This is the key and overriding element of the innovation essentials. You can have the best definition, strategy and process in place, but without a strong culture, innovation will fail or not deliver consistently to its potential.

For an innovative organisation, culture should be as important as training is to an athlete; it is the key attribute that supports healthy innovation and must be set by the leadership. The culture in an organisation is obvious to everyone in that organisation, and those who work with them; it must be authentic and consistent. A positive innovation culture is created by leaders understanding what motivates their people. This is not pay, bonus, progression and other forms of compensation — these are important but are hygiene factors in any organisation — it is about feeling that they are supported in an organisation that has shared values aligned to their own, a sense of mission or purpose in the work, and a sense of pride and belonging.

McGregor and Doshi (2015) report that organisational culture directly influences the quality of employee motivation, which in turn drives performance. They identify six core motives for why people work—play, purpose, potential, emotional pressure, economic pressure, and inertia. The first three are motivators that significantly enhance performance; the latter three undermine it. High-performing cultures are those that maximise play, purpose, and personal potential, and minimise pressure-based motives. Culture is not a vague concept but a set of organisational processes, and leaders can enhance culture by designing roles, evaluation systems, and environments that strengthen intrinsic motivation to enhance innovation and growth. Simple carrot-and-stick approaches to creating a culture don't have lasting effects (Lai, 2017) because people stay motivated when they feel their work matters, not when they are pressured, bullied or bribed. This should be considered in performance and progression systems when designing an organisation. Leaders must provide context, remove barriers and recognise contributions to create motivated teams who feel a sense of being valued.

Kirsner (2018) outlines how innovation is often derailed not by a lack of ideas but by internal dynamics such as politics, turf wars, risk-averse mindsets, and cultures built for operational excellence rather than experimentation. These behaviours inhibit collaboration and prevent organisations from acting on clear signals about the future. For innovation to thrive, leaders must address these blockers by clarifying roles, reducing territorial battles, creating space for experimentation, and fostering diverse viewpoints to allow the organisation to be hospitable, not hostile to new ideas.

To overcome internal frictions, companies have used the approach to form an Innovation Pod to create ground-breaking ideas. An Innovation Pod is a small team of talented individuals who are taken out of the organisation to develop ideas in an environment where they are not held back by the internal frictions like politics, turf wars and business-as-usual distractions. They are given a problem to solve, with the resources and permission to go ahead without interference from the mothership. Lockheed Martin's Skunk Works pioneered this, and its first project was to develop America's first jet fighter plane in 1943 (the P-80 Shooting Star). It was completed in 143 days, beating the 150-day deadline, and shows what can be achieved by a motivated, adequately resourced and talented team given a problem to solve (Lockheed Martin, 2016).

Nestlé developed Nespresso using a similar approach by briefing an Innovation Pod to transform their instant coffee offer into a barista-level experience (Cumming, 2020). These innovations demonstrate how ground-breaking innovation can thrive when teams are motivated and trusted to work on top-priority projects with little or no oversight. It may be a luxury to form Innovation Pods in resource-constrained environments, but the elements of trust, inspiring project briefs, teamwork and minimal interference can be recreated in any organisation to support a positive innovation culture.

In practice, leaders must be open, curious and supportive by:

- Demonstrating genuine interest in ideas and challenges to the status quo, and modelling curiosity themselves.
- Encouraging experimentation and being genuinely accepting of failure.
- Providing context rather than control by explaining the 'why' behind decisions and allowing autonomy over the 'how'.
- Recognising contributions in real time and showing appreciation for creative effort, not just outcomes.
- Ensuring that values, behaviours and incentives align, so employees see that innovation is valued.

In the Innovation Fitness Test, assessing culture involves examining whether the organisation provides psychological safety, intrinsic motivation, cross-silo collaboration, and genuine reinforcement of innovation behaviours. Leadership capability—particularly in emotional intelligence, communication, and empowerment—is a central diagnostic factor.

Ultimately, an innovation culture is about creating the conditions in which people want to innovate. Structures and processes can enable or constrain, but only a culture set by committed, emotionally intelligent leadership unlocks the motivation that propels successful innovation.

## Level 1: Stimulus and Insight

With the innovation essentials in place as the foundation to support innovation, we now move on to the day-to-day activity of innovation with Level 1 (Stimulus and Insight). Individuals responsible for innovation must be involved in the continual collection of stimulus and insight (S&I). This becomes the raw material to solve problems and create new ideas. In a strong innovation culture, everyone in an organisation should be collecting S&I, and this should be managed in such a way that it is shared and available to everyone to catalyse innovation. Innovation is not just brainstorming and coming up with new ideas, but rather it is the disciplined every day activity of curiosity, collecting stimulus and generating insight. Innovation is rarely a spontaneous flash of inspiration — it is most often the result of patient collection of knowledge in the form of S&I over a period of time that begins to pool and clarify to form new ideas and innovation. We shouldn't misunderstand innovation as just idea-creation. In practice, ideas come last and are formed from the knowledge created by S&I.

High-performing innovation teams and organisations create a culture where everyday curiosity is expected. Conn and McLean (2020) identify being ever-curious as one of the six mindsets of their model to solve inscrutable problems (Figure 2). This relates directly to the culture of innovation where teams must be inspired and motivated to explore ideas and ask endless questions, with the psychological safety to be able to suggest and advocate new ways of doing things. All organisations must have the capability to gather and use S&I.

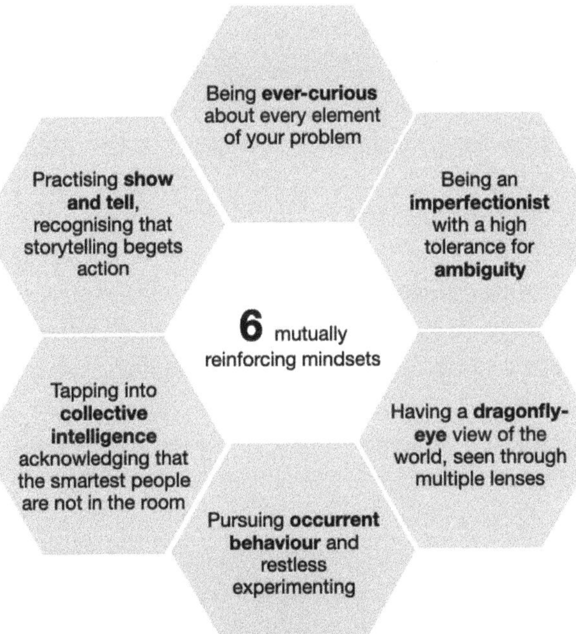



Figure 2. Faced with an inscrutable problem? Try a more creative approach Conn and McLean (2020).

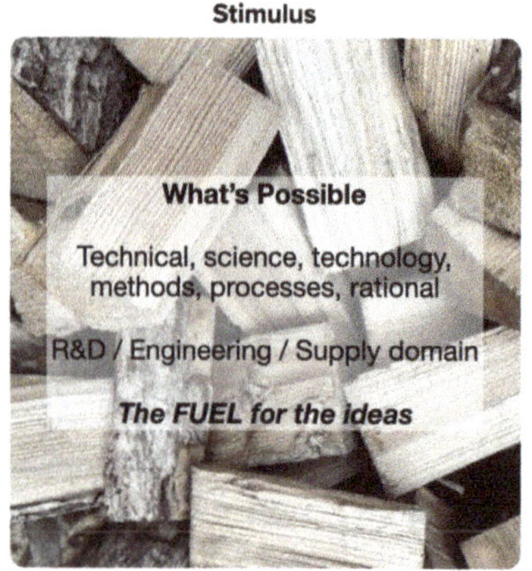

Figure 3. Stimulus and Insight Defined.

Stimulus and insight are different complementary types of information. Stimulus is technically driven and captures what is possible, whereas insight is customer/consumer or market driven and captures the 'why' of innovation. [Note: customer and consumer are used interchangeably in this chapter, although they are subtly different, the customer being the purchaser and the consumer being the user]. Stimulus is the technical knowledge we gather on a topic, and insight is the commercial knowledge. The best ideas are led by insight and combine with stimulus to create solutions. With a deep understanding and insight into the consumer, we can define their problems with a high degree of confidence and use our technical knowledge (stimulus) to solve them. We can think of stimulus as the fuel for ideas and insight as the spark that sets an idea alight (Figure 3).

Over time, S&I becomes a valuable source of corporate intellectual property that allows you to solve problems, innovate and grow. Organisations that systematically collect S&I build a comprehensive view of the consumer, market and an armamentarium of technological knowledge within their sector. This builds up over years and enables the organisation to out compete competitors with innovation. It also helps create a learning organisation where teams can access knowledge generated by their predecessors to learn from the past and avoid repeating mistakes and reinventing ideas. This is especially useful where turnover of staff is high. Strong archives of S&I are competitive moats that competition cannot easily or quickly replicate. The depth of understanding enables faster decision making, allowing the detection of signals to be acted upon faster.

Of key importance when collecting S&I is to go beyond the obvious sources, as this allows you to generate novel insights to stay ahead of the competition, who will be attending the same conferences, reading the same journals and meeting the same experts as you. Most companies in a sector go to the same sources and arrive at the same conclusions; advantage emerges when organisations deliberately seek to go beyond these obvious sources. It pays to get closer to the consumer or consumer to really uncover the most valuable insights, especially in the moment they use your product. Conn and McLean's (2020) "dragonfly-eye" supports this by encouraging companies to look at the problem from multiple perspectives to uncover unseen opportunities.

Insight is fundamentally about understanding people, not just demographics, to uncover the emotions that drive them and allow you to establish consumer empathy. Human decision-making is complex and driven by subconscious actions influenced by experiences, values, traditions and beliefs. This makes it highly individualised and super-personal; the best insight aims to tap into this understanding and inevitably is hard to gain, but it is rewarded by creating highly emotive interactions with your consumers. Standard consumer groups are useful but rarely lead to such empathetic connections. The best innovators should find other ways to connect with their consumer at a more personal and emotional level.

Stimulus and Insight form the daily activity of the IMS, building the organisation's ability to think differently, develop proprietary knowledge and innovate with success. When gathered continuously, interpreted thoughtfully, and focused on human empathy, they are a distinctive source of value and a growing body of organisational intelligence growing over time. By going beyond the obvious, organisations can stay ahead of the competition to create novel, valuable innovation pipelines. With S&I embedded as everyday practice, the innovation moves from episodic activity to a sustained capability.

## Level 2: Innovation Sprint

In the IMS the innovation sprint is the process that converts the raw materials of innovation activity, stimulus and insight, into new ideas to solve business problems and create an innovation pipeline. The innovation sprint is designed to be flexible and may be deployed quickly or run over a number of days, depending on the time available. It could be run over a week, using a day for each step, or be run in a few hours in response to an urgent issue.

But an innovation sprint is a process run in response to a problem statement to create ideas to respond to that challenge.

The key to a successful innovation sprint is preparation. A checklist to consider for a successful sprint is:

- Attendees: ensure you have the skills and knowledge available for a successful outcome, and have enough people to work through the issues.
- Venue and resources: it may pay to hold sprints off-site to remove people from distractions. Ensure the venue has space to work comfortably and has the capacity to present ideas and work creatively.
- Experts: consider whether external expertise is needed to get a good outcome.
- Consumers: bringing in consumers is a great opportunity to learn first-hand their frictions and generate insight in real time.
- Materials: it is often necessary to provide in-depth materials to lead people through a session, which may mean converting s timulus and i nsight relevant to the topic into presentations, posters, physical samples or other immersive materials like video, audio or interviews.
- Forming teams: using teams working in parallel but independently is a good way to maximise success, and it creates a sense of competition that tends to elevate the quality of the ideas.

The sprint has 5 elements:

## Download

Step one aims to get everyone to the same level of understanding of the issue which is the subject of the sprint. This generally means sharing relevant stimulus and insight relating to the topic that will give the participants the knowledge to solve the issue. This might include pre-work for the participants to bring to share with colleagues in the sprint or inviting guest speakers to share presentations and materials relevant to the topic. The Download sets the tone for the overall sprint and high-quality, immersive, inspiring content will elevate the outputs and solutions. Concentrating on consumer insight and unmet needs will allow you to immerse participants in the user context and reframe the problem with deep discovery. This aligns with Design Thinking principles (Brown, 2008) and helps ensure solutions are rooted in consumer needs.

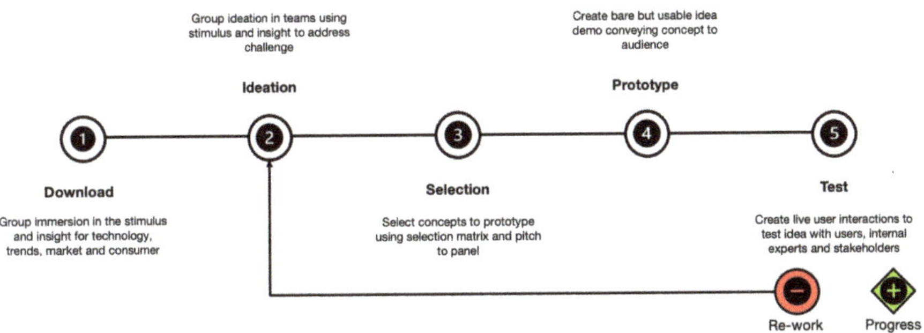


Figure 4. Innovation Sprint Process.

## Ideation

This is the process where the attendees devise ideas to solve the problem. This part of the process is divergent, and the more ideas you have, the better. If you have multiple teams working on the issue, you may generate a large number of ideas, which is beneficial at this point. Ideation can be done in an unstructured manner, simply collecting ideas as they occur, but it is often better to create a structured approach to the process to help guide the teams and ensure the key elements of the problem are addressed. The Doblin model is one such tool that can help guide teams to create ideas as it forces them to look at problems through different lenses and work on product, customer and business structure to solve problems (Keely et al., 2013). Discipline is needed to record ideas legibly with enough detail to aid comprehension later when ideas are processed.

## Selection

Selection is the step where the process becomes a convergent evaluation and prioritisation exercise. In a session, you may generate tens or potentially hundreds of ideas, many of which will be good, and some great, but you can only progress one, so selection needs to be applied. This can be done very simply by attendees voting for the ideas they prefer by marking the ones they like. This has the advantage of being fast and easy, and it feels democratic. But it is hard to evaluate ideas properly using this method and good ideas might be lost as they are not well explained in this fast process. Selection deserves some time and is done well by applying simple assessment criteria to score the ideas, which leads to a better outcome. For example, simple criteria could be:

- How well does the idea solve the problem?
- How resource-intensive (time and money) is the idea?
- What is the level of risk?

Each criterion can be scored 1–5 and the best-scoring idea is progressed. These simple evaluation matrices can be adapted to suit your use case, offering a fair and measured selection methodology.

## Prototype

In the prototype stage, we create a representation of the selected idea that gives enough information to test it. We can create an actual prototype if you have the wherewithal to do that — for example, a 3d printed model; a prototype APP; or a simply constructed engineered solution. But this can also be done effectively using visual means like a flip chart, presentation software or using a concept artist. The prototype needs to convey what the idea is, how it works to solve the issue, how it is used and how it generates value. In other words, the key points that must be conveyed to pitch the idea in the next phase, which is Test. Ries (2011) emphasises that prototyping is a key principle in Design Thinking and Agile methodologies as it allows you to test assumptions quickly.

## Test

In the test phase, we are evaluating the prototype to check that the idea is viable to move into the next stage of development, which is a live project to be delivered. At this point, it would enter the project management process normally deployed by the organisation, testing aims to create interactions with three groups to test the idea.

## Experts

These are internal colleagues with responsibility for key aspects of the business like Supply Chain, Research and Development, Sales, Marketing, Legal, Regulatory, etc. We check with them that there are no internal show stoppers for the idea as a basic check of feasibility.

## Stakeholders

These are leaders in the business who hold the budget, resources or own the overall strategy for the organisation. We need their buy-in to progress ideas.

## Consumers

These are the people who will use the innovation and are the most important group in the test phase. We need to understand whether or not the idea meets their needs and whether it can deliver the value we promised.

Following this, we have a Go/No-go outcome. Ideas that test positively go into full development. Ideas that fail can be re-worked by going back to an earlier stage of the process; for example, choose an idea from the pool generated during ideation if it addresses feedback raised during the test phase. Ideas can loop through the process several times but eventually should be killed or archived when it is clear they are unsuitable. All ideas should be managed in some way in an archive to be referred to in the future, and form part of the formal record of Stimulus and Insight, which may be useful later.

## Level 3: Tools

Tools are the practical mechanisms, techniques and methods your innovation team can use to aid the various levels of the IMS, ensuring that innovation activity is consistent, repeatable and scalable. They are the enablers of the whole system and will be developed to meet your individual organisational needs. In this section, we will look at some useful tools that work for most organisations, but you should develop your own as you develop your innovation function and IMS.

## Open Innovation (OI)

Open Innovation or Outside Innovation is the practice of sourcing ideas and solutions from outside of the organisation. It is a practical tool within the Innovation Management System to expand an organisation's access to ideas, technologies, and expertise beyond its own boundaries. It operates on the principle that no matter how capable an organisation is, there is infinitely more knowledge outside, which can be leveraged by bringing in solutions to solve internal problems. These solutions are generally proven and so reduce risk and timelines compared to generating new solutions internally. By engaging with start-ups, universities, suppliers, customers, or research institutes, organisations can accelerate learning, tap into fresh stimulus, and uncover insights that internal teams would not generate alone. Mechanisms such as challenge briefs, scouting networks, joint development agreements, and accelerator partnerships become part of the OI toolkit, enabling faster experimentation and reducing development risk.

Open Innovation helps counter internal barriers such as narrow thinking, organisational inertia, and political resistance by introducing diverse perspectives and new sources of value. However, it works only when framed by clear strategic intent, defined problem statements, and disciplined engagement models. Open Innovation is a tool to increase options and ensure the organisation is never restricted to its existing knowledge base.

## Doblin

The Doblin Ten Types of Innovation framework (Keeley, 2013) broadens the traditional view of innovation that tends to focus on product alone, to include configuration (business model, networks, structure, processes), offerings (product performance and product systems), and experience (service, channels, brand, customer engagement). The core principle is that the most powerful innovations rarely emerge from a single dimension but happen when an organisation deliberately combines multiple types of innovation in ways that competitors find hard to replicate. Doblin forces organisations to look through ten different lenses to build their innovation and shows that, based on their forty years of research, the most successful innovations leverage at least four lenses (Figure 5).

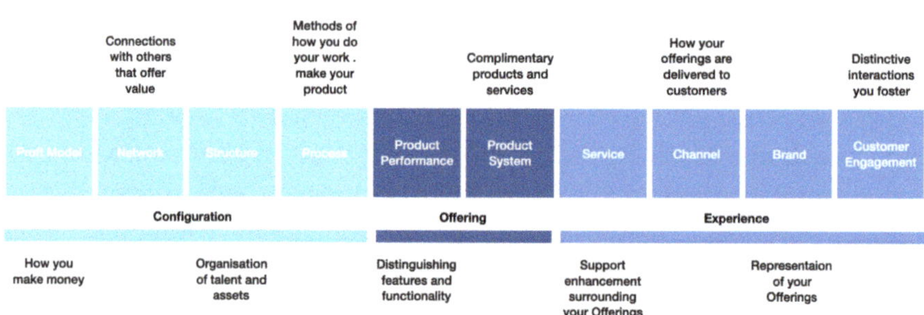


Figure 5. Doblin Innovation Lenses Kelley, (2013).

Doblin helps teams analyse their existing innovation activity, where effort is often concentrated on product performance, while other high-value forms of innovation remain underused. When applied to your IMS, Doblin encourages organisations to deliberately mix types of innovation, improving the value potential of their innovation.

## Customer Empathy Mapping

Customer empathy maps help organisations collect Insight and establish consumer empathy – key elements of the IMS — by allowing them to see issues from the perspective of their customers. A customer empathy map creates a template for generating consumer insight as an innovation tool (Figure 6).

This model allows you as an organisation to build up customer personas and predict what they want in terms of innovation and understanding of their unmet needs. This is a powerful tool to gain empathy with them.

The tools you use as part of your IMS will grow over time and become a valuable asset for your teams to innovate and generate growth. You can develop your own or utilise the myriad of tools available in the literature and on the market. Over time, the assets and methods you create as tools become a way of working that can improve your innovation output and allow you to innovate faster than your competitors.

## Level 4: Innovation Portfolio Management

Innovation Portfolio Management is the lens through which we can look at our innovation pipeline to assess its balance, and it is the tool that allows us to monitor its health. We must ensure there is a balance of short and long-term opportunities that support growth. In most organisations, there is no shortage of ideas; the problem is choosing which to progress and which to de-prioritise. Fundamentally, a balanced pipeline protects an organisation from disruption by balancing looking after the business today and placing bets for the future. At this point, let's consider Disruptive Innovation as a concept.

Disruptive Innovation was raised as a concept by Clayton Christensen (1997, 2015) as he investigated why large organisations fail as new technologies develop. He observed that new technologies enter the market below the radar of incumbents and have low performance and value. But over

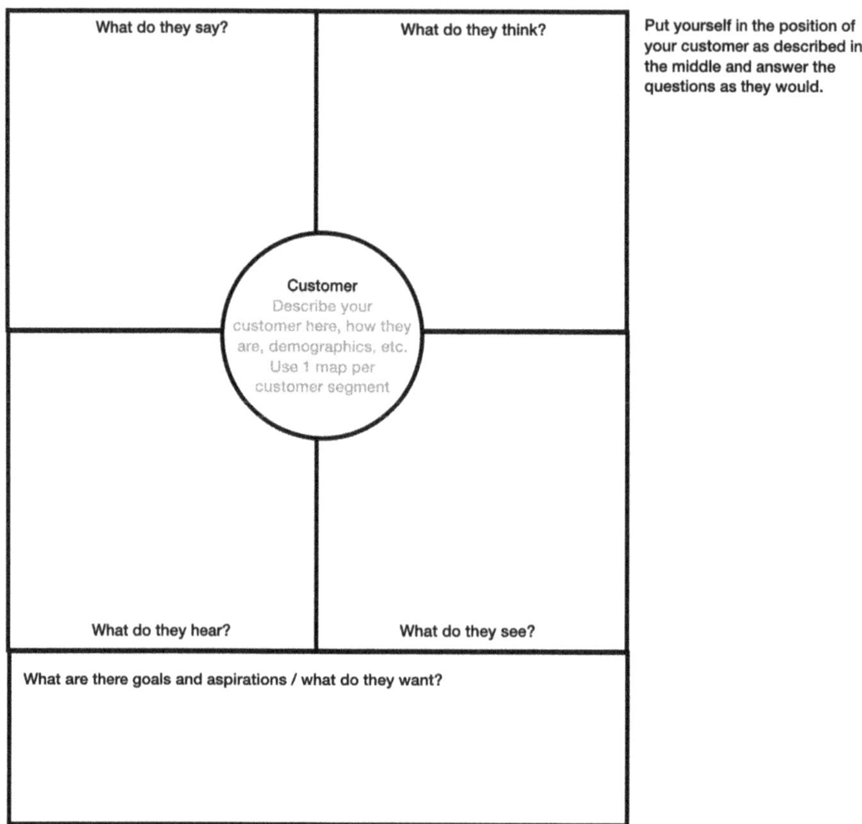


Figure 6. Customer Empathy Map.

time their performance and value increase whilst remaining invisible to the incumbent, until performance and value cross the incumbent at the Point of Disruption. At this point the disruptor continues on an upwards trajectory, and the incumbent's trajectory falls and they are disrupted by the new technology (Figure 7).

Incumbents tend to fail to spot disruptors because they are comfortable in their dominant positions, and often if they do detect disruptors, they fail to imagine how they could be dethroned by them. Fundamentally, incumbents tend to adopt a "playing not to lose" approach to innovation, and disruptors who are not held back by their dominant position tend to "play to win" when it comes to innovation. This gives disruptors the energy, confidence and freedom to disrupt often very large incumbents. In your assessment of

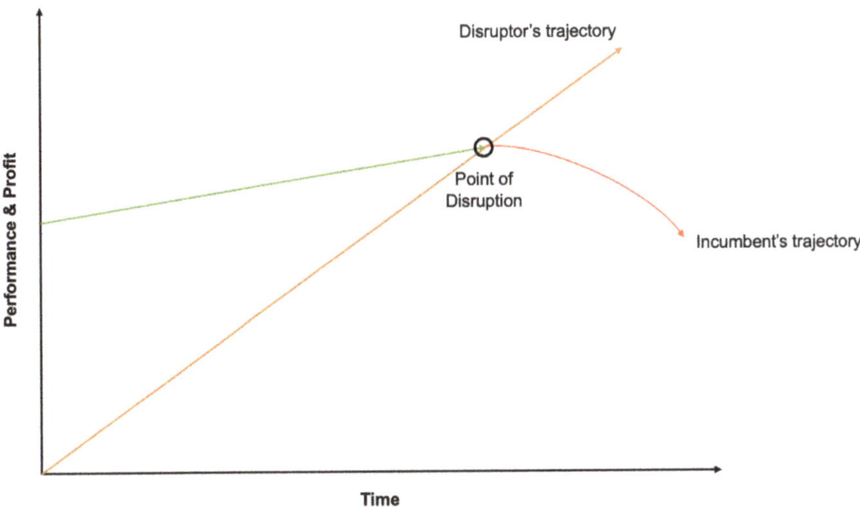



Figure 7. Disruptive Innovation Trajectory (Christensen, 2015).

Innovation Fitness, consider how you can adopt a 'play to win' mentality as part of your culture. The following unattributed quote sums this up well:

"Legacy businesses have too much to gain from the present to think too much about the future".

If this statement resonates with you, then you should look to address this in your innovation culture and create an Innovation Portfolio that plots ambitious future innovations. This is the best defence against disruption by new technologies and disruptive business models.

Nagji and Tuff (2012) describe an innovation horizon model with three horizons of innovation — Incremental, Adjacent and Radical. After studying the most innovative and successful companies, they determined the ideal balance of Incremental, Adjacent and Radical innovation for success (Figure 8). Their research shows that the best performing companies allocate 70% of resources to Incremental, 20% to Adjacent and 10% to Radical Innovation. This means that they are looking after their existing business and keeping it fresh with Incremental innovation, taking advantage of accessing innovations that are proven in some way with Adjacent innovation, but also placing bets for the future by investing in Radical innovation. Interestingly, their study shows that 70% of the returns and growth came from the 10% of resources allocated to Radical innovation. This is the incentive to stretch your innovation into the Radical horizon as they add more value.

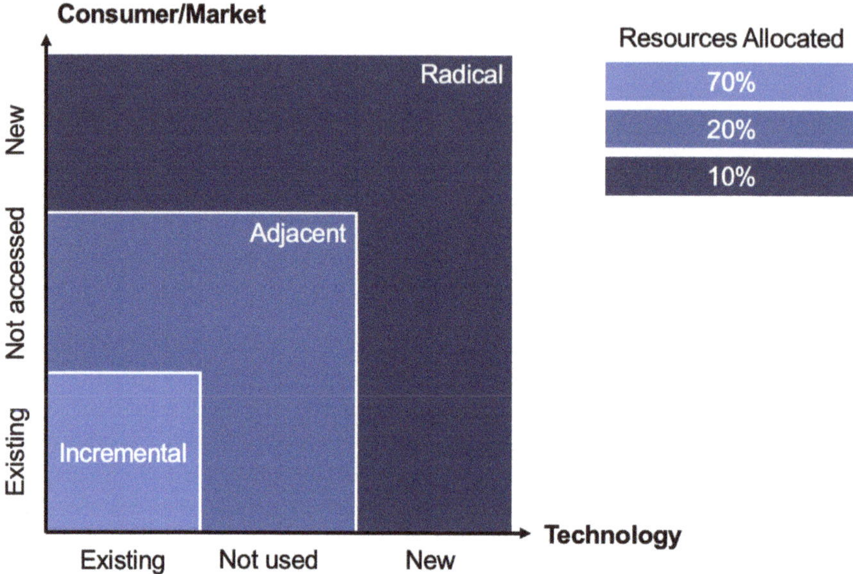


Figure 8. Innovation Horizons - How Successful Companies Allocate Innovation Resources.

Existing means already in the business; Not Used/Not Accessed means exists in the world but is not used in the business; New means new to the world (or sector).

The percentage allocation to the different horizons and the definitions of what is 'new' in the model can be adapted to suit an organisation's maturity, status and priorities. But a balanced, healthy innovation portfolio should ensure that they have each horizon populated with projects to maintain growth and defend against competition or disruption.

This view of the overall pipeline should be monitored regularly, and action should be taken to balance the pipeline at times when it does not meet the targeted balance. For example, if the pipeline is deficient in Radical innovation, then they should take action to fill that gap. This could be to run an innovation sprint to create a Radical project opportunity for the organisation.

## Conclusion

### *Building and Sustaining Innovation Fitness*

Innovation fitness is a practical measure you can apply to your organisation to assess whether you are equipped to create value amid complexity, volatility, and accelerating technological change. The Innovation Management System (IMS) provides a structured framework on which to build innovation capability. Each level of the IMS, from clarifying what innovation means and why it matters, through establishing the essential foundations of definition, strategy, process, and culture, to the operational disciplines of stimulus and insight generation, ideation, portfolio management, and delivery, represents a component of organisational fitness that must be consciously designed rather than left to chance.

The Innovation Fitness Test operationalises this framework. By comparing an organisation's current practices, behaviours, and structures against the IMS, leaders gain a clear view of where they are robust, where they should improve, and are able to create a prioritised plan to address gaps to improve the innovation function.

Innovation fitness is not about achieving perfection across all IMS elements. Indeed, few if any organisations have full maturity in every domain. But fitness should be applied to the context of the organisation, and leaders should decide which capabilities best support their strategy, markets, and ambition. The IMS helps leaders make informed decisions, ensuring they invest in the elements that will enhance value creation and support current priorities.

Used as a continuous improvement tool, the Innovation Fitness Test supports organisations in building innovation capability over time. It shifts innovation from a sporadic activity to a disciplined, systemic organisational skill. It encourages reflection on whether leaders and structure enable or inhibit creativity; whether culture motivates or demoralises; whether strategy inspires or confuses; and whether process accelerates innovation or stifles it.

Ultimately, innovation fitness creates organisational resilience. In a world where business models and sources of advantage are at risk and subject to turbulent change, the ability to innovate well establishes long-term relevance and growth. The IMS and Innovation Fitness Test allow organisations to understand not only how innovative they are today, but also how to develop and grow innovation capability to match future ambition.

## References

Business Development Bank of Canada (2020). 'What Is Innovation?' BDC.ca. Available at: www.bdc.ca/en/articles-tools/business-strategy-planning/innovate/what-is-innovation, viewed 21 November 2025.

Bolton, Robyn (2024). 'Council Post: Back to Basics: What Is Innovation?' *Forbes*, available at www.forbes.com/councils/forbesbusinesscouncil/2019/12/30/back-to-basics-what-is-innovation/, viewed 21 November 2025.

Brown, Tim (2008). 'Design Thinking.' *Harvard Business Review*, available at www.hbr.org/2008/06/design-thinking, viewed 8 November 2025.

Christensen, Clayton M. (1997). *The Innovator's Dilemma: When New Technologies Cause Great Firms to Fail.* Boston, Mass.: Harvard Business Review Press.

Christensen, Clayton M., et al. (2015). 'What Is Disruptive Innovation?' *Harvard Business Review,* available at www.hbr.org/2015/12/what-is-disruptive-innovation, last viewed 2 November 2025.

Conn, Charles, and Robert McLean (2020). 'Six Problem-Solving Mindsets for Very Uncertain Times.' McKinsey & Company, available at www.mckinsey.com/capabilities/strategy-and-corporate-finance/our-insights/six-problem-solving-mindsets-for-very-uncertain-times#/, viewed 20 November 2025.

Cumming, Ed. (2020). 'How Nespresso's Coffee Revolution Got Ground Down.' *The Guardian,* available at www.theguardian.com/food/2020/jul/14/nespresso-coffee-capsule-pods-branding-clooney-nestle-recycling-environment, viewed 20 November 2025.

Herzlinger, Regina E., et al. (2024). 'The Middle Path to Innovation.' *Harvard Business Review*, available at www.hbr.org/2024/07/the-middle-path-to-innovation, viewed 20 November 2025.

Keeley, Larry, et al. (2013). *Ten Types of Innovation: The Discipline of Building Breakthroughs.* Hoboken, New Jersey: John Wiley & Sons.

Kirsner, Scott (2018). 'The Most Commonly Cited Barriers to Innovation in Large Companies? Internal Politics.' *Harvard Business Review*, available at www.hbr.org/2018/07/the-biggest-obstacles-to-innovation-in-large-companies, viewed 20 November 2025.

Lai, Lisa (2017). 'Motivating Employees Is Not about Carrots or Sticks.' *Harvard Business Review,* available at www.hbr.org/2017/06/motivating-employees-is-not-about-carrots-or-sticks, viewed 20 November 2025.

Lockheed, Martin (2016). 'Missions Impossible: The Skunk Works Story.' Lockheed Martin, available at www.lockheedmartin.com/en-us/news/features/history/skunk-works.html, viewed 20 November 2025.

Magids, Scott, et al. (2015). 'The New Science of Customer Emotions.' *Harvard Business Review,* available at www.hbr.org/2015/11/the-new-science-of-customer-emotions, viewed 10 November 2025.

McGregor, Lindsay, and Neel, Doshi (2015). 'How Company Culture Shapes Employee Motivation.' *Harvard Business Review*, available at www.hbr.org/2015/11/how-company-culture-shapes-employee-motivation, viewed 20 November 2025.

McKinsey & Company (2022). 'What Is Innovation?' Www.mckinsey.com, available at www.mckinsey.com/featured-insights/mckinsey-explainers/what-is-innovation, viewed 18 November 2025.

Nagji, Bansi, and Geoff Tuff (2012). 'Managing Your Innovation Portfolio.' *Harvard Business Review*, available at www.hbr.org/2012/05/managing-your-innovation-portfolio, viewed 21 November 2025.

Pisano, G. (2019). 'The Hard Truth about Innovative Cultures.' *Harvard Business Review*, available at www.hbr.org/2019/01/the-hard-truth-about-innovative-cultures, viewed 18 November 2025.

Ries, Eric. (2011). *The Lean Startup*. London: Portfolio Penguin.

UK Government (2021). 'UK Innovation Strategy Leading the Future by Creating It.' Gov.uk, available at assets.publishing.service.gov.uk/government/uploads/system/uploads/attachment_data/file/1009577/uk-innovation-strategy.pdf, viewed 31 October 2025.

Viguerie, P. (2017). 'Corporate Longevity Forecast: Creative Destruction Is Accelerating.' Innosight, available at www.innosight.com/insight/creative-destruction/, viewed 18 November 2025.

Waytz, A. (2023). 'Beware a Culture of Busyness.' *Harvard Business Review*, available at www.hbr.org/2023/03/beware-a-culture-of-busyness, viewed 10 November 2025.

# THE SPHERE ECONOMY
## Christopher Gleadle

*To all the complexity of the physical world of weather, crops, ores, and factories, you add the psychological complexity of humans acting on their fleeting expectations of what may or may not happen*

*Benoît Mandelbrot (2004)*

Thriving in today's complex business landscape requires organisations to prioritise adaptive capacity over traditional risk management or predictive approaches (Tinch et al., 2015). Why? Because, in an environment marked by diversity, interdependence, ambiguity, and flux, successful organisations foster distributed intelligence and enable flexible, collaborative responses to emerging challenges (Amann, Nedopil and Steger, 2011).

The failures observed during recent global crises, such as economic, climate and pandemic, reveal that entrenched hierarchies and reductionist strategies are inadequate for managing systemic risk and complex inter-connected challenges like inequality, climate change, and institutional fragility (Silman, 2022). Instead, a "Sphere Economy" framework (Gleadle, 2018) is proposed, promoting systems thinking that maps value chains, integrates diverse forms of capital, and encourages learning, improvisation, and resilience.

This approach centres on understanding and acting upon feedback loops, while acknowledging that economic, social, and environmental outcomes are inseparable. Recognising complexity as a constant, and crises as systemic rather than anomalous, leaders can cultivate environments that reward experimentation, empower teams, and build trust.

Furthermore, the Sphere Economy distinguishes competence from knowledge and highlights the importance of multidimensional skills for decision-making in dynamic contexts. Ultimately, the Sphere Economy champions integrated, adaptive approaches that enhance systemic viability, sustainability, and equitable value creation across interconnected organisational and societal systems.

## Introduction

Coping with complexity in today's business environment centres on building adaptive capacity in individuals and organisations, rather than just predicting the future or only managing risk (Seijts, 2011). The global economic crisis exposed the fact that poor risk management is often a symptom of a deeper inability to handle complexity; an environment marked by unpredictable, interconnected, and fast-changing sociotechnical issues as key causes of the current crisis, including weaknesses in managerial risk perception, firms' risk appetite frameworks, governance structures and risk cultures and inflexible/silo-based corporate structures that have hindered both risk management and reporting (Ashby, 2010). Effective leadership now requires recognising and responding to complexity as a defining feature of the modern landscape.

Four major drivers amplify organisational complexity: diversity, interdependence, ambiguity, and flux. Diversity encompasses conflicting demands from stakeholders across varied products, markets, and cultures. Interdependence reflects "small world" effects decisions or disruptions in one area rapidly reverberate globally. Ambiguity arises from overwhelming, often contradictory data, making causation and action difficult to judge. Finally, flux denotes relentless change, forcing organisations to reconsider assumptions and operate at higher speeds (Amann, Nedopil and Steger, 2011).

Traditional hierarchical controls and standardised processes fail to foster the creativity and innovation needed for dynamic environments (Laker, 2024). Instead, leaders should set minimal strategic and process frameworks, enabling distributed intelligence and flexible responses. This is important, because from my experience working with clients, information travels vertically through an organisation like a one-way street, leaving employees feeling distant and out of touch with other parts of the business for which they feel they have no expertise and therefore no connection. But what this has actually achieved is to kill off practical on-the-ground insights, innovation and opportunity from stifled information flow (Gleadle, 2018). Consequently, organisational learning and improvisation are crucial: leaders must design psychologically safe workplaces where experimentation, open communication, and real-time collaboration thrive. Expertise remains important but must balance with improvisation and the ability to pivot quickly as situations evolve.

It follows that effective complexity management distributes leadership, empowering teams to act autonomously and innovatively. Successful companies like Google foster open cultures, delegate authority, and reward frontline creativity (Aksu, 2024). In complex environments, leaders that promote adaptability, facilitation of learning, rapid information sharing, and collective problem-solving foster a deeper collaborative culture within organisations, which, from my experience, increases motivation, information flow, lowers personnel churn, and further eliminates waste, cost and risk, uncovering opportunity.

Ultimately, mastering complexity is about nurturing continuous organisational learning and resilience, blending structured guidance with improvisational capacity to seize opportunities and embrace uncertainty.

Traditional decision-making often focuses on one issue and one set of metrics, while not taking notice of the relationship between other events and numbers, risking harm to value. For example, reducing carbon emissions without addressing overall waste or supply-chain effects can cause problems such as ignoring other waste streams like isolated projects or supply-chain clashes. It can also cause friction between functions and decisions that run on different times, different scopes, or KPIs that instead of measuring success are targeting, for example, capacity in renewable energy when customers want to know about dispatch, or what will actually be delivered. Such isolationist siloed ways of working create cost, risk and waste that goes unaccounted. In contrast the Sphere Economy encourages businesses to see how their actions impact economic, social, and natural capital together by mapping their value chains, using new metrics, and optimising sustainable practices like sourcing from fair-labour suppliers (Beazley, 2024) therefore linking multiple circular economy initiatives to understand and measure overall outcomes, both positive and negative. This integrated approach creates resilient, sustainable supply chains, benefiting local and global economies and the environment. It helps leaders navigate markets systemically, innovatively and socially responsibly, aiming for a sustainable, equitable, viable higher performing future.

**The Sphere Economy** Model (**TSE**) is a defined holistic management model that helps organisations see how decisions and actions interact over time.

## Organisational Clarity

TSE helps organisations understand feedback loops between decisions and actions. By tracking overall performance and redefining key performance indicators (KPIs), organisations can assess policies, projects, teams, products, and services as an interconnected whole rather than as isolated initiatives.

This matters because a defined holistic view can reveal when a portfolio that looks successful at project level is actually destroying value through hidden waste, unnecessary cost, unmanaged risk, and missed opportunities. TSE makes these issues visible so leaders can address them systemically.

Consequently, mapping all of an organisation into TSE, leaders can take in the full picture of obstacles and opportunities and begin not just looking for patterns but understand relationships between patterns, which can be useful in gaining advantage to capture, create and deliver more value.

TSE has been applied in multiple contexts and has been shown to help organisations become sustainably viable (Gleadle, 2018). In this sense, if an organisation is not sustainable and viable, it is not truly sustainable.

## Key Elements

- Enhanced agility: TSE improves individuals and multidisciplinary teams' agile adaptability to define clearly and address problems and realise opportunities across different domains.
- Reduced risk: TSE increases the decision space to visualise interdependent issues that conspire to destroy value, speeding up response times and reducing risk issues cascading to create new risks.
- Reduced waste: by helping diverse individuals and teams visualise how multiple isolated and independently measured efforts can destroy value. How to create value, effectively resolving issues across the whole.
- Reduced cost: TSE reduces cost by reducing waste in all its forms by reducing friction between multiple events, teams and individuals.
- Improved innovation: TSE helps improve innovation by reducing risk cost and waste and opening up fresh opportunity by showing how efficiency without effectiveness, and merely scaling to larger, can most often mean less due to increased waste.

## Crisis, What Crisis?

*Any fool can tell a crisis when it arrives. The real service is to detect it in embryo.*

*Isaac Asimov (1951)*

Complexity is not a single space in time but changes over time. It follows that it is important to understand what factors appear to have conspired to cause a crisis and what could have been done to see it and prevent it again.

Right now, we are living in an age of polycrisis: a state where multiple crises, such as social, political, economic, environmental, are interdependent and create compound effects. For example, the war in Ukraine triggered immediate geopolitical instability, disrupted global food and energy markets, causing inflation and cost-of-living crises worldwide. Covid 19 caused health and economic disruptions, leading to widespread job losses, business closures, and increased poverty. Climate change leads to more frequent and severe weather events, damaged crops, and increased water stress, which then reduce food and energy production. These come under greater stress from rising demand such as data centres, green industrialisation and alternative fuels, that compete for energy and water. Each feedback loop turns on itself, creating economic fragility, conflict, poverty, inequality, ultimately weakening resilience, creating a fertile ground for future crises, as recent blackouts in Chile and the Iberian Peninsula illustrate how quickly energy interruptions cascade, affecting millions of businesses and people (IEA, 2025).

But crises are nothing new… what is interesting is that extreme inequality shows up regularly in crises over time (Marçal, 2012). And what we see is repeating patterns of behaviour. The United Nations Research Institute for Social Development (UNRISD) notes that today's extreme inequalities are not a flaw but a feature of the current system, requiring large-scale systemic change to resolve (UNRISD, 2023).

For example, "a fundamental characteristic of our economy is that the financial system swings between robustness and fragility, and these swings are an integral part of the process that generates business cycles" (Minsky, 1974). Reflect on the financial crisis of 2008/9 and its ripples are still being felt. Financial markets are deeply siloed with artificial boundaries separating asset classes. This fragmentation distorts pricing, creates inefficiencies, and obscures true value (Jane, 2022).

## Tackling complex multiple crises

While we do face novel challenges such as the frequency and scale of ecological disasters, our systems (global production, food and mineral supply chains, economic systems, the international political order, trade and so on…) are more hopelessly entangled.

As inequality further marginalises sections of society (World Inequality Report, 2022), so greater strains are being applied to systems such as health, which is set only to get worse since greater poverty tends to lead to ever worsening health outcomes (Raleigh, 2024). Hence, in the words of Harry Burns, "It's time to make the NHS [National Health Service, UK] a well-being service not a sickness service." (Burns, 2015).

A clear illustration of complexity is The 'Understandascope' (Leunig, 1984)

This depicts a solitary figure peering through a telescope-like device at a complex, chaotic scene of human interaction and conflict below. The figure represents an observer trying to understand the messy reality of human

Figure 1. The Understandascope (Leunig, 1984)

behaviour and society. This metaphor illustrates a lens through which one tries to grasp complexity. However, true understanding is not simply about distant observation; it requires recognising the inseparability of the observer from the observed; where both observer and observed are merging and interpenetrating aspects of one whole reality, which is indivisible and unanalysable (Bohm, 1980). To be engaged with and interpret the complex context rather than a detached analysis alone.

Of course, it might be argued that some interconnections between the observer and observed are more significant than others. Vickers (1972) claims that interconnections between the observer and observed are relatively trivial (to scientific observation), while the interconnections between humans in social systems are strongly implicated in social-scientific observations. Thus, decisions to undertake observations must take account of these interconnections, and observations of them can feed back to transform what is observed (Midgley, 2008).

It follows that a shock in one crisis reverberates in others. So, the war in Ukraine affected global food supply and energy prices.

Other examples include:

- Economic, social and climate effects of COVID-19
- Volatility in global food and energy markets
- Geopolitical conflict
- Civil unrest arising from economic insecurity ideological extremism
- Political polarisation
- Tariff wars and protectionism
- Increasingly frequency and intensity of devastating weather events.

This list is not exhaustive; you will think of many others in your fields of study. In isolation, each has terrible effects but as illustrated, they are interdependent and feedback into one another, exacerbating the impacts of the whole over time.

At the time of COVID, in the US and the UK, pressures such as inequality and partisan conflict were already high and growing before the first outbreak. Large numbers of impoverished people were vulnerable to the disease. Political in-fighting resulted in slow government response times, and poor, confusing, and contradictory communication (Blundell et.al., 2022).

Many countries that lacked strong social cohesion and trust in leadership during COVID-19 were unable to implement and manage effective strategies, which worsened tensions, amplified pre-existing inequalities, and led to higher death rates (Shokri, 2022). Social cohesion weakened further when government responses were perceived as inadequate or unfair, deepening feelings of exclusion among marginalised groups (Hallett, 2025).

Unless we adopt a systems approach, unless we employ systems thinking, we will fail to understand the world we are living in. This is a world made up of complex systems, systems of systems interacting with each other, and changing each other by that interaction and the links between them. (OECD, 2020)

Hence, inflexible systems and policies that do not adapt to realities like climate change and socio-economic shifts will typically increase damage and suffering leading to disasters at multiple scales — environmental, social, and economic (Fletcher, 2024). Thus, applying the thinking that caused the crises is not the thinking to solve them. Yet decision makers continue with mechanistic management practices, while all evidence shows an over-reliance on engineering-style design, rigid methodologies, and one-size-fits-all change programs suppress learning, adaptation, and human judgment, which in turn produces shallow "average" performance rather than excellence (Snowdon, 2021).

## A Perfect Storm

The origins of our climate and biosphere problems lie in the failure to understand nature's complexity and the three-dimensional interrelatedness of feedback loops between economic decision-making and environmental change. Instead of seeking more integrated decision-making, a two-dimensional "cause-and-effect" framework within which the climate crisis is most often analysed is still applied as the main approach to tackling its problems. Yet complex systems have no linear material causality [and] all forms of root cause analysis should be abandoned (Snowdon, 2021). The result is that a multitude of fragmented micro-solutions remain oblivious to the interconnectedness of feedback loops. In contrast, the Sphere Economy recognises complexity, so that focusing on one level, or one theme, does not reduce or eliminate the multi-dimensionality, non-linearity, interconnectedness, or unpredictability encountered at the multidimensional levels. With human systems, the whole is present in the parts (Midgley, 2016).

## The Difficulty with Hierarchical Structures

Outcomes of current hierarchical structures tend to fail to generate cross-structural, feasible action plans and expose a lack of diverse practical critical thinking in decision-making. Already existing fragmented strategies are implemented with little desire for structural change and a unification of strategies.

For example, errors in carbon accounting are a cause of concern since climate impact can be underreported. For instance, the Kyoto Protocol of 1997, which defined wood, or biomass, as a renewable energy source equal to wind and solar, has led to the EU, along with the UK (biomass now accounts for 13–14 % of energy generation (Carbon Brief, 2024)), and others, committing to burning forest biomass to replace coal. But burning wood produces more emissions than coal per unit of electricity made. As a result, burning forest biomass is not carbon neutral because burning emits carbon simultaneously, while forests need decades, if not centuries, to regrow to offset emissions (Joint Research Centre, 2021). This is important because trust in carbon-neutrality cannot happen from burning wood pellets if the emissions and reduction of biodiversity services are not accounted for from that deforestation.

## Mistrust… and the Negative Impacts between Power Groups

Corporations and national economies find themselves caught in a competition spiral that compels them to perpetuate various forms of degradation and to amplify social and environmental inequalities. Therefore, global value chains are structured and governed by powerful and highly influential actors that are not adequately incentivised to design and implement closed loop systems, for example, the food system and the interaction between agriculture, processing, logistics, storage, retail, and service. To put this another way, how actors in a value chain behave (operate internally and interact externally) depends on their incentives (prices of inputs and outputs, elements of risk, culture, personal preferences, attitudes and transaction costs) and their capacities (financial, human, physical, social, informational, etc.) (Neven, 2014).

Accordingly, the urge to measure everything leads to the injudicious use of tools — AI or otherwise — that do not require awareness of possible side effects and reactions. Indiscriminate use [of tools] may result in side effects and reactions outweighing the benefits... The cure is sometimes worse than the disease (Ridgeway,1956). This is currently the outcome for tackling the climate crisis since despite all the money spent, technological advancement, digitalisation, and the increasing culture of sustainability and Environmental Social Governance (ESG):

- Emissions are still rising
- The services of the biosphere are still declining
- Productivity is poor
- All societies are fractured.

## The Sphere Economy: Advancing Solutions to Complex Wicked Problems

The notion of what we call "wicked problems" – social, cultural, economic, and environmental problems that appear difficult to solve — and their explicit connection with complexity and system-wide breadth now has a language and development path through sustainable viability and the Sphere Economy (Figure 1): we move from linear modes of analysing issues to more systemic approaches that allow for the relationships within and between both organisations and the external environment. As a result of understanding the feedback loops, the inverse is also true; that we understand and

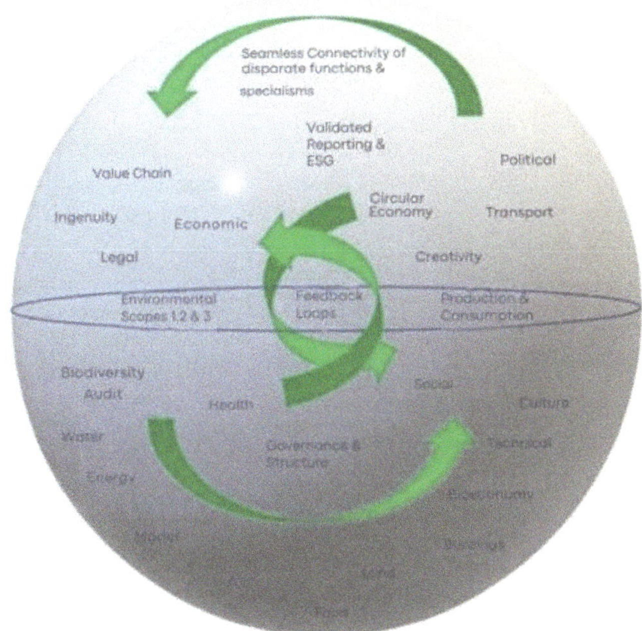


Figure 2. The Sphere Economy

can value the relationships of and between ecosystems of the biosphere and their effect on organisations of humankind. Sometimes it's not about things, but the relationship between things.

I don't think systems thinking can ever replace the experience or knowledge of context that a leader or a decision-maker has, but I do think it can help their thinking (Jackson, 2024).

## The Sphere Economy: Making Sustainability Viable

Complex connected events do not take place on a straight line. They go out into all directions. The circle exists in the two-dimensional plane, but, like any curve, is itself a one-dimensional object. A sphere consists of all the points in three-dimensional space (Frieburger and Thomas, 2025). Likewise, earth's biosphere, as well our economy, should be imagined as three-dimensional spaces. Three-dimensional thinking, which is a model applied in various different sciences, demands more theoretical effort than linear (cause-and-effect) thinking and requires some training before an individual is comfortable to apply it flexibly to complex problems: the climate crisis being only one major problem field systems thinking can and should be applied to (Gleadle, 2022).

## Science of Systems Thinking

The roots of systems thinking are often traced to the theoretical biologist Ludwig von Bertalanffy, who developed the General Systems Theory (GST) in the 1930s. Systems thinking then emerged as an interdisciplinary movement to address the limitations of traditional reductionist science, which studies phenomena by breaking them down into parts. Systems thinking has revolutionised the way that problems, analysis and ultimately approaches to solutions are garnered in equal measure. It has thus been developed as a methodology and as a means to address complex issues that relate to multiple interacting investment, organisational, environmental, governance and social ecosystems; the actions of each affects the many and feedback loops inform better decision-making to reduce impact between functions.

*I think it's very important to have a feedback loop, where you're constantly thinking about what you've done and how you could be doing it better. I think that's the single best piece of advice: constantly think about how you could be doing things better and questioning yourself.*

*Elon Musk*

It appears that Elon Musk understands that permanent decisions cannot be made upon temporary information. It's complex. With all the interactions between skills, functions, people and the environment it's not possible to predict the actions of others with any certainty. There is entropy, a term borrowed from physics, which is a measure of disorder and in a comparable manner, there are a great many possibilities for how its information can be arranged (Gleadle, 2023).

Entropy delivers increasing chaos and disorder. Reflect on the quote by Mandelbrot at the start of the chapter. When embracing complexity, accepting imperfection, and checking assumptions, you open yourself to feedback.

Hence, work on one Sustainable Development Goal (SDG) can impact on another – positively or negatively. This matters because transitioning towards more sustainable and resilient societies also requires an integrated approach that recognises that these challenges – and their solutions – are interrelated (Zhenmin, 2018).

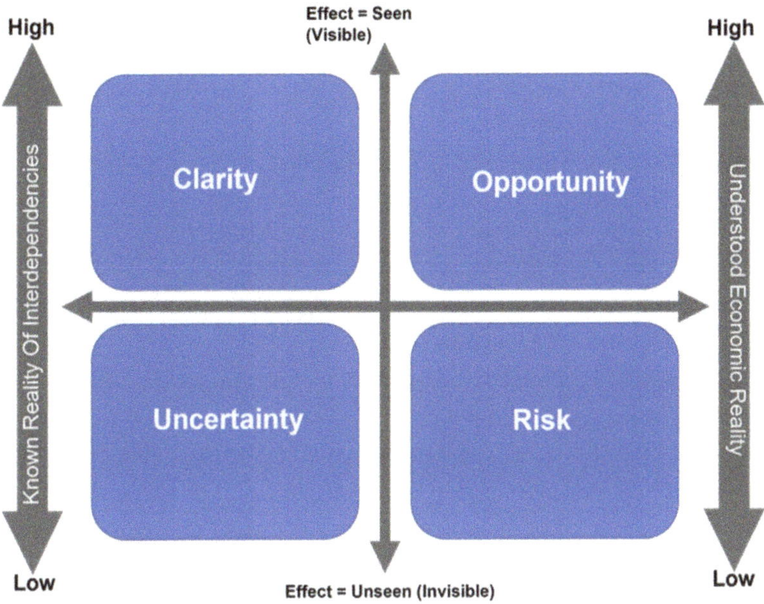


Figure 3. Uncertainty and Entropy (Gleadle, 2015)

For example, current overfocus on greenhouse gas emissions as a carbon footprint portraying them as the sole expression of emission impact limits the decision space to optimise climate projects because it disassociates itself from other potentially more harmful waste stream impacts to the biosphere and society. It follows the Sphere Economy will elevate the efficiency and productivity of resource use since feedback will be optimised (Gleadle, 2022), creating a movement away from the indiscriminate use and undue confidence and reliance on performance tools that results in naïve modelling (Gleadle, 2020) with insufficient knowledge of the full effects and consequences.

Complexity is a core feature of most policy issues today and in this context traditional analytical tools and problem-solving methods no longer work.

*(OECD, 2017)*

The Sphere Economy helps make sense of applying systems thinking effectively. Thus, for present-day and future leaders, it is desirable to expand their decision space as far as possible: to open all the possible options that should be assessed and to identify all the factors that may impact upon the decision and forensically examine their assumptions, check bias, and reflect: "could it be anything else?"

In applying the Sphere Economy multidimensional approach decision makers can demonstrate:

- A thinking shift toward zero waste systems.
- A move away from single data points to data networks to release greater value performance.
- The ability to visualise cross functional/cross policy impacts that destroy value.
- The ability to reveal feedback loops that identify value cycles equitably across systems turning waste streams into profit centres.
- The integration of new wisdom into financial and management systems.

## Measuring

What you measure badly, you manage badly: what tools, metrics, and digital analysis to use in measuring impact and opportunity is critical. It follows that these tools and metrics are applied in a systemic way to broaden the decision space, improve modelling and aid more inclusive and complete decisions that signal decision sequence vital for optimisation.

For example, to measure environmental return on investment in a manner like financial return on investment but expanded to understand the economic profit (measuring all inputs and opportunities and the comparison on decisions foregone) opens the decision space to see decisions and actions collectively rather than in isolation (Gleadle, 2018). As a result, the efficiency and productivity of resource use and feedback can be maximised. Accordingly, holistic measurements such as Global Warming Potential (GWP) can help by allowing for impact equivalence across systems.

## Embracing complexity

The struggle is twofold: decision-makers have to negotiate their ways into viable strategies, and then tactically implement them. At the same time, the public must support them. Yet decision-makers who are re-elected have their hands tied. Many voters struggle to form a truly informed opinion on

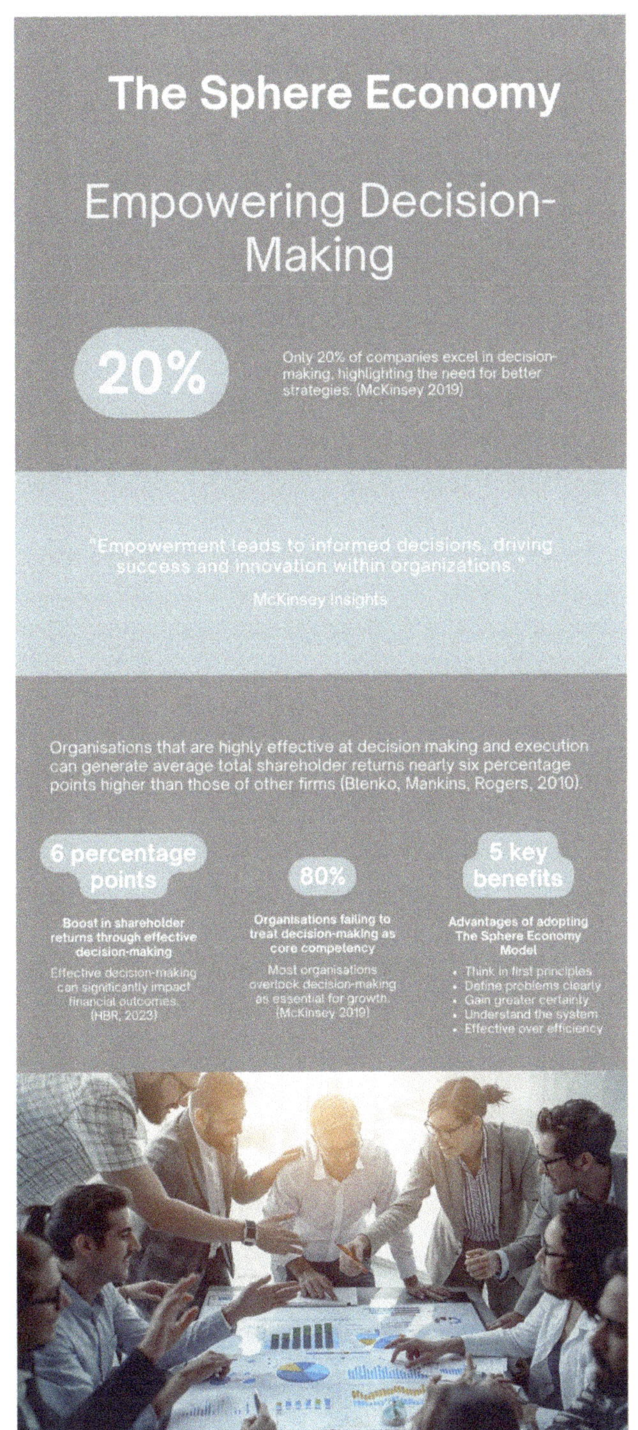
The Sphere Economy

Empowering Decision-Making

20%

Only 20% of companies excel in decision-making, highlighting the need for better strategies. (McKinsey 2019)

"Empowerment leads to informed decisions, driving success and innovation within organizations."

McKinsey Insights

Organisations that are highly effective at decision making and execution can generate average total shareholder returns nearly six percentage points higher than those of other firms (Blenko, Mankins, Rogers, 2010).

6 percentage points

Boost in shareholder returns through effective decision-making

Effective decision-making can significantly impact financial outcomes. (HBR, 2023)

80%

Organisations failing to treat decision-making as core competency

Most organisations overlook decision-making as essential for growth. (McKinsey 2019)

5 key benefits

Advantages of adopting The Sphere Economy Model

• Think in first principles
• Define problems clearly
• Gain greater certainty
• Understand the system
• Effective over efficiency

climate-related issues because climate-related issues–as well attempts to solve them – seem to quickly disintegrate into a confusing amount of smaller problems, the more aspects are considered (Fabian and Gleadle, 2022). Causal relations between fragmented problems become harder to trace back; stakeholders' interests seem to become more contradictory the more responsible actors we add to the equation. The result is discouraging for everybody involved: policymakers are left with a complex mega-puzzle, businesses are left with a decreasing range of movement, and the public has an increasingly hard time to understand how it all concerns them. This undermines trust in all directions; in a democracy, it also brings more volatility to the political status quo. The decline of public trust in political authorities is central to the challenges facing democratic governments in many countries today (Valgarðsson, 2025).

Helping the wider public befriend the complexity of climate-related issues is crucial to enable independent opinion-building, critical thinking, and smart decision-making in democratic societies. Tools like infographics, animated videos, and data visualisations simplify complex climate concepts, while interactive approaches such as virtual simulations, remote-sensing images, and 3D models make them more tangible (Current Conservation, 2025). After all, within their own range of activities, voters make decisions daily in their work lives and for their businesses, their consumption and mobility habits, their lifestyles, their choice of sources of information, and their choice to trust certain politicians over others. Understanding how complex

a decision truly is, and what drives that complexity, is critical to improving our ability to make better choices. Without such a Sphere Economy framework, decision-makers often misjudge the difficulty, risks, and resources needed, leading to suboptimal outcomes (Bareš, 2025). On the other hand, to embrace complexity means a hugely enlarged freedom of choice for the individual. Thus, the implementation of change does not solely depend on 'professional' decision-makers who currently apply the same problem-solving and analysis techniques upon the complex environmental, economic and social puzzle that caused the problem in the first place. Accordingly, the crucial issue at hand is how to move beyond "we've always done it this way" to see behind the complexity barrier.

## Move forward with viable climate action

Systems thinking is based on the idea of interrelatedness; here, for example, that of environmental and economic decision-making. The common (2D) approach to thinking, seeing action and reaction, cause and effect, as a linear chain of events, each of them with a clear beginning and end is, with the Sphere Economy, replaced by an interactive iterative spherical (3D) space (Gleadle, 2018) of activity where any action is simultaneously connected to a multitude of other actions in the same space, connected through feedback loops.

When there are nonlinear relationships, which is usual in reality, changes in output are disproportionate to changes in input and causes are interlinked in complex feedback structures (Strogatz, 2004). Positive (reinforcing) and negative (self-regulating) feedback loops abound (Jackson, 2024).

In the Sphere Economy model, feedback loops replace the notion of singular cause-and-effect-chains with morphing networks of complex change impulses that reflect back on each other. It serves to visualise why so many problems seem to ping-pong back and forth between environmental and economic decision-making processes that destroy value in the sense of economic value and healthy environmental commons, as well as the access to both.

Consequently, in advancing action to decipher the climate puzzle, decision-makers need to move from the traditional methods of problem solving and analysis to multidimensional methods. This will require a greater reliance upon practical and diverse experience rather than just academic and theoretical knowledge since sustainable, viable systems thinking requires a broad spectrum of experiential knowledge that can reflect the real world. As the great American philosopher John Dewy once said, "We do not learn from experience; we learn from reflecting on experience."

This does not mean being all-knowing and all-seeing. True intuitive expertise is learned from prolonged experience with good feedback on mistakes (Kahneman, 2011), giving the feel for what feedback loops will and won't lead to. Systemic thinking ignites imagination, a skill which, in this author's experience, is seldom used in decision making. It also gives greater insight to know what questions to ask of experts to bring ideas and technologies together to deliver robust action today and not at some vague point in the future.

## Complex decision-making

To give one example of the capacity-opening qualities of systemic thinking, let us recount a situation that required three-dimensional systems thinking and a diverse practical team willing to embrace this kind of complexity. Apollo 13 was launched on April 11th, 1970 (Daise, 2023). On board were astronauts James A. Lovell, John L. Swigert, and Fred W. Haise. Two days into the mission and 200,000 miles from Earth, oxygen tank No. 2 ruptured in the spacecraft. Swigert called mission control: "Houston, we've had a problem here." The requisite supply of oxygen, electricity, light, and water had been seriously degraded.

The astronauts and mission control were now faced with huge logistical problems: how to stabilise the spacecraft and its environment, as well as provide enough energy to bring it home with re-entry into the Earth's atmosphere: and all this to be achieved when navigation was now also another problem.

The astronauts and teams at mission control had to come up with emergency procedures founded on a very clear and agreed outcome. Apollo 13's course was dramatically and repeatedly corrected with untested manoeuvres. Multiple issues were overcome simultaneously. For example, by overriding the broken environmental control unit to reduce $CO_2$ in the cabin immediately and for the journey home using only what they had, they integrated differently by understanding feedback loops. Odyssey, the damaged spacecraft – or mothership – continued to the moon and circled it, so that it could be propelled on its long journey back to Earth. On April 17th, tragedy turned to triumph as Apollo 13, with its complement of astronauts, touched down safely in the Pacific Ocean.

This was a triumph based on leadership, cool heads, and managing resources with logical systemic problem-solving that embraced complexity as a friend by understanding feedback loops. For what was also vital to bring the mission home was to make not just any decision that prioritised certain parts of the system over others but to make sustainable viable decisions in the right order for a solution to work optimally, immediately, and with a long-lasting integrative effect that comprised many parts of the system and how they related.

## Spherical thinking

Decision-makers are not expected to be omniscient, but there is a skills gap between where many decision makers currently are and where they need to be. And while we cannot expect that they think through all relevant possible feedback loops simultaneously and in their entirety, the attempt to do so, as previously exampled by Elon Musk, is good practice for anyone who seeks to understand smart decision-making. The idea of interconnectedness in the model challenges the subject to include a wider range of factors into their task-related decision-making. Adaptations may be small at first, but they can open up space for alternative ideas; change follows attention. Learning how to place our attention on bigger and more complex dimensions can train us, step by step, to think more complexly in general.

Complex thinking allows for more complex solutions: seeing the relationship between objects and patterns rather than just the objects and patterns themselves. Steve Jobs once explained:

*You can't connect the dots looking forward; you can only connect them looking backwards. So, you have to trust that the dots will somehow connect in your future.*

*Steve Jobs (2005)*

This emphasises the importance of trusting that seemingly random experiences will eventually form a meaningful story.

It is a process, a tedious one perhaps, but we have to think of sustainability in multidimensional ways: a viable sustainability climate strategy that doesn't also include a sustainable viable economic strategy, for example, cannot function, and vice versa.

If it's not sustainable and viable, it's not sustainable.

Experience has shown that insights, and action founded on systems thinking, diversity and feedback loops of and between decisions, of and between life cycles, can serve to create climate, economic and social value at the intersection of functional problems and development of well-being, security, human rights, and economic resilience. Such action protects humanistic values and shows how through those values, when harmonised and understood from the Sphere Economy, action can be accelerated toward an equitable, just, inclusive, fair, and authentic net-zero world. For example, it enhances both the visibility and the need for systemic collaboration to build upon the essential values of equality, and community, where opportunity is for all. It can help to develop talents, foster diversity and nurture creativity sustained by a strong market economy that offers real choices to many. As an approach The Sphere Economy speeds actions required to tackle effectively diversity, interdependence, ambiguity, and flux.

## People complicate complexity: they may not mean to, but they do.

Mix conflicting world events from a financial crisis, climate change, loss of biosphere service levels, war and so on… and what is exposed are serious weaknesses and vulnerability in business models. No industry or sector is immune.

What has been laid bare are vulnerabilities and weaknesses within the considered wisdom of structures, and isolated systems of finance, technology, productivity, climate and so on. Consequently, there is a lack of foresight against the relentless march of crises. Lessons not learned!

Resilience planning has now become important, in order to build robust, sustainably viable futures. And this should be inclusive of the potential for failures being always considered in risk assessment and decision making (Clearfield and Tilksic, 2018).

We need to develop the kinds of competencies and tools that businesses need in order to thrive in a complex world. This requires relational knowledge and skills to position organisations at the forefront of digital, educational and performance transformations.

However, it is not untypical to find sustainability shifts from an essential inherent property of all subjects to being siloed, blinkering the ability to tackle the visible complexity that is fundamental to addressing interlocked personal and organisational performance with the global challenges that we all face – ecological, societal, and personal. This begs the questions: what has failed in our learning to have created the situation in which we consume the present at the expense of the future? To not be prepared for pandemics, wars, fractured societies, climate and biosphere degradation, migration, human rights abuses, inequity and so on? That for all the wealth generation, and technological advance, why are inequalities so stark, and planetary damage so profound? And what can we do about it… at speed?

## Competence vs Knowledge

Competence is a broader notion than knowledge (Gleadle, 2015). And, in the workplace, competence is more desirable. Competence is the ability to integrate and apply contextually appropriate knowledge, skills and psycho-social factors (e.g., beliefs, attitudes, values and motivations) to consistently perform successfully within a specified domain (Cambridge, 2022).

Naturally, it is important to understand too that knowledge and competence are bounded by time:

1.  The rate of change that makes sector specific knowledge redundant.
2.  The rate of change in the education system to keep up with knowledge redundancy.

Competence in professional sectors is increasingly bounded by time due to rapid technological change, which drives sector-specific knowledge toward redundancy at historically unprecedented rates. The education system is under pressure to adapt quickly enough to equip individuals with useful, up-to-date knowledge as these shifts accelerate, but the response pace often lags behind industry needs (Keep & Brown, 2018).

## *As Descartes wrote:*

The mind has within itself ideas of numbers and figures, and it has likewise among its common notions the principle that if equals be added to equals the wholes will be equal and the like; from which it is easy to demonstrate that the three angles of a triangle are equal to two right angles, etc. Now, so long as we attend to the premises from which this conclusion and others similar to it were deduced, we feel assured of their truth; but, as the mind cannot always think of these with attention, when it has the remembrance of a conclusion without recollecting the order of its deduction, and is uncertain whether the author of its being has created it of a nature that is liable to be deceived, even in what appears most evident, it perceives that there is just ground to distrust the truth of such conclusions, and that it cannot possess any certain knowledge until it has discovered its author.

*(Descartes, 1641)*

In other words: check your assumptions, context, fundamentals, relationships and sequence.

## Complexity and the misinterpretation of holism

Misinterpreting 'holistic' and 'holism' introduces significant risk of tackling complexity effectively by importing preexisting biases into analysis or decision-making frameworks. Holism properly emphasises integrated consideration of whole systems, including their environment and interconnected activities, while the term 'holistic' is often misunderstood as simply a synonym for some whole if we zoom out far enough. But this is not how cognition or the universe works. Every whole is part of another whole, which too is part of something else. The part-whole structure repeats infinitely from the quantum to the observable universe. Such distortions can

**Spheres at the quantum level**

shift focus away from actual systemic relationships, overshadowing context with personal, cultural, or theoretical biases. This can be seen within organisational contexts as cognitive biases: for example, the halo effect (refers to the tendency to allow one specific trait or our overall impression of a person, company or product to positively influence our judgment of their other related traits (Perera, 2023)) or attribution bias (includes the fundamental attribution error, where people tend to attribute others' actions to their personality or character while overlooking situational factors. This can cause individuals or organisations to interpret holistic information through a lens of personal or cultural assumptions (Kahneman, 2011))

Consequences of Misinterpretation:

- Using 'holistic' narrowly encourages fractured or systematic thinking, missing the intended integration of environment, context, and relationships.
- Viewing holism as vague or overly broad can weaken precise professional practice or research, generating perceptions that these perspectives are not evidence-based or are unscientific.
- When holistic processing in perception or cognition is misunderstood or simplistically applied, implicit social or cultural biases can influence outcomes, such as favouring one's own group or overgeneralising from familiar contexts.

## Mechanisms of Bias Import

- Failing to distinguish between holistic (systems-oriented) and non-holistic (reductionist or linear) approaches results in unintentional integration of reductionist assumptions, limiting true systems understanding.
- Biases, both implicit and explicit, shape how interconnected systems are framed, such as which elements are emphasised or ignored, and which causal relationships are prioritised.

The lack of clear boundaries in holistic concepts allows personal or cultural attitudes to influence what is included as part of 'the whole', potentially reinforcing preexisting stereotypes or omitting relevant context.

## Fads and Fashions

The raft of conflicting complexities of the world around us continues to expose limitations and inefficiencies to current strategy and tactical implementation, since they remain disconnected. Separation of the two creates an execution gap formed from the erosive action of opportunities foregone from the frictional interaction between the two. Lack of relational interaction leaves essential components of the system left to run on different

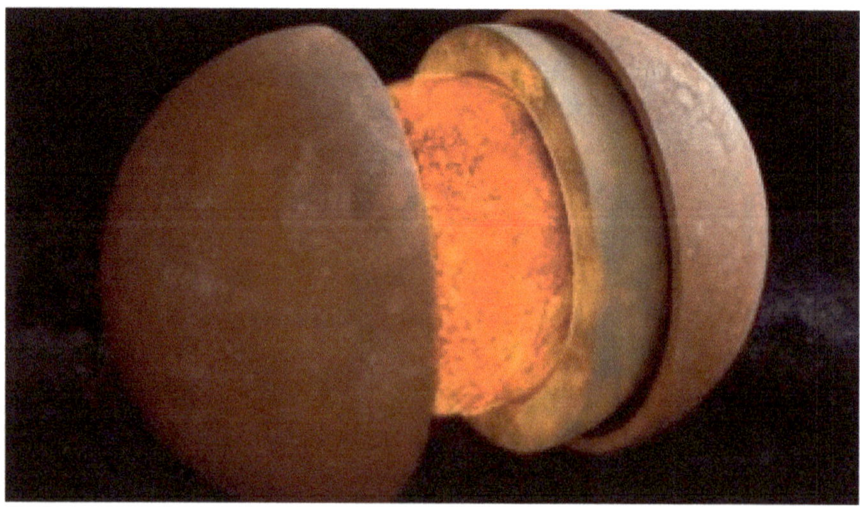

Spheres at the cosmic level

decision cycles, different time boundaries, different stakeholder boundaries, and adherence to different process boundaries and so on. The result is blurred decision sequence clashes that destroy value and fail to visualise anything different.

## Welcome to the Machine

Careful, explicit definition and application of holism are essential to prevent unwanted bias import. Instead of defaulting to popular uses or limited interpretations, practitioners must rigorously clarify what is meant by a holistic approach, focusing on and objectively accounting for relationships, context, and interactions within a system, while remaining vigilant to cultural, theoretical, and methodological sources of bias.

Appropriately, the Sphere Economy approach to AI can help solve the complexity of converting large quantities of data into reliable, clear information that is currently problematic since compilation and interpretation are subject to many influences such as personal biases and intent. For example, the intent of analysts and decision makers may not always be as aligned as it could be. It is not uncommon to find other agendas embedded in the output information that perhaps serve some concealed purpose.

Conventional wisdom considers that training artificial intelligence on evermore data can help fix issues with replicating and amplifying biases. However, this conventional wisdom is being proved wrong. For example, AI trained on larger datasets was shown to be twice as likely to put black female faces in the criminal category and, black male faces were five times more likely to be placed in the same category. (Jeremy Hsu, 2023).

Consequently, AI can have its own problems amplifying errors and dealing with complexity since it has no way of telling whether the generated text corresponds to reality. As a result, more misinformation can be generated. It follows that a lot of noisy data or unreliable data may be as unsuitable for humans as it is for training AI models. You will not solve the problem with the thinking that caused it.

Researchers have looked at solutions where machines do not have to embark on explorations uninformed. Armed with sophisticated language models, researchers could add a pre-training step. Automated pre-training could mean watching. AI only needs to build intuition for how humans behave: build intuition by asking, what would a human do in this scenario? (Zhong, 2021)

It follows that creating more AI generalists could be a big leap from what standard reinforcement learning does, and would allow more generalist managers to make better more informed, more complete intuitive systemic spherical decisions.

## It's the Economy Stupid

Critical information is often unknown at the time or unknowable, concealed, misrepresented, and/or misunderstood.

Unlike most complex physical systems, the agents of an economy, and perhaps to some extent the economy itself, have an extra ingredient and an extra degree of complexity. This ingredient is misbehaviour (Thaler, 2015) which in itself is at the heart of all risk management optimal performance strategies.

Humans develop averages and methods to place things in boxes because, as discussed, people typically feel comfortable with straight line cause and effect. One box to another. The frame becomes normal.

Normal distribution is derived from taking random samples from single events that have no correlation between them. For example, if you were to

flip a coin, the coin will follow a pattern of normal distribution of heads and tails. But this does not mean that winning on one table in a casino, you will, as a result, win on another.

We do not live in a linear world. It is human behaviour that has created narrow linear processes and forced them upon a spherical, three-dimensional, looped, feedback world. On this basis, the siloed thinking of 'green', 'low-carbon' energy, water etc, when treated separately will, at best, deliver *not as bad*.

In contrast, the Earth's surface and all living things upon it are incredibly diverse. The Earth presents a vast geology, physical oceanography and limnology, and a climate that varies on a scale from the largest oceans, continents, lakes and rivers to the tiniest microsites. Billions of individual organisms belonging to millions of species are distributed over the Earth. These act upon one another interdependently.

It follows that natural complex systems offer many orders of magnitude and provide a means for extrapolating between scales: between the large scale of the globe, region, ecosystem or habitat where ecological relationships appear to be complex. The study of scaling is a way of simplifying ecological complexity and of understanding the human, physical

and biological principles that regulate biodiversity. Vivid biological patterns emerge from even subtle interactions. Similar phenomena are seen in the emergence of order in economic, social and political systems (Haseloff, 2013).

Mixed with the complexity of nature's systems is intentional human impact upon those systems and the economies [of scale], that along with the resources of the planet, help provide for the well-being and growth of communities intermingled with the creation of self-sustaining systems.

Using tools of probability, investors can evaluate the odds of an outcome. Yet as discussed, tools can be misused. For example, a financial trader needs to obtain information that can provide some confidence in the immediate future of a stock. This is often based upon repeating patterns from the past. If the normal distribution is applied perfectly, the probability of the 2008/9 financial crisis would have been considered nearly impossible. But, since multiple 'six-sigma' events occurred in close succession, with correlations between asset classes spiking precisely when diversification was most needed, the crisis highlighted how traditional risk management approaches often fail during times of severe market stress (Avenue Investment Management, 2025). In a complex world, the greater dynamic systems that will affect value in the future will have little to do with the 'normal' distribution patterns of the past.

## Financial Crisis and Silo Mentality

When, on a visit to the London School of Economics, the Queen asked of the assembled dignitaries of the economics and financial worlds, "why did you not see it coming?" After some thought and discussion, the Royal Academy wrote a response and in conclusion explained:

"Your Majesty, the failure to foresee the timing, extent and severity of the crisis and to head it off, while it had many causes, was principally a failure of the collective imagination of many bright people, both in this country and internationally, to understand the risks to the system as a whole."

*(Besley and Hennessy, 2009).*

This failure highlighted the need for a defined holistic approach to economics, bridging finance and macroeconomics, moving beyond narrow models and assumptions. Behavioural finance and diversity of thought include hiring non-economists – critical steps to prevent silo thinking.

## Conclusion: Toward Sustainable Viability

To reflect upon where we started:

*To all the complexity of the physical world of weather, crops, ores, and factories, you add the psychological complexity of humans acting on their fleeting expectations of what may or may not happen.*

*Benoît Mandelbrot (2004).*

The Sphere Economy model transforms hierarchical information flows into rich, cross-team communication networks, reducing bottlenecks and missed opportunities. Connecting individuals across silos allows for fast, entrepreneurial innovation while maintaining freedom for experimentation.

A Sphere Economy advances not just economic growth but ecological integrity and social equity through multidimensional systems thinking. Adaptive capacity, critical engagement, diverse experiential learning, and feedback-centric metrics nurture sustainability and resilience within complexity. Rejecting reductionism for defined holistic integration, societies and organisations can respond effectively to crises, innovate collaboratively, and thrive amidst uncertainty.

Ultimately, adopting and operationalising the Sphere Economy is a chance to transform our capacities for sustainable development, equitable value creation, and planetary stewardship, providing a robust academic and practical argument for its essential role in navigating the complexity of the modern world.

## References

Aksu, H. (2024). Google's Innovation Culture: Fuelling Creativity and Disruption in the Digital Age. Available at https://digitopia.co/blog/google-innovation-culture/ (Accessed: 5th December 2025)

Amann, W, Nedopil, C and Steger, U (2011). The Meta-Challenge of Complexity for Global Companies: Springer Nature, Volume 18, pp. Pages 200–204.

Aminov, I. et al. (2019). Decision Making in the Age of Urgency: McKinsey.

Ashby, S. (2010). The 2007–09 Financial Crisis: Learning the Risk Management Lessons. University of Nottingham

Avenue Investment Management (2025) Fat Tail Risk. Available at: https://avenue-investment.com/tail-hedging/fat-tail-risk/ (Accessed: 5th December 2025)

Azimov, I. (1951). *Foundation*. Panther Science Fiction

Bareš, J. (2025) Decision Complexity. European Nexus For Strategic Intelligence. Available at: https://www.intelligencestrategy.org/blog-posts/decision-complexity (Accessed: 5th December 2025)

Beazely Group (2024). Lloyds Underwriters. Guide to Sustainable and Ethical Sourcing. Available at: https://www.beazley.com/en-US/esg-centre/articles/your-guide-to-sustainable-and-ethical-sourcing/. (Accessed: 5th December 2025)

Besley T, Hennessy, P (2009). The Global Financial Crisis – Why Didn't Anybody Notice? The British Academy.

Blundell, R. et al. (2022). Inequality and the COVID-19 Crisis in the United Kingdom. Institute For Fiscal Studies.

Blenko, M. Mankins, M. and Rogers, P. (2010). The Decision-Driven Organization. *Harvard Business Review.* Available at: https://hbr.org/2010/06/the-decision-driven-organization (Accessed 5th December 2025).

Bohm, D. (1980). *Wholeness and the Implicate Order*. Routledge Classics.

Burns, H. (2015). Make the NHS a Well-Being Service not a Sickness Service. New Scientist. Available at: https://www.newscientist.com/article/dn27197-make-the-nhs-a-well-being-service-not-sickness-service/. (Accessed 5th December 2025).

Carbon Brief (2024) Analysis: UK emissions fall 3.6% in 2024 as coal use drops to lowest since 1666. Available at: https://www.carbonbrief.org/analysis-uk-emissions-fall-3-6-in-2024-as-coal-use-drops-to-lowest-since-1666/. (Accessed 5th December 2025)

Clearfield, C, and Tilcsic, A. (2018) *Meltdown*. Penguin Books.

Current Conservation. (2025). Sailing Through Change: Climate Communication for Coastal Communities. Available at: https://www.currentconservation.org/sailing-through-change-climate-communication-for-coastal-communities/ (Accessed 5th December 2025).

Deiss. H. (2023). NASA. The Hard-Won Triumph Of The Apollo 13 Mission. Available at: https://www.nasa.gov/missions/apollo/the-hard-won-triumph-of-the-apollo-13-mission-45-years-later/ (Accessed 5th December 2025).

Fletcher, C. et al. (2024). Earth at risk: An urgent call to end the age of destruction and forge a just and sustainable future. Available at: https://doi.org/10.1093/pnasnexus/pgae106

Descartes, Meditations on First Philosophy (1641), University of Lancaster (2003), History of Philosophy in the 17th & 18th Centuries, Descartes' Principles of Philosophy, University of Lancaster. Available at https://www.lancaster.ac.uk/

users/philosophy/courses/211/Descartes'%20Principles.htm (Accessed: 5th December 2025)

Dewey, J. (1933). *How We Think*. Boston: DC Heath & Co.

Freiberger, M. and Thomas, R. (2025). Plus, Millenium mathematics Project. University of Cambridge.

Gleadle, C. (2018). The Five Essential Steps to Sustainable Viability (2018). SSRN: https://ssrn.com/abstract=4005250 or http://dx.doi.org/10.2139/ssrn.4005250

Gleadle, C. (2020). Naïve Modelling. Long Finance. Available at: https://www.longfinance.net/news/pamphleteers/naïve-modelling-and-covid-19/ (Accessed 5th December 2025)

Fabia, N. and Gleadle, C. (2022). The Climate Puzzle. Fredrich Naumann Foundation. Available at: https://www.freiheit.org/european-union/launch-solving-climate-puzzle-how-systems-thinking-supports-environmental-decision (Accessed 5th December 2025)

Gleadle, C. (2015). Making Education Sustainably Viable – Bridge The Gap. Available at: https://thepaddyashdownforum.org/blog/2022/07/20/making-education-sustainably-viable-bridge-the-gap/ (Accessed 5th December 2025)

Gleadle, C. (2022). What Gets Measured Gets Managed…Oh Really? Long Finance. Available at: https://www.longfinance.net/news/pamphleteers/what-gets-measured-gets-managedoh-really/ (Accessed 5th December 2025)

Gleadle, C. (2023). ESG and Net-Zero. Whose Truth? Long Finance. Available at: https://www.longfinance.net/news/pamphleteers/esg-and-net-zero-whose-truth/ (Accessed 5th December 2025)

Guo, L. and Pankaj, K. (2022). Market Fragmentation and Price Impact. American Economic Association.

Hallett, Baroness DBE. (2025). UK Covid 19 Enquiry. Crown Copyright 2025.

Haseloff, J. (2013). Fractal patterns spontaneously emerge during bacterial cell growth. University of Cambridge.

Hsu, J. (2023). How this moment for AI will change society forever (and how it won't). *New Scientist*. Available at: https://www.newscientist.com/article/mg25834352-800-how-this-moment-for-ai-will-change-society-forever-and-how-it-wont/ (Accessed 5th December 2025).

International Energy Authority (2025). World Energy Outlook. IEA.

Jackson, M. C. (2024). *Critical Systems Thinking: A Practitioners Guide*. Wiley Blackwell.

Jackson, M. (2024). Interview by Martin Reeves, 1st October 2024

Jobs, S (2005). Stanford University. Available at: https://www.youtube.com/watch?v=5BSbOc5VYY8 (Accessed 5th December 2025).

Joint Research Centre (2021). Environmental Sustainability of Energy Generation From Forest Biomass. EU Commission

Kahneman, D. (2011). *Thinking Fast and Slow*. Penguin Books.

Keep, E. and Brown, P. (2018). Rethinking the Race Between Education and Technology. National Academy of Sciences, Arizona State, Vol. XXXV, No. 1, Fall 2018

Kyoto Protocol, 1997. United Nations Framework Convention on Climate Change. UNFCCC

Laker, B. (2024). Why Rigid Hierarchies Might Be Killing Your Team's Creativity. Forbes. Available at: https://www.forbes.com/sites/benjaminlaker/2024/08/15/why-rigid-hierarchies-might-be-killing-your-teams-creativity/ (Acessed 5th December 2025)

Leunig, M. (1984) The Understandascope. *The Age Newspaper*, Melbourne.

Katrine, M. (2012) *Who Cooked Adam Smith's Dinner?* Albert Bonniers Förlag.

Mandelbrot, B. and Hudson, R. (2004). *The (Mis)Behaviour Of Markets*. Profile Books.

Midgley, G. (2008). *Systems thinking, complexity and the philosophy of science. Emergence: Complexity and Organization.* Emergent Publications.

Midgely, G. (2016*). Four Domains of Complexity*. Emergent Publications.

Minsky, H. (1974). Our Financial System Is Fragile. *New York Times*. Hyman P. Minsky Archive. 346. https://digitalcommons.bard.edu/hm_archive/346 (Accessed 5th December 2025)

Neven, D. (2014). Developing Sustainable Food Value Chains: Guiding principles. Food and Agriculture Organisation of the United Nations.

OECD. (2017). Systems Approaches To Public Sector Challenges. OECD Observatory of Public Sector Innovation.

OECD. (2020). Systemic Thinking for Policy Making. OECD and International Institute for Applied Systems Analysis (IIASA).

Perera, A. (2023). Halo Effect i n Psychology: Definition and Examples. Simply Psychology. Available at: https://www.simplypsychology.org/halo-effect.html (Accessed 5th December 2025)

Raleigh, Veen. (Kings Fund, 2024). Available at: https://www.kingsfund.org.uk/insight-and-analysis/long-reads/whats-happening-life-expectancy-england

Ridgeway, V. (1956). Dysfunctional Consequences of Performance Measurements. *Administrative Science Quarterly* Vol. 1, No. 2 (Sep.,1956), pp. 240–247 (8 pages)

Seijts, G., Crossan, M. and Billou, N. (2011). Coping w ith Complexity. Forbes. Available at: https://www.forbesindia.com/article/richard-ivey/coping-with-complexity/21732/1 (Accessed 5th December 2025)

Sillmann, J. et al. (2022). Briefing note on systemic risk, Paris, France. International Science Council. Available at: https://doi.org/10.24948/2022.01

Shokri, A, et al. (2022). Has Covid 19 Affected the Social Cohesion. National Library of Medicine. Available at:https://doi.org/10.18502/ijph.v51i2.8705 (Accessed 5th December 2025)

Snowdon, D. (2021). The Cynefin Framework. The Cynefin Company.

Strogatz S. (2004). *The Emerging Science of Spontaneous Order*. London. Penguin Books.

Thaler, R. (2015). *Misbehaving: The Making of Behavioural Economics*. Allen Lane.

Tinch, R. et al. (2015). Applying a Capitals Framework to Measuring Coping and Adaptive Capacity in Integrated Assessment Models. *Climatic Change* 128, pp.323–337.

UNRISD, (2023). Crises of Inequality Shifting Power for a New Eco-Social Contract. United Nations Research Institute For Social Development.

Valgarðsson, V. (2025). *A Crisis of Political Trust? Global Trends in Institutional Trust from 1958 to 2019*. Cambridge University Press.

Vickers, G. (1972) *Freedom in a Rocking Boat: Changing Values in an Unstable Society*. Cambridge University Press.

Vitello, S. Greatorex, J. (2022). What is competence? A shared interpretation of competence to support teaching, learning and assessment. University of Cambridge.

World Of Inequality Report (2022). World Inequality Lab.

Zhenmin, L. (2018). Under-Secretary-General for Economic and Social Affairs, United Nations Sustainable Development Goals Report. United Nations.

Zhong, V. (2021). The Multi-environment Symbolic, Interactive Language Grounding Benchmark. Cornell University. arXiv:2110.10661

# ARTIFICIAL FLAVORS IN ORGANISATIONS

## Raluca Bochis

## Introduction

Given the rising prevalence of Artificial Intelligence (AI) in organisational processes, and the fact that this disruption is likely still in incipient stages, organisational structures, hierarchies and identities will be also impacted dynamically. This chapter will explore possible ways in which quintessentially human characteristics that give the flavor of organisations (such as trust, psychological safety, community) might evolve, and how these changes may impact organisational structures, hierarchies and identities. The study is grounded in complexity theory and starts from the premise that organisations are c omplex Adaptive systems, or networks of interconnected nodes, the human element being central to the shared identity of a company. While this topic is significant for all of us humans operating in various organisational forms, it is especially critical for leaders to orient themselves in the midst of a technological revolution, to be able to catch the wave of emergence and navigate it in a way that allows their organisations not just to survive but to thrive in the new world taking shape. Leaders must do so while preserving or enhancing innovation, adaptability and carving out the right place for the human spirit. The paper offers reflections and recommendations for leadership in managing the AI "flavored" organisation.

## Organisations as Complex Human Systems

The study is grounded in complexity theory, viewing organisations as complex a daptive s ystems. These systems are present in a wide variety of contexts, from the natural world, biology, and climate, to the socially constructed world, social media, and communities. Complex systems display several defining characteristics: they consist of a large number of elements connected in networks via nonlinear dynamics, they are self-organizing and they exhibit emergent behaviors and structures, which are not fully ordered nor fully disordered. These systems continuously adapt, exapt, and evolve (Taylor and Bochis, 2025).

The elements composing complex adaptive systems continuously interact with each other "at multiple touchpoints and across layers" (Allan et al., 2013) and in doing so, impact each other and the overall system (Lewin and Regine, 2003). There is a *continuous dance of evolution* between system states and interactions, as interactions change the state of the system and those states in turn determine future interactions (Thurner et al., 2018). Organisational design therefore is constantly evolving into the shape that is most appropriate for the evolving circumstances (Jackson, 2003). Organisations are living networks, more than the sum of individuals, and they are the product of their interactions (Espejo, 2003).

Taylor and Bochis (2025) identify several markedly human factors that power organisations as complex adaptive systems:

- **Communities of practice**. Organisations display layers of networks. What is a sub-network at one level becomes a node at the level above, in what Beer (1984) calls levels of recursion. Drawing on Wenger's (1998) concept of communities of practice (CoPs), which are groups of individuals bound by shared expertise and practice, we can see how such communities are fundamental sub-systems of organisations. In fact, it is argued that organisations are essentially networks of communities of practice, or even communities of communities of practice (Brown and Duguid, 2001). Communities of practice self-organise and continuously renegotiate their structure and objectives, generating localised knowledge and feedback loops, that promote adaptability (Taylor and Bochis, 2025) and represent the recursive DNA of the organisation. These informal groups of people and the collection of interactions between their sub-cultures often drive the course of action more than formal policies or strategies do (Schein, 2010).
- **Relationships based on trust**. More than contractual or rules driven interactions, trust serves as a major lubricant of social systems (Arrow, 1974) and is the foundation for collaboration. Environments of high trust foster decentralised decision-making and enable a higher

degree of risk appetite, which in turn fuels the emergence of innovation. Lewin and Regine (2003) highlight that respect, care and trust form the foundation of relationships are the core of effective management practice.

- **Meaningful interactions**. Seeing organisations through the lens of complex adaptive systems, inherently human phenomena such as reflexivity, intentionality, emotion and intuition (MacLean and MacIntosh, 2003) become critical considerations. The human element in business (Taylor and Bochis, 2025) brings qualities such as consciousness, self-awareness and a sense of agency or free will (Basios, 2017) as characteristics particular to this subset of complex adaptive systems. More than a shared purpose, reducible to survival and adaptation to changing conditions, these complex social systems (Mitleton-Kelly, 2003) are bound together by a shared sense of meaning that is co-created and re-emerges through time as foundational for their identity.

- **Psychological safety**. Defined by Edmondson (2004) as a climate where people feel safe expressing their thoughts and making mistakes without fear of punishment, psychological safety encourages experimentation, learning through failure, and diminishes the reputational risk attached to trying out new ideas. A psychologically safe team is more likely to act, take the lesson, freely discuss the errors made, and try again, thereby fostering an environment conducive to innovation (Taylor and Bochis, 2025). Psychological safety can be viewed as progressing through stages: starting with the safety to be yourself, then safety to learn and experiment, to safety to contribute with own input, and finally, at the highest level, the safety to challenge the status quo (Clark, 2020).

- **Strength in the heterogeneity of perspectives**. Complex adaptive systems benefit from heterogenous elements. Diversity in cognitive, experiential and cultural perspectives ensures the variety needed for a system to adapt to changing circumstances in their environment, as maintained by Ashby's Law of Requisite Variety (Ashby, 1956). Stacey et al. (2000) argue that new organisational developments can occur only if the people comprising the organisation are different from one another. Diversity creates the adaptive tension (Allen, 2001) that fuels change and prevents groupthink (Janis, 1972).

Therefore, human interactions, informed by inherently human characteristics, drive learning and innovation, continually shaping and reshaping the organisation as order emerges in a constant flux in these *complex human systems*.

## Enter Artificial Intelligence

Technological advancements, coupled with societal, geopolitical and climate changes, provide constant input to alter existing conditions and drive organisations to change. Among these forces, Artificial Intelligence has the potential to drastically transform organisations, driving an evolutionary leap towards new structures, processes, dynamics and overall shape. However, AI's rise also carries the risk of leaving behind those who are not prepared to shed old identities in favour of AI-infused ones.

In keeping with the nature of complex systems, the outcomes of introducing AI at scale are not easy to predict; AI is not contained nor are its effects easily understood. Following Snowden's Cynefin framework (Snowden, 2004) for complex domains, attention must be focused on *probing* to detect emerging patterns, *sensing* the specifics of the disruption that AI brings about, and then *responding* by placing informed bets on which waves would be more beneficial to exploit and which to counteract. AI will undoubtedly shape the future, and the future will depend on how we leverage it, recognizing its potential as both a weapon and a tool (Taylor and Bochis, 2025).

This raises the question: what does a *complex human system* look like with "artificial flavoring"? Organisational design, hierarchies, processes and structures are all likely to change drastically. We can either brace for impact or probe, sense and respond to channel this emergence; most likely, we must do both. In the last days of 2025, Satya Nadella, Microsoft's CEO, reflected in the inaugural post of his new personal blog (Nadella, 2025) that as we gain a better sense of where technology is headed, the more important challenge is figuring out how to shape its impact, or, rephrasing in complexity terms, how to channel emergence. Nadella's core position is that AI serves as a scaffolding for human potential and not a substitute for human cognition. He encourages the shift from considering AI models as ends in themselves to seeing them as agents orchestrated in complex systems.

One of the first noticeable changes in an AI-infused organisation is the surge in process automation and the use of AI personal assistants, all in pursuit of greater efficiency. However, AI's impact will extend far beyond efficiency—and in fact, single-mindedly chasing efficiency is a trap as it moves strategic focus away from innovation (Taylor and Bochis, 2025).

Indeed, AI is likely to challenge existing business models, obliterate established processes (Hammer, 1990), and radically transform organisations to leverage network effects in capturing value. By consolidating autonomous networks within organisations, AI can serve as a powerful tool for facilitating emergence and driving innovation. Traditional hierarchies are already challenged as even large corporations seek the agility of smaller firms; AI is expected to accelerate this shift, and promote flatter, more networked structures (Baumann and Wu, 2023). Information disseminates faster through networks, leading to a higher degree of responsiveness and promoting organisational flexibility and resilience. On the other hand, an over-reliance on rigid algorithms could actually decrease flexibility and make the organisation less adaptable to changing conditions in its environment, which would make the case for intentionally injecting novel human input into AI models.

When information no longer needs to flow top-down or bottom-up, decisions can be delegated and informed by a universally available AI "modus operandi", applicable not just to operational procedures (how we *do* things here) but also to decision-making (how we *think through* things here). Less need for hands-on operational control is likely to translate into fewer managerial layers (Felten et al., 2019). Large organisations might retain just enough hierarchy to ensure strategic coherence (Foss and Klein, 2023), while smaller and more agile organisations could adopt structures that are virtually flat.

When algorithms assign tasks, monitor their execution, and enforce rules, they effectively act as supervisors, enabling what is known as algorithmic management (Duggan et al., 2020). Gig economy platforms already operate this way, with ride-sharing apps managing work via software and minimal human oversight. As algorithmic management slowly permeates more traditional organisations, the role managers play will change. A potentially significant part of their jobs, operational control, may be transferred to AI, meaning managers may end up with a broader span of supervision but with less hands-on oversight (Baumann and Wu, 2023) or a role focusing more on handling and training the AI on exceptions (Colbert et al., 2016). The removal of management layers, instead of leading to decentralisation and empowerment, can result in *more* centralisation of decision-making at top leadership levels, enabling micro-management at scale by senior leaders.

While the full implications of such a transition on management roles are yet to be discovered, the impact on the teams that will take instructions and guidance from AI, in terms of work quality, performance, and motivation, is no clearer. On the one hand, people could end up feeling they belong to a more democratic structure, where everyone receives guidance from the same unbiased system. On the other hand, they might feel a reduced sense of belonging to what has become a code-driven organisation. The less optimistic scenario is shown to be the case for ride-sharing companies such as Uber, where multiple case studies document reduction in worker autonomy (Duggan et al., 2020), erosion of community (Möhlmann and Zalmanson, 2017) and a diminished sense of belonging (Rosenblat and Stark, 2016). The efficiencies created by removing human management layers must be carefully considered against the potential loss of engagement and motivation in the workforce.

## Artificial Flavors to the Complex Human System

### Trust

In traditional organisational structures, trust was earned in a process of interrelating and represented the foundation for solid relationships, collaborative behavior, and coordinated action. If there are less opportunities to build and exercise human trust, due to fewer interactions, and no need to trust the human to therefore trust the decision made, as decisions get increasingly made by data-driven systems, do people still need trust to function? And if so, who or what do they trust?

We already trust non-human algorithms with critical tasks: we rely on them to detect strokes in brain scans; to fly planes and coordinate landings; to move large quantities of goods through manufacturing facilities. The more we trust in data-informed algorithms, the less we rely on human decision-making. In turn, this leads to less human repository of experience, experimentation, and accumulated expertise, which further increases reliance on the system. By diminishing the opportunities to interact in processes that now become fully automated, and by making it easy to just ask AI instead of leveraging a colleague's expertise, there are fewer opportunities to earn trust, and the bonds between colleagues become weaker. In this way, trust begins to shift away from humans and toward the system itself.

When AI makes decisions, it is arguable that formal authority matters less than technical authority, and leaders hold less real control than data scientists. If decisions are seen as impersonal, employees may place less trust in management, eroding the relationship as well as the employee's engagement and motivation. To prevent this, it is critical to ensure oversight and transparency in AI-driven decisions, to actively promote trust in the system for all layers in the organisation (Toreini et al., 2020). For example, data-driven hiring or promotion tools can reduce subjective biases and require less trust in the fairness of the hiring manager but can also be infused with algorithmic biases or lack the nuanced human intuition that is not necessarily grounded in algorithm-ready data. Therefore, transparency about how they work and human oversight of their outputs are essential for trust.

## Psychological Safety

Psychological safety, the shared belief that it is safe to voice your opinion without fear of retribution (Edmondson, 2004), could either be diminished or enhanced by the presence of AI.

On the one hand, the perception of constant AI surveillance can erode psychological safety and discourage experimentation. In an environment where every mistake is visible, monitored, and potentially punished by an algorithmic metric, people become less willing to engage in *safe-to-fail* experiments (Snowden, 2004) and develop a lower appetite for risk (Taylor and Bochis, 2025), which in turn decreases human-driven innovation. Also, given challenger safety is the highest level of safety to attain (Clark, 2020), it is hard to challenge others and even harder to challenge AI as the perceived authority making high-quality, data-driven decisions. To prevent AI from hindering psychological safety, rules can be established to encourage people to express where they disagree with the AI recommendations. This can be done more effectively where there is already a climate of high psychological safety, where people would be more open to express disagreement anyway. Conversely, where psychological safety is low, introducing AI could further diminish people's willingness to speak up.

On the other hand, AI can be leveraged as a tool to promote psychological safety. Google provides an excellent example of how this can be done. After identifying psychological safety as the most important trait of successful teams, in their internal "Project Aristotle" research (Osmani, 2024), the company followed up by implementing AI-assisted tools to analyse variations in the degree of psychological safety displayed by their teams such as pulse surveys, mood barometers, and AI sentiment analysis in meetings (Markland, 2025). It can also be argued that while this does not increase psychological safety per se, AI can counter the effects of a lower level of safety by providing safe virtual spaces for experimentation and unlimited scenario-testing opportunities. In these virtual environments, it becomes risk-free to try out things, not because the community would not punish failure but because there is no tangible failure to punish.

## Communities of Practice

Communities of practice traditionally create and exchange knowledge, both *explicitly*, through documentation, databases, recordings, and *tacitly*, via storytelling, shadowing activities, and shared practice. Knowledge is created and spread through interactions between members (Snowden, 2002). AI is very adept at aggregating and disseminating knowledge at scale, thus having the potential to substitute some of the functions served by communities of practice, specifically the formal knowledge management capabilities (storing, categorizing, retrieving, maintaining knowledge artifacts). However, when it comes to tacit knowledge, its value is more limited. AI can answer questions like an experienced colleague but cannot act as a mentor; can mimic live customer interaction for training purposes, but cannot provide the contextual cues that only shadowing a coworker can; it is able to generate stories, but is not able to convey the same nuance and elicit the same emotional reactions as real "war stories" coming from more experienced community members do.

Brown and Duguid's (2001) networks of practice, looser and more dispersed knowledge networks compared to communities of practice, can benefit greatly from AI. The system can reach in, identify a knowledge gap in a piece of work, and surface hidden expertise in other parts of the company, suggesting experts who can be contacted for help. It can create new networks of practice, it can revive old ones, and it can break through traditional silos and create a sharing ground for skills that would have been difficult to meet otherwise. The result is more nodes identified in a network, and more connections being formed between them, which improve the strength of the complex system and its capacity for innovation (Boisot and McKelvey, 2011). Such networks of practice can be internal to the company but also can expand over the limits of the organisation into broader professional and industry forums.

While the merits of AI are unquestionable, knowledge is not just about what is *known* but also what is *knowable*. The value of a community extends beyond the knowledge it currently holds and can share, into what can emerge as new knowledge. An AI-informed community of practice can represent the actual enactment of a global knowledge village, and at the same time, lose its identity. A true community may need a sense of *communion* among its members, and the more a community is scaled up, the less communion is possible, to the point of turning the community concept meaningless. We may all be connected through the internet, but we are not a global community of internet citizens. AI-driven communities of practice would need to complement interpersonal trust with trust in the algorithm, but this would still not make up for what is lost in terms of engagement, commitment, and the simple joy of connection.

A key risk is that in the absence of human connection, and with the convenience of just getting an instant answer without engaging in in-depth reasoning, people will start to outsource their thinking to AI, including creation of knowledge. Knowledge remains both a "thing" and a "flow" (Snowden, 2002) and requires the active human practices of sense-making, debating, storytelling for new knowledge to emerge and for the organisation to learn and evolve. Without its dynamic aspects, knowledge is nothing more than a museum artifact, no matter how many times it can be repackaged by AI. To counter this, communities should question and refine what AI suggests, keeping a human-in-the loop element to breathe life into knowledge and maintain it relevant as a tool for growing and maintaining organisational adaptive capabilities.

## Heterogeneity

Nurturing and leveraging diverse human perspectives is even more important in the age of AI. While starting out as a wide exploration of vast data sets, AI outputs tend to converge with every iteration, as the diversity of data diminishes. This creates what Pentland (2013) calls an "echo chamber", where the same ideas get recycled to the point of cutting off social learning opportunities and insulating from the environment which would otherwise contribute with cues of emerging variation, thus violating Ashby's Law of Requisite Variety (Ashby, 1956). To counteract this, the utilisation of multiple AI models, and focus on providing access to fresh sets of data sources can instil the required heterogeneity in the AI itself and improve the output.

Convergent thinking in AI solutions becomes a greater problem when coupled with convergent thinking in the human teams. Solvingproblems is proven to be more effective (Pentland, 2013) in heterogenous groups, as the diversity of ag ents is more important than their expertise (Boisot and McKelvey, 2011). The diversity provided by the human-in-the-loop hybrid setup is not sufficient; the humans in the loop need to be diverse to achieve optimal results. Diverse teams are more likely to identify where the AI solution is flawed or biased, and less likely to have convergent thinking, or engage in groupthink (Janis, 1972). Dissenting opinions, in the presence of the psychological safety to challenge (Clark, 2020), create the adaptive tension for change (Allen, 2001).

Heterogeneity fuels collective intelligence (Taylor and Bochis, 2025) as diverse perspectives generate more innovative solutions. A practical strategy could be to use AI for routine idea generation, and then have diverse human teams filter through them with a broad evaluation lens. The use of heterogenous teams in training AI will also provide a wider set of perspectives, helping to make AI less biased and driving more acceptance of results as being fair. IBM's AI ethics princis, for example, (Rossi, 2020), translate into an intentional approach towards mitigating that human bipleases are picked up and amplified by AI. Additionally, cultural and regional heterogeneity in global teams can be fostered by leveraging AI tools in bridging language barriers. However, it is also possible that regional voices become even less prevalent in the presence of an AI "source of truth" that is developed by and reflects the cultural norms of Western cultures. Ensuring global diversity is truly represented in AI systems is therefore critical.

Leadership Getting oriented in the midst of a technological revolution is critical for leaders so that they can catch the wave of emergence and navigate it in a way that will allow their organisations to not just survive but thrive in the new world taking shape. A strategy for AI adoption should focus on preserving or enhancing innovation, promoting adaptability and carving out the right place for the human spirit within the organisation.

Leaders now need to actively facilitate the transition to AI-embedded organisations. They should seek to channel emergence for the most adaptive response and assess whether the new patterns and behaviors truly enable innovation and creativity, redirecting them if they do not (Stacey, 2007).

Leading through disruption means *riding* the wave of change, not trying to escape or overpower it (Lewin and Regine, 2000). The leader as a facilitator of emergence should promote self-organizing principles (Burnes, 2004) and identify the minimal conditions necessary for structure. They must broadly disseminate the core functioning principles: purpose (priorities), account-ability, and communication as the node connector (Brown and Eisenhardt, 1997). With AI now in the mix, human control over the core functioning principles must be defended and emphasised by leaders. Employee com-mitment to the organisational mission and values depends on the employee feeling valued, feeling valuable and feeling included in a mission broader than what individuals can achieve on their own, within a living company, displaying human signs of vitality. People are not inspired by machines, but by other people.

Trust remains foundational and sustaining it in an AI-driven environ-ment requires multiple layers of transparency. One layer is the transparency of the AI systems themselves; what informs them, what data sets are lever-aged, what the main algorithmic principles are, in order to actively educate employees and build trust in AI so that they embrace it. Another layer of transparency is from leadership on how and why AI is leveraged in the func-tioning of the organisation. Leaders need to dispel any suspicion of surveil-lance or lack of respect for privacy by clearly communicating the purpose of AI deployments and their limits. Also, leaders should be open about how AI is utilised in decision-making, especially where decisions affect employ-ees such as promotions, rewards, restructuring, by clarifying principles of fairness, equity and reasoning involved. In fact, to increase the level of psy-chological safety and trust, leaders should invite input from everyone when implementing AI and ensure they act on employee feedback. Governance structures (like AI ethics committees or review boards) should also be set up so that employees can trust that AI is being used responsibly.

A third layer of transparency concerns the norms for operating in hybrid teams, with both human and artificial intelligence elements, orchestrating human-AI interactions. Leaders should encourage and model fallibility and openness to challenge the AI, making it clear it is expected and acceptable to question AI. They should recognize employees who experiment with AI and acknowledge the trial and error that are inherent to learning new technology. By focusing too much on accelerating the pace of adoption, leaders may mistakenly augment the benefits and the soundness of reasoning of the mod-els, inadvertently discouraging employees from questioning their outputs or sharing problems in using AI. This could erode psychological safety and discourage the experimentation that leads to innovation.

AI needs to be positioned as a tool to leverage and control, not as the ultimate source of truth and judgement; or in the words of Nadella (2025), think of AI as "scaffolding for human potential", or "bicycles for the mind", rather than a substitute for human cognition. AI is there to augment, not replace human judgement.

Given the acceleration of the pace of change, leaders benefit from what Tushman and O'Reilly (1996) call *ambidexterity*: the capability to combine incremental improvements with fostering radical innovation. This requires the double ability to exploit AI for efficiency to ensure current viability (Levinthal and March, 1993), while simultaneously exploring the new opportunities AI opens in pursuit of future organisational viability. Concretely, leaders should ensure people get the training and education necessary to integrate AI into today's operations effectively, while also providing room for *safe-to-fail* experimentation (Snowden, 2004). Such experiments might spark novel ideas and lead to transformative outcomes.

As Artificial Intelligence gets more imbedded in organisational practices and processes, the company's culture – the shared norms and values underpinning it s identity – serves as the compass to guide AI implementation and the ensuing hybrid AI-human functioning. The leadership human touch becomes even more critical in guiding the complex adaptive system that is a modern organisation through the disruptive force of artificial intelligence.

To keep employees committed and engaged, it is vital that the leader reasserts the organisation's purpose and values and explains how AI supports the company's mission. Purpose is the overarching reason for the company's existence, a profoundly human construct. To create a sense of shared purpose, meaningful interactions are foundational, built on respect, care and trust. When people understand the value they bring to the company and the value they get by belonging to it, they are more likely to find meaning in their work and connect with the broader mission. If AI is introduced without this context, simply focusing on automating tasks, optimis ing workflows, and potentially facilitating decisions, employees might feel threatened or alienated from the organisation. Feeling as if they are part of a soulless machine, they could struggle to see the impact of their work and question the value they bring.

To mitigate for these risks, the human element must be reinforced and emphasised. The following recommendations can inform management practice in channelling the benefits of artificial intelligence by leveraging the human elements that keep organisations truly alive:

- Communicate clearly and consistently about the purpose of the company, the role of AI as a tool to free people from mundane tasks and to unlock opportunities for experimentation and innovation; this improves employee engagement and connection to the overarching purpose.
- Establish clearly that accountability stays with the human. Use AI to inform decisions, not act as decision-maker. Consider presenting AI and human perspectives side by side to promote transparency and trust.
- Position AI as a scaffolding for human potential—augmenting cognition, not replacing it—and redesign roles to elevate human creativity, judgment, and agency in a hybrid human-AI system.
- Promote psychological safety by creating a climate where people feel safe to express disagreement with AI recommendations, share concerns, and challenge the status quo without fear of retribution.
- Intentionally nurture heterogeneity of perspectives—cognitive, experiential, and cultural—to fuel adaptive tension, prevent groupthink, and enhance the system's capacity for innovation and resilience.
- Lead as a facilitator of emergence by setting minimal conditions for structure (purpose, accountability, communication), enabling self-organisation, and sensing which patterns to amplify or dampen as the system evolves.
- Intentionally create opportunities for connection such as recognition events, team-building programs, mentorship and coaching, to offset the increasing depersonalisation of work and sustain the human fabric of the organisation.
- Leverage the power of storytelling, ensuring personal messages are personally crafted without the assistance of AI, to nurture the emotional aspects of work and reinforce shared meaning.
- Use engagement surveys, ensuring they capture sense of purpose, belonging and psychological safety, during and post-AI implementation. Carry out sentiment analysis on internal communication (AI-driven) to detect early signals of declining connection.
- Use town halls, skip-level meetings, focus groups, community of practice meetings, and lessons-learned sessions as opportunities to engage in healthy debate, strengthen relationships and build trust.

- Redesign processes with human-in-the-loop or better, diverse humans-in-the-loop, ensuring that AI serves as a tool not a replacement for the team. Review periodically and adjust by adding or removing human checkpoints to maintain the appropriate degree of oversight.
- Reinforce a people-centric culture. Invest in both technical upskilling and in soft skills development to reinforce the need for specialisation and that human capabilities remain irreplaceable.
- Build AI literacy. Provide practical training on AI capabilities. Train managers on leading AI-infused teams.
- Get buy-in through transparency and inclusion. Engage employees early and co-create the path forward.
- Balance performance reviews by evaluating behaviours alongside output metrics, recognizing collaboration, adaptability, and ethical judgement as core to success.
- Encourage experimenting with AI, publicly discuss failures and lessons learned from AI projects.
- Include employees in AI decision boards and evaluation processes to democratis e AI governance, incorporate diverse perspectives, and build trust in the technology shaping their work.
- Use AI to strengthen communities of practice, not to replace them, by enhancing knowledge flows, surfacing hidden expertise, and enabling the emergence of dynamic networks of practice.
- Treat AI adoption like a journey of discovery. Continuously iterate and adapt. Implement feedback loops for the human-AI interface. Experiment and test for fitness. Frame errors as necessary for learning. Question assumptions, evolve structures, norms and processes as AI continues to evolve.

## Conclusion

The integration of AI is about to reshape organisations in profound ways, but viewing these changes through the lens of complexity theory reveals a consistent theme: human-centric elements remain critical to sustained success. Trust, psychological safety, communities of practice, and heterogeneity are not elements of the past but essential drivers of collective learning, innovation, and resilience in an AI-driven environment. The key insight is that organisations function as complex adaptive systems where emergent outcomes depend on the interplay of technology and human agency. Leaders, therefore, must navigate this emergent landscape by balancing technological advancement with human values, maintaining transparency to build trust, fostering a culture of open experimentation to preserve psychological safety, and using AI as an augmentative tool rather than a replacement for human judgment and creativity. By channelling AI's capabilities while reinforcing purpose, meaning, and connection, leaders can shape AI's impact in ways that allow their organisations to thrive. Those organisations that leverage AI to enhance the human dynamics of collaboration and adaptation will be best positioned to innovate and prosper in the complex, ever-evolving future of work.

## References


Allan, N., Cantle, N., Godfrey, P. and Yin, Y. (2013). 'A review of the use of complex systems applied to risk appetite and emerging risks in ERM practice: Recommendations for practical tools to help risk professionals tackle the problems of risk appetite and emerging risk'. *British Actuarial Journal*, 18(1), pp.163–234.

Allen, P. M. (2001). "A complex systems approach to learning in adaptive networks". *International Journal of Innovation Management*, 5(2), pp.149–180.

Arrow, K. J. (1974). *The limits of organization*. New York: W. W. Norton & Company.

Ashby, W. R. (1956). *An introduction to cybernetics*. London: Chapman & Hall.

Basios, V. (2017). 'Complexity and consciousness: A conceptual analysis'. *Journal of Consciousness Studies*, 24(1–2), pp. 8–28.

Baumann, O. and Wu, B. (2023). 'Managerial hierarchy in AI-driven organizations.' *Journal of Organization Design*, 12(1), pp.1–12.

Beer, S. (1984). 'The viable system model: Its provenance, development, methodology and pathology'. *Journal of the Operational Research Society*, 35(1), pp. 7–25.

Boisot, M. and McKelvey, B. (2011). 'Connectivity, extremes, and adaptation: A power-law perspective of organizational effectiveness'. *Journal of Management Inquiry*, 20(2), pp.119–133.

Brown, J. S. and Duguid, P. (2001). 'Knowledge and organization: A social-practice perspective'. *Organization Science*, 12(2), pp. 198–213.

Brown, S. L., and Eisenhardt, K. M. (1997). 'The art of continuous change: Linking complexity theory and time-paced evolution in relentlessly shifting organizations'. *Administrative Science Quarterly*, 42(1), pp. 1–34.

Burnes, B. (2004). 'Emergent change and planned change – competitors or allies? The case of XYZ construction'. *International Journal of Operations & Production Management*, 24(9), pp. 886–902.

Clark, T. R. (2020). *The 4 stages of psychological safety: Defining the path to inclusion and innovation*. Oakland: Berrett-Koehler Publishers.

Colbert, A., Yee, N. and George, G. (2016). 'The digital workforce and the workplace of the future'. *Academy of Management Journal*, 59(3), pp. 731–739.

Duggan, J., Sherman, U., Carbery, R., and McDonnell, A. (2020). 'Algorithmic management and app-work in the gig economy: A research agenda for employment relations and HRM'. *Human Resource Management Journal*, 30(1), pp. 114–132.

Edmondson, A. C. (2004). 'Psychological safety, trust, and learning in organizations: A group-level lens'. In R. M. Kramer and K. S. Cook (Eds.), *Trust and Distrust in Organizations: Dilemmas and Approaches* (pp. 239–272). New York: Russell Sage Foundation.

Espejo, R. (2003). 'The viable system model: A briefing about organizational structure'. In H. Yolles (Ed.), *Knowledge cybernetics: A new metaphor for social collectives* (pp. 45–60). London: Springer.

Felten, E. W., Raj, M. and Seamans, R. (2019). 'The occupational impact of artificial intelligence: Labor, skills, and polarization'. NYU Stern School of Business.

Foss, N. J. and Klein, P. G. (2023). 'Why managers still matter as applied organization (design) theory'. *Journal of Organization Design, 12*(1), pp. 7–18.

Hammer, M. (1990). 'Reengineering work: Don't automate, obliterate. *Harvard Business Review*, 68(4), pp. 104–112.

Jackson, M. C. (2003). *Systems thinking: Creative holism for managers*. Chichester: Wiley.

Janis, I. L. (1972). *Victims of groupthink: A psychological study of foreign-policy decisions and fiascoes*. Boston: Houghton Mifflin.

Levinthal, D. A. and March, J. G. (1993). 'The myopia of learning'. *Strategic Management Journal*, 14(S2), pp. 95–112.

Lewin, R., and Regine, B. (2000). *The soul at work: Embracing complexity science for business success*. New York: Simon & Schuster.

Lewin, R. and Regine, B. (2003). The core of adaptive organisations. In E. Mitleton-Kelly (Ed.), *Complex systems and evolutionary perspectives on organisations: The application of complexity theory to organisations* (pp. 167–184). Oxford: Elsevier.

MacLean, D. and MacIntosh, R. (2003). 'Complex adaptive social systems: Towards a theory for practice'. In E. Mitleton-Kelly (Ed.), *Complex systems and evolutionary perspectives on organisations: The application of complexity theory to organisations* (pp. 149–165). Oxford: Elsevier.

Markland, D. (2025). 'Google Project Aristotle Psychological Safety Guide 2025'. *Noomii Leadership Coaching*. November 14, 2025. Available at: https://orgs.noomii.com/google-project-aristotle-psychological-safety/.(viewed January 11, 2026).

Mitleton-Kelly, E. (2003). Ten principles of complexity and enabling infrastructures. In E. Mitleton-Kelly (Ed.), *Complex systems and evolutionary perspectives on organisations: The application of complexity theory to organisations* (pp. 23–50). Oxford: Elsevier.

Möhlmann, M. and Zalmanson, L. (2017). 'Hands on the wheel: Navigating algorithmic management and Uber drivers' autonomy'. *Proceedings of the International Conference on Information Systems (ICIS)*, Seoul, South Korea.

Nadella, S. (2025). *On shaping the impact of AI*. Satya Nadella's Blog. Available at: https://satyanadella.blog (viewed January 2, 2026).

Osmani, A. (2024). *Leading effective engineering teams: Lessons for individual contributors and managers from 10 years*. Sebastopol: O'Reilly Media.

Pentland, A. (2013).'Beyond the echo chamber'. *Harvard Business Review,* (November).

Rosenblat, A. and Stark, L. (2016). 'Algorithmic labor and information asymmetries: A case study of Uber's drivers'. *International Journal of Communication,* 10, pp. 3758–3784.

Rossi, F. (2020). 'Building trust in AI: The role of ethics and transparency'. *IBM Research Blog.* https://ibm.com/blogs/research (viewed January 3, 2026).

Schein, E. H. (2010). *Organizational culture and leadership* (4th ed.). San Francisco: Jossey-Bass.

Snowden, D. J. (2002). 'Complex acts of knowing: Paradox and descriptive self-awareness'. *Journal of Knowledge Management*, 6(2), pp. 100–111.

Snowden, D. (2004). 'Multi-ontology sense-making: A new simplicity in decision making'. *Management Today*, 20(10), 44–48.

Stacey, R. D. (2007). *Strategic management and organisational dynamics: The challenge of complexity to ways of thinking about organisations* (5th ed.). London: Pearson Education.

Stacey, R. D., Griffin, D. and Shaw, P. (2000). *Complexity and management: Fad or radical challenge to systems thinking?* London: Routledge.

Taylor, A. and Bochis, R. (2025). *All In: A Complexity Guide to Digital Disruption.* London: Buckingham University Press.

Thurner, S., Hanel, R. and Klimek, P. (2018). *Introduction to the theory of complex systems*. Oxford: Oxford University Press.

Toreini, E., Aitken, M., Coopamootoo, K., Elliott, K., Zelaya, C. G. and van Moorsel, A. (2020). 'The relationship between trust in AI and trustworthy machine learning technologies'. In *Proceedings of the 2020 Conference on Fairness, Accountability, and Transparency* (pp. 272–283). ACM.

Tushman, M. L. and O'Reilly, C. A. (1996). 'Ambidextrous organizations: Managing evolutionary and revolutionary change'. *California Management Review,* 38(4), pp. 8–30.

Wenger, E. (1998). 'Communities of practice: Learning as a social system.' *Systems Thinker,* 9(5), pp. 2–3.

# DESIGNING ORGANISATIONS FOR THE AGE OF AGENTIC AI

Jonathan Melhuish

## Introduction

Agentic AI—Artificial Intelligence that autonomously takes actions – has massive potential to improve efficiency and deliver better, cheaper and faster products and services. Yet many organisations risk getting agentic AI wrong, because they will deploy it using the same approaches that worked for previous generations of business software.

If they run it as a traditional software project, manage it through existing hierarchies, and treat workforce concerns as a communications problem to be handled after the fact, they will e nd up with expensive implementations that capture only a fraction of the technology's potential (McKinsey, 2025b) while generating employee resistance, knowledge loss, and customer experience failures. Research suggests that employees who feel threatened by AI don't just disengage — they actively hide the knowledge organisations need most (Kim, 2024), sometimes deliberately providing incorrect information (Connelly et al., 2012).

This matters because agentic AI is a fundamentally different category of technology. Unlike tools that wait for human instruction, agentic systems act autonomously — booking appointments, resolving complaints, coordinating workflows, making decisions with real consequences. I argue that agentic AI functions less like software and more like a new class of employee: capable of independent judgement, prone to occasional errors, requiring oversight rather than operation.

Crucially, AI is a complex system rather than a complicated one and as such, its behaviour emerges from interactions that cannot be fully specified in advance (Merali, 2006), which means the corporate instinct to control it through rigid rules and predetermined responses fundamentally misunderstands its nature.

Now more than ever, business leaders need to understand that AI, especially agentic AI, is a disruptive technology that will not only change technical architectures but also professional roles and organisational structures. Over the next few years, many roles will transition from hands-on work to supervising increasingly autonomous AI agents -so it's crucial that we get this transition right.

## From craftspeople to supervisors

AI might not take your job, but it will fundamentally change it.

Unlike previous waves of workplace technology that put tools in workers' hands, agentic AI represents something more profound: a shift from the majority of an organisation's workforce being involved in the direct execution of tasks to the management of teams of AI agents — a role I will refer to as "AI Manager". Gartner (2025) estimates that agentic AI will automate 15% of day-to-day work decisions by 2028, up from essentially zero in 2024.

Although we're in the early phases of implementation, the large majority of businesses plan to adopt this technology. Research from Salesforce (2025) surveying 200 HR executives found that 80% believe most workforces will have humans and AI agents working together within five years. Chief Human Resources Officers project 327% growth in AI agent adoption by 2027, and 86% say that integrating digital labour alongside their existing workforce will be a critical part of their job.

This isn't the run-of-the-mill digitalisation or automation project we've grown used to. A gentic AI is flexible artificial intelligence technology that can draw knowledge from multiple sources, make decisions automatically and take action on its own. This is less like running a piece of code, and more like hiring a new kind of employee. One that, inevitably, needs careful supervision as they learn the ropes.

Yet this analogy, while useful, isn't perfect. Even experienced managers need to learn about the capabilities and limitations of AI systems in order to be able to supervise them effectively. McKinsey (2025a) research suggests that in their experience, a human team of two to five people can already supervise an agent factory of 50 to 100 specialised agents running end-to-end processes such as customer onboarding, product launches, or financial closing.

As McKinsey (2025b, p18–19) puts it,

*Agents won't just assist humans—they'll act alongside them. This raises nuanced questions about interaction and coexistence: When should an agent take initiative? When should it defer? How do we maintain human agency and oversight without slowing down the very benefits agents bring? Building clarity around these roles will take time, experimentation, and cultural adjustment.*

The challenge facing organisations is therefore as much cultural as technological; employees can't all be expected to easily adjust or embrace this new role. Many workers were recruited specifically for their ability to execute tasks effectively and genuinely enjoy the craftsmanship of doing so. Wrzesniewski and Dutton (2001) capture this beautifully when recounting the research of Fine (1996):

*The cooks used their own artistic standards in trying to create a product worthy of pride. As such, the cooks Fine studied experienced "flow" as they executed their work tasks, paying attention to their own artistic vision rather than management policy regarding cooking. Cooks often tried new food combinations, creating novel dishes in order to meet job demands in ways that allowed them to experience the work as meaningful and creative, rather than scripted and uninspired.*

My personal experiences working with software developers mirror this. It takes a special kind of brain to reliably weave the magic spells that make computers do interesting things, and over the past few decades these computer wizards have enjoyed high salaries and good employment prospects.

AI hasn't automated the whole software development process — there's still a lot of complexity around requirements gathering, architecture decisions, permissions management and testing that requires human input — but it's getting good at writing the actual code. And looking at the rapid rate of improvement of Large Language Models (LLMs) on coding benchmarks and the billions of dollars being poured into solving this problem, most programmers realize that AI is quickly becoming faster and cheaper than them at writing code.

The problem is that coding is generally the part of the job that they find most rewarding. Watching an AI rapidly spit out code and then cleaning up its mess is not nearly as satisfying to a 'code poet'. I've also worked with multiple engineers who *have* moved into management but would quite obviously prefer to return to writing elegant code than sitting patiently in their seventh meeting of the day.

Furthermore, even if they wanted to transition to managing AI agents, not all programmers are the ideal candidates for the job. While not all management skills are essential for working with AI agents, the role centres on managing complexity, interacting with stakeholders and facilitating participatory design processes — not skills that engineers automatically excel at. This example is not atypical; many staff will need significant upskilling to become AI agent managers, or transition to roles that automation will impact more slowly. But will employees enthusiastically embrace this transition?

## Lessons from the Luddites

The term "Luddite" has become shorthand for irrational technophobia, yet this caricature fundamentally misrepresents a sophisticated labour movement that represents a historical lesson that may well be repeated if workers' concerns about AI are not heard.

The real story of the Luddites is that between 1811 and 1816, skilled textile workers in England systematically destroyed automated machinery in what Hobsbawm characterised as "collective bargaining by riot" — a rational strategy when formal unions were illegal (Hobsbawm, 1952).

McGowan and Geobey's examination reveals workers who "made multiple attempts to work within Parliament", sending "petition after petition... without the slightest hint of support" before resorting to machine-breaking (McGowan and Geobey, 2022, pp. 306–320).

Crucially, Lancashire machine-wreckers spared spinning jennies under 24 spindles (suitable for domestic use) whilst destroying larger factory-scale equipment (Hobsbawm, 1952). Griffin's recent synthesis confirms that protests "tended not to oppose technological innovation but rather challenged the ways in which machinery impacted upon labour and wider social relations" (Griffin, 2025). The Luddites' actions reflected strategic judgement about power and distribution rather than opposition to technology itself. As Hobsbawm concluded: "in none of these cases was there any question of hostility to machines as such" (Hobsbawm, 1952).

Contemporary workers facing AI automation are currently encountering similar dynamics, and I believe that organisations that misdiagnose worker resistance as technophobia will replicate historical failures. McGowan and Geobey argue that transformation attempts favouring elite arrangements face structural resistance, warning this represents "a cautionary tale for those interested in a just transition" (McGowan and Geobey, 2022, p.307).

## Worker anxiety reflects reality

The mainstream narrative around AI seems to be gradually evolving from the somewhat fantastical, extreme and simplistic "AI utopia" and "AI doom" storylines previously favoured by mainstream sci-fi and legacy media. Instead, we're seeing a more nuanced narrative emerge that echoes that of the Luddite movement.

Specifically, we're currently seeing the emergence of a much more well-grounded argument that the way that AI is being developed — principally by well-funded tech companies, with little regard for the disruption to the artists and writers whose work has been hoovered up to train AI systems and with a liberal interpretation of copyright law — is unjust and should be resisted. Even for those who don't make their living from art or words, it requires little imagination to consider that this 'AI steamroller' could be coming for them next, whether they like it or not.

Pew Research Center (2025) found that 52% of U.S. workers are worried about AI's workplace impact, with only 6% believing it will create more opportunities for them personally. Among creative workers, the anxiety is even more pronounced. An Authors Guild (2023) survey of more than 1,700 writers found 69% believe their careers are threatened by AI. Equity UK conducted a survey which found that 65% of performers responding thought the development of AI technology poses a threat to employment opportunities in the performing arts sector, rising to 93% for audio (e.g. voice) artists.

This anxiety is not only understandable but also firmly grounded in reality. The World Economic Forum's (2025) Future of Jobs Report, surveying 1,000 employers representing 14 million workers, found that 47% of employers plan to transition employees from AI-disrupted roles to other positions while 41% expect to downsize their workforce as AI capabilities expand.

Considering this growing sentiment, leaders should probably not expect employees to embrace agentic AI with the same enthusiasm as previous digital tools that more clearly put humans in direct control and didn't aim to replace the cognitive skills for which many professionals have largely been valued for the last century or so. I posit that aggressive top-down implementation of agentic AI is therefore likely to backfire.

Later in this chapter, I explore how participatory design and grassroots adoption support, alongside UX design using an "augmented intelligence" rather than "artificial intelligence" lens, offers a potential solution. But first, let's explore how the necessary shift in employee roles towards the supervision of agentic AI systems could create significant pushback.

## AI manager or lowly data labeller?

How the AI supervision role is presented and framed is likely crucial to its attractiveness and rate of adoption within organisations. The same role — of giving feedback to the AI system on its actions or plans — has often been referred to as "data labelling", a task often outsourced to low-paid labour in developing countries (Posada, 2021).

Alternatively, the exact same task could be reframed as "AI Manager", in which employees are supervising their "team" of AI agents to continually monitor and improve their performance. As management roles are generally valued more highly in hierarchical organisations, I suggest that the latter framing is more likely to be considered attractive.

The importance of the framing of the role is not limited to staff feeling a little prouder of their status within the organisation. Staff who are ignored, threatened with replacement, or not offered appropriate training are unlikely to offer full insights to guide the AI agents and may even undermine AI implementation efforts. A 2024 time-lagged study of 402 South Korean employees found that AI-induced job insecurity positively relates to knowledge-hiding behaviour directly and through reduced psychological safety (Kim, 2024). Their study showed that this is a result of employees feeling "left behind" in the AI transition:

*The moderation analysis revealed a significant interaction effect between AI-induced job insecurity and self-efficacy in AI learning on psychological safety (b = 0.274, p < 0.001). This finding aligns with social cognitive theory, which indicates that individuals with higher self-efficacy in AI learning are better equipped to maintain psychological safety even amid AI-induced job insecurity… Employees with greater confidence in their ability to learn and adapt to AI technologies are more adept at preserving their psychological safety, even amid job insecurity.*

Research by Connelly, Zweig, Webster and Trougakos (2012) also observed "knowledge hiding": an intentional attempt by individuals to withhold or conceal knowledge as a documented organisational behaviour, including evasive hiding and providing incorrect information.

Considering the crucial importance of proprietary data and domain knowledge to the performance of AI systems, I argue that it's therefore essential that employees feel this career transition represents progression into a management role, not regression from empowered decision-maker to lowly data labeller, even though the same role transition could be framed either way. But even more crucial than the job title is that the "AI Manager" role must be carefully constructed to be rewarding and meaningful.

## "AI Manager" must be a desirable new role

The Job Characteristics Model (Hackman and Oldham, 1976) proposes that five core job dimensions — skill variety, task identity, task significance, autonomy, and feedback — influence critical psychological states (experienced meaningfulness, experienced responsibility, and knowledge of results), which in turn affect personal and work outcomes, including internal work motivation, job satisfaction, work quality, and absenteeism, with these relationships moderated by individual growth and the need for strength.

If the new role of AI Manager is not carefully designed, all five of these core job dimensions are potentially threatened by a transition from performing the task directly to supervising an AI agent:

- **skill variety**, if the role focusses on routinely monitoring the output of the AI agent to identify occasional errors, many of which are likely to be repetitive as they reflect the technical limitations of the underlying technologies.
- **task identity** and **feedback**, especially in the case of performing ongoing monitoring of a swarm of AI agents, each of which may be responsible for a complete task, but the human supervisor only observes part of the process before switching to attending to the needs of another agent, without receiving feedback on the ultimate outcome of the task.
- **task significance**, when taking the perspective that the AI agent now performs the creative hands-on work for which they have been previously valued and around which they may have constructed their self-identity, and now they are merely a "babysitter" to AI agents.
- **autonomy**, as it can easily feel that they're a "slave to the machine", as the AI agent is in control of the workflow while the human supervisor must attend to the needs of the AI agent whenever required.

However, each of these dimensions can be addressed by careful design of the AI Manager role, for example:

- **skill variety**: by broadening the role to encompass related activities beyond the AI's capabilities, including tasks that are not purely judging existing output but include creative acts, social interactions, physical activities etc., as appropriate to the business context; in a software development context this might include stakeholder engagement, user research etc.
- **task identity** and **feedback**: by incorporating milestones and clear success feedback (e.g. aligned to customer goals) into the supervision task, even if not strictly necessary as no action is required.
- **task significance**: by recognising the value of the supervision task, e.g., by drawing parallels to management roles that are generally regarded as "superior" within hierarchical organisations.
- **autonomy**: by incorporating flexibility into how the supervisor performs their role, e.g., the order in which they attend to the AI agents and prioritise tasks, the ability to perform additional inspections even when not deemed necessary by the AI, and the ability to start and stop supervision as they require.

In this context, it may be useful to focus less on the concept of "Artificial Intelligence," which places emphasis on the replication of human behaviour, often with the goal of replacing human involvement, and instead on "Augmented Intelligence". This is an approach to AI design that positions the technology as enhancing and supporting human capabilities and decision-making rather than replacing human judgment and control.

## Designing AI supervision for human abilities

The design of supervision tasks should take a human-centred approach. Of particular concern is striking a careful balance between the dangerous tedium of monitoring a system that functions correctly 99% of the time and the unsettling chaos of managing AI that behaves too randomly.

The tedium of monitoring an automated system can lead supervisors to lose focus and try to perform other tasks at the same time. For example, even while using automation as limited as Adaptive Cruise Control (a driver assistance system that maintains a set speed, reducing it as necessary to maintain a minimum distance to the vehicle ahead), drivers showed a 50% increase in the odds of engaging in any secondary task, and an 80% increase in engaging in visual/manual secondary tasks compared to manual driving, as well as taking more frequent and longer glances away from driving-related tasks (Dunn et al., 2019).

Conversely, it should be considered that the AI system may often have superhuman abilities that can make it difficult for a human to supervise. This challenge is fundamentally difficult to solve, despite the fact that it has been understood for decades; it was clearly described by Bainbridge (1983):

*A more serious irony is that the automatic control system has been put in because it can do the job better than the operator, yet the operator is being asked to monitor that it is working effectively.*

For example, an autonomous vehicle may be able to observe multiple directions simultaneously and make a decision to proceed through an intersection in a fraction of a second, but its human supervisor cannot turn their head that fast. The vehicle should proceed more slowly than it is safely able, in order to allow the human to supervise effectively. This requirement is specifically mentioned in Article 14 of the EU's Artificial Intelligence Act:

*High-risk AI systems shall be designed and developed in such a way, including with appropriate human-machine interface tools, that they can be effectively overseen by natural persons during the period in which they are in use.*

Some employees will inevitably not want to make the transition, regardless of how the role is formulated. They may be more passionate about or skilled in task execution rather than managing AI agents, which requires different competencies, even though domain knowledge remains useful, while others might not want to take responsibility for the machine's actions.

Competitive forces will push companies to transition these employees to roles not yet suitable for automation or, failing that, to separate from them. McKinsey Global Institute (2024) estimated that up to 30% of current hours worked could be automated by 2030, requiring up to 12 million occupational transitions in Europe and the United States each. They estimate that workers in lower-wage jobs in the US are up to 14 times more likely to need to change their occupation compared to the highest-wage workers.

Individual workers might be able to make the necessary transition into new and adapted roles for this age of agentic AI. But if we zoom out and consider the culture and structure of our organisations, will they be fit for purpose?

## The structural incompatibility of hierarchy and agentic AI

Many large, hierarchical organisations face fundamental challenges in making this transition successfully. Agentic AI, by definition, takes actions with real consequences, both positive and negative. At the edges of its capability, it still requires human oversight of its actions, input into the most unfamiliar decisions, and feedback that it can learn from. And in many contexts, it's necessary for a human to ultimately take responsibility; it is either unsatisfactory or illegal to assign ultimate culpability to the machine.

For organisations to fully embrace the technology's potential, oversight must be widely distributed among frontline staff with the greatest contextual knowledge. Modern AI, being biologically inspired by neural networks, is a complex system at its core, and agentic AI adds to this complexity by implementing multiple independent agents that work concurrently and usually interact with other systems and software services, both internal and external.

Complex adaptive systems require distributed control for effective adaptation — rigid hierarchical structures that concentrate decision-making authority fundamentally impair the system's capacity to respond to dynamic environments.

Merali (2006, p. 220) defines complex adaptive systems as:

*...open, non-linear dynamical systems that adapt and evolve in the process of interacting with their environments — they have the potential (capacity) for adaptation and transformation. Adaptation at the macro-level (the 'whole' system) is characterised by emergence and self-organisation based on the local adaptive behaviour of the system's constituents. The emergent global systems behaviour is very sensitive to initial local conditions.*

Though they were considering a society-level rather than company-level perspective, the need for an adaptable approach to the supervision of complex systems such as AI, rather than a one-off definition of rules to govern its operation, is echoed by Kolt et al. (2025):

*According to these principles, governance mechanisms that aim to regulate complex systems should not be static institutions but rather feedback-driven processes that iteratively respond and adapt to new information while preserving overarching societal goals and values.*

Based on my experience as an AI Service Designer, frontline employees are more likely to be willing to take responsibility for the impact of a new system if they are actively included in the design, implementation and refinement of that system, as part of a participatory design approach. Yet corporate cultures often block the effective implementation of such participatory design approaches.

Within hierarchical cultures, middle managers often oppose or obstruct digital implementation to protect personal interests. Research by Bagrationi and Thurner (2023) found that middle managers often exhibit resistance to change and that their resistance can create a ripple effect, as middle managers transmit their own resistance to their subordinates, thereby hindering the overall digital transformation process and ultimately affecting the overall performance and adaptability of these organisations.

The problem is compounded by leadership using AI deployment as an opportunity to gain more power within their organisation. One leader I worked with in the IT department of a large corporation neatly captured the message in a single bar chart: placing our team's relatively meagre budget for AI development against the vast operational cost of the call centre. Although he diplomatically stopped short of directly calling for job cuts, the implication was clear: redirecting the budget from operations to AI innovation can reduce overall costs in future. I'm sure he was right, and of course I'd have appreciated an increased budget for my team, but it's easy to see how this could be met by fear and resistance in a corporate culture that was already quite divided along tribal lines.

## The challenge of maintaining customer focus

While leading the implementation of new AI systems, I've also found that middle management frequently intercepts attempts to directly involve frontline employees in design activities, ensuring that development work serves management's interests rather than empowering frontline employees to shape the AI development and take on expanded roles in its deployment. In this way, the hierarchy reasserts itself, leading to frontline employees understandably feeling that agentic AI is being forced upon them with the intention to replace rather than support them.

This hampers efforts to take a needs-based approach to AI software development, as managers are often more familiar with current processes than with the nuance of the customer's goals. Although it's important to also understand the company's objectives, the more important and difficult challenge of a user-centred designer is usually to understand the varying needs of different customer groups and key stakeholders. If the design process loses this focus, it often becomes derailed into unresolvable conflict between internal stakeholders, each believing that their functional requirements are more important than those of other departments.

The need to stay focussed on the customer's desired outcomes is especially important in the adoption of agentic AI, which requires companies to rethink and redesign processes if they are to take full advantage of its capabilities while effectively managing its limitations.

The growing popularity of OKRs (Objectives and Key Results) is a welcome step in the right direction, but I feel that many managers still need to get comfortable with setting sufficiently "loose", qualitative, aspirational objectives that allow teams (and AI agents) to take advantage of opportunities to improve the customer experience through novel processes and approaches. This requires an appropriate level of trust, which in turn requires managers to understand the nature of agentic AI, and continually update this knowledge as its capabilities improve.

Considering the rapidly evolving nature of this technology, and the value of real-world experience both in training AI and shaping product development, playing it too safe is likely to result in nimbler and braver competitors taking market share as they more quickly discover ways to exploit agentic AI effectively.

An effective approach to this learning is implementing "safe to fail" experiments a little beyond the organisation's comfort zone. Safe-to-fail experiments are small-scale, contained probes designed so that failure will not cause catastrophic consequences to the system. These experiments allow organisations to explore the interesting emergent properties of networked AI agents while minimising the negative impact of unintended consequences.

But why is this type of experimentation particularly essential in the context of agentic AI?

## AI is complex to its core; agentic AI, doubly so

The overwhelming majority of the progress made in the last few decades of AI can be attributed to (broadly) nature-inspired approaches that exploit the emergent properties of complex systems. The clearest example is Artificial Neural Networks, in which a relatively simple component — the neuron — can be copied millions of times to produce behaviour far more complex than any individual part. The same principle operates at a higher level in Multi-Agent Reinforcement Learning, where multiple AI agents interact within a shared environment and collectively produce emergent behaviour.

In general, this more nature-like quality makes these approaches well suited to modelling real-world situations that are themselves complex, such as markets, societies, ecosystems, etc.

The agentic AI systems I've been involved in building are typically affected by the complex interactions between streamed or batched data (including data quality issues and limitations), user input, non-deterministic AI models, continual or incremental upgrades of components (e.g., cloud AI services) and network issues (e.g. latency, service unavailability, rate limits), to name but a few.

Increasingly, systems are deployed as loosely coupled multi-agent systems in order to segregate functionality (even inside a single component, e.g. the Mixture of Experts approach used by leading LLMs), enable easier troubleshooting and replicate the structure of human teams (which can enable better use of training data). This multi-agent approach allows greater adaptability and allows switching out components in a vendor-agnostic manner as better alternatives emerge, but also further increases complexity.

## Managing complexity requires a fundamentally different approach

Snowden and Boone's Cynefin framework provides essential guidance for understanding the governance requirements of AI. In complex domains, such as AI systems, Snowden & Boone (2007, p.5) state that

*We can understand why things happen only in retrospect. Instructive patterns, however, can emerge if the leader conducts experiments that are safe to fail.*

The framework distinguishes between ordered contexts (simple and complicated) where cause-and-effect relationships are perceptible, and unordered contexts (complex and chaotic) where "there is no immediately apparent relationship between cause and effect, and the way forward is determined based on emerging patterns" (Snowden & Boone, 2007, p.4).

For AI governance, this distinction is critical: rather than seeking predetermined solutions according to established procedures or industry best practice, managers must "probe first, then sense, and then respond" (Snowden and Boone, 2007, p.5). This probe-sense-respond approach involves conducting experimental interventions, observing what patterns emerge from the system's response, and then amplifying successful patterns whilst dampening unsuccessful ones. The approach acknowledges that AI systems operating in complex environments cannot be fully controlled or predicted, requiring instead a pattern-based leadership style that creates "environments and experiments that allow patterns to emerge" (Snowden and Boone, 2007, p.7).

Merali's research on information systems also provides valuable insights relevant to managing AI as complex adaptive systems. Traditional approaches to systems development have been "predicated on designing for complexity reduction" through decomposition and hierarchical control, while she argues that complex systems "demand designs for complexity accommodation" that embrace rather than suppress emergence (Merali, 2006, pp.223–224).

This shift is particularly relevant for AI governance, where "the emergent, bottom-up network dynamics challenges the classical top-down paradigm" of control (Merali, 2006, p.219). Critically for networked AI systems, she writes that "it is impossible for any one agent in the network to have complete knowledge of the state of the whole network at any given time" (Merali, 2006, p.218). Although she was writing about human agents, I argue that it is equally applicable to AI agents; this fundamental constraint requires governance frameworks that can function under conditions of distributed knowledge and emergent behaviour, where no single authority possesses the complete information necessary for centralised decision-making.

Ostrom's framework of polycentric governance offers a robust approach for managing complex systems through distributed authority. "Polycentric" refers to centres of decision-making that are formally independent of each other yet function as an interdependent system through competitive relationships, contractual arrangements, and conflict resolution mechanisms (Ostrom et al, 1961, p.831).

Adaptive governance provides the operational framework for implementing polycentric approaches for the effective governance of complex AI systems:

*Adaptive governance of interdependent social and ecological systems is key to address complex interactions and to manage uncertainty and periods of change. A central characteristic of such adaptive governance is collaborative, flexible and learning-based issue management across different scales. (Stockholm Resilience Centre, 2012, p.1).*

This literature on governance of complex systems suggests that rather than pushing restrictive ex-ante regulation or centralised control, effective AI governance requires: (1) pattern-based sense-making that distinguishes between contexts requiring different responses; (2) designs that accommodate rather than suppress complexity; (3) multiple independent but coordinated centres of authority; and (4) multilevel networks that enable learning and adaptation. This approach acknowledges that AI systems will generate emergent behaviours that cannot be fully anticipated, requiring governance structures capable of responding to patterns as they arise whilst maintaining coordination across scales.

This lies in stark contrast with the typical *modus operandi* of most businesses. The ineffectiveness of controlling AI through fixed operational rules is inherently in opposition to AI's complex nature. Unlike complicated systems whose behaviour can be predicted by logical inference, complex systems exhibit emergent behaviours and non-linear interactions that cannot be predicted. Edge cases aren't simply overlooked details — they represent the unpredictable situations that arise from complex real-world interactions. This is exactly the kind of complex pattern employees tend to "get a feel for" after years on the job.

## The cost of losing tacit knowledge

Frontline employees develop tacit knowledge precisely because they've learned to navigate this real-world complexity through direct experience. By contrast, systems designed by middle management capture the predictable paths but miss the adaptive responses that make the difference between routine operations and chaos.

Top-down implementation of agentic AI may allow organisations to cut frontline employees, but at the expense of the customer experience. In markets where customers have free choice of competitive alternatives, I believe this will inevitably lead to companies losing ground to competitors who succeed in retaining embedded knowledge and transitioning employees to AI supervision roles. These competitors ensure sufficient capacity to deal with the edge cases that AI cannot handle, which as a result provides more valuable training data for AI improvement. They can offer the same or improved quality of service at lower cost, potentially winning increased market share and expanding revenues without requiring additional staff.

Klarna learned this lesson the hard way: after proudly proclaiming that their new AI could "replace the work of 700 staff", they were then forced to re-hire human agents after receiving complaints from customers about the poor standard of customer service received (Bloomberg, 2025). CEO

Sebastian Siemiatkowski admitted that "cost unfortunately seems to have been a too predominant evaluation factor when organizing this; what you end up having is lower quality… really investing in the quality of the human support is the way of the future for us".

Companies taking a top-down approach to implementing agentic AI may struggle to incorporate the tacit knowledge of frontline employees into their AI systems. Instead, systems risk being created based on business processes described by middle management, which tend to capture typical or optimal process paths while omitting edge cases that are currently dealt with ad hoc, through human judgement.

Hadjimichael and Tsoukas (2019) argue that contextually sensitive practitioners remain necessary to judge whether AI is relevant to a problem, make sense of AI outputs, and undertake appropriate action, particularly in open-ended tasks. Being skilled is therefore not merely about knowing facts, but knowing which facts are relevant to each situation and acting on that knowledge competently through judgment rather than rule-following. Rather than making tacit knowledge irrelevant, AI increases the need for practitioners who can maintain situational discretion and human meaning-making in both deploying AI and using its outputs. They conclude that AI's ability to analys e vast amounts of data does not diminish the organisational importance of tacit knowledge — the experiential understanding that enables humans to navigate the complexity and unpredictability that AI cannot handle.

## Learning from historical failures in AI deployment

The evolution of corporate chatbots offers an instructive lesson in another important way that organisational culture impacts AI implementation.

While renewed interest in natural language interfaces was sparked by advances in neural network-based systems, corporate implementations of online customer service chatbots in the 2010s still often relied on predefined scripts and rule-based systems that merely spit out predetermined responses, similar to the ELIZA chatbot created in 1964. This approach created clunky, repetitive conversations that could be very frustrating for customers.

Why did companies roll out such restricted implementations when clearly superior, more flexible technology existed? The answer is cultural, not technological: these companies could not accept the risk of a machine answering rudely or incorrectly, so they rejected the complex (and effective) solution in favour of a complicated (but ineffective) one that they could exert more control over.

This direct impact of the rigid governance approach destroys the value of modern AI, by trying to control it the same way as traditional software, i.e., by specifying behaviour in every situation. The rigid scripting approach enforced deterministic cause-and-effect, while, as discussed above, the power of modern AI systems comes from emergent properties that can't be fully predicted or prescribed.

The lesson is clear: organisations that attempt to maintain industrial-era control over inherently probabilistic technologies create worse outcomes for customers while delaying learning.

On the contrary, companies that successfully embrace AI realise that it requires comfort with experimenting in public because that's generally how real data gets gathered.

Amazon has a strong culture of continual experimentation, and has done for over a decade, running thousands of experiments per year (Bezos, 2014). Each variation alters how the user interface functions or how the products are presented, for example. Some experiments lose money by harming sales compared to the previous version, but Amazon knows the long-term value of these data make small, short-term risks worthwhile.

To take an example from the cutting edge of AI, Tesla's "Full Self-Driving" (FSD) autonomous vehicle development provides another illuminating case study.

Inevitably, early versions of the software tended to exhibit somewhat erratic behaviour, requiring careful and patient supervision by an attentive driver. Faced with the same challenge, most other autonomous vehicle manufacturers restricted access to teams of paid "safety drivers". This allowed them a higher degree of control, both over the drivers and over their public image. However, it meant that their cost of collecting driving data remained high.

Tesla took a different approach, releasing their FSD software (in the form of a driver assistance system) publicly on consumer vehicles in the USA in 2020. In this model, drivers are not paid for their time and cover the cost of their own vehicles. This was a much riskier approach but allowed them to collect vastly more data than any of their competitors at a fraction of the cost, including valuable supervision data such as when the driver decided to take over from the system and correct its behaviour (Tesla, 2021).

Despite its initial flaws, FSD still delivered enough value to some customers, including the novelty of using the latest technology and successfully automating the most tedious parts of driving, to motivate sufficient participation for data collection. At time of writing, Tesla customers have now driven over 7.3 billion miles using FSD, giving Tesla access to vast amounts of data (Tesla, 2026). In fact, this approach creates so much data than Tesla doesn't even store it all; instead, they built a "Data Engine" system that sends requests to the cars to send back data only on specific objects or situations that will be most valuable for training the next version of the AI (Tesla, 2021). Additionally, they only use supervision data from the most skilled drivers, discarding the rest.

Although this example involves customers rather than employees, it relies on the same cultural factors, including an appreciation of the significant value of the training data produced by careful supervision of AI systems in real world situations, and a willingness to endure potential short-term harm to the customer experience, public image and profit margins in order to gain valuable training data and feedback.

Companies wanting to fully harness agentic AI need to help frontline staff feel equally safe and motivated to participate in this experimental process, even when AI behaviour occasionally disappoints or surprises. And the company needs to be willing to take some risks.

## Two reasons startups adapt faster

I believe startups are generally better positioned to harness the power of agentic AI for several interconnected reasons. Structurally, they lack the legacy infrastructure, technical friction, hierarchical approval processes and interdepartmental competition that slows adaptation.

Foundational work on complex adaptive systems demonstrates that effective adaptation emerges from distributed control rather than centralised authority, with coherent behaviour arising through self-organisation as agents compete or collaborate. As Dooley (1997) puts it:

*Meta-agents help distribute and decentralize functionality, allowing diversity to thrive and specialization to occur. In organizational systems, distributed and decentralized control enhances reaction speed and robustness, diversity ensures robustness and creativity, and specialization enhances requisite variety.*

It's for precisely this reason that multi-agent approaches to AI are becoming increasingly popular in order to adapt to the complexity and unpredictability of real-world contexts. Often one of the agents will act as the "orchestrator" (meta-agent), for example selecting the correct expert to invoke in a Mixture of Experts LLM, or which AI agent in a team where each has a specialist role (e.g., software engineer or QA tester). Organisations where this approach is already embedded into the culture will likely find it much easier to adapt to this architecture, both as the technical architecture or for human supervisors to play the role of meta-agent.

The danger of organisations becoming "fossilized" and unable to effectively adapt to new technologies such as agentic AI that demand new decision-making structures has long been understood. As described by Virany, Tushman, & Romanelli (1992, p.74):

*The longer that executive teams are in place, the less turnover in the team and the more homogeneous the team members become with respect to experiences and understandings (Tushman and Keck, 1990). Over time, first-order learning processes overwhelm whatever diversity of experience and knowledge may have characterized the team early on. Habit, SOPs, history, and institutionalization drive out vigilant problem solving... Inertia associated with first-order learning anchors the organization to its past even in the face of environmental change (e.g., Morison 1966). The benefits of first-order learning are achieved at the price of decreased ability to adapt as an ever more redundant experience base drives out an executive team's ability to learn outside a given frame.*

They go on to describe the disruptive innovation and experimentation that is required, which they term second-order learning (p.87):

*When environments are turbulent, however, second-order learning is required to alter established decision-making patterns (Lant and Mezias, 1992). Second-order learning involves an explicit change of core organization assumptions, as well as experimentation with alternative decision-making premises.*

This is analogous to what Argyris and Schön term "double-loop learning" (1978, p.2–3):

*Single-loop learning is like a thermostat that learns when it is too hot or too cold and turns the heat on or off. The thermostat can perform this task because it can receive information (the temperature of the room) and take corrective action. Double-loop learning occurs when error is detected and corrected in ways that involve the modification of an organization's under-lying norms, policies and objectives.*

Organisations stuck in first-order learning are likely to miss out on the full power of agentic AI, instead merely deploying AI tools that remain in the firm grasp of a human operator and which do not overly disrupt staff roles or organisational hierarchies. The power of agentic AI will only be fully unleashed by those organisations bold enough to question their fundamental assumptions, rules, and frameworks that guide how and why they make decisions.

McKinsey (2025b) estimates that in a typical call centre example, deploying genAI tools to assist human operators can improve resolution times by as little as 5%, while redesigning the process around agentic AI could lead to improvements of 60–90%. They explain:

*Reinventing a process around agents means more than layering automation on top of existing workflows—it involves rearchitecting the entire task flow from the ground up. That includes reordering steps, reallocating responsibilities between humans and agents, and designing the process to fully exploit the strengths of agentic AI: parallel execution that collapses cycle time, real-time adaptability that reacts to changing conditions, deep personalization at scale, and elastic capacity that flexes instantly with demand.*

## How to adopt agentic AI successfully

To fully benefit from the power of agentic AI, I believe organisations must fundamentally rethink their approach.

First, they must use participatory design to get frontline employees genuinely on board, ensuring AI develops as a tool to empower them in expanded roles rather than replace them. This requires moving beyond token consultation to meaningful co-design that incorporates frontline employee insights throughout development. Successful AI implementation depends on the interaction of social and technical elements, with organisations needing to carefully choose and curate training data whilst appropriately managing how AI interacts with its surroundings — processes that require frontline knowledge to be effective.

Second, organisations must provide real incentives for frontline employees to voluntarily move into AI Agent Manager roles, giving them appropriate training that combines managerial skills with knowledge of AI capabilities and limitations, along with ongoing support. The World

Economic Forum (2025) found that skill gaps are categorically considered the biggest barrier to business transformation, with 63% of employers identifying them as a major barrier.

Alternatively, organisations should help employees to transition or broaden their roles so they aren't displaced. Middle management could potentially deliver this training by complementing their management knowledge with AI awareness and pedagogical skills, allowing them to play an important role, so they're more likely to buy into the transition rather than blocking co-design efforts.

Third, by creating the AI Agent Manager role, organisations must ensure there's always a human willing to take responsibility for AI actions, who has genuine control and influence over those actions. When AI inevitably fails, customers are reassured to find a human employee willing to take responsibility and rectify the situation.

Fourth, organisations should establish peer support communities among AI Managers to avoid loneliness and increase learning, while actively supporting an experimental culture that drops the requirement to "look busy" and encourages learning from failure. This allows deployment of cutting-edge agentic AI in safe-to-fail but realistic, often public, contexts.

Complex adaptive systems learn and evolve through variation and selection processes. Experimental cultures that embrace failure as feedback enable this evolutionary adaptation. Projects and contracts with external suppliers must therefore be managed as continual series of small experiments rather than using an industrial-era mindset demanding long-term planning and budgeting. The technology and customer expectations move too quickly for that to work.

Organisations unable to shift culture quickly should consider establishing a skunkworks or collaborating with startups who can be given enough independence to experiment safely without threatening the core brand or operations, but with a clear path to later incorporating new ways of working into the main organisation. A skunkworks is a small, autonomous group within an organisation that operates outside normal bureaucratic structures and constraints to rapidly develop innovative products or solutions. This type of "protected niche" allows innovative experimentation to occur without being prematurely snuffed out by organisational inertia.

Successful AI implementation also requires establishing clear boundaries within which the AI system operates. Skunkworks provide exactly such bounded environments where organisations can learn to balance AI performance with risk mitigation before scaling to core operations.

Lastly, organisations must adopt measurement approaches suited to AI's inherent complexity. As an inherently black-box technology in similar ways to humans, AI should be managed like companies manage employees who they want to be creative and innovative: by setting vision, goals and metrics while allowing freedom within fairly unrestrictive limits as to the approach employed. As shown above, prescriptive control of complex systems proves counterproductive — the valuable but hard-to-predict element is precisely the emergent behaviour between multiple AI agents and humans working together. In complex adaptive systems, control must be distributed rather than concentrated, with coherent behaviour arising through processes of self-organisation as agents compete or collaborate — attempting to impose centralised control suppresses this adaptive capacity. This means effective measurement of outcomes rather than actions, valuing results while accepting process variation, much like companies that value creativity in their human employees.

Therefore, in order to imbue the system with their full knowledge, AI Agent Managers also need genuine authority to guide AI behaviour based on outcomes rather than being constrained by rigid process specifications.


## The Path Forward

The transition to agentic AI represents a fundamental shift in how organisations operate, comparable in magnitude to previous industrial revolutions. Yet unlike purely mechanical automation or "traditional" software (imperative programming), agentic AI requires organisations to embrace complexity, distribute decision-making authority, and genuinely empower frontline employees in new, expanded roles.

The evidence from decades of organisational behaviour research, historic social movements, recent AI deployment experiences, and analogous technology transitions converges on a clear message: top-down implementation that threatens rather than supports employees will fail to capture the full value of these technologies.

Organisations that succeed will likely be those that recognise agentic AI as fundamentally sociotechnical rather than purely technological. They will invest in participatory design, provide genuine incentives for role transitions, establish supportive peer communities, and embrace experimental cultures that treat failure as learning. They will measure outcomes rather than dictating processes, select employees for their AI management potential, and understand that the competitive advantage lies not in firing employees but in orchestrating effective collaboration between human and artificial intelligence.

The evidence suggests that this path, while fundamentally challenging for traditional hierarchical organisations, offers substantial rewards. Companies that successfully navigate this transition will achieve improved customer experiences, operational efficiency, and market position while building more resilient, adaptive organisations prepared for continued technological evolution.

Meanwhile, those that cling to industrial-era management approaches risk not only failing to capture AI's benefits but actively harming their competitive position as knowledgeable employees block progress, hide knowledge or leave the company, and rigid systems of control prove unable to handle the complexity of real-world operations.

The future belongs to organisations that recognise their frontline employees as essential partners in the AI transition, not obstacles to be overcome or costs to be eliminated. This requires courage to challenge entrenched hierarchies, humility to learn from the expertise of those on the ground, and wisdom to invest in human capability even as artificial capabilities expand.

## References


Argyris, C. and Schön, D.A. (1978). *Organizational learning: A theory of action perspective.* Reading, MA: Addison-Wesley.

Authors Guild (2023). *Survey reveals 90 percent of writers believe authors should be compensated for the use of their books in training generative AI.* Available at: https://authorsguild.org/news/ai-survey-90-percent-of-writers-believe-authors-should-be-compensated-for-ai-training-use/

Bagrationi, K. and Thurner, T. (2023). 'Middle Management's Resistance to Digital Change', *Foresight and STI Governance*, 17(2), pp. 49–60. doi: 10.17323/2500-2597.2023.2.49.60.

Bainbridge, L. (1983). 'Ironies of automation', *Automatica*, 19(6), pp. 775–779. doi: 10.1016/0005-1098(83)90046-8.

Bezos, J. (2014). *Amazon.com 2013 Annual Report - Letter to Shareholders.* U.S. Securities and Exchange Commission. Available at: https://www.sec.gov/Archives/edgar/data/1018724/000119312514137753/d702518dex991.htm

Bloomberg (2025). *Klarna turns from AI to real person customer service.* Available at: https://www.bloomberg.com/news/articles/2025-05-08/klarna-turns-from-ai-to-real-person-customer-service

Connelly, C.E., Zweig, D., Webster, J. and Trougakos, J.P. (2012). 'Knowledge hiding in organizations', *Journal of Organizational Behavior*, 33(1), pp. 64–88. doi: 10.1002/job.737.

Dooley, K.J. (1997). 'A Complex Adaptive Systems Model of Organization Change', *Nonlinear Dynamics, Psychology, and Life Sciences*, 1(1), pp. 69–97.

Dunn, N., Dingus, T. and Soccolich, S. (2019). *Understanding the Impact of Technology: Do Advanced Driver Assistance and Semi-Automated Vehicle Systems Lead to Improper Driving Behavior?* Technical Report. Washington, D.C.: AAA Foundation for Traffic Safety.

Equity UK (2023). *Survey of audio artists on AI employment threats.* Available at: https://committees.parliament.uk/writtenevidence/111017/pdf/

Gartner (2025). *Gartner predicts over 40% of agentic AI projects will be canceled by end of 2027.* Press Release, 25 June. Available at: https://www.gartner.com/en/newsroom/press-releases/2025-06-25-gartner-predicts-over-40-percent-of-agentic-ai-projects-will-be-canceled-by-end-of-2027

Griffin, C.J. (2025). 'Luddism, Machine-Breaking and the Swing Riots', *Revue Française de Civilisation Britannique*, XXX(1). doi: 10.4000/133dc.

Hackman, J.R. and Oldham, G.R. (1976). 'Motivation through the design of work: Test of a theory', *Organizational Behavior and Human Performance*, 16(2), pp. 250–279. doi: 10.1016/0030-5073(76)90016-7.

Hadjimichael, D. and Tsoukas, H. (2019). 'Toward a better understanding of tacit knowledge in organizations: Taking stock and moving forward', *Academy of Management Annals*, 13(2), pp. 672–703. doi: 10.5465/annals.2017.0084.

Hobsbawm, E.J. (1952). 'The Machine Breakers', *Past & Present*, 1(1), pp. 57–70. doi: 10.1093/past/1.1.57.

Kim, B.-J. and Kim, M.-J. (2024). 'How artificial intelligence-induced job insecurity shapes knowledge dynamics: The mitigating role of artificial intelligence self-efficacy', *Journal of Innovation & Knowledge*, 9(4), 100590. doi: 10.1016/j.jik.2024.100590.

Kolt, N., Shur-Ofry, M. and Cohen, R. (2025). 'Lessons from complex systems science for AI governance', *Patterns*, 2666389925001898. doi: 10.1016/j.patter.2025.101898.

Kudina, O. and van de Poel, I. (2024). 'A sociotechnical system perspective on AI', *Minds and Machines*, 34(3), 21. doi: 10.1007/s11023-024-09680-2.

McGowan, K. and Geobey, S. (2022). '"Harmful to the commonality": the Luddites, the distributional effects of systems change and the challenge of building a just society', *Social Enterprise Journal*, 18(2), pp. 306–320. doi: 10.1108/SEJ-11-2020-0118.

McKinsey & Company (2025a). *The agentic organization: Contours of the next paradigm for the AI era*. Available at: https://www.mckinsey.com/capabilities/people-and-organizational-performance/our-insights/the-agentic-organization-contours-of-the-next-paradigm-for-the-ai-era

McKinsey & Company (2025b). *Seizing the agentic AI advantage*. Available at: https://www.mckinsey.com/capabilities/quantumblack/our-insights/seizing-the-agentic-ai-advantage

McKinsey Global Institute (2024). *A new future of work: The race to deploy AI and raise skills in Europe and beyond*. 21 May. Available at: https://www.mckinsey.com/mgi/our-research/a-new-future-of-work-the-race-to-deploy-ai-and-raise-skills-in-europe-and-beyond

Merali, Y. (2006). 'Complexity and information systems: the emergent domain', *Journal of Information Technology*, 21(4), pp. 216–228.

Ostrom, V., Tiebout, C.M. and Warren, R. (1961). 'The Organization of Government in Metropolitan Areas: A Theoretical Inquiry', *American Political Science Review*, 55(4), pp. 831–842.

Pew Research Center (2025). *U.S. workers are more worried than hopeful about future AI use in the workplace*. February. Available at: https://www.pewresearch.org/social-trends/2025/02/25/u-s-workers-are-more-worried-than-hopeful-about-future-ai-use-in-the-workplace/

Posada, J. (2021). 'The Coloniality of Data Work in Latin America', in *Proceedings of the 2021 AAAI/ACM Conference on AI, Ethics, and Society (AIES '21)*, 19–21 May. doi: 10.1145/3461702.3462471.

Salesforce (2025) *Research on agentic AI's impact on the workforce*. Available at: https://www.salesforce.com/news/stories/agentic-ai-impact-on-workforce-research/

Snowden, D.J. and Boone, M.E. (2007). 'A leader's framework for decision making', *Harvard Business Review*, 85(11), pp. 1–9.

Stockholm Resilience Centre (2012). *Adaptive governance (Insight #3)*. Stockholm University. Available at: https://www.stockholmresilience.org/download/18.3e9bddec1373daf16fa439/1459560363382/Insights_adaptive_governance_120111-2.pdf

Tesla (2021). *AI Day*. Available at: https://www.youtube.com/watch?v=j0z4FweCy4M

Tesla (2026). *Full Self-Driving Safety*. Available at: https://www.tesla.com/fsd/safety

Virany, B., Tushman, M.L. and Romanelli, E. (1992). 'Executive succession and organization outcomes in turbulent environments: An organization learning approach', *Organization Science*, 3(1), pp. 72–91.

World Economic Forum (2025) *Future of Jobs Report*. Available at: https://www.weforum.org/publications/the-future-of-jobs-report-2025/

Wrzesniewski, A. and Dutton, J.E. (2001). 'Crafting a job: Revisioning employees as active crafters of their work', *Academy of Management Review*, 26(2), pp. 179–201. doi: 10.5465/amr.2001.4378011.

# PLATFORM POWER: BUILDING RESILIENT BANKING ECOSYSTEMS IN THE AGE OF DISRUPTION

## Raluca Muresanu

We are living in an era where the pace of change is relentless, and the rules of competition are being rewritten almost overnight (McKinsey Global Institute, 2023). Terms like disruption, first-mover advantage, digitalisation, adaptation, and—perhaps most overused—resilience have become part of the everyday language of leaders across industries (World Economic Forum, 2023, Network for Greening the Financial System, 2019). Yet beneath these buzzwords lies a deeper challenge: how can organisations prepare for the next wave of disruption? When and how will the very markets that sustain us be transformed? Is the sustainability trend the next "green swan" on the horizon?

Throughout different domains, leaders are grappling with these fundamental questions that comes with the rapid changes. However, nowhere is this more evident than in the banking sector—a field once defined by stability, regulation, and incremental innovation (Deloitte Insights, 2018, McKinsey & Company, 2021). Today, banks face a perfect storm: rapid digitalisation, evolving customer expectations, increased phenomenon of using smart devices to do banking, new fintech, more agile competitors, and the social and regulatory pressure to mitigate environmental risks (Maklan et al., 2017, Gomber et al., 2018, Sivarajaha et al., 2020).

This chapter proposes a possible strategic approach for banks seeking to thrive amid such complexity. Rather than focusing solely on incremental improvements or defending existing business models, banks are encouraged to reimagine their role: not just as providers of financial products, but as orchestrators of broader ecosystems. By leveraging their core competencies, using a platform strategy (Prahalad and Hamel, 1990) and exploiting network effects (Kelly, 1999, Zhu and Iansiti, 2019) to make a different value proposition, banks can position themselves at the centre of new value chains—facilitating sustainable investments, connecting diverse stakeholders, and creating resilient profit centres that are less vulnerable to traditional risks.

The ideas and framework proposed here are illustrated using an East European Bank's context (further named LB), the local market leader, but the recommendations are designed to be broadly applicable. Any bank—or indeed, any organisation facing the threat of disruption—can draw inspiration from this approach. Thus, whether you lead a financial institution, a retail giant, or a technology startup, the ability to sense, adapt, and respond to complexity will define your success in the years ahead. The goal is to offer a roadmap and to inspire leaders who are ready to embrace complexity—not as a threat, but as a catalyst for innovation and growth and to have a different approach to build adaptive organisations ready for the next wave of change.

LB is a strong candidate for this framework because although it is the market leader, the recent digitalisation wave—amplified by the COVID-19 pandemic—proved that size and a leading position are not enough as during that crisis smaller competitors that adopted early digital strategies were able to adapt far more quickly. This experience highlights a critical lesson: anticipating and preparing for the next disruptive force is essential. Today, that force may be climate change—once considered a peripheral issue, now a central concern for risk management, regulatory compliance, and long-term profitability. The bank's strategic leaders must think what are the options for the bank to become more resilient to environmental risks and to, as far as possible, transform these threats into opportunities.

The significance of this endeavour becomes clear when considering the consequences of inaction. Without a proactive strategy, banks expose themselves to mounting financial pressures. As climate change intensifies and new sustainability regulations emerge, the likelihood increases that some borrowers will struggle to meet their obligations, leading to higher provisions for non-performing loans. This scenario threatens not only profitability but also the capital strength that underpins the bank's stability. Moreover, hesitation or delayed action can have profound competitive repercussions. If management waits until competitors have already moved, the bank risks missing out on valuable opportunities and forfeiting the advantages that come with being a first mover. Such delays can erode market share and diminish the institution's relevance in a rapidly evolving landscape.

Beyond financial and competitive risks, there is also a strategic imperative for leadership development. Engaging with complex, uncertain scenarios now allows leadership teams to practice and internalize emergent practices—an essential capability recommended by frameworks like Cynefin for navigating complexity. By confronting these challenges head-on, leaders not only prepare their organisations for disruption but also cultivate the adaptive mindset needed to thrive in an unpredictable future. In short, the cost of waiting is high. The time to experiment, adapt, and lead is now— before the next wave of disruption turns today's strengths into tomorrow's vulnerabilities.

To begin with, we challenge the LB's leaders, when strategising, to use the lens "we are in the services business" instead of "we are in the financial services business or just narrowing to the banking industry", to avoid "marketing myopia, or just being product orientated instead of customer orientated" (Review et al., 2013). Furthermore, to avoid becoming obsolete, any strategist should follow Chandler's advice (1963) to have client obsession at the centre of all strategies and long-term goals and objectives. Therefore, the suggested lenses are: "We are in the business of serving customers".

This way of looking at the business model is all the more important because the ability to interact, communicate, advise and find solutions alongside call centre and branch experience, all-in-one relationship management is for LB's clients one of the main aspects appreciated and confirmed by the yearly annual survey conducted by the bank and therefore one of *the core competences* of the Bank, which "should constitute the focus for strategy at corporate level" and the "wellspring of new business development" (Prahalad and Hamel, 1990).

In complex situations, the most effective leadership approach is not to dictate solutions from the top, but to create conditions for experimentation, learning, and adaptation. The Cynefin framework (Snowden and Boone, 2007), a complexity science tool, advocates for a "probe-sense-respond" strategy: leaders should encourage safe-to-fail experiments, observe emerging patterns, and amplify what works while dampening what doesn't. This approach not only builds organisational resilience but also fosters innovation, as new solutions emerge from the collective intelligence of diverse teams and partners.

At the same time, we aim to identify alternative profit centres with lower risks associated and sense new channels to deliver value to customers, therefore impacting the business model (Teece, 2010), leveraging the

Bank's core competencies and using associate thinking to make a Gavetti "cognitive leap" (2011) to identify opportunities missed by not being "cognitively close" to banking.

Currently, LB already has in place a strategy to increase its resilience to climate change risks, focusing on decreasing Scope 3 carbon emissions generated by the loans granted to its clients in line with the European Commission's Action Plan on Financing Sustainable Growth (2018). However, since the majority of the Bank's customers are individuals and SMEs, the demand for green loans is currently low. For these clients, progressively reducing their carbon footprint is not a top priority, and suppliers often overlook SMEs as a potential emerging market.

A valid sustainability strategy must start from the client's needs when planning and implementing an investment project designed to improve their business' sustainability or, in the case of individuals, their quality of life.

Several impediments and unsatisfied customer needs persist in the LB's market, particularly regarding green projects. For example, there is a lack of awareness and information. To counteract this, the Bank can go online and use a digital platform to increase the dissipation of information, boosting access through available technology. For Relationship Managers from the national network of the Bank, one of LB's core competencies could become an extremely efficient information distribution channel for advice on green projects. They benefit from clients' trust, are easy to reach, and have historically solid communication channels.

During sustainability-themed workshops organized by the bank with its SME clients, another challenge was identified: the local "sustainability" ecosystem is still in the creation phase, fragile, and has low credibility in the eyes of SME customers due to the small number of sustainable projects implemented. The market needs more feedback loops from previous experiences and greater trust in existing suppliers. Clients need more information and connections to implement sustainability plans easily, but their energy-efficient investment plans often have budgets too small to attract consultants or supplier's attention. Moreover, the local "sustainability" ecosystem, including specialised suppliers, local and national authorities, regulators, auditors, clients, and software companies, are not yet well connected according to the findings of these sessions.

Here, the Bank can become a sustainability ecosystem orchestrator. By acting as an aggregator of supply and demand in this niche, the Bank can bridge clients—providing increased visibility and access to suppliers and other mandatory partners in any project of this type—and suppliers, expanding their access to customers at the national level. Mentally, using associative thinking, the Bank may become the next Amazon for sustainability partnerships, linking customers, producers, connected service providers, and authorities. To amplify confidence in the ecosystem, the Bank can provide related services: for example, sending confirmations to suppliers at the time of placing the order that there are liquidities for making payments on delivery through the Bank's core products (such as escrow accounts, good payment guarantee accounts, issuing letters of guarantee, or confirmation of loan approval to buy green equipment). To increase the credibility of suppliers, the Bank may also apply (on demand) a "vetting" system and centralize customer feedback by implementing a public review system.

Another barrier is the lower return on investment of the SME's small-scale projects which significantly delays managers' decision for such investments. Smaller projects involve a higher cost of equipment because such projects are managed by intermediaries (involving the payment of an additional margin) and without the possibility of obtaining the discounts that producers grant to large projects. In addition, such projects have a higher unit transport cost as the transport companies charge per kilometre, not per quantity (Jaramillo, Sossa, Mendoza, 2018). The Bank may intervene by aggregating the demand. In such a way, the Bank can manage orders made simultaneously, allowing customers to associate in "order baskets" to reach the minimum order value to benefit from discounts from suppliers and facilitate transport groups to make transport more cost-efficient. Management of group orders and obtaining financial benefits from managing larger volumes coming from different clients is a capability that the Bank already has (especially used in the Treasury area).

The needs of individuals are addressed even less than those of SMEs. Although in recent years individuals have benefited from government subsidies to improve the energy efficiency of their homes, there remain a cluster of customers partially overlooked by specialis and suppliers due to the small business volumes they generate. By aggregating requests from multiple customers and increasing product exposure using the Bank's national network and the network effect from its digital platforms, the Bank can play a decisive role in bringing this niche market to the fore, solving addressability and market access issues.

Crafting one single service for companies and individuals is a deviation from the conventional pipeline business model, which focuses on products by customer type (Ayadi et al., 2016). Each segment business division usually has its own approach and strategy for creating "green products" and a proposed business model to address this need. However, because the fundamental needs of customers are similar—regardless of whether they are retail or corporate—and they are part of the same "sustainability" ecosystem (with the same consultants, intermediaries, maintenance companies, and banks providing financing), a paradigm shift is needed. Exiting the silo business model and breaking departmental boundaries to achieve a unitary approach would be more lucrative. Creating a "new value proposition" by participants from different divisions (who are used to serving only retail or only corporate clients) can help avoid "tunnel view" (Vroom and Yago, 1988) and the "echo chamber" syndrome (Pentland, 2013). However, when forming "mixed" teams from different segment business units, leaders must be aware that unit managers are often protective of "their" people, which can result in imprisoned competencies (Hamel and Prahalad, 1996).

Another known limitation of the local market is that there are few consultants who specialise in conducting energy audits and feasibility studies for energy efficiency projects and, for the most part, they are geographically located in the country's big cities. Additionally, although it is a technical field, energy engineers (who need more communication skills or customer care abilities) are not involved in collecting information or discussions with customers. Instead, sales-skilled people with no technical background manage client relations, offering advice to complete the questionnaires needed to identify a technical best-fit solution. Moreover, consultants use a software application for small projects to establish the technical solution, involving the engineers only to validate the proposal. Even so, only a few such consultancy companies have offices in more than one city. Therefore, their business model is geographically limited, missing contracts and opportunities. On the other hand, for an SME to access a well-known consultancy firm means supporting extra charges for the consultant's travel expenses.

To address these issues, the Bank can use its core competence in alliance with consultancy firms and exploit different existing capabilities. Consulting firms benefiting from no significant investments in creating their own offices will gain access to the entire national market through the Bank's Relationship Managers (existing capabilities, which can thus be capitalised with a minimum of training in order to be able to advise the completion of specific questionnaires online or in the branch). The Bank's clients or potential new clients will have access to expertise from consulting firms without supporting the travel additional costs. Furthermore, the access of consultancy firms to a larger market, generating higher sales and obtaining economy of scale, means that the Bank can negotiate lower consulting fees for its clients served through this business model, increasing SME accessibility to such projects.

Building on the Bank's existing capabilities—such as its positive experience in creating small ecosystems, its digital marketplace for retail customers and especially its core competencies in relationship management and solution selling—the Bank is well positioned to capitalise on these strengths in a diversification strategy.

Thus, the proposal is to create and capture value within digital networks by expanding the Bank's existing digital platforms, where the Bank acts primarily as orchestrator and secondarily as lender and supplier of other basic banking products necessary for contracts brokered on the digital platform. Rather than simply offering products or services, a platform approach positions the organisation as an orchestrator: a connector of diverse stakeholders, a facilitator of value-creating interactions, and a catalyst for innovation.

In banking, this means moving beyond the classic pipeline model, where value flows linearly from the bank to the customer. Instead, the bank becomes the hub of a dynamic ecosystem, enabling collaboration among customers, suppliers, consultants, regulators, and technology partners. By leveraging digital platforms, banks can aggregate demand, connect clients with vetted suppliers, and provide access to specialized expertise and services that would otherwise be out of reach—especially for individuals and small businesses.

This ecosystem approach is particularly powerful in the context of sustainability. By orchestrating a digital sustainability ecosystem, the bank can address the market's identified pain points—offering education, facilitating group purchasing, and building trust through transparent feedback and vetting systems.

The proposed strategy, analysed from the perspective of Ansoff's matrix (1957), is at the boundary between Market Penetration and Diversification. Simultaneously, the Bank consolidates its digital sales channels for existing products and partners with suppliers in the ecosystem created to offer customers attractive price campaigns to encourage them to access green loans offered by the Bank and other related classic banking products. Therefore, all these actions aim to increase the market share of existing products. However, because the Bank primarily acts as the "administrator" of a digital ecosystem, which will revolve around it, it generates a new type of service in a new market (database management, digital platform administration). Nonetheless, the customers served in this new market are the same as the core business line, which partially decreases the risk of entering a new market. Another mitigant for entering a new market is that the Bank already has the necessary competence to manage digital platforms. Another result of the Project is a product improvement as a complementary service (such as access to the ecosystem created around the Bank on its digital platform) with important benefits for customers upgrading the "green loan" (for both retail and corporate customers), who are thus sensitive to buy from LB instead of their competitors. However, we do not consider the proposed strategy mainly Product Development because non-clients of the Bank will also access the created ecosystem and because the Bank has the option to attract into the ecosystem other financiers, marching on the idea of cooperation instead of competition (Ritala, Golnam, Wegmann, 2014).

The intention is not to create a new product that is more competitive because it could soon be copied by the competition, outdated by better offerings and thus would return to the category of commodities, losing its disruptive effect. We aim to apply a platform strategy to obtain a long-term disruptive potential, switching the focus to managing resources through a digital platform business model that, enhanced by network effects, will grow fast, manifesting increasing returns (Arthur, 1996) and thus creating "a winner-takes-most environment" (Kelly, 1999). LB will primarily facilitate participants' interactions, as the value creation model revolves around transactions between the ecosystem's participants (providers and consumers). The more interactions between them (not necessarily financed by the Bank, which is only a plus), the more valuable the network is because its value increases exponentially with incremental costs (Kelly, 1999), as the "cost of serving an additional user is negligible" (Zhu and Iansiti, 2019). The strategy aligns with a global shift in management literature from focusing "solely on the firm as an organisation unit to focusing on networks of firms" (Merali and McKelvey, 2006).

On the other hand, success depends on the Bank's ability to manage the five fundamental properties of a platform business model, depicted in Table 1. The Bank must act as a magnet for clients and suppliers, a matchmaker facilitating valuable connections, and a platform company focused on user experience, timely offers, data exchange, and open architecture.

Ultimately, the value proposition of the ecosystem will depend on the orchestrator's capacity to recruit and manage participants, foster collaboration, and co-create value at every level. This requires a shared vision, ecosystem-specific investments, and agile problem-solving to maintain stability. The health, defensibility, and dominance of the ecosystem will determine the long-term success of the business model.

The benefits of such a strategy are significant. The bank diversifies its revenue streams, reduces risk by spreading exposure across a broader network, and strengthens its brand as a leader in innovation and sustainability. At the same time, the platform model creates network effects: as more participants join, the value of the ecosystem grows, attracting even more users and partners. This virtuous cycle can establish the bank as a market leader, difficult for competitors to dislodge.

**Table 1. Five fundamental proprieties of the network (Zhu and Iansiti, 2019)**

| Fundamental proprieties of network | Details and proposals to fulfil the requirements |
| --- | --- |
| Network effects | The network has "self-reinforcing virtuous circles. Each additional member increases the network's value, attracting more members, initiating a spiral of benefits" (Kelly, 1999). However, the online marketplace, part of the "sustainability" ecosystem, has a limitation because the products are sophisticated with long-term use and presumably, a customer will only buy it once every ten or twenty years. Due to this limitation, the network effect will not be similar to, for instance, Amazon. Nonetheless, the value of the network will increase with each new member, which can lead to expanding it further by attracting additional attachments, from the network or nodes owned by the latest added node, according to Metcalfe's Law (Iansiti and Lakhani, 2017). |
| Clustering | The network design is national, with customers from the entire country and mainly local suppliers. When group ordering per quarter reaches the threshold value imposed by equipment producers, the network may also interest them. Thus, the network will expand into international grounds. The proposed network structure is not fragmented in local clusters; therefore, it will not be easily challenged. |

| Risk of disintermediation | The risk of bypassing the platform is diminished by additional features provided: |
|---|---|
| | • special pricing negotiated for Bank's clients,<br>• the additional services provided<br>• the review system— only clients that make the transaction through the platform can rate a service or a product.<br><br>The review system has a crucial value for online acquisitions and the network users, as they exchange through the review system information that becomes "unique, exceptionally valuable resources" (Uzzi and Dunlap, 2006).<br><br>• access to group ordering with better prices for products, transport, and insurance of equipment during transport.<br><br>In this case, the Banks act as an "economic catalyst" (Schmalensee and Evans, 2007) that facilitates value-creation interaction between two or more clients who need each other to place a common order to obtain better prices. On the other hand, a marketplace where clients collaborate to obtain better discounts is an opportunity for the platform to attack new users and grow faster, similar to the classic example of China's Pinduoduo (Roggio, 2022), to reach that critical mass of users, that tipping point when the network effect becomes an entry barrier for similar products (Sironi, 2021). Platforms try to capture our time by providing us with as many diversions and as much utility as possible.<br>Because of the high value, clients do not purchase equipment related to green projects on the spot. Furthermore, as a general rule, the acquisition intentions of a customer reach the status of the firm order only after its acceptance by intermediaries and producers within 30 days. Thus, we appreciate that the opportunity to access a better price based on a group order (facilitated by the Bank) in exchange for waiting an additional 15 days is a strong incentive based on the equipment's important share in investment budgets.<br><br>• Connection with companies specialised in obtaining from local and national authorities the authorisations for the operation or commissioning of special equipment.<br><br>The risk of connecting directly with a supplier from the platform can only occur in the case of clients who self-finance their investment because otherwise if the financing is blocked in escrow accounts or is financially supported by credit, the Bank has the legal obligation to track the destination of the amounts. Thus, such a bypass attempt would be easily identified. |

| Vulnerability to multi-homing | Customers currently can purchase "green" equipment from other e-markets. The proposed strategy includes "locking customers" through related products: financing, issuing guarantees, guaranteeing transactions, mediating supplier disputes, managing returns, and specialised call centres. In addition, the platform benefits from the Bank's brand awareness, from the fact that the Bank's presence in the intermediation of the transaction brings security elements in compliance with GDPR rules, cyber security, and payment security. Moreover, we appreciate that multi-homing risk occurs mainly on platforms that capitalise on inferior products or services (value, utility, ease of switching) with repetitive use. |
|---|---|
| Bridging to multiple networks | Bridging multiple networks is necessary, as networks reinforce "one another's market position, helping each network sustain its scale" (Zhu and Iansiti, 2019, p.9). Initially, the platform will benefit from LB's existing network. However, to grow, the platform needs to bridge other industries and different products to maintain high traffic and transactions. A potential extension of the platform is towards offering accounting services, financial audit, cash-flow analysis, and invoice services for SMEs to explore a digitally underserved segment further, bridging in this way to new service industries. |

Crucially, this model is not limited to banking. Any organisation facing disruption can draw on the same principles: leverage core competencies, build digital platforms, and orchestrate ecosystems that create value for all participants. In a complex world, those who connect, facilitate, and adapt will shape the future.

The platform model is not new. Consider how Amazon transformed retail: rather than simply selling products, Amazon built a marketplace where third-party sellers, logistics providers, and customers interact. The company's role as orchestrator allows it to benefit from every transaction, even those it does not directly fulfil. Similarly, Alibaba's ecosystem in China connects manufacturers, retailers, logistics, and financial services, creating a network effect that is difficult for competitors to replicate. In healthcare, platform strategies are emerging as well, offering digital platforms where patients can consult with doctors, access pharmacies, and manage their health data. Ride-sharing companies like Uber and Bolt have also adopted the platform orchestrator model. They connect drivers, riders, payment providers, and even food delivery services within a single digital ecosystem. The value comes not just from matching supply and demand, but from enabling new services, gathering data, and fostering innovation across the network.

These examples show that the orchestrator model is adaptable and powerful. For banks, adopting this approach means leveraging existing strengths—such as trust, regulatory expertise, and customer relationships— while embracing new roles as connectors and facilitators. For leaders in any sector, the lesson is clear: in a complex world, those who build and nurture ecosystems will be best positioned to create value, adapt to change, and lead their industries into the future.

However, the strategy comes with its own challenges. The leader of such an ecosystem seeking to obtain emergent new value or innovation should focus on three dynamic capabilities: "facilitating the formation of a shared vision (sensing), inducing others to make an ecosystem-specific investment (seizing) and engaging in ad hoc problem solving to maintain stability" (Foss, Schmidt and Teece, 2023). Suppose the leader cannot develop common ground between connected suppliers and specific investments or parties cannot coordinate, the costs will increase, and even the existence of the ecosystem will be in danger. Furthermore, the business model's success "depends heavily on the health, defensibility, and dominance of the ecosystem in which it operates" (Zhu and Iansiti, 2019).

Furthermore, the proposal to launch the platform-powered ecosystem backed by the existing linear business comes with its one challenge. While it is easier to use the existing customer base (Sironi, 2021) and upgrade an already in-place platform, benefiting from the already formed network and the Bank's brand power compared to creating a new one from scratch, the level of openness required from an ecosystem leader exerts substantial pressure on the organisational boundaries (Merali, 2002), that if unsolved may lead to organisational identity issues, integrity problems, even disruption and cultural change. However, "isolationism is no longer a viable strategy" (Merali, 2022) to address the changes a networked global world brings, but at the same time, "the risks attendant upon the change may have to be weighed against other risks arising from maintaining the same state of affairs" (Burns and Stalker, 1968, p. 21).

The business model proposed involves the interaction of many actors and part of the ecosystem; it includes a non-linear business model where the network value is not the sum of the participants, and the emergent value proposition is still unknown. Thus, we conclude that these are characteristics of a complex situation (Snowden and Boone, 2007) and traditional leadership, revolving around insisting on a previous action plan, applying historical best practice, or a command-and-control approach will most likely fail because in such context into "domain of emergence" the best approach is probe-sense-respond (Snowden and Boone, 2007). Furthermore, the same authors advise leaders to create safe-to-fail environments to experiment with ideas obtained from open conversations with all partners part of the ecosystem (which will benefit from a cross-industry view, a diverse group that has a common goal), where patterns can emerge (2007, p.7). Before starting any testing, management must have a contingency plan set to amplify (if the emerging pattern is favourable) or, on the contrary, a damping strategy to limit its negative impact.

Leaders should also be mindful of the resistance to change within the organisation, as the project proposed involves a significant cognitive-associative leap, which the organisation may still need to achieve (Gavetti, 2011).

Despite these challenges, the rewards of overcoming them are substantial. Organisations that successfully break down internal silos, foster a culture of innovation, and build trust with external partners position themselves to lead in a complex, rapidly changing world. The key is to approach these barriers not as roadblocks, but as opportunities for learning and adaptation—hallmarks of resilient, future-ready leadership.

The journey toward building and orchestrating ecosystems in banking offers lessons that extend far beyond the financial sector. In today's volatile and interconnected world, every leader—regardless of industry—faces the challenge of navigating complexity and anticipating disruption.

One of the most important lessons is the necessity of vigilance. Disruption rarely announces itself in advance. Another key insight is the value of ecosystem thinking. No organisation operates in isolation. By embracing partnerships, fostering collaboration, and building platforms that connect diverse stakeholders, leaders can unlock new sources of value and resilience. The orchestrator model—so powerful in banking—can be adapted to retail, healthcare, mobility, and beyond. It is about creating the conditions for innovation, not controlling every outcome.

To make such a model work, adaptability is also essential. In complex environments, rigid plans quickly become obsolete. Leaders must be comfortable with experimentation, learning from failure, and iterating rapidly. The "probe-sense-respond" approach, borrowed from complexity science, encourages organisations to test ideas in small, safe-to-fail ways, observe what works, and scale successful patterns.

Finally, by internalizing these lessons, leaders in any sector can transform complexity from a source of anxiety into a wellspring of opportunity. The future will belong to those who are not only prepared for disruption, but who are willing to shape it.

## References


Ansoff, H. I. (1957). 'Strategies for Diversification'. *Harvard Business Review.* 35(5), pp. 113–124.

Arthur, W.B. (1996). 'Increasing Returns and the New World of Business'. *Harvard Business Review.* July-August 1996, pp. 100–109.

Ayadi, R., De Groen, W., Sassi, I., Mathlouthi, W., Rey, H. and Aubry, O. (2016). *'Banking Business Models Monitor 2015 Europe'.* SSRN Elictronic Journal. [online]. Available at: https://papers.ssrn.com/sol3/papers.cfm?abstract_id=2784334 (Accessed: 22 July 2025).

Bolton, P., Despres-Luiz, M., Pereira Da Silva, L.A., Samama, F., and Svartzman, R. (2020). *The Green Swan. Central banking and financial stability in the age of climate change'* [online]. Available at: https://www.bis.org/publ/othp31.pdf (Accessed: 8 July 2023).

Bonchek, M., and Choudary, S.P. (2013). Three elements of a successful platform strategy. *Harvard Business Review.* January, [online]. Available at: https://hbr.org/2013/01/three-elements-of-a-successful-platform. (Accessed: 9 July 2023).

Burns, T. and Stalker, G.M. (1968). *The Management of Innovation.* London: Tavistock Publishing Limited.

Chandler, A.D. (1963). *Strategy and Structure: Chapters in the History of American Enterprise.* Cambridge, Mass MIT Press.

Chaffey, D., and Ellis-Chadwick, F. (2016). *Digital Marketing: Strategy, Implementation and Practice.* 6th ed. Harlow: Pearson Education Limited.

Deloitte Insights. (2018). *Accelerating digital transformation in banking* [online]. Available at: https://www2.deloitte.com/us/en/insights/industry/financial-services/digital-transformation-in-banking-global-customer-survey.html (Accessed: 08 July 2023).

Foss, N.J, Schmidt, J, and Teece, D.J. (2023). Ecosystem leadership as a dynamic capability. *Long Range Planning,* 56(1), pp. 5–24.

Gavetti, G. (2011). 'The New Psychology of Strategic Leadership'. *Harvard Business Review.* 89(7–8), pp. 118–5, 166.

Gomber, P., Kauffman, R.J., Parker, C., and Weber, B.C. (2018). 'On the Fintech Revolution: Interpreting the Forces of Innovation, Disruption, and Transformation in Financial Services', *Journal of Management Information Systems*. 35(1) pp. 220–265.

Hamel, G., and Prahalad, C. (1996). 'Competing for the Future'. *Harvard Business Review Press*. Available at: https://www.perlego.com/book/836827/competing-for-the-future-pdf (Accessed: 25 June 2023).

Iansiti, M., and Lakhani, K.R. (2017). 'Managing our hub economy'. *Harvard Business Review*. September-October 2017.

Jaramillo, J.A., Sossa, J.W.Z., and Mendoza. G.L.O. (2018). 'Barriers to sustainability for small and medium enterprises in the framework of sustainable development—Literature review'. *Business Strategy and the Environment*. 28(4).

Kamalaldin, A., Linde, L., Sjödin, D., and Parida, V. (2020). 'Transforming provider-customer relationships in digital servitisation: A relational view on digitalisation'. *Industrial Marketing Management*. 89, pp. 306–325.

Kelly, K. (1999). *New Rules for the New Economy*. London. Penguin Publishing Group.

Maklan, S., Antonetti, P., and Whitty, S. (2017). 'A Better Way to Manage Customer Experience: Lessons from the Royal Bank of Scotland'. *California Management Review*, 59(2), pp. 92–115.

McKinsey &Company. (2021). '*The Great Divergence-McKinsey Global Banking Annual Review*

*2021*'. [online]. Available at: https://www.mckinsey.com/~/media/mckinsey/industries/financial%20services/our%20insights/global%20banking%20annual%20review%202021%20the%20great%20divergence/global-banking-annual-review-2021-the-great-divergence-final.pdf (Accessed 14 January 2023).

McKinsey Global Institute. (2023). *The State of Organizations 2023*. [online]. Available at: https://www.mckinsey.com/capabilities/people-and-organizational-performance/our-insights/the-state-of-organizations-2023#/ (Accessed: 22 December 2025).

Merali, Y. (2002). 'The role of boundaries in knowledge processes'. *European Journal of Information Systems*. 11(1), pp. 47–60.

Merali, Y. (2022). 'Complex Adaptive Systems in a Contentious World'. *New England Journal of Public Policy*. 34(2). Available at: https://scholarworks.umb.edu/nejpp/vol34/iss2/3 (Accessed: 14 January 2023).

Merali, Y., and Mckelvey, B. (2006). 'Using Complexity Science to effect a paradigm shift in Information Systems for the 21st century'. *Journal of Information Technology*. 21(4), pp. 211–215.

Miehé, L., Palmié, M., and Oghazi, P. (2023). 'Connection successfully established: How complementors use connectivity technologies to join existing ecosystems – Four archetype strategies from the mobility sector'. *Technovation*. 122(C).

Mintzberg, H. (1979). *The Structuring of Organization*. Englewood Cliffs: Prentice Hall.

Network for Greening the Financial System. (2019). *NGFS First Comprehensive Report. A Call for Action - Climate Change as a Source of Financial Risk*. [online]. Available at: https://www.ngfs.net/en/first-comprehensive-report-call-action (Accessed: 9 July 2023).

Pentland, A.S. (2013). 'Beyond the Echo Chamber'. *Harvard Business Review*. November 2013.

Porter, M.E. (2008). 'The Five Competitive Forces That Shape Strategy'. *Harvard Business Review*. Jan 2008, 86(1), pp. 78–93.

Prahalad, C.K., and Hamel, G. (1990). 'The core competence of the Corporation'. *Harvard Business Review*. May-June 1990.

Review, H. B. et al. (2013). HBR's 10 Must Reads on Strategic Marketing (with the featured article 'Marketing Myopia,' by Theodore Levitt). *Harvard Business Review Press*. [online] Available at: https://www.perlego.com/book/837108/hbrs-10-must-reads-on-strategic-marketing-with-featured-article-marketing-myopia-by-theodore-levitt-pdf (Accessed: 2 October 2022).

Ritala, P., Golnam, A., and Wegmann, A. (2014). 'Coopetition-based business models: The case of Amazon.com'. *Industrial Marketing Management* 43.

Roggio, A. (2022). '*Network Effects Drive E-commerce Marketplace Growth*'. [online]. Available at: https://www.practicalecommerce.com/network-effects-drive-ecommerce-marketplace-growth (Accessed:16 July 2023).

Sivarajaha, U., Irani, Z., Gupta, S., and Mahroofa, M. (2020). 'Role of big data and social media analytics for business-to-business sustainability: A participatory web context'. *Industrial Marketing Management*, 86, pp. 163–179.

Schmalensee, R., and Evans, D.S. (2007). 'Industrial Organization of Markets with Two-Sided Platforms', *Competition Policy International*, 3(1), s pring 2007.

Sironi, P. (2021). *Banks and Fintech on Platform Economies*. 1st ed. Wiley. Available at: https://www.perlego.com/book/3053892/banks-and-fintech-on-platform-economies-contextual-and-conscious-banking-pdf (Accessed: 29 June 2023).

Snowden, D.J. and Boone, M.E. (2007). 'A Leader's Framework for Decision Making'. *Harvard Business Review*. November 2007.

Teece, D.J. (2010). 'Business Models, Business Strategy and Innovation'. *Long Range Planning*. 43 (2), pp. 172–94.

UNEP FI. (2021). *Decarbonisation and Disruption: Understanding the financial risks of a disorderly transition using climate scenarios*. [online]. Available at: https://www.unepfi.org/industries/banking/decarbonisation-and-disruption/ (Accessed: 8 July 2023).

Vreugdenhil, A. (2021*). The power of platforms and how banks can become one*. [online]. Available at: https://www.finextra.com/the-long-read/225/the-power-of-platforms-and-how-banks-can-become-one (Accessed:15 July 2023).

Uzzi, B. and Dunlap, S. (2006). 'How to Build Your Network'. *Harvard Business Review*. 83(12), pp. 53–60, 151.

Vroom, H. V., and Yago, G.J. (1988). *The new leadership: managing participation in organisations*. Englewood Cliffs, NJ: Prentice Hall.

Zhu, F. and Iansiti, M. (2019). 'Why Some Platforms Thrive... and Others Don't'. *Harvard Business Review*. January-February 2019.

World Economic Forum. (2023). *The Global Risks Report 2023*. 18th ed. [Online]. Available at: https://www.weforum.org/reports/global-risks-report-2023/ Accessed on 8 July 2023.

# COMPLEXITY IN PRACTICE: CREATING CONDITIONS FOR EMERGENCE IN AN EFFICIENCY-FOCUSED ORGANIZATION

**Cătălina Vescan**

## 1. Introduction

This chapter presents a case study of a multinational utilities organisation with well-established procedures and a strong efficiency mindset that faced a significant challenge. Despite continuous lean optimisation efforts, it struggled to adapt to the emerging complexity of its operational environment. Interventions incorporated Critical Systems Practice, the EPIC framework (Jackson, 2024), Complex Adaptive Systems (CAS) (Holland, 1995), double-loop learning (Argyris, 1977), the Cynefin framework (Snowden and Boone, 2007), organisational routines, and building adaptive capacity. It revealed that the real challenge was achieving greater adaptability rather than pursuing efficiency alone. The organisation needed to rethink how it addressed the new challenges and move from a Lean framework (Saurin, Rooke, and Koskela, 2013) suitable for ordered domains to a Complex Adaptive Systems (CAS) framework suitable for unordered domains, a framework designed for emergence and resilience.

---

**Disclaimer:** This case study is based on a real organisational transformation in a large multinational utilities organisation. However, organisational names, specific programme names, precise performance metrics, and identifying details have been modified or generalised to protect commercial confidentiality and proprietary information. The core concepts, frameworks, and learning journey remain authentic and are presented to illustrate complexity thinking in practice.

The case study documents each phase of the journey. First, it describes the context that made transformation necessary, challenging the "this is how we've always done it" mindset. Then, it outlines the methodology chosen to guide the intervention and the design of the multimethodological intervention strategy that would bring clarity, accountability, purpose, enable conditions for self-organisation, and make space for reflection and emergence. Next, it details the pivotal shift from efficiency to emergence and how it happened. Finally, it ends with the importance of continuously sensing and reflecting to build and maintain the capacity to adapt.

Early results exposed a paradox, while the organisation fostered conditions for emergence, it struggled due to the lack of a shared language for identifying and addressing different kinds of problems. The intervention flexibility, demonstrated early, was particularly important.

Over time, sense-making capability spread beyond the initial program, scaling through distributed learning.

This is not a blueprint to copy. Instead, it is a learning journey showing how an efficiency-focused organisation can evolve into a resilient, adaptive system through an iterative dance between structure and emergence.

## 2. Context

To understand how this transformation unfolded, it is first important to understand the organisational context and the systemic pressure that led to this intervention.

For years, the organisation had been recognized internally as a model of efficiency; processes were standardised, performance indicators clearly defined, and decision-making followed well-established routines. This model had been highly successful in predictable periods where the relationship between cause and effect could be analysed and optimised. Efficiency was not just a goal, but part of the organisation's identity.

In recent years, the environment changed in ways that the existing model was not designed to handle. Customers' needs were continually evolving, market pressure demanded faster responses, frequent regulatory changes increased complexity, impacting complaint handling, and the competition intensified. High pressure persisted, as customer experience was a big differentiator. On top of this, internal fatigue and demotivation were more evident due to the overall decrease in customer satisfaction metrics regarding complaints.

Organisational level initiatives to build awareness about the volatile, uncertain, complex and ambiguous (VUCA) world we live in were implemented (Syamsir, Saputra and Anzanello, 2025). However, nothing fundamentally changed in the way of thinking, as pressure to deliver results increased, and there was little to no time for reflection. Although we were aware of the need to adapt, we ended up doing the opposite of building resilience. Instead, we went overboard with current practices, focusing more than ever on improving efficiency and on KPI targets. As a result, routines became even more tightly coupled than before, and the current system was not allowing learning to happen.

The Complaints Resolution Program then began to witness the consequences of forcing lean optimisation onto a system that actually needed adaptive capacity. Early signs were that KPIs started to decline compared to the previous year. The number of complaints increased. Frontline teams and experts found themselves unable to properly analyse and address the identified problems, not because of the lack of effort, but because the problems were becoming more and more complex, and the system was designed for complicated ones. In this context, complicated problems could still be solved by experts working together and using existing practices, but complex problems involve many interacting causes, unpredictable effects, and not only a single right answer, making linear approaches less effective (Snowden and Boone, 2007). Fatigue, frustration, and demotivation spread across the team. Not properly acknowledging the disordered domain it was currently in and continuing with ordered domain practices, the organisation was close to falling into chaos. Leaders at the organisational level, on the other hand, saw a performance dashboard that overall still looked acceptable; the customer satisfaction metrics for complaints handling were just slightly below organisational targets, but at the operational level, effort was compensating for structure. A comprehensive description of the situation will occur later during the Explore Stage of the EPIC framework (Jackson, 2024).

The challenge was not simply to fix what was broken, but to confront the possibility that some of the underlying assumptions about how work should be organised no longer held. And at a time when the pressure of delivering results was high, trusting a radical change that comes with letting go of control was very low.

In this intervention, I led the customer listening initiative for the Complaints Resolution Program. I developed and monitored the redesign of the Program together with the product lead and process facilitator of the dedicated cross-functional agile team, under the sponsorship of a senior customer management director. I collaborated closely with customer relations and support team coordinators and subject matter experts across multiple customer-facing and operational departments, which positioned me as both a participant and an observer in the transformation process. Due to my position, I was able to both shape the program's design and implementation and gather information on its impact on employees and customers.

The central question became how an organisation that was designed for control and stability can develop the capacity to adapt and learn without triggering organisational chaos or paralysis. How could you maintain efficiency that still worked while opening space for experimentation in domains where it didn't?

Addressing these challenges required more than a single method or framework. It demanded further iterative exploration and the willingness to introduce a new perspective as the situation revealed was needed. How we found the right approach to respond to all these needs is presented next.

## 3. Our approach

As the presented context became increasingly tightly coupled and lean optimisation increased the system's vulnerability (Saurin, Rooke, and Koskela, 2013), the decision to redesign the Program emerged gradually rather than as a single, well-planned change initiative. It was triggered by a series of discussions in cross-functional sessions with the agile team, where we repeatedly acknowledged that the current practice was no longer working: the volume of complaints was rising, KPIs were slipping, and the team was increasingly demotivated, frustrated and fatigued as their effort grew while the results worsened. A process facilitator noted that "we are working harder every month, yet complaints are increasing and becoming more difficult to solve, and we are unable to really get to the root cause". A customer support team coordinator observed that "we might be solving the specific situation for the customers in question, but this kind of problem reappears frequently". These conversations, combined with senior leadership's increasing awareness of the Complaints Resolution Program's results, led to shared recognition that a more loosely coupled, adaptive approach was needed. Therefore, by making the transition, the goal of the redesigned program was to navigate complexity and build adaptive capacity in the organisation.

Rather than prescribing specific solutions upfront, I proposed to redirect our attention from Lean Practices to the contemporary Critical Systems Practice developed by Michael C. Jackson (2024), building on ideas I had explored in MBA modules and in informal exchanges with alumni from my MBA Community. I had become increasingly convinced, through both theory and experience, that tools designed for ordered domains were no longer sufficient for the complex, evolving nature of our complaints environment. More concretely, attempts to optimize the existing approach were yielding diminishing returns and increasing stress on the colleagues involved, signalling that working harder on the current approach was failing. In this context, the EPIC framework (Explore, Produce, Intervene, Check) provided a structured yet flexible process for sense-making, continuous adaptation, and experimentation which seemed better aligned with the organisational need to build adaptive capacity. The next sections describe in detail how the framework was introduced and applied in the Complaints Resolution Program.

We treated EPIC (Jackson, 2024) not as a linear project methodology but as an iterative cycle, allowing additional methodologies and patterns to emerge as our understanding deepened. It represented a good start, as it was important to conduct a multidimensional diagnosis before entering the design phase. Emphasising the complexity of our situation, the importance of a multi-lens diagnosis is evident. The essence of Michael C Jackson's framework is that:

> *There are no simple ways to improve complex situations. They constitute multidimensional messes which cross boundaries and where technical, economic, organizational, human, cultural, political, and environmental elements interac.* (Jackson, 2024, p. 72).

The framework considers the situation from multiple perspectives and employs a range of methodologies, models, and intervention strategies to maximise results. So, in the end, there should be a balanced evaluation of the outcomes and suggestions for what needs to be done next, to ensure its durability and continuous adaptation.

While the Critical Systems Practice approach suited our context, no one-size-fits-all formula exists. Each situation must be analysed individually, even if it shares similarities with those in our context.

Figure 1. The four EPIC stages of Critical Systems Practice (Jackson, 2024), p. 74

Additionally, as Dave Snowden pointed out, believing we can fully understand or predict behaviour with enough mapping is not true.

*Though a complex system may, in retrospect, appear to be ordered and predictable, hindsight does not lead to foresight because the external conditions and systems constantly change.* (Snowden and Boone, 2007, p. 3)

We acknowledged this critique. Yet exploration and mapping of the current situation were needed. This allowed us to create an intervention strategy that fit the Complaints Resolution Program needs. Jackson (2024) recommends using a variety of methodologies, models, and methods to maximize benefits. Therefore, introducing complexity through double-loop learning (Argyris, 1977), CAS (Holland, 1995), Cynefin (Snowden and Boone, 2007) and routines as needs emerged was important.

Another critique comes from Michael Quinn Patton's public debate with Michael C. Jackson (Schmidt-Abbey, 2023). Patton argues that this framework is too complicated and hard to apply in the real world. He also says it has a mechanistic, stage-based approach that contradicts Jackson's critique and undermines the critical nature of systems practice. While this may be true at a theoretical level, I see Jackson's work as an "ideal type" primarily used for reflection rather than something you should rigorously follow for success.

Some critics say that mapping in a complex environment will not provide a full understanding because complexity is emergent (Snowden and Boone, 2007). Others claim this framework is too complicated to use in the real world (Schmidt-Abbey, 2023). Despite debates about applicability and complexity, in our situation, it was a good combination. The structure offered guidance but allowed us to choose methodologies from complexity science that fit our needs. This provided a broad approach, not a restrictive, standardised one. Flexibility allowed us to make space for emergence, while the structure helped us engage stakeholders who needed clarity, roadmaps, and numbers. The EPIC framework (Jackson, 2024) made it easier to secure buy-in and make space for experiments that built resilience.

## 4. Learning about the system

The Explore stage requires moving from superficial symptom identification to engaging in genuine sense-making. To deliberately seek to understand not only what was happening, but why the existing approaches were not working as before. Double-loop learning (Holland, 1995) is a powerful tool for reflection, as it helps you deeply understand the underlying assumptions, values, and beliefs behind what we do, and we used it throughout this stage.

Double-loop learning was introduced by Chris Argyris and Donald Schön (1978) and represents a transformative approach to problem-solving by questioning and altering the underlying assumptions, norms, and objectives that govern actions. Argyris and Schon (1978) define organisational learning as a process of detecting and correcting errors. They claim there are two possible responses to correcting an error, represented by single-loop learning and double-loop learning. The first type of response (SLL) implies that individuals search from other action strategies to achieve the same desired consequence but in the second type of response (DLL), individuals do more than that, they also examine the appropriateness and propriety of their chosen ends. Double-loop learning occurs when "mismatches are corrected by first examining and altering the governing variables and then the actions" (Argyris, 1999). This process is crucial for addressing complex problems

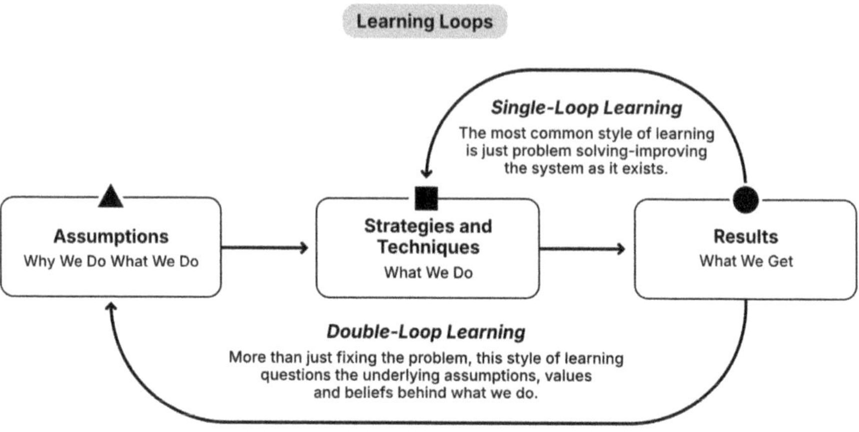


Figure 2. Learning loops – Adapted from Argyris (1991).

and fostering innovation as it moves to a more profound reframing of the situation. Through this process, tacit knowledge becomes more explicit, enabling individuals not only to solve existing problems but also to change the way they approach future challenges.

To define the context, we analysed various perspectives and data. This analysis showed we are in a complex system, demanding a new approach. A clear sign was the failure of best practices; the current lean framework was no longer working. There was also visible entanglement and interconnectedness—the number of complaints and their complexity were increasing because different systems that had to work together were becoming increasingly entangled. Cause and effect were only visible in retrospect. With the previous approach, the number of times when the root cause was difficult to identify increased, despite multiple experts from different fields working together. Moreover, the monthly customer satisfaction metrics results showed a significant decrease compared to the previous year. Customer feedback revealed more complex situations, as issues touched many systems. Non-linearity was more visible, and unintended consequences were more frequently observed as a consequence of the actions taken during the weekly problem-solving sessions mentioned earlier. This created even more complexity and fatigue for the involved experts, as a lot of effort yielded little to no results.

Ultimately, we recognized that we had been applying tools designed for an ordered world to a disordered reality, mistakenly treating a complex situation as if it were merely complicated (Snowden and Boone, 2007).

More precisely, by applying double-loop learning (Argyris, 1978) and examining the situation through all 5 lenses of the EPIC framework (Jackson, 2024), we discovered that our system was dysfunctional, and each lens revealed how a mechanistic, efficiency-driven approach failed in an increasingly complex, interconnected environment.

- The mechanistic lens revealed that current routines designed for stable conditions and unclear roles had become rigid obstacles rather than enabling structures. New routines that shift from controlling to shaping and predicting to navigating were necessary.
- The interrelationship lens had uncovered a cascade of coupled feedback loops across human and technological systems where quality was degraded not by a single element failure but by the reinforcing interactions between them. The organisation lacked the systemic understanding of how each component influences the whole, and it required deep mapping of system flows and interdependencies.
- The organismic lens showed that pursuing efficiency and KPI targets stripped the organisation of adaptive capacity. Genuine agility was replaced by reactive, speed-driven responses that left no time for reflection or experimentation, both essential for learning in uncertain domains.
- The purposeful lens exposed how the combination of unsustainable effort, unrelenting pressure, and visible failure had eroded team morale and sense of agency, transforming the organisation's promise of meaningful work into a cycle of helplessness and demotivation, which paradoxically undermined the results-oriented approach that created it.
- The societal lens called for amplifying all stakeholders' voices (employees, customers, regulators, partners), recognizing that durable solutions emerge from bottom-up optimisation and inclusive dialogue that honour diverse perspectives.

The exploration stage ends when those involved in the exploration process can identify the primary and secondary issues in the situation of interest. The primary issue is the one that needs the most urgent attention, and secondary issues are those ruled out of immediate action but that should be kept in mind, as their turn might come when the framework is revisited. It's important for the participant to take a broad look at the situation and focus on the issues that are most crucial at the point in its evolution (Jackson, 2024).

In our case, the primary issue was the lack of time for reflection and deep thinking about complicated and complex problems, rooted in a deeply held belief that control and efficiency were the best response in every situation, even when the context had become highly complex and fast-changing. By complicated problems, we refer to issues that can be analysed and solved by experts using good practices, while complex problems involve many interacting factors, uncertain cause and effect relationships and patterns that evolve and cannot be fully predicted in advance (Snowden and Boone, 2007). This tension became visible in the increase in the number of customer feedback expressing dissatisfaction, as well as routines focused on efficiency rather than learning. We concluded that intervention efforts should redirect organisational energy from mechanistic control to emergent adaptation, from imposed solutions to participatory sense-making, and from unsustainable intensity toward sustainable learning.

As Michael C. Jackson (2024) notes, success in "holistic flexibility" depends more on nurturing appropriate cognitive skills than on methodologies, frameworks, and prescriptions. Instead of searching for a fixed recipe for exploring the situation, we focused on seeing the world through diverse systemic perspectives. This stage provides only a general orientation within the EPIC framework, as the following stages will put this thinking into practice.

## 5. Producing a multimethodological intervention strategy

One can only hope to solve the identified issue in one iteration, as in complex systems, this is quite impossible. In the current situation of interest, we are facing multiple stakeholders who are affected by the outcomes of the organisation's current routines, and an abrupt change would not only be rejected by the organisation but might also paralyse the programme.

> *Change is not a big event around which processes and structures are transformed, but a rhythmic succession of small and large changes connecting the present to the future.* (Taylor and Bochis, 2025, p.78).

First, when developing an intervention strategy, we need to consider all the actors involved in the routines we intend to change and determine why the existing approaches are no longer working. An important element in creating an appropriate intervention strategy (similar to the explore stage) was applying double-loop learning (Argyris and Schön 1978). This approach has made a big difference in both understanding the situation and shifting people's perspectives, which also helped secure their buy-in for the proposal. During the process, the main question asked to all stakeholders repeatedly, until we managed to make a satisfactory amount of tacit knowledge explicit, was "Why do we do what we do?".

As the system we are in has become more entangled, with no space for change without creating disturbance, and has been visibly affecting efficiency and failing to respond to complex situations, we directed our focus to frameworks used to understand complexity. The Complex Adaptive System (CAS) framework (Holland, 1995) suited our need to make space for reflection and deep analysis of the complicated and complex problems we were identifying through our customer feedback.

Lewin and Regine (2003, p. 168) argue that "complex adaptive systems composed of a diversity of agents that interact with each other, mutually affecting each other, and in doing so generate novel behaviour for the system as a whole, such as in evolution, ecosystems, and the human mind" and Jackson (2003) states that complex evolving systems are the ones that have

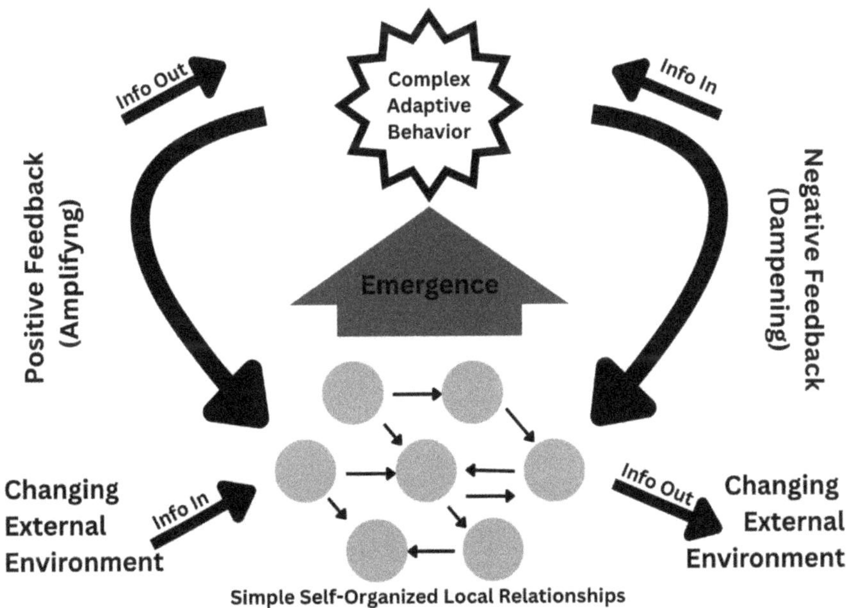


Figure 3. Complex Adaptive System – Adapted from Holland, (1995)

the capacity to transform their structure as they grow and can adapt to what is most suitable for the evolving circumstances.

A more practical view comes from Taylor & Bochis (2025) who recommend viewing organisations as complex adaptive systems, as it helps shape management practices, create safe spaces for experimentation, and thereby leverage existing capabilities in novel ways.

Complex adaptive systems (Holland, 1995) imply being more aware of interconnections, self-organising, creating the context for emergent behaviour to happen, and measuring the impact to amplify or dampen it. In our case, it would mean moving from a tightly coupled system typical of Lean to a loosely coupled system that serves as a container for emergence. It replaces end-to-end control, enabling a more generative function and making space for self-organisation.

Using the CAS framework (Holland, 1995) was important for building resilience in the system and for addressing the increasingly complex situations we were facing, but we also needed small incremental changes to get us there. That's why the next step (intervene flexibly) plays a crucial role in translating the thinking into a practice that is adopted, and it works: "In theory, there is no difference between theory and practice, while in practice, there is." (Brewster, 1882, p. 202)

Because the organisation has been working for many years in an environment optimized for efficiency and variance reduction, transitioning to a complex adaptive system optimised for adaptability and emergence, is a significant shift that requires time and cannot be done overnight. It cannot be achieved simply by communicating new organisational routines. So we needed to start moving from current good practices to the new practices.

To do that, we started thinking of improved routines that would be refined weekly, as positive results would be visible and new data would be available. This way, we could create a structural intervention that forced the system to observe its own emergent patterns (Krings-Klebe, 2021). Choosing this incremental approach stemmed from resistance to change, even in a time of significant constraints, as efficiency and high standardisation had been, until now, the way to success. So, we started by focusing on methods, frameworks, and methodologies that could improve efficiency but, most importantly, create the needed space for reflection and deep analysis, without the feeling of an abrupt change or a total lack of control. This respects both the CAS framework of emergent behaviour and flexibility while working on transforming the efficiency focused organisation into a resilient adaptive system.

Drawing from the work of John H Holland (1995) on the CAS framework, we also understood its limitations as Philip Anderson (1999) states organisations can't rely solely on CAS for strategic direction as it gives little to no concrete guidance but plays an important role in building resilience. We also acknowledged that as Brian Arthur said, "Complexity, the overall subject, as I see it is not a science, rather it is a movement within science." (2021, p. 136). More recent work about organisations experiencing high levels of complexity that are built around the themes of emergence, decentralis ation, antifragility and critique traditional management styles has led to more concrete guidance: "Real adaptability comes from the core: from rethinking not just what the organisation delivers, but how it is structured to learn." (Krings-Klebe, 2025, para.10)

To build the structure, we moved further with the following multimethodological intervention.

- Introduce a CAS approach – enable constraints as we understand that self-organising does not mean the absence of a structure but has a structure that enables autonomy by giving clear roles, purpose, and specific desired outcomes. This aligns with Jackson's organismic perspective (Holland, 1995; Jackson, 2024)
- Redesign organisational routines – to embed structured reflective practices, enabling double-loop learning and iterative adaptation (both to improve problem solving and routines) (Argyris, 1999; Krings-Klebe, 2025)
- Establish small self-organizing structures governed by enabling constraints – clear roles, purpose, and desired outcomes, that bound autonomy while facilitating emergent problem solving and innovation (Holland, 1995; Krings-Klebe, 2025).

The intervention objectives were:

- Develop organisational resilience – enhance the capacity to respond to volatility and unexpected challenges and changes by reducing time to adapt and increasing the number of innovative initiatives proposed by first-line colleagues.
- Embed Adaptive Capacity in the Customer Management Department – transform the reflective practices from facilitated interventions to autonomous practices, achieving self-sustaining capacity beyond intervention.

- Demonstrate performance impact–show measurable program performance improvement from the first month to build momentum, and secure stakeholders' buy-in to further develop the program in the CAS direction.

## 6. From efficiency to emergence

This stage focuses on implementing the previously agreed intervention. The main message is to execute the intervention while staying committed to pluralistic intentions and adapting to real-world situations. Flexibility is crucial for success at this stage.

As Jackson states (2024, p.159), "The main problem at the Intervene stage is to remain true to CSP's commitment to systemic pluralism. Intervene is guided but not determined by the nature of the primary and secondary issues surfaced by Explore and the appropriate intervention strategy agreed on during Produce. It is Intervene itself that will give rise to the greatest learning about which systems approaches are most useful and what improvements are possible in the situation of interest." And in our situation, it was indeed what happened.

To help ensure pluralism and responsiveness, flexibility requires frequent revisiting of the Explore and Produce stages. In our case, this was achieved through monthly assessments of the intervention, which served both as proof of impact and as a basis for improving the intervention strategy.

Moving to how we should make space for reflection in our routines, by applying double-loop learning in all our interactions with all stakeholders inside the organisation from the beginning, we found out that many aspects of the current routine were rooted in "because this is how we have been doing it until now." The decisions were not based on current needs or the situations we were going through, and the structure was rigid, causing the goal of each step of the routine to get lost in the process.

Double-loop learning (Argyris, 1977) is a powerful tool for reflection, as it helps you deeply understand the underlying assumptions, values, and beliefs that underpin what we do. By making them explicit, the stakeholders were more easily convinced that to create real change and improvements, we had to move from a Lean to a CAS (Holland, 1995) framework and embrace the complexity.

The hardest part was giving up control and designing new routines without knowing exactly how emergence would happen. Accepting and trusting the shift from prediction and control to creating the conditions and sensing what emerges in a large organisation is not only organisational but also cultural.

Here is where structure and creating new routines that build small self-organising structures play a crucial role in the intervention's success. It's a fine line between unleashing chaos and creating a structure that brings real growth. The secret was flexibility and adaptability – the ability to make changes quickly at this stage and having a hypercare system in place to closely monitor interactions and quickly sense if the results are not going in the intended direction.

In a large organisation with well-established procedures, a clear path had to be defined for how the new routines would unfold, and the roles and desired outcomes of the small self-organising structures were well documented. However, throughout this process, an important aspect was mentioned. We were paying attention to what was emerging and made adjustments as appropriate (Jackson, 2024). Ultimately, we we re looking to build the capacity to adapt, not to embed a specific practice through rigid routines and high levels of standardisation (Krings-Klebe and Schreiner, 2025).

After the first month with the new routines, we saw a significant improvement in programme efficiency, measured by monthly improvements in problem analysis, identification of solutions and implementation rates using existing resources differently, enabling self-organisation, and clarifying roles and desired outcomes. These results served multiple purposes simultaneously. Operationally, it proved that the intervention worked, and politically, it gave sponsors the confidence to continue. Psychologically, it gave first-line colleagues visible proof that change was possible. Systematically, it suggested that when problems sit in complex domains, a pragmatic path to building resilience can begin through efficiency improvements, freeing up time and attention for learning. On our way to building resilience, we were building trust, step by step, as people needed time to transition to the CAS mindset (Holland, 1995). Doing things right (single-loop learning) before doing the right things (double-loop learning) is important in order to create the much-needed space both in physical time and mentally in the experts involved to work on it (Argyris and Schön, 1978).

What made this approach successful is the capacity to understand the needs of all stakeholders involved in the intervention, while not losing sight of the end goal (Hazy, Goldstein and Lichtenstein, 2007). People need small wins and signals that we are going in the right direction to trust such a big transition from control to self-organisation (Kotter, 1995).

After analysing the results from the first month, although our efficiency metrics were excellent (significant efficiency improvement), we saw little evidence of improvement in experimentation and the emergence we were looking for. Teams were executing better but not thinking differently. They were still highly reliant upon best practices and quick fixes. We had created the conditions for emergence, but we lacked a shared language for recognising and responding to the different types of problems emerging. That's when we decided to include the Cynefin Framework in our routines, Cynefin (Snowden and Boone, 2007) as a decision-making filter, to help us categorise situations and choose an appropriate response based on their context. Taylor & Bochis (2025) state that the real value of the Cynefin Framework is recognising that most of the time managers are in the zone of disorder; that

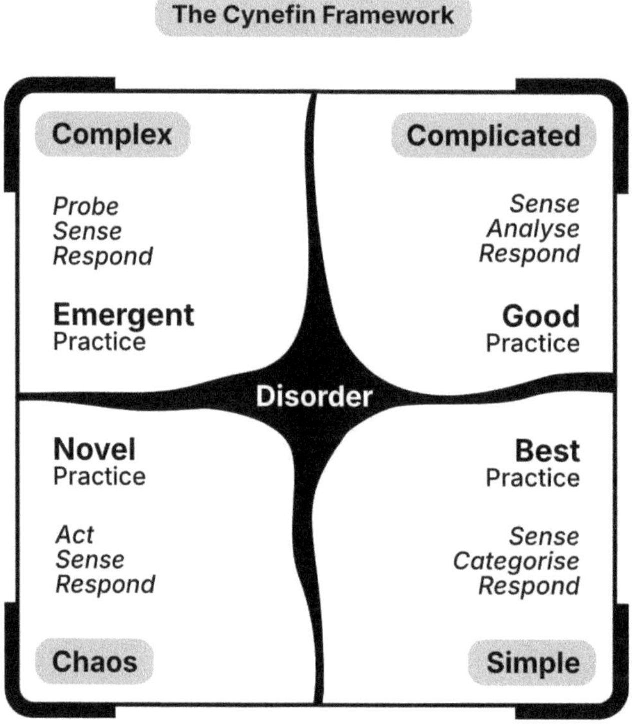


Figure 4. Cynefin Framework

is, not knowing in which space you find yourself in, or in our case, with the problems of our customers. For us, this was true, as we were not disagreeing about solutions, we were disagreeing about the nature of the problem itself. Through this framework, we had a pre-step to first understand the type of problem we were discussing.

The Cynefin Framework was created by Dave Snowden and Mary Boone (2007) and has been widely popularized since 2007. They developed the Cynefin Framework to help managers identify the nature of the problems they face before rushing into applying best practices. Building on this, the framework provides a structure for thinking before acting (Taylor and Bochis, 2025) which was exactly what we needed to move from only improving efficiency and numbers to creating meaningful change.

The framework categorises systems based on causal relationships: clear, complicated, complex, chaotic, and disorder. In ordered domains (clear and complicated), causality is predictable, allowing leaders to rely on best practices or expert analysis. In unordered domains (complex), causality is only evident retrospectively, requiring an experimental "probe-sense-respond" approach to foster emergent solutions rather than having predefined answers. By correctly identifying the domain, organisations can shift from rigid adherence to efficiency toward the adaptive resilience necessary for uncertain environments (Snowden and Boone, 2007).

We integrated the Cynefin Framework during our weekly reflection sessions. When analysing our customer feedback and understanding the situation end-to-end, we identified together which domain a situation fell into, asking simple but powerful questions about the relationship between cause and effect. This way, besides ensuring we were not overlooking or simplifying complex situations, we collectively learned to look at problems when returning to our day-to-day activities and facing different situations. Over the weeks, people started to internalise this thinking and find it useful in their daily work, not only in our weekly problem-solving sessions. This was an important step in escaping single-loop learning in weekly sessions and questioning our assumptions.

Starting to identify complex problems correctly has enabled a more structured approach to creating well-defined experiments that can be measured and amplified or damped accordingly. Otherwise, many situations we were trying to make sense of were considered from ordered domains (complicated or clear) for which we already have a good practice that solves them. Indeed, a large proportion of the problems were from clear and complicated domains, and we could apply best practices, or, with the right experts at the table, identify the root cause and apply good practice. But we needed to be able to point out the complex situations, to give us space to explore them further, and create the experiments, all of which couldn't be done during the weekly sessions. This approach at first looks as if it slows you down, but over time, we found that it does the opposite, as you can respond better and faster in times of uncertainty.

The clarity of "what we're trying to achieve" actually created the context for people to experiment with "how we achieve it" and as a conclusion the impact of this new routine transcended the barriers of the intended program due to the self-organising mini structures that started to apply this thinking in other contexts. Without any formal rollout and training, it was scaled through distributed learning. We closed the year with a visible improvement across channels in the way we thought and acted, and visible results in not only being faster but also in solving problems more effectively.

Recognizing the ongoing nature of this journey, we acknowledged that this is not sufficient when it comes to working with complexity; the job here is not done. As Jackson (2024) states, this framework requires frequent re-visiting of the explore and produce stages, along with flexibility and adaptation, as complexity is ever-changing. The journey continues, we've built the adaptive capacity, and now we are focusing on how to sustain this practice of adaptation as pressure increases and old habits can resurface.

## 7. Maintaining an adaptive capacity

*It seems to us that life in organizations is essentially paradoxical. Managers are supposed to be in charge, and yet they find it difficult to stay in control. The future is recognizable when it arrives, but in many important respects not predictable before it does. We sense the importance of difference but experience the pressure to conform* (Stacey, et al., 2000, p. 5).

Complex adaptive systems thrive on adaptation (Holland, 1995). However, organisational change initiatives must stabilise to become embedded. This stabilisation helps maintain the organisation's ability to probe, sense, and respond instead of preserving specific practices. It also enables double-loop learning to propagate across other business areas.

Organisational transformation from lean to complex adaptive systems is about navigating a fundamental paradox, and embedding new ways of working while preserving the flexibility for continuous adaptation. Unlike traditional change management models that hold on to the new organisational state in complexity, we are looking at building the capacity to adapt, not to embed a specific practice. This chapter addresses two critical mechanisms for maintaining this adaptive orientation, adaptive stakeholder management and adaptive capacity building.

- In the current environment, sustaining the shift requires reframing stakeholder management. It should be seen as an ongoing sense-making process, not just a static mapping exercise carried out in the early stages of the change. Freeman's stakeholder theory (1984) argues that organisational success depends on relationships with all parties affected by organisational decisions, shifting the focus beyond the traditional narrow definition of stakeholders. In complex systems, stakeholders' attributes shift dynamically as organisational conditions evolve (Mitchell, et al., 1997), making the stakeholders' positions inherently unstable. Bryson (2004; 2011) offers a framework for inclusive engagement that supports learning and adaptation. This framework emphasises iterative stakeholder engagement and provides practical techniques for multi-stakeholder contexts. Jackson (2024) adds that stakeholder engagement must address the underlying power dynamics and competing interests systematically. So, rather than seeking consensus around predetermined visions, continuous adaptation uses stakeholders' diversity as a generative resource for continuous learning and improvement.
- Building organisational adaptive capacity is the second main pillar for dancing with complexity in the long term (Krings-Klebe and Schreiner, 2025). Teece's (2007) dynamic capabilities framework provides the theoretical foundation for understanding how organisations maintain adaptation over time and other complementary frameworks strengthen this view (Cohen and Levinthal, 1990; Zahra and George 2002), stating that absorptive capacity enables organisations to identify, assimilate and apply knowledge, while organisational ambidexterity (March, 1991) balances exploitation of current capabilities with exploration of new possibilities. Also, Feldman's (Feldman, 2000) work demonstrates that organisational routines are themselves

a continuous source of change rather than a source of rigidity. To add, from the Communities of Practice theory (Wenger, 1998), the communities of practice model proves essential for embedding learning capacity throughout the organisation through social learning systems that distribute knowledge and capability development in a self-organised way while maintaining a well-defined purpose. So, successfully navigating complexity requires organisations to build adaptive capabilities. By self-organising around a clear purpose, remaining receptive to feedback, creating safe environments, and continuously providing value to stakeholders, organisations can foster an environment open to ongoing learning and adaptation.

To develop adaptive stakeholder management and build organisational adaptive capacity, we must create the right conditions. Drawing from Krings-Klebe's and Schreiner's (2025) concept of "dancing with complexity," organisations build resilience not through rigid controls, but through institutionalised flexibility. This enables emergence and self-organisation. Sustainable change embeds adaptive mechanisms, transforming them into permanent organisational features. Integrating the work of Jackson, Snowden, Holland, and Krings-Klebe in our situation of interest demonstrates that the shift from lean to complex adaptive systems is not a destination, it is a continuous practice of sensing emerging challenges, continuously adapting organisational routines through engaged stakeholder self-organised structures, and evolving organisational capabilities.

## 8. Continuous sensing and reflection

The last stage of the EPIC framework (Jackson, 2024), check on progress, requires evaluating the improvements we have achieved, reflecting on the learnings we have gained and discussed, and agreeing on the next steps. From the practical standpoint, it's important to deliver tangible results after a full cycle in order to build credibility of the approach, to scale it, to prove that it's worth all the effort, or to understand what went wrong, what stakeholders we didn't take into consideration, and what perspectives are not seeing the intended improvements. This is how organisations work, and this is how you move further.

Still, our job is never done in a complex system. You can't simplify it or truly solve all problems. As Dave Snowden states (2025, para. 2), in complexity "the only thing we can say with certainty is that there will be un-intended consequences". For this reason, this stage is important and should not be done only once; it should be present throughout all stages, sensing and reflecting on whether the direction we are heading is the desired one – in our case, moving from a lean mindset to a CAS one.

*Good behaviour more often emerges from rituals and habitual patterns of behavior, not rules. By focusing on interaction (human-human, human-AI), we build systems resilient in the tail, where most disasters lurk. The goal isn't perfect control but adaptive capacity: the ability to reconfigure roles and heuristics when the unpredictable strikes.* (Snowden, 2025, para. 25)

## 9. Conclusions

This case study is not about a recipe for success. Instead, it should be perceived as an attempt to transform established ideas about complexity and adaptation into practice – real action that solves the challenges organisations face today. It was written to encourage leaders to shift from control to shaping the right conditions. It's about trusting their people as key sources of knowledge, making space for them to try experiments that can influence the system without causing major disturbances or paralysis. Human and political factors are as important as methods, because leaders need certainty, to trust others to make decisions, and achieve quick, visible successes that increase the sense of safety needed to trust new approaches.

Emergence is not about abandoning structure. It is about finding the right rhythm between structure and flexibility. It involves a redesign that balances routine with flexibility while still preserving boundaries, just not rigid rules. Structures that once limited change now serve as a support for creating small, self-organised structures that enable people to experiment. This experiment demonstrates that efficiency and emergence can support each other when routines are seen as clear guides that give you the purpose and define roles, but do not dictate behaviour.

Moving away from a focus on control, the organisation should build its ability to experiment, sense, reflect, and adapt. This capacity adds to efficiency, making people more adaptable and resilient, shifting the way people think about accountability rather than just relaxing rules. Shifting to a complex adaptive systems mindset is not a method of change that can be done quickly, but a way an organisation should learn to navigate complexity and handle uncertainty. The real learning happened through actions and mistakes. Not giving the ability to apply knowledge results in regurgitating what we already know.

This work is not the end, but an ongoing journey, since adaptation in a complex system is never finished. Having a linear approach to this transformation results in falling back into old habits, when it should be a constant process of adjustment and improvement.

For organisations focused on efficiency that face similar challenges, this case study shows that resilience comes from making structures that support emergence and not by solely removing them. While using the frameworks and methods discussed, it's important to pay attention to using them when the system is ready and not forcing them as a key to success in becoming a resilient organisation.

Finally, real work with complexity requires both courage and patience. Courage to loosen the control in the right places and to believe you can make a difference despite the constant pressure to deliver business results. Patience, while still remaining alert, to let small successes, new ways of working, and new routines change how an organisation both thinks and acts.

## References


Anderson, P. (1999). 'Perspective: Complexity Theory and Organization Science'. *Organization Science,* 10(3), pp. 216–232.

Argyris, C. (1977). 'Double-Loop Learning in Organizations'. *Harvard Business Review,* 55(5), pp. 115–125.

Argyris, C. and Schön, D. (1978). *Organizational Learning: A Theory of Action Perspective.* Reading: MA: Addison-Wesley.

Argyris, C. (1999). *On Organizational Learning.* 2nd Edition ed. Oxford: Blackwell.

Arthur, W. (2021). 'Foundations of Complexity Economics'. *Nature Reviews Physics,* 3(2), pp. 136–145.

Brewster, B. (1882). 'Theory and Practice'. *The Yale Literary Magazine,* 47(5), p. 202.

Bryson, J. (2004). 'What to Do When Stakeholders Matter: Stakeholder Identification and Analysis Techniques'. *Public Management Review,* 6(1), pp. 21–53.

Bryson, J. (2011). *Strategic Planning for Public and Nonprofit Organizations: A Guide to Strengthening and Sustaining Organizational Achievement.* 4th Edition ed. San Francisco: CA: Jossey-Bass.

Cohen, W. and Levinthal, D. (1990). 'Absorptive Capacity: A New Perspective on Learning and Innovation'. *Administrative Science Quarterly,* 35(1), pp. 128–152.

Feldman, M. (2000). 'Organizational Routines as a Source of Continuous Change'. *Organization Science,* 11(6), pp. 611–629.

Freeman, R. (1984). *Strategic Management: A Stakeholder Approach.* Boston: Pitman.

Hazy, J., Goldstein, J. and Lichtenstein, B. (2007). *Complex systems leadership theory: New perspectives from complexity science on social and organizational effectiveness.* Mansfield: MA: ISCE Publishing.

Holland, J. (1995). *Hidden Order: How Adaptation Builds Complexity.* Reading: MA: Addison-Wesley.

Jackson, M. (2003). *Systems Thinking: Creative Holism for Managers.* Chichester: John Wiley & Sons.

Jackson, M. (2024). *Critical Systems Thinking.* Hoboken: John Wiley & Sons Inc.

Kotter, J. (1995). 'Leading change: Why transformation efforts fail'. *Harvard Business Review,* 73(2), pp. 59–67.

Krings-Klebe, J. (2021). *'Serving People – 6. Revolutionizing Leadership Development'.* [Online] Available at: https://www.druckerforum.org/retrospective/2021/www.druckerforum.org/blog/serving-people-6-revolutionizing-leadership-development/ [Accessed 20 December 2025].

Krings-Klebe, J. and Schreiner, J. (2025). *The Antifragile Organization: From Hierarchies to Ecosystems.* London: LID Publishing.

Krings-Klebe, J. (2025). *Why Our Organizations Break – and What It Takes to Make Them Whole.* [Online] Available at: https://www.thedigitaltransformationpeople.com/channels/people-and-change/why-our-organizations-break-and-what-it-takes-to-make-them-whole/ [Accessed 20 December 2025].

Lewin, R. and Regine, B. (2003). 'The core of adaptive organizations'. In *Complex systems and evolutionary perspectives on organisations: The application of complexity theory to organisations,* pp. 167–184.

Maclean, K., Cuthill, M. and Ross, H. (2014). 'Six attributes of social resilience'. *Journal of Environmental Planning and Management,* 57(1), pp. 144–156.

March, J. (1991). 'Exploration and Exploitation in Organizational Learning'. *Organization Science,* 2(1), pp. 71–87.

Mitchell, R. K., Agle, B. and Wood, D. (1997). 'Toward a Theory of Stakeholder Identification and Salience: Defining the Principle of Who and What Really Counts'. *Academy of Management Review,* 22(4), pp. 853–886.

Saurin, T. A., Rooke, J. and Koskela, L., (2013). 'A complex systems theory perspective of lean production'. *International Journal of Production Research,* 51(19).

Schmidt-Abbey, B. (2023). *In Search of a Golden Mean for Systemic Evaluation – a public debate between Michael Quinn Patton and Mike C. Jackson hosted by EES.* [Online] Available at: https://europeanevaluation.org/2023/03/29/in-search-of-a-golden-mean-for-systemic-evaluation-a-public-debate-between-michael-quinn-patton-and-mike-c-jackson-hosted-by-ees/[Accessed 20 December 2025].

Snowden, D. and Boone, M. (2007). 'A Leader's Framework for Decision Making'. *Harvard Business Review,* 85(11), pp. 68–76.

Snowden, D. (2025).*The Cynefin Co.* [Online] Available at: https://thecynefin.co/the-limits-of-rules/ [Accessed 20 December 2025].

Soliman, M., Saurin, T. A. & Anzanello, M. (2018). 'The impacts of lean production on the complexity of socio-technical systems'. *International Journal of Production Economics,* Volume 197, pp. 342–357.

Stacey, R. D., Griffin, D. and Shaw, P. (2000). *Complexity and Management: Fad or Radical Challenge to Systems Thinking?* London: Routledge.

Syamsir, S., Saputra, N. and Mulia, R. A. (2025). 'Leadership agility in a VUCA world: a systematic review, conceptual insights, and research directions'. *Cogent Business & Management,* 12(1).

Taylor, A. and Bochis, R. (2025). *All in.* London: University of Buckingham Press.

Teece, D. (2007). 'Explicating Dynamic Capabilities: The Nature and Microfoundations of (Sustainable) Enterprise Performance'. *Strategic Management Journal,* 28(13), pp. 1319–1350.

Wenger, E. (1998). *Communities of Practice: Learning, Meaning, and Identity.* Cambridge: Cambridge University Press.

Zahra, S. and George, G. (2002). 'Absorptive Capacity: A Review, Reconceptualization, and Extension'. *Academy of Management Review,* 27(2), pp. 185–203.

# FROM BOUNDARIES TO FUSION: HOW WORKATIONS REDEFINE PERFORMANCE AND BELONGING IN THE DISRUPTION ERA

## Raluca Gheorghes

Lund et al. (2021) argue that the pandemic transformed the geography of work while altering its meaning and structure. What once relied on predictable rhythms, clear routines and the reassurance of shared spaces became exposed to volatility, as Al-Habaibeh and Wilkesmann (2021) observe. The separation between professional and personal spheres gradually weakened, and the familiar language of balance began to lose relevance. Individuals started to seek coherence, a form of alignment in which purpose, autonomy and belonging could coexist within a single lived experience (Haeger and Lingham, 2014).

Within this transition, a practice once viewed as peripheral gained conceptual and managerial visibility: **the workation** (Wilkesmann and Bassyiouny, 2025). Defined as a structured interval during which employees perform their regular duties from a leisure-oriented location, the workation blends work and vacation in ways that support well-being and work-life fusion (Gheorghes, 2023). It occupies an intermediary position between remote work and digital nomadism. Unlike remote work, it implies a deliberate change of environment designed to enhance recovery and focus; unlike digital nomadism, it preserves organisational anchoring, continuity and shared expectations (Pecsek, 2018; Bassiouny and Wilkesmann, 2023).

Scianna and Patti (2023) describe workations as adaptive mechanisms that allow organisations to test flexibility, engagement and creativity in uncertain contexts. This is particularly visible in knowledge-intensive and digital sectors, where the pressure to innovate intersects with the need to retain talent. In Central and Eastern Europe, and especially in the Romanian IT and creative industries, firms have begun to move beyond the traditional outsourcing logic, where cost arbitrage was the primary comparative advantage. As Gheorghes (2023) points out, competitiveness now depends on the ability to create environments that sustain learning, collaboration and psychological presence. Within this landscape, workations function as controlled experiments that reveal how trust, autonomy and team cohesion translate into measurable performance (Rao, 2016).

The following chapter examines two such experiments implemented by Company L, a small digital firm based in Cluj-Napoca, Romania. The two trials, referred to as Greece 1.0 and Greece 2.0, took place in 2022 and were envisioned as structured interventions rather than leisure escapes (Gheorghes, 2023). The first involved twenty-two people who worked remotely for eight days in Greece, resulting in a total of ten days including travel. The second, organised four months later, expanded participation to thirty-four individuals. This extension signalled a deepening of organisational trust

Figure 1: Personal Archive, Greece (2022) Gheorghes (2023), p. 3

**Table 1. Overview of the Greece 1.0 and 2.0 Workation Trials**

| Experience | Duration | Costs | Facilities | Transport |
|---|---|---|---|---|
| Greece 1.0 | 8 days | 385€/person | Accommodation & 3 meals per day | Personal cars |
| Greece 2.0 | 11 days | 300€/person | Only Accommodation | Personal cars |

| Experience | Total participants | Direct participants | Indirect participants |
|---|---|---|---|
| Greece 1.0 | **22 people** | 20 employees | 2 life partners |
| Greece 2.0 | **34 people** | 27 employees | 7 life partners |

| Survey Number | Date | Respondents |
|---|---|---|
| 1. Post Greece 1.0 | May 2022 | 20 employees |
| 2. Post Greece 2.0 | September 2022 | 21 employees |
| 3. Long-term post event | May 2023 | 28 employees |

Source: Gheorghes (2023)

and reflected the firm's growing openness toward integrative well-being practices. Participation remained voluntary and self-funded, which reinforced the personal commitment of those involved.

Data collected through FocusD, the company's internal AI-based analytics platform (see Figure 7), provided tangible insights. Stress peaks were lower, task efficiency increased and collaboration indicators improved when compared with standard office periods (Gheorghes, 2023). What began as a functional pilot soon evolved into a shared experience that reshaped perceptions of identity, belonging and collective performance. Table 1 presents the main parameters of the two interventions, including their structure, duration and evaluation cycles.

Ultimately, the case of Company L illustrates both the promise and the limits of human-centred transformation. Change arose less from new technologies than from collective reflection and shared awareness. The trials showed that performance and belonging are not competing objectives but interdependent dimensions of organisational sustainability (Haeger and Lingham, 2014; Gheorghes, 2023). Yet their replication depends on cultural readiness and sectoral maturity. In a world of constant disruption, the ability to pause, reflect, and reconnect may prove to be the most critical form of organisational intelligence. This chapter explores how workations function as living laboratories for organisational learning in post-pandemic digital firms.

## Theoretical Anchors – Reframing Performance and Belonging

The theoretical perspectives guiding this chapter operate as multiple, inter-linked lenses that illuminate how performance and belonging evolve within contemporary organisations. These lenses are necessary because the Greece trials did not merely illustrate behavioural change; they revealed the underlying mechanisms through which performance and belonging became mutually reinforcing. Read together, they map a progression from individual motivation to collective learning and, ultimately, to the ethical boundaries that protect sustainable well-being. Soft human resource management (HRM) and Social Exchange Theory form the first interpretive layer, positioning employees as active contributors whose motivation emerges from trust, recognition and participation (Truss et al., 1997; Gill, 1999; Blau, 1967). Within this view, commitment grows through reciprocity rather than supervision, a dynamic that becomes particularly visible in settings where autonomy is central to daily work.

A second lens derives from experiential and triple-loop learning frameworks, which explain how individuals and teams reinterpret assumptions, behaviours and shared norms when placed in unfamiliar or decoupled environments (Kolb, 1984; Argyris and Schön, 1978; Bateson, 1972). Through repeated cycles of action and reflection, groups develop new collaborative patterns that endure beyond the immediate moment and become embedded in practice.

A third lens introduces ethical calibration through Siegrist's Effort–Reward Imbalance model, emphasising the strain that arises when autonomy is not matched with recovery, recognition and structural support (Siegrist, 1996). This perspective helps explain why flexible work systems can simultaneously enable creativity and generate vulnerability.

Taken together as a single conceptual architecture, these lenses clarify why the Greece workation trials produced shifts in cohesion, identity and perceived purpose. They reveal how autonomy, reciprocity and reflective practice interacted to transform a short-term relocation into a living learning process and organisational behaviour that strengthened both performance and belonging.

The Greece Workation initiatives reflected this orientation in practice. Traditional supervision was replaced with peer accountability and self-management (Gheorghes, 2023). Employees organised their daily schedules independently while maintaining collective objectives. This distributed

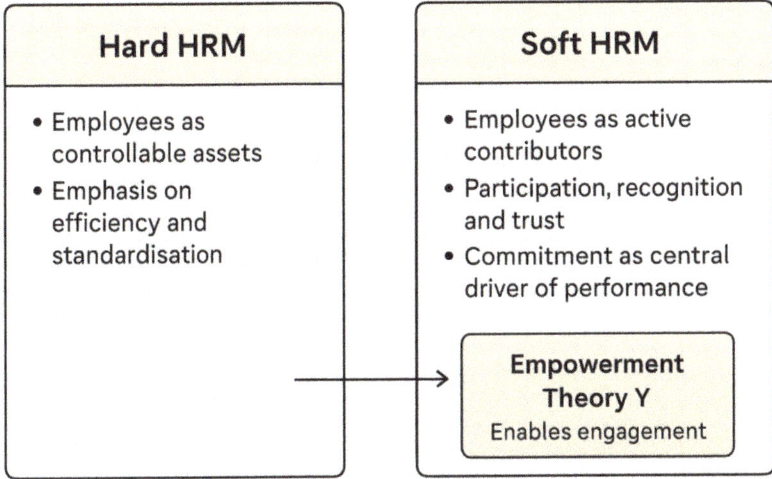


**Figure 2. Soft vs. Hard HRM: Empowerment and Theory Y Integration**

Source: Generated by author with the help of AI.

autonomy resulted in measurable improvements in satisfaction, creativity, and perceived purpose. Similar outcomes are documented in hybrid work research, which suggests that autonomy is most effective when supported by clarity, communication, and trust-based coordination (Lojeski and Reilly, 2020).

The interplay between autonomy and accountability can be further explained through Social Exchange Theory (SET) (Blau, 1967). SET conceptualises employment not as a transactional contract but as a reciprocal relationship in which perceived fairness generates intrinsic motivation. When individuals feel trusted and valued, they reinvest trust through loyalty and performance (Bakker and Leiter, 2010). During the Greece trials, participants consistently described the experience of being trusted to self-manage as a catalyst for engagement and identification with the company (Gheorghes, 2023). The sense of belonging that followed was the tangible outcome of reciprocity. These findings confirm that psychological and relational dimensions of work, often dismissed as "soft", can yield measurable productivity gains, a conclusion consistent with current analyses of remote engagement systems (Brecheisen et al., 2022). Yet reciprocity rarely unfolds on neutral ground. As Foucault's (1977) notion of disciplinary power reminds us, freedom within organisations often functions as a subtle technology of control. In hybrid regimes, visibility metrics, digital footprints, and peer comparison

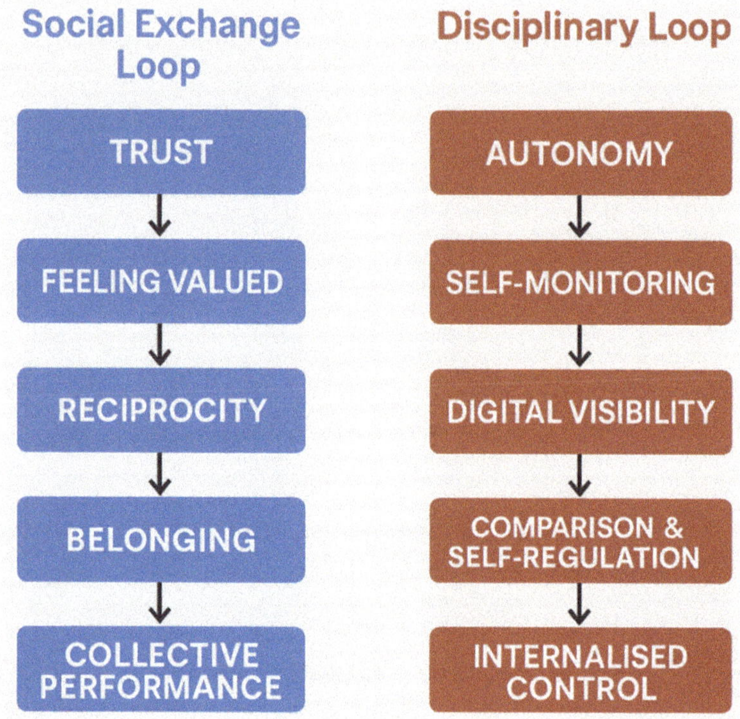



**Figure 3. The Trust–Control Paradox in Hybrid Work: A Social Exchange Perspective**

Source: Generated by author with the help of AI (based on Blau, 1967; Foucault, 1977; Fleming, 2020).

sustain a form of "panoptic flexibility" (Fleming, 2020) in which self-monitoring replaces overt supervision. Recognising this helps counterbalance the overly optimistic readings of trust-based management.

Learning rather than control thus becomes the connective tissue between performance and belonging. Kolb's experiential learning theory provides a valuable interpretive lens, describing learning as a continuous cycle of action, reflection, conceptualisation, and experimentation (Kolb, 1984; McLeod, 2023). When applied to workations, this model explains how exposure to new environments disrupts established cognitive patterns and promotes adaptive thinking. Participants in the Greece trials intuitively moved through these stages, experimenting with new routines, reflecting individually and collectively, and translating insights into new collaborative norms

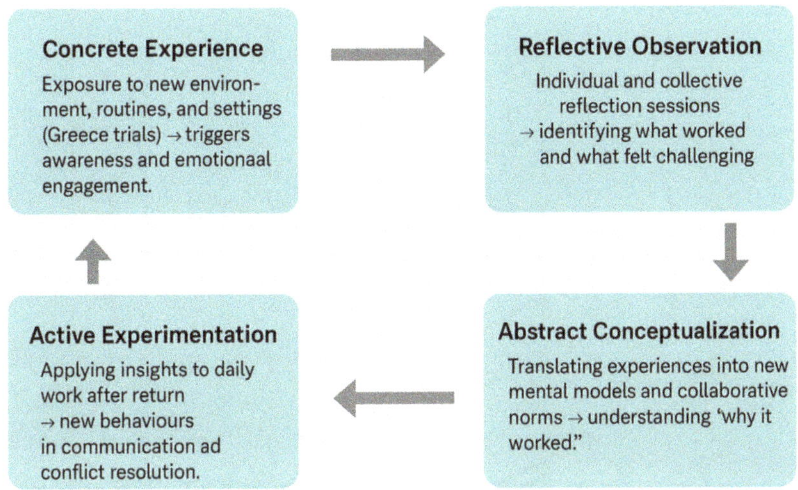


**Figure 4. Experiential Learning Cycle Applied to Workation Contexts**

Source: Generated by author with the help of AI (based on Kolb, 1984; Haeger and Lingham, 2014; Gheorghes, 2023).

(Gheorghes, 2023). Learning became embedded in daily practice rather than confined to formal training. The persistence of these patterns months later, visible in communication and conflict-resolution dynamics, suggests that experiential processes can generate durable behavioural shifts (Haeger and Lingham, 2014).

Building on the earlier discussion of multi-loop learning and its role in reflective practice, this section extends the analysis by positioning Kolb's experiential framework (1984) as complementary to the triple-loop learning perspective. Whereas previous arguments focused on the structural logic of learning loops, the emphasis here shifts toward the *depth* and *lived quality* of transformation. In this view, experiential cycles such as Kolb's (1984) describe *how* learning unfolds through action and reflection, while the triple-loop framework (Bateson, 1972; Argyris and Schön, 1978; Torbert, 2004; Tosey et al., 2012) illuminates *why* such learning reshapes identity, values, and collective meaning. In the Greece trials, this deeper level of reflection became visible as participants questioned long-held assumptions about productivity, time, and self-worth. Many described rediscovering intrinsic motivation, empathy, and a renewed sense of collective purpose. Through recursive dialogue and shared sense-making, learning transcended

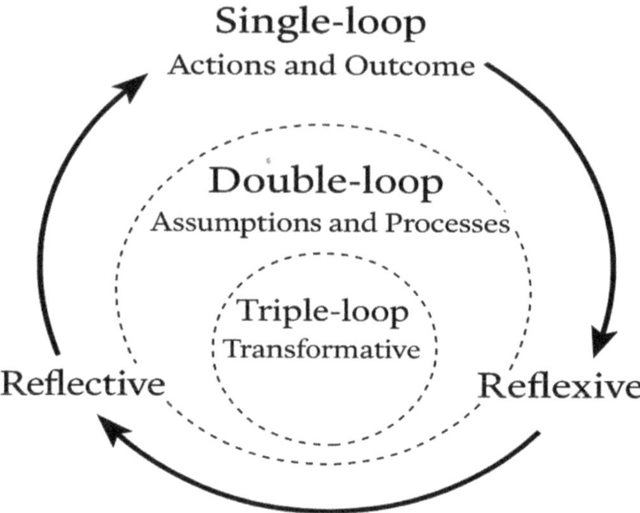


**Figure 5. Triple-Loop Learning and Identity Shift**

Source: Generated with AI based on Gheorghes (2023), adapted from Argyris and Schön (1978) and Kolb (1984).

individual performance to become *identity work*, a space where personal and organisational boundaries blurred, and transformation was internalised as a new way of being (Gheorghes, 2023). This evolution from *doing* to *thinking* to *becoming* reflects the essence of *triple-loop learning*: an awareness that growth is sustained through continuous self-inquiry and relational meaning-making (Torsey et al., 2012).

Figure 5 conceptualises the Greek projects across three layers of reflection, illustrating how experiential cycles evolved into deeper reflexive processes that redefined individual and organisational awareness. From a systems perspective, these loops operate as *feedback circuits* that sustain organisational viability (Beer, 1972) and enable adaptation in complex environments (Snowden, 2003). In this light, reflection is no longer a side activity but an *operational mechanism*, a dynamic process that links learning to resilience, a theme further developed in the findings section.

While the convergence of Soft HRM (Truss et al., 1997; Gill, 1999), Social Exchange Theory (Blau, 1967), and experiential learning frameworks (Kolb, 1984; Argyris and Schön, 1978) highlights the emancipatory potential of autonomy, it also exposes a latent tension. The optimism of human-centred models presupposes reciprocity and trust, yet autonomy can easily evolve into self-surveillance when organisational cultures valorise visibility and emotional labour. Critical management scholars have long argued that discourses of flexibility may conceal new forms of control, shifting responsibility for well-being from institutions to individuals (Fleming, 2014; Costea, Crump and Amiridis, 2008).

In hybrid and post-pandemic contexts, this paradox becomes sharper: employees internalise managerial expectations under the guise of freedom, echoing Foucault's (1977) notion of productive power, understood as a mode of control that operates through internalised norms and self-regulation rather than direct supervision, and neo-Marxist critiques of self-exploitation in cognitive capitalism, which describe how knowledge workers may over-extend themselves when performance and availability become closely tied to personal identity (Han, 2017). Situating workations within this critical lens enables a balanced interpretation, recognising both their liberating and disciplinary potentials.

Yet as in all adaptive systems, growth also brings vulnerability. The Effort–Reward Imbalance (ERI) model (Siegrist, 1996) offers a crucial lens for understanding this tension. ERI conceptualises strain as the result of a mismatch: when high effort is not met with proportional reward (recognition, support) or recovery, individuals experience emotional exhaustion and disengagement (Kunz, 2019). The Greece follow-up data illustrated this mechanism with precision. Although most participants described the workation as energising and autonomy-enhancing, several reported difficulties in re-adjusting to conventional routines and in disconnecting from work afterwards (Gheorghes, 2023). In other words, the same autonomy that supported growth during the experience also blurred boundaries upon return. Thus, the ERI model reinforces that sustainable well-being in flexible work systems depends on maintaining a dynamic balance between effort, reward, and rest. This was evident in the May 2023 follow-up survey, where multiple respondents noted challenges in re-establishing personal and professional limits once back in standard work environments.

Taken together, these frameworks (Soft HRM, Social Exchange Theory, Experiential Learning, Triple-Loop Learning, and Effort–Reward Imbalance) form a coherent theoretical foundation for understanding workations as both individual and organisational phenomena. They collectively demonstrate that performance emerges not from control but from reflection, and that belonging grows not from hierarchy but from reciprocity. In a context defined by disruption, these insights reaffirm that resilience depends less

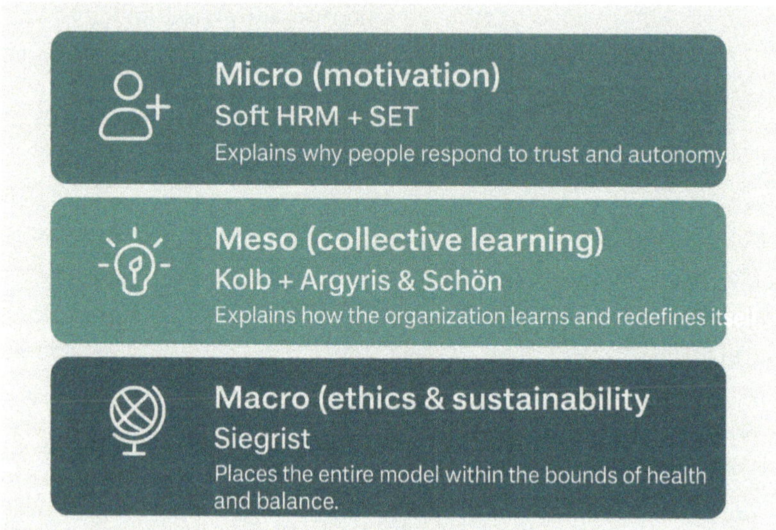


**Figure 6. Multi-Level Theoretical Architecture**

Source: Generated by the author with the help of AI (ChatGPT, 2025).

on stability than on a collective capacity to learn, unlearn, and reconstruct meaning together (Rao, 2016; Marr, 2023).

Figure 6 summarises the multi-level architecture underpinning the analysis. At the micro level, Soft HRM and Social Exchange Theory explain individual motivation through trust and reciprocity. At the meso level, Kolb and Argyris and Schön capture the collective learning dynamics that sustain adaptation. At the macro level, Siegrist's Effort–Reward framework outlines the ethical boundaries within which autonomy remains viable. Together, these levels form an integrated learning system in which performance, reflection, and well-being co-evolve.

## Methodological Lens and Case Context – Workations as Living Systems

The empirical foundation of this study is grounded in an interpretivist and case-based research design, where observation, reflection, and meaning-making were central to understanding the human dynamics behind organisational adaptation. The Greece Workation initiatives of *Company L* were not designed as discrete HR projects but as evolving social experiments embedded in the firm's strategic and cultural fabric. This approach reflects the interpretive tradition in organisational research, which conceives reality as co-constructed through interaction, dialogue, and shared sense-making (Lincoln and Guba, 1985). The inquiry, therefore, did not aim to isolate variables or identify causal mechanisms, but to explore how experience and context interacted to produce new forms of learning, engagement, and belonging.

*Company L* is a small digital enterprise based in Cluj-Napoca, Romania, employing around forty professionals across software development, design, and project management. Like many technology-driven firms in Central and Eastern Europe, it faced post-pandemic fatigue, employee turnover, and the erosion of informal cohesion caused by prolonged remote work (Al-Habaibeh and Wilkesmann, 2021). In early 2022, the leadership team, initially cautious about unconventional HR practices, agreed to pilot a short-term workation in Greece. The initiative, later known as *Greece 1.0*, brought together twenty-two volunteers who relocated their work environment for ten days. Because participants covered their own expenses, the trial was experienced as a voluntary learning journey rather than a company-funded incentive (Gheorghes, 2023).

The first trial combined remote work during standard hours with peer-led evening reflections. Participants used their usual digital collaboration tools while dedicating time to structured discussions about productivity, motivation, and team cohesion. The environment itself became an instrument of inquiry. By stepping outside routine settings, participants observed their behaviours and relationships in new configurations, revealing both individual and collective learning loops. Data from Greece 1.0 included three complementary sources: structured post-event surveys, field notes, and analytics from *FocusD*, an internal AI-based platform monitoring stress and concentration. The FocusD data showed a measurable decline in stress indicators compared with baseline office periods, corroborated by qualitative reflections that described higher creativity, psychological safety, and mutual trust (Gheorghes, 2023).

Encouraged by these outcomes, the organisation launched Greece 2.0 in September 2022, expanding participation to thirty-four individuals, including several partners and collaborators. The inclusion of partners introduced a new social variable, family integration within the work environment, which reinforced perceptions of work–life fusion and inclusivity (Haeger and Lingham, 2014). This second phase incorporated structured reflection workshops based on Kolb's experiential learning cycle, encouraging participants to transform insights into actionable commitments. One-month follow-up reflections indicated that improvements in focus, collaboration, and morale were sustained beyond the event (Gheorghes, 2023).

The methodological orientation followed a mixed-method logic that integrated quantitative, qualitative, and reflexive components. Three surveys were conducted at distinct time points: immediately after *Greece 1.0*, following *Greece 2.0*, and one year later, in May 2023. This temporal layering allowed the study to capture both short-term impressions and long-term behavioural shifts. The first survey examined efficiency and emotional well-being, the second explored collaboration and creativity, and the third assessed sustained commitment and cultural alignment. Each combined Likert-scale measurement with open-ended responses, enabling both statistical and thematic interpretation. Thematic coding of open-ended data followed Braun and Clarke's (2006) principles of inductive analysis, identifying recurrent patterns related to trust, motivation, and self-efficacy. Participants represented diverse functional roles within Company L, including software developers (40%), project managers (25%), designers (20%), and support staff (15%). Gender distribution was balanced (52% female, 48% male), with an average tenure of 3.2 years. The Likert-scale items ranged from 1 ("strongly disagree") to 5 ("strongly agree"), and Cronbach's alpha coefficients exceeded 0.80 across scales, ensuring internal consistency.

To complement the subjective data, *FocusD* analytics provided continuous behavioural insights into cognitive strain and productivity. This triangulation strengthened the study's validity by linking self-reported perceptions to quantifiable indicators, an increasingly recommended approach in contemporary research on organisational well-being (Bakker and Leiter, 2010). To enhance reliability, the thematic codes were independently reviewed by a second researcher familiar with qualitative methods, and discrepancies were resolved through discussion. This double-coding process reduced subjectivity and increased analytical robustness. The research design also explicitly recognised the reflexive role of the author. Acting as both initiator and observer, the researcher occupied a dual position of insider-participant and analytical interpreter. This positionality enabled direct observation of team interactions while preserving critical distance through systematic journaling and structured post-event interviews. Reflexivity functioned not as a methodological disclaimer but as an analytical tool, ensuring that meaning was co-created transparently and grounded in context (Finlay, 2002).

Ethical integrity was maintained throughout. Participation was voluntary, written informed consent was obtained, and all data were anonymised and securely stored. Participants were informed that the findings would be used exclusively for academic and organisational learning purposes. The study followed the ethical standards of Babeş-Bolyai University and complied with GDPR data-protection principles (Gheorghes, 2023).

Viewed through a methodological lens, the two Greece Workations can be interpreted as iterative design experiments situated within a living organisational system. Each iteration constituted a learning loop testing hypotheses about engagement and well-being, observing outcomes, and integrating feedback into subsequent cycles. The leadership's progression from scepticism to sponsorship mirrored the recursive structure of organisational learning described by Argyris and Schön (1978), where action and reflection become mutually reinforcing.

The integration of quantitative, qualitative, and reflexive methods transformed the workations from HR initiatives into instruments of diagnosis and renewal. They demonstrated that an organisation can learn not merely about its members but *through* its members. By treating experience as data and reflection as analysis, the project blurred conventional distinctions between work and inquiry. In doing so, it aligned with systems-thinking perspectives that view organisations as living entities capable of self-observation and adaptive transformation (Senge, 1990). The methodological design thus operated as both research process and intervention, evidence that the act of studying a system can itself become a moment of collective learning.

## Findings – The Adaptive Journey from Doing to Being

The Greece Workation initiatives revealed not a linear project but an unfolding process of organisational self-discovery. Performance and belonging, once treated as separate domains, became intertwined practices through which people learned how to think, act, and be together. The two editions formed successive loops of adaptation, each deepening awareness and redefining what it meant to work well. The process echoed Argyris and Schön's (1978) concept of *learning-in-action*, in which behaviour, cognition, and identity evolve along a single experiential continuum.

The first edition, *Greece 1.0*, embodied the **doing phase**. It began as an act of curiosity, a willingness to test what flexibility could mean in real time. For many participants, it was their first experience of working abroad, and

Table 2. Comparative Evolution of Key Performance and Well-being Indicators across Workation Phases

| Indicator | Office Baseline | Greece 1.0 | Greece 2.0 | Δ Change |
|---|---|---|---|---|
| Stress peaks | 72% | 41% | 38% | ↓47% |
| Collaboration | 58% | 74% | 87% | ↑29% |
| Self-efficacy | 64% | 81% | 90% | ↑26% |

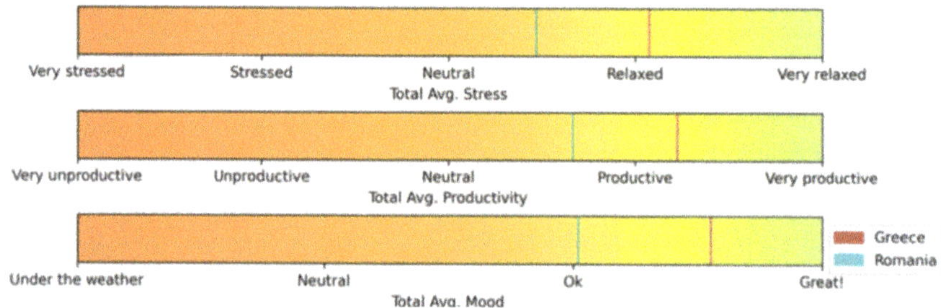


Figure 7. FocusD Dashboard – Stress, Productivity, and Mood Comparison (Greece vs. Romania)

Source: Generated with FocusD analytics, adapted from Gheorghes (2023), internal survey dataset.

the novelty brought both excitement and disorientation. Quantitative data confirmed a visible uplift: task completion rates increased, focus sharpened, and 80 percent of respondents rated their productivity above their usual average. *FocusD* analytics recorded lower stress peaks and steadier concentration levels (Gheorghes, 2023).

This table summarises the quantitative shifts observed between the office baseline and the two Greece Workation editions. Stress peaks dropped by nearly half, while collaboration and self-efficacy increased by more than a quarter, signalling measurable progress along the *doing–thinking–being* continuum. These data provide the empirical foundation for Figure 3, which visualises the same patterns captured by FocusD analytics.

Figure 7 summarises aggregate changes across both workations. Stress indicators decreased by almost half, while collaboration and self-efficacy rose by more than a quarter. These metrics substantiate the qualitative accounts of renewed energy and team cohesion observed during and after the trials. Participants repeatedly described the ability to "get things done without interruption." The change of environment catalysed creativity and perspective, supporting Rainoldi and Ladkin's (2022) argument that mobility enhances cognitive agility. Yet this freedom also carried a subtle cost. Several participants reported difficulty drawing boundaries between work and leisure, signalling the early presence of *effort–reward imbalance* (Siegrist, 1996). The same energy that sustained focus risked tipping into overcommitment. Freedom, it seemed, could both liberate and consume.

One participant reflected: *"It felt like rediscovering colleagues as people, not just names on Slack."* Another wrote: *"Working under the same sun where we shared breakfast turned deadlines into conversations."* Such remarks illustrate how emotional proximity and informal learning reshaped both task focus and belonging. Not all participants experienced the transition as effortless. A minority (approx. 12 %) reported post-workation fatigue and difficulty readjusting to office rhythm. Within the Effort–Reward Imbalance model, these accounts underline the risk of over-identification with work, where emotional energy continues to exceed perceived reward once the immersive context ends.

The second edition, *Greece 2.0*, shifted into the **thinking phase**. Informed by the first trial's lessons, the programme was redesigned around reflection, feedback, and collective inquiry. Sessions structured around Kolb's experiential learning cycle prompted participants to analyse what had worked, what had failed, and why. The inclusion of partners added an emotional dimension, reinforcing the idea of work–life fusion as lived experience rather than abstract ideal (Haeger and Lingham, 2014).

Quantitative data confirmed a new layer of depth. 94 percent of participants reported stronger team cohesion; 87 percent observed improved communication and trust (Gheorghes, 2023). Qualitative narratives revealed a cognitive shift from individual performance to collective intelligence. Employees described *Greece 2.0* as "a living workshop in collaboration," where productivity no longer depended on metrics but on connection. These accounts resonate with Edmondson's (1999) theory of *psychological safety*, which identifies trust and openness as conditions for innovation. Informal dialogues, often over shared meals or evening walks, became the generative ground for creative problem-solving, reflecting Craddock's (2021) insight that relational proximity amplifies team learning.

This second phase also reconfigured leadership. What began as an employee-led experiment evolved into a co-owned practice endorsed by management. The shift closed the Social Exchange Theory (Blau, 1967) feedback loop: trust, initially offered by employees, was reciprocated institutionally. The mutual recognition transformed autonomy into alignment, validating the soft HRM premise that commitment and empowerment strengthen each other (Truss et al., 1997). Leadership, in this context, became less about direction and more about resonance about creating the conditions under which others could thrive (Bakker and Leiter, 2010). This evolution was also reflected in participants' experiences, many noting that they "felt seen, trusted, and supported" in ways that strengthened their confidence in the company's direction. The shift from supervision to relational presence signalled a leadership style grounded not in oversight, but in attunement and shared ownership.

The final phase, captured by the follow-up survey in May 2023, represented "being", the internalisation of new attitudes and collective identity. Eight months after the last workation, engagement levels remained higher, burnout scores lower, and emotional attachment to the company stronger (Gheorghes, 2023). 92 percent of respondents stated they felt closer to their colleagues and more motivated to contribute. Thematic analysis surfaced recurring words (belonging, trust, renewal), signalling that reflection had become part of the organisational DNA.

Across both projects, a unifying thread emerged, psychological safety as both precondition and outcome. The workations created a space where vulnerability could coexist with ambition. In the absence of rigid hierarchy, dialogue replaced instruction, and authenticity became a form of collective intelligence. Participants recounted moments of breakthrough insight born from casual exchanges, reinforcing the principle that trust is not an accessory to performance but its infrastructure.

Still, the findings reveal a tension intrinsic to autonomy. The very freedom that nurtures innovation also exposes fragility. Post-workation surveys captured this paradox: while the majority experienced empowerment, a few described difficulty returning to conventional routines or maintaining focus afterward. This *post-workation fatigue* echoes Siegrist's (1996) warning that when effort outpaces recognition or rest, motivation erodes. Autonomy without containment risks collapsing under its own weight. As an insider researcher, I was aware that my dual role (both facilitator and analyst) could influence participants' openness. To mitigate bias, reflective journaling was used to capture observations and emotions in real time, later triangulated with anonymised survey feedback. This reflexive approach ensured that the analysis remained both empathetic and critical, acknowledging the interpretive nature of insider inquiry (Finlay, 2002).

Context also matters. Nevertheless, the benefits of such autonomy presuppose access to portable work and stable connectivity, privileges not equally distributed across labour markets. Future iterations should therefore integrate inclusion criteria and digital-equity safeguards to prevent reinforcing structural divides within and beyond the organisation. The workation model thrives in knowledge-intensive, digitally enabled industries but remains impractical where performance depends on physical coordination or fixed outputs (Bassiouny and Wilkesmann, 2023). Participants themselves acknowledged this limitation, situating their experience within a privileged context of technological infrastructure and cultural readiness for flexibility.

Taken together, the data portray the workation not as an HR experiment but as a living system, one that learns, adapts, and redefines its own logic. Through iterative cycles of experience, reflection, and identity-building, *Company L* transformed a logistical initiative into a collective act of sense-making. Performance became relational, belonging became operational, and learning became cultural.

In tracing this adaptive journey, from doing to thinking to being, the Greece Workations illustrate that resilience is not built by resisting

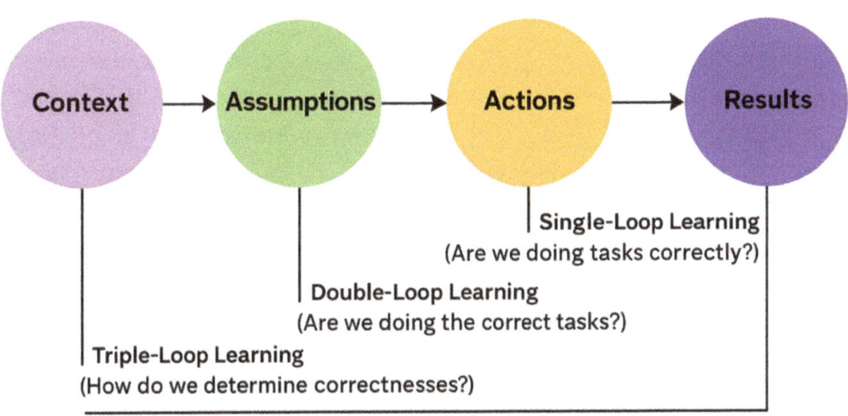


Figure 8. Adaptive Learning Path across Workation Cycles

Source: Generated with AI based on Gheorghes (2023), adapted from Argyris and Schön (1978), Kolb (1984), and Atkinson (2019)

uncertainty but by metabolising it. Adaptation, in this sense, is less a response to disruption than its re-interpretation as opportunity. As Rao (2016) suggests, truly adaptive organisations do not learn to survive change; they learn to inhabit it.

This visual summarises the integrated process of experiential and reflexive learning observed during the Greece 1.0 and 2.0 trials, illustrating the progression from single-loop (action) to double-loop (reflection) and triple-loop (identity reconstruction) learning. It bridges the empirical findings with the forthcoming discussion on purposeful design and strategic adaptation.

Given the space constraints of a book chapter, the analysis presented here synthesises only the most representative patterns emerging from the three survey waves and the FocusD analytics. The complete dataset, including descriptive statistics, long-term tracking results, thematic codes, and the full qualitative corpus can be explored in detail in the author's dissertation, *Exploring the Impact of Workation Initiatives: Insights from the Greece Workation Trial Projects* (Gheorgheş, 2023).

## Discussion – From Flexibility to Purposeful Design

As a microcosm of the Romanian digital and creative sectors, Company L's experience reflects a broader regional shift: from outsourcing efficiency to learning-oriented organisational ecologies that internalise talent sustainability in volatile markets. The findings of the Greece Workations suggest that flexibility alone does not create meaningful change; it is the structure behind flexibility that determines whether new work models can sustain engagement and performance. While the two workations began as creative responses to post-pandemic fatigue, their success was ultimately shaped by design rather than spontaneity. This resonates with Senge's (1990) argument that learning organisations thrive when systems and culture are aligned around a shared purpose. In the case of Company L, the workations served as design experiments in human-centred performance combining autonomy with reflection, and personal well-being with collective accountability.

The results demonstrated that belonging can function as a performance driver rather than a secondary outcome. As Blau (1967) explains through Social Exchange Theory, reciprocity is a fundamental element of sustainable motivation: people give back to systems that invest in them. Employees who felt trusted to self-manage during the workations reciprocated with higher

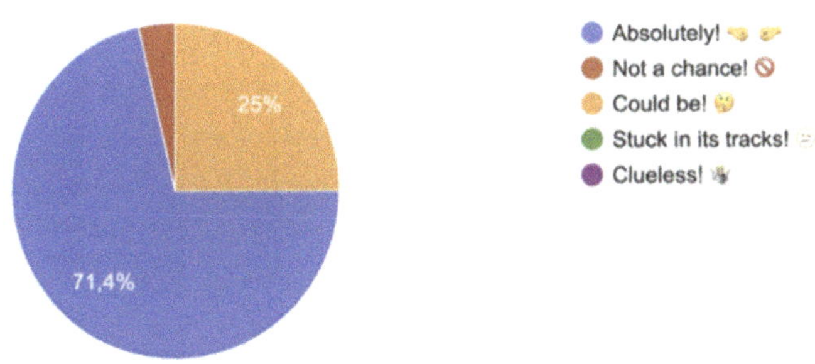


**Figure 9. Perceived Impact of the Greece Workation on Work–Life Fusion**

Source: Adapted from Gheorghes (2023), internal post-workation survey (n = 28).

engagement and innovation (Gheorghes, 2023). This exchange extended beyond the individual to the collective, turning trust into an organisational resource. The sense of shared ownership created during Greece 1.0 evolved into institutional confidence by Greece 2.0, confirming Truss et al.'s (1997) view that soft HR practices build long-term commitment by empowering employees to act from intrinsic motivation. When trust is institutionalised, it becomes a source of structural stability in volatile environments (Marr, 2023).

As illustrated in Figure 9, more than 70% of participants perceived a clear improvement in their work–life fusion following the Greece workation, reinforcing the qualitative findings on engagement and belonging.

At the same time, the findings highlight the limits of flexibility as a universal solution. Workations require specific conditions, digital maturity, adaptable leadership, and psychological safety to succeed (Edmondson, 1999). The model works best in knowledge-based sectors, where outcomes depend on collaboration and cognitive effort rather than physical production (Bassiouny and Wilkesmann, 2023). For industries that rely on standardisation or regulatory constraints, such as healthcare or manufacturing, the same level of autonomy may be neither feasible nor desirable. As Siegrist (1996) warned, when effort outweighs reward or when boundaries remain unclear, the motivational benefits of autonomy can transform into chronic strain. The experience of a few participants who reported post-workation fatigue illustrates this paradox. What empowers some can overwhelm others if organisational structures fail to contain the emotional demands of continuous flexibility.

The findings also point to a deeper transformation in the nature of leadership. In traditional settings, leaders manage performance through oversight and control. Within the Greece Workations, leadership was distributed and relational. Senior managers who initially doubted the project became facilitators of learning, embodying what McGregor (1960) conceptualized as Theory Y leadership: the belief that people perform best when trusted to take responsibility. This shift from supervision to facilitation represents a subtle but powerful evolution in organisational culture. It supports the view that modern HR systems must move from *management of people* to *partnership with people*, where leaders act as sensemakers rather than controllers (Gill, 1999).

A critical insight emerging from the discussion is that flexibility, to be sustainable, must evolve into purposeful design. Haeger and Lingham (2014) describe *work–life fusion* as the intentional blending of professional and personal roles in a way that enhances both. The Greece Workations provided this intentionality by embedding reflection within the workflow. Structured group discussions and personal journals turned flexibility into a guided process of sensemaking. This aligns with Kolb's (1984) experiential learning cycle, where experience without reflection remains incomplete. The design of the workations translated reflection into performance metrics and belonging into a cultural resource. Participants learned to associate well-being not with the absence of work but with the quality of connection, both human and organisational.

The discussion also reveals that organisational transformation depends on what Argyris and Schön (1978) termed *double-loop learning*: the ability to question underlying assumptions. For Company L, this meant re-examining the implicit belief that productivity requires physical proximity and managerial control. The data from FocusD and post-surveys challenged this assumption empirically. Employees performed effectively in decentralised settings, suggesting that structure can exist without hierarchy. This realisation redefined the company's understanding of performance as a function of clarity, not presence. In doing so, it positioned belonging as an operational capability, an enabler of adaptability in uncertain conditions.

A further implication concerns leadership communication and inclusion. The decision to involve partners in Greece 2.0 expanded the emotional ecosystem of the company, bridging personal and professional spheres. This inclusion humanised corporate culture and strengthened psychological safety. It demonstrated that the boundaries between work and life are not obstacles to performance but potential sources of creativity when managed with empathy (Haeger and Lingham, 2014). The initiative blurred the traditional distinction between employee and person, turning individuality into a source of innovation.

Nevertheless, the workation model carries risks of overextension. As Rao (2016) notes, agility must not be confused with instability; without balance, rapid adaptation can lead to organisational fatigue. The sustainability of workations, therefore, depends on institutionalising pauses, or moments where the organisation reflects collectively before scaling new practices. Reflection, not acceleration, becomes the mechanism of growth. The success of Greece 1.0 and 2.0 was not the result of continuous expansion but of iterative refinement. The leadership team's willingness to learn from feedback and adjust scope between editions transformed the project from an experiment into a replicable model of adaptive HR design.

From a strategic perspective, the workation model represents a shift from flexibility as benefit to flexibility as learning architecture. It reframes autonomy as a structured process supported by measurement, dialogue, and ethics. This approach connects directly to the principles of sustainable HRM, which emphasise employee well-being as a precondition for long-term organisational performance (Bakker and Leiter, 2010). In essence, the Greece Workations turned disruption into design: they transformed the uncertainty of hybrid work into a disciplined practice of reflection. By doing so, they demonstrated that the future of HR is neither hard nor soft, but *boundless*, capable of bridging autonomy and care through deliberate, ethical systems of engagement. Despite its insights, this study remains contextually bounded. Company L represents a small-sized digital enterprise operating within a relatively high-trust culture and advanced technological infrastructure, factors that may not generalise across industries or geographies. Future research could explore longitudinal impacts of workations across multiple sectors or examine how cultural and generational differences mediate the relationship between autonomy, belonging, and performance.

# Learning Beyond Boundaries: Strategic Implications for Sustainable Workations

The Greece Workation initiatives demonstrate that flexibility alone cannot sustain transformation; it becomes valuable only when embedded within a coherent system of purpose, structure, and reflection. In this sense, flexibility functions less as a benefit and more as a test of organisational design maturity. The trials revealed that learning organisations, those able to integrate experience into adaptive systems, can turn uncertainty into discipline and autonomy into capability (Senge, 1990; Gheorghes, 2023).

## Purpose-driven design

The Greek experience confirmed that purpose gives direction to flexibility and prevents it from dissolving into superficial change. Organisations that approach workations as morale boosters tend to reproduce existing patterns rather than reform them. The Company L trials succeeded because intent preceded logistics: the programme was designed to tackle burnout, restore cohesion, and stimulate creative focus. Kolb's (1984) experiential learning cycle (experience, reflection, conceptualisation, and experimentation) provided the interpretive spine of this design. The process demonstrated that reflection cannot remain an add-on; it must be operationalised as part of the workflow. Practically, this means that preparation and post-event integration are as strategic as the event itself. Sustainable design, therefore, depends on embedding cycles of reflection that transform insight into institutional knowledge.

## Leadership readiness and governance

Leadership proved decisive not as authority but as presence. The Greece trials showed that flexibility without leadership engagement risks ambiguity and cultural drift. As Edmondson (1999) observes, psychological safety emerges not from permission but from participation. When senior managers moved from oversight to involvement, working alongside their teams, sharing reflections, and modelling vulnerability, they redefined control as sensemaking. This shift aligns with McGregor's (1960) Theory Y and Gill's (1999) argument that facilitative leadership transforms motivation into ownership. Yet participation alone is not sufficient: governance provides the scaffolding that keeps experimentation accountable. Clearly defined decision-making norms and risk protocols allow freedom to coexist with clarity. A practical solution drawn from Company L's case was the creation of "reflection stewards" responsible for capturing learning and translating it into tangible post-workation improvements.

## Cultural and infrastructural readiness

Readiness emerged as a double condition, technological and cultural. While digital infrastructure enables distributed collaboration, it is the cultural architecture that sustains trust and coherence (Bassiouny and Wilkesmann, 2023). The Greece projects revealed that autonomy without relational clarity leads to friction. Pre-departure workshops, conducted to align expectations, transformed potential uncertainty into shared responsibility (Gheorghes, 2023). This shows that readiness is not an audit of systems but a negotiation of meaning. As such, one practical recommendation is that organisations conduct *cultural readiness dialogues* alongside technical assessments before launching hybrid or off-site initiatives. By doing so, they ensure that freedom is experienced as partnership rather than exposure.

## Well-being governance and ethical design

Every model of autonomy carries an ethical dimension. Siegrist's (1996) Effort–Reward Imbalance theory cautions that enthusiasm can collapse into fatigue if the energy invested exceeds recovery or recognition. Data from the Greece trials showed precisely this duality: while motivation spiked during the workations, several participants reported post-event exhaustion (Gheorghes, 2023). Sustainable flexibility, therefore, requires intentional recovery cycles with lighter workloads before departure, decompression days after return, and structured reflection debriefs to consolidate learning. These elements are not auxiliary; they constitute the ethical infrastructure of sustainable HRM. As Bakker and Leiter (2010) argue, well-being is not the absence of strain but the presence of resources that enable renewal. From a governance standpoint, HR leaders should treat well-being as a strategic KPI, embedding rest, reflection, and recognition into every cycle of experimentation.

## Measurement and continuous learning

Measurement was another point where the Greece initiatives departed from standard practice. Many organisations rely on anecdotal satisfaction surveys, which capture sentiment but not system learning. Company L integrated FocusD analytics, tracking stress and concentration patterns with qualitative reflection sessions, generating evidence for double-loop learning (Argyris and Schön, 1978). This hybrid method not only measured performance but also interrogated the assumptions behind performance itself. Data became dialogue, enabling the team to adjust processes in real time rather than retrospectively. For future practice, measurement should evolve from evaluation to co-reflection: combining behavioural analytics with qualitative insight to capture both the cognitive and affective dimensions of performance.

## Scalability and inclusion

Finally, the Greece model highlighted that scalability is as much a question of fairness as feasibility. While the format thrived in a digital, mid-sized enterprise, replication across sectors requires differentiation. Hybrid models, such as rotating participation or local reflection hubs, can maintain the core learning dynamic without disrupting operational continuity (Bassiouny and Wilkesmann, 2023). Yet inclusion must go beyond logistics. Those unable to travel should still engage in the reflective and social elements virtually, preserving collective belonging as a shared right rather than an earned privilege (Edmondson, 1999). Inclusivity, when embedded structurally, transforms workations from experiments in flexibility into cultures of learning.

Taken together, these findings underscore that workations succeed not because they disrupt routines but because they redesign the architecture of learning. Their sustainability depends on six interlocking levers: clear purpose, participatory leadership, cultural readiness, ethical well-being governance, integrated measurement, and inclusive scalability. Each lever balances autonomy with structure, ensuring that freedom does not drift into fragmentation. The Greece trials demonstrate that flexibility becomes strategic only when it is both designed and disciplined anchored in purpose yet adaptive to context. In this sense, the future of HR lies not in creating looser structures but in cultivating systems capable of reflection, renewal, and responsibility. When organisations design for learning rather than control, flexibility ceases to be a response to disruption and becomes a capability for evolution itself (Senge, 1990; Gheorghes, 2023).

## Summarising the Learning Journey: Towards a Fusion Mindset

The Greece Workation initiatives revealed more than functional flexibility; they showed how organisations learn to redesign themselves through experience. Across the two experiments, performance evolved from task efficiency into shared reflection, and belonging shifted from sentiment into structure. This progression confirmed that adaptation is not a technical process but a cognitive and emotional one; organisations do not transform by adding systems, but by reinterpreting what they already know (Senge, 1990; Gheorghes, 2023). Learning, in this context, becomes both method and outcome: awareness institutionalised as practice. In knowledge-based economies such as Central and Eastern Europe's digital sector, workations exemplify how small firms can pioneer systemic learning architectures ahead of institutional HR transformation.

To situate these findings within the broader transformation of work, Ulrich's (2024) **STEPED framework** offers a valuable interpretive lens. It highlights six interconnected forces: Social, Technological, Economic, Political, Environmental, and Demographic that reshape organisational capability and redefine what sustainable human resource management entails.

### STEPED

1. **Social trends**: expectations, mental health, engagement, burnout, mobility, belonging, trust, 100-year life expectancy
2. **Technology and AI trends**: AI changes in accessing information for decisions (genAI) and efficiency (agenticAI), robotics, quantum computing
3. **Economic trends**: uncertainty, shorter life cycles (speed), increased intangible value, ecosystems
4. **Political trends**: trade wars, geo political conflicts, regulation, human capital reporting (SEC), refugees, immigration, politicalization, nationalism
5. **Environmental trends**: social citizenship, planet stewardship, climate, stakeholder capitalism
6. **Demographic trends**: multiple generations in the workforce, birthrate fluctuations, have vs. have nots

**Figure 10. STEPED Framework – External Drivers of HR Evolution**

Source: Adapted from Ulrich (2024), "How Do You Feel About the Future of HR?", LinkedIn Pulse

Viewed through this framework, the Greece Workations emerge as a microcosm of systemic adaptation. Socially, they addressed the post-pandemic erosion of connection, transforming belonging into a governance mechanism rather than a cultural afterthought. Technologically, they demonstrated how data can evolve into dialogue: the FocusD analytics platform turned AI-driven metrics into reflective learning tools. Economically, they reframed well-being not as an expenditure but as a productivity strategy, showing that engagement and performance are mutually reinforcing. Politically, the voluntary, participatory nature of the workations reflected a form of internal micro-democracy, where employees co-authored the boundaries of autonomy and accountability. Environmentally, the very act of working from Greece brought the ecological dimension of mobility into focus, inviting reflection on the sustainability of work-travel models. Demographically, the inclusion of diverse age groups and family structures illustrated that flexibility must adapt to different life stages, needs, and rhythms of participation.

Analysed critically, STEPED situates the Greece trials as anticipatory responses to macro-level disruptions. What appeared locally as HR innovation represented, in fact, an organisational rehearsal for the complex equilibrium that global work systems must now achieve, balancing autonomy with care, efficiency with empathy, and innovation with ethical constraint. The framework thus bridges micro-practice and macro-tendency, revealing how reflective learning at the organisational level mirrors structural evolution in society at large.

At the same time, the Greece experience exposed the fragility of human-centred design. The workations succeeded precisely because they were intentional, bounded, and inclusive. Without such design integrity, autonomy risks collapsing into fatigue; without empathy, systems harden into bureaucracy; without reflection, innovation dissolves into noise. The balance of these tensions between doing and being, freedom and care, individual and collective, defines what this study terms a *fusion mindset*. This mindset is not a management technique but a mode of consciousness: the ability to transform paradox into purpose.

For leaders, this implies reimagining flexibility as a governance principle rather than a benefit. The integration of Kolb's (1984) experiential learning cycle, Blau's (1967) reciprocity logic, and Truss et al.'s (1997) soft-HRM foundations provides a pragmatic architecture for operationalising trust without losing coherence. Yet, as Siegrist (1996) reminds us, commitment must remain balanced by reward and recovery. Institutionalising rest, fairness, and reflection with the same rigour as performance metrics safeguards this balance and preserves the ethical dimension of flexibility.

Ultimately, the Greece Workations suggest that innovation in work design is less about *place* than about *consciousness*. They signal a transition from managing performance to cultivating reflection as a strategic capability (Rao, 2016). When re-examined through the STEPED lens, they appear as a micro-model for the adaptive organisation of the future, one that learns to absorb disruption without losing integrity. Summarising this journey, the central argument becomes clear: the future of work will not be defined by its format, hybrid, remote, or flexible, but by its mindset. It will be reflective by design, integrating performance and belonging as inseparable dimensions of the same living system. Building on these findings, future research should investigate how reflective work models can be institutionalised within hybrid organisations beyond pilot projects. Longitudinal comparisons between firms that integrate structured reflection (such as workations or learning retreats) and those that rely solely on remote policies could illuminate how adaptive capacity evolves over time. In this sense, workations may represent not the end point of flexibility, but the starting point of a new organisational learning paradigm grounded in consciousness, care, and co-creation.

In conclusion, the Greece Workation Trials illustrate how workations can serve as micro-systems of adaptive learning where doing, thinking, and being converge into sustained belonging. Theoretical implications extend beyond HR practice: workations reveal the organisation as a living system capable of self-correction through reflexive experience. Future research should examine comparative models across industries and cultures, employ quantitative validation of adaptive-learning outcomes, and pursue longitudinal tracking beyond twelve months to evaluate behavioural persistence and systemic maturity.

## Acknowledgement

*Editorial refinements, grammar, and visual formatting were supported by OpenAI's ChatGPT (GPT-5, 2025), while all theoretical synthesis, analysis, and interpretive insights remain entirely the author's own.*

# References


Al-Habaibeh, A., Watkins, M., Waried, K. and Bathaei Javareshk, M. (2021). 'Challenges and opportunities of remotely working from home during Covid-19 pandemic', *Global Transitions*, 3, pp. 99–108. Available at: https://doi.org/10.1016/j.glt.2021.11.001 (Accessed: 4 November 2025).

Argyris, C. and Schön, D. (1978). *Organizational Learning: A Theory of Action Perspective.* Reading, MA: Addison-Wesley.

Bakker, A. B. and Leiter, M. P. (2010). *Work Engagement: A Handbook of Essential Theory and Research.* New York: Psychology Press.

Balzac, S. R. (2014). *Organizational Psychology for Managers.* New York: Springer.

Bass, B. M. (1990). 'From transactional to transformational leadership: Learning to share the vision', *Organizational Dynamics*, 18(3), pp. 19–31. doi: 10.1016/0090-2616(90)90061-S.

Bassiouny, M. and Wilkesmann, M. (2023). 'Going on workation – Is tourism research ready to take off? Exploring an emerging phenomenon of hybrid tourism', *Tourism Management Perspectives,* 45, pp. 1–9. DOI: 10.1016/j.tmp.2023.101096.

Bateson, G. (1972). *Steps to an Ecology of Mind.* San Francisco: Chandler.

Bennie, L. (2015). *The Value of Wellness in the Workplace: A Perspective of the Employee–Organisation Relationship in the South African Labour Market.* Singapore: Springer Nature.

Blau, P. M. (1967). *Exchange and Power in Social Life.* 2nd edn. New Brunswick: Transaction Publishers.

Carter, D. R. et al. (2020). 'Functional leadership in interteam contexts', *Current Directions in Psychological Science*, 29(5), pp. 1–7.

Costea, B., Crump, N. and Amiridis, K. (2008). 'Managerialism, the therapeutic habitus and the self in contemporary organizing', *Human Relations*, 61(5), pp. 661–685. doi: 10.1177/0018726708090533.

Edmondson, A. (1999) 'Psychological safety and learning behavior in work teams', *Administrative Science Quarterly,* 44(2), pp. 350–383.

Finlay, L. (2002). 'Negotiating the swamp: The opportunity and challenge of reflexivity in research practice', *Qualitative Research,* 2(2), pp. 209–230.

Fleming, P. (2014). *Resisting Work: The Corporatization of Life and Its Discontents.* Philadelphia: Temple University Press.

Foucault, M. (1977). *Discipline and Punish: The Birth of the Prison.* New York: Pantheon Books.

Gheorghes, R. (2023). *Exploring the Impact of Workation Initiatives: Insights from the Greece Workation Trial Projects.* Master's Thesis. Cluj-Napoca: Babeş-Bolyai University.

Gill, C. (1999). *Use of hard and soft models of HRM to illustrate the gap between rhetoric and reality in workforce management.* RMIT Business Working Paper Series. Melbourne: RMIT Business, Graduate School of Business.

Haeger, D. L. and Lingham, T. (2014). 'A trend toward work–life fusion: A multi-generational shift in technology use at work', *Technological Forecasting and Social Change,* 89, pp. 316–325. doi: 10.1016/j.techfore.2014.08.009.

Han, B.-C. (2017). *Psychopolitics: Neoliberalism and New Technologies of Power.* London: Verso Books.

Jenkinson, J., Oakley, C. and Mason, F. (2013) 'Teamwork: The art of being a leader and a team player', *Advances in Psychiatric Treatment*, 19(3), pp. 221–228. doi: 10.1192/apt.bp.111.009639.

Katsande, R., Farhana, N. and Devi, A. (2022). 'Hybrid models for remote work practices in the post-pandemic era: Prospects and challenges', *International Journal of Academic Research in Business and Social Sciences*, 12(11), pp. 430–443. doi: 10.6007/IJARBSS/v12-i11/15582.

Kolb, D. A. (1984). *Experiential learning: Experience as the source of learning and development.* Englewood Cliffs, NJ: Prentice-Hall.

Kroeber, A. L. and Kluckhohn, C. (1952). *Culture: A critical review of concepts and definitions.* Cambridge, MA: Peabody Museum Press.

Kunz, C. (2019). 'The influence of working conditions on health satisfaction, physical and mental health: Testing the effort–reward imbalance (ERI) model and its moderation with over-commitment using a representative sample of German employees (GSOEP)', *BMC Public Health*, 19, 1009. doi: 10.1186/s12889-019-7289-1.

Lund, S., Madgavkar, A., Manyika, J., Smit, S., Ellingrud, K. and Robinson, O. (2021). *The future of work after COVID-19.* McKinsey Global Institute. Available at: https://www.mckinsey.com/featured-insights/future-of-work/the-future-of-work-after-covid-19 (Accessed: 4 November 2025).

Lojeski, K. S. and Reilly, R. R. (2020). *The Power of Virtual Distance: A guide to productivity and happiness in the age of remote work.* Hoboken, NJ: John Wiley & Sons.

Marr, B. (2023). 'The eight biggest HR trends in 2024', *Forbes*, 18 December. Available at: https://www.forbes.com/sites/bernardmarr/2023/12/18/the-eight-biggest-hr-trends-in-2024/ (Accessed: 4 November 2025).

McGregor, D. (1960). *The Human Side of Enterprise.* New York: McGraw-Hill.

McLeod, S. (2025). 'Kolb's learning styles and experiential learning cycle', *Simply Psychology.* Available at: https://www.simplypsychology.org/learning-kolb.html (Accessed: 4 November 2025).

Muscalu, E. (2014). 'Organizational culture change in the organization', *Land Forces Academy Review*, 19(4), pp. 392–396.

Pecsek, B. (2018). 'Working on holiday: The theory and practice of workcation', *Balkans Journal of Emerging Trends in Social Sciences*, 1(1), pp. 1–13. doi: 10.31410/Balkans.JETSS.2018.1.1.1-13.

Rainoldi, M., Ladkin, A. and Buhalis, D. (2022). 'Blending work and leisure: a future digital worker hybrid lifestyle perspective', *Annals of Leisure Research*, 27(2), pp. 215–235. doi: 10.1080/11745398.2022.2070513.

Rao, T. V. (2016). *Performance Management: Toward Organizational Excellence.* New Delhi: SAGE Publications India.

Roger, L. M. (2022). 'Talent management – The real secret to retaining talent', *Harvard Business Review,* March. Available at: https://hbr.org/2022/03/the-real-secret-to-retaining-talent (Accessed: 4 November 2025).

Patti, I. and Scianna, P. (2023). 'Work and Vacation become Workation: new HR trends and practical implications', *Lexology*, 8 June. Available at: https://www.lexology.com/library/detail.aspx?g=bdd83b2e-4b0d-44d7-a124-9eba2e9ffe19 (Accessed: 4 November 2025).

Senge, P. M. (1990). *The Fifth Discipline: The Art and Practice of the Learning Organization.* New York: Doubleday.

Siegrist, J. (1996). 'Adverse health effects of high-effort/low-reward conditions', *Journal of Occupational Health Psychology,* 1(1), pp. 27–41. doi: 10.1037/1076-8998.1.1.27.

Thompson, B. Y. (2019). *The Digital Nomad Lifestyle: (Remote) Work/Leisure Balance, Privilege, and Constructed Community.* Cham: Springer Nature.

Torbert, W. R. (2004). *Action Inquiry: The Secret of Timely and Transforming Leadership.* San Francisco, CA: Berrett-Koehler Publishers.

Tosey, P., Visser, M. and Saunders, M.N.K. (2012). 'The origins and conceptualizations of "triple-loop learning": A critical review', *Management Learning*, 43(3), pp. 291–307.

Truss, C., Gratton, L., Hope-Hailey, V., Stiles, P. and Zaleska, J. (1997). *Soft and Hard Models of Human Resource Management: A Reappraisal.* London: Chartered Institute of Personnel and Development.

Ulrich, D. (2024). *'How Do You Feel About the Future of HR? Introducing Insights from the Inaugural STEPED Framework'*, LinkedIn Pulse, April. Available at: https://www.linkedin.com/pulse/how-do-you-feel-future-hr-introducing-insights-from-inaugural-ulrich-djzec/ (Accessed: 4 November 2025).

Voll, K., Gauger, F. and Pfnür, A. (2022). 'Work from anywhere: Traditional workation, coworkation and workation retreats: A conceptual review', *World Leisure Journal*, pp. 1–25. doi: 10.1080/16078055.2022.2134199.

Wilkesmann, M. and Bass iouny, M. (2025). 'From leisure to labor: How workations are reshaping hospitality and destination marketing in the era of New Work'. *Journal of Destination Marketing & Management*, 36, 100991.

# NAVIGATING COMPLEXITY: GROOVE-IN DYNAMICS ACROSS STARTUPS AND STATES

Laura Dragos-Radoi

*We can't control systems or figure them out. But we can dance with them!*

*— Donella Meadows*

This chapter explores how startups and state institutions navigate complexity through groove-in dynamics, the processes by which innovations become contextually embedded within their operational habitats. Drawing on the Cynefin framework, complexity theory, and organisational learning, it compares an entrepreneurial case (G-Start, a UK-based AI startup) with public sector digitalisation trajectories in Estonia and Romania. The analysis reframes groove-in from a narrow notion of adoption and increasing returns (Arthur, 1996) to a systemic model of co-evolution between actors and environments. Deliberately comparing entrepreneurial and governmental contexts reveals how complexity navigation principles transfer across domains while implementation must remain contextual. The central argument:

---

**Disclaimer:** This chapter draws on insights from entrepreneurial and public sector contexts. The startup case is based on direct observation and participation in an AI venture (2024), while the public sector analysis reflects experience in digitalization programs. Cases have been anonymised appropriately and represent illustrative examples rather than comprehensive empirical studies.

both startups and states face parallel challenges in navigating complexity, avoiding groupthink, and building adaptive capacity, but their solutions must differ according to habitat characteristics — market velocity versus democratic accountability, rapid iteration versus institutional trust. In doing so, it identifies the core competencies and learning architectures that enable resilience across both domains, while diagnosing how groupthink and institutional inertia inhibit adaptation. The chapter concludes by outlining a Startup-State Mindset: a shared set of principles for navigating complexity that emphasizes safe-to-fail experimentation, distributed sense-making, and trust-based systemic embedding.

## 1. Introduction: Sensing the Complexity Landscape

### 1.1. *The Emergence of Complexity as a Defining Feature*

Innovation today fails less from bad technology and more from bad embedding. The 21st-century landscape for innovation is increasingly shaped by complexity rather than complication. As change accelerates in both entrepreneurial and public contexts, traditional management tools fall short. Complexity, unlike complication, implies that outcomes are emergent, feedback is nonlinear, and pathways are unpredictable (Holland, 2006).

The distinction between complicated and complex systems is fundamental to understanding contemporary organisational challenges. A complicated system, such as a mechanical watch or an aircraft engine, may have many parts and require expertise to understand, but its behaviour remains predictable and can be decomposed into constituent elements. A complex system, by contrast, exhibits properties that cannot be reduced to the sum of its parts; it displays emergence, nonlinearity, and path dependence (Holland, 2006). The global economy, urban ecosystems, and digital platforms all exemplify complex systems where traditional reductionist approaches prove inadequate.

Today, both startups and governments are being pulled into this space more than ever. Digital transformation, artificial intelligence, platform economies, and geopolitical uncertainty are creating fast-moving conditions where linear cause-effect thinking no longer suffices. Even the best-laid plans can be rendered obsolete by sudden shifts in user behaviour, technology stacks, or regulatory environments. In such contexts, adaptability is not a competitive advantage but a survival mechanism.

This chapter deliberately juxtaposes startup and state contexts, not because they are similar, but because they face parallel complexity challenges under radically different constraints. Startups operate in market-driven chaos with rapid feedback loops but limited resources. States navigate institutional weight with democratic accountability but glacial timelines. By examining both, we reveal universal principles of complexity navigation while exposing why context-blind imitation fails. A startup cannot simply "move fast and break things" when deployed at state scale, just as governments cannot expect Estonian blueprints to work on Romanian soil. The comparison illuminates what transfers across domains and what remains stubbornly contextual.

## 1.2. *The Cynefin Framework as a Sense-Making Tool*

The Cynefin framework (Snowden and Boone, 2007) offers a way to sense and respond to such environments. Developed by David Snowden in 1999 while working at IBM Global Services, Cynefin, a Welsh word meaning 'habitat', provides executives with a decision-making framework that distinguishes between simple, complicated, complex, and chaotic domains, helping decision-makers determine the most appropriate course of action.

The choice of 'habitat' as the framework's name is deliberate and profound. A habitat is not merely a location; it is an ecosystem of relationships, dependencies, and evolved adaptations. Just as a biological habitat shapes the organisms within it, our organisational and institutional habitats shape our capacity to perceive, decide, and act. This ecological sensibility becomes essential when we examine how innovations, whether startup products or public sector initiatives, must not simply enter a market or institution, but must groove into their habitat.

Cynefin distinguishes simple, complicated, complex, and chaotic contexts (Figure 1). In the simple and complicated domains, we apply best practices or expert analysis; in complex domains, we probe-sense-respond with safe-to-fail experiments; in chaos, we act to stabilize. Most failures stem from misdiagnosis, using best practices for complex problems or over-analyzing simple ones. The framework also includes a fifth space called 'disorder,' representing situations where it is unclear which domain applies.

This chapter extends Arthur's (1996) concept of groove-in, originally describing increasing returns and lock-in effects in technology adoption, to encompass a broader view of how innovations embed themselves within

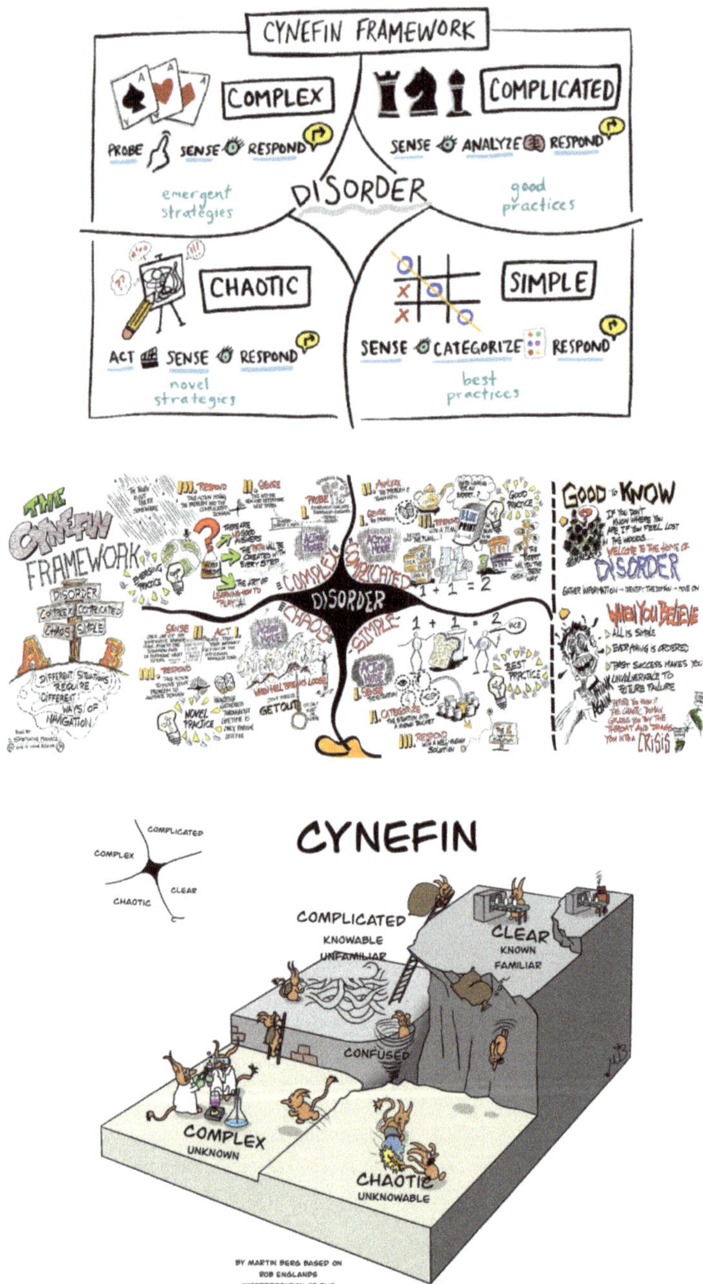



Figure 1. The Cynefin Framework (adapted from Snowden and Boone, 2007), various interpretations from sources as Francisco Cárcamo, Edwin Stoop and Martin Berg

their operational habitats. **Groove-in** in this chapter means: *the process by which an innovation becomes contextually embedded in its habitat such that switching costs, norms, and workflows co-evolve to make it integral rather than peripheral.* This definition shifts perspective from mechanism to habitat, from adoption to embedding, from individual to systemic.

In the startup context, groove-in manifests as the increasing switching costs and network effects that lock users into a platform or service. In the context of state digitalization, groove-in takes on a different character, requiring achievement of alignment among diverse stakeholders around a shared vision for technology adoption. Unlike the market-driven adoption dynamics of startups, public sector groove-in requires navigation of political legitimacy, institutional trust, procedural norms, and democratic accountability (see Figure 2 for how organisations progress through these domains).

## 1.3. *Core Competencies as Survival Mechanisms in the AI Era*

The urgency of understanding groove-in dynamics has intensified dramatically with the rise of artificial intelligence and its disruptive effects across industries. In this new landscape, core competencies function as organisational moats, the defensive barriers that protect value creation from rapid erosion. For established companies with decades of accumulated knowledge and coordination capabilities, these competencies represent substantial advantages. But for newly born startups, the dynamics are fundamentally different and far more precarious.

Startups face a temporal paradox in the AI-disrupted environment. On one hand, they require time to develop genuine core competencies; the 'collective learning' that Prahalad and Hamel (1990) describe cannot be rushed or purchased – it must be cultivated through repeated practice and organisational coordination. On the other hand, the velocity of technological change and competitive dynamics demands rapid traction. A startup that takes too long to groove-in may find its market position pre-empted by faster movers or rendered obsolete by technological shifts.

This creates a critical challenge: how do you build moats when you're still building the castle? Traditional startup advice emphasizes speed, 'move fast and break things', but this approach often sacrifices the deeper capability development necessary for sustainable competitive advantage. Conversely, focusing too much on capability building without market validation leads to well-engineered solutions in search of problems. The startups that successfully navigate this paradox are those that identify their core competencies early, articulate them clearly, and align their go-to-market strategies around them.

## 1.4. *Scope and Methodological Approach*

This chapter uses case study methodology to examine how startups and state institutions navigate complexity, develop core competencies, manage emergence, and avoid common traps such as groupthink. The startup analysis draws from an AI and data analytics venture whose journey illustrates the challenges of groove-in in complex entrepreneurial environments. The public sector analysis contrasts Estonia's successful digital transformation with Romania's ongoing struggles, revealing how institutional context fundamentally shapes groove-in possibilities.

The cases selected represent typical rather than exceptional instances, providing insights that may transfer to similar contexts. Following scholars of organisational learning and complex adaptive systems, the analysis emphasizes processes and patterns rather than seeking generalizable laws. The comparative approach recognizes that while startups and public institutions operate under fundamentally different constraints, they share common challenges in navigating complexity and building adaptive capacity.

This chapter contributes to the literature on complexity by extending Arthur's (1996) concept of increasing returns into a systemic framework of *groove-in dynamics*, a model linking adaptive embedding processes across entrepreneurial and institutional systems.

## 2. Groove-In Dynamics in Startup Habitats

## 2.1. *Initial Conditions and Lost in Complexity*

An AI and data analytics startup founded in 2023 illustrates these dynamics vividly. The company emerged from a university research context, where the founding team had developed novel algorithms for processing unstructured data. The technical innovation was genuine, the algorithms demonstrated superior performance on benchmark datasets, but the path from technical capability to commercial viability remained unclear.

Superior algorithms didn't translate into traction. The team cycled through pitch circuits and conflicting mentor advice, pivoting reactively. Agile motion without strategic coherence produced noise, not learning. The missing piece was an integrated core competency linking technical skill to a specific user, workflow, and value proposition.

Initially aspiring to become a 'ChatGPT for enterprises,' the startup attempted to cover all organisational expertise domains. This broad ambition positioned them firmly in Cynefin's complex domain, a space where the very problem being solved remained unclear and constantly shifting. After one year of conducting various proofs of concept across different industries, the team remained unable to demonstrate sustainable value or achieve groove-in. By mid-2025, G-Start's focused pivot enabled the company to secure six-figure pre-seed funding and its first three recurring medical-sector clients, signalling the onset of measurable groove-in traction.

Drawing on Complex Adaptive Systems theory (Holland, 2006), we can see that their efforts to probe and adapt were active but not yet producing emergent order. What was missing was the organisational capability to coordinate technical skills with market understanding, user experience design, and business model development. Their expertise remained siloed rather than integrated, limiting their ability to create distinctive value.

## 2.2. *The Pivot: From Complex to Complicated*

The turning point came through customer discovery interviews, initially resisted by technical founders who believed their technology 'spoke for itself.' The team began to understand that their true competency lay in rapidly customizing solutions for specific data problems in professional services, particularly in the medical industry. By focusing specifically on clinical text classification for pathology reports, they began defining their customer persona, clarifying their value proposition, and discovering repeatable processes.

In Cynefin terms, the startup moved from the complex domain (where cause and effect are only apparent retrospectively) to the complicated domain (where cause and effect are discoverable through analysis). By constraining their problem space, they could identify patterns, develop specialized knowledge, and create replicable solutions. The groove-in process accelerated dramatically.

Focus unlocked four shifts: deep domain know-how (medical data structures, regulatory requirements, clinical workflows), standardised delivery (PoCs transformed into productised rollouts with predictable timelines), adjacency referrals (success in pathology created referrals to nearby departments), and natural switching costs from workflow embedding.

The case reveals a crucial insight: core competencies based solely on technical capability are insufficient for startup survival. The competencies only became valuable when integrated with market insight, domain expertise, and strategic focus. The core competency that ultimately enabled groove-in was 'rapidly customizing AI solutions for specific medical data challenges', a capability combining technical skill, domain knowledge, user experience design, and business model clarity.

As of 2024–2025, the pivot is recent and long-term validation remains ongoing. However, initial market response suggests sound strategic direction. The company secured initial funding and began attracting sustainable customer relationships, transitioning from perpetual pilots to subscription contracts, tangible signals of emerging groove-in.

## 2.3. *Learning Processes and Double-Loop Learning*

The journey involved significant personal and organisational learning. The founders had to confront their own biases and assumptions, a process that Argyris (1991) terms 'double-loop learning.' Rather than simply adjusting strategies while maintaining underlying beliefs (single-loop learning), they questioned whether their fundamental assumptions about market needs were valid.

Single-loop learning asks 'are we doing things right?' while double-loop learning asks 'are we doing the right things?' The startup's initial year represented extensive single-loop learning, improving pitch decks, refining algorithms, optimizing sales processes, while maintaining flawed assumptions. The pivot required double-loop learning: acknowledging that their entire approach needed fundamental reconsideration.

This illustrates how Cynefin's 'probe-sense-respond' approach operates in practice. Initial probes yielded signals requiring interpretation. The sensing phase involved making sense of contradictory feedback and recognizing which signals mattered most. The response phase required courage to act on insights even when they contradicted initial assumptions.

## 2.4. *Lessons: What Enables Startup Groove-In*

This journey reveals several principles for startup groove-in. First, strategic focus precedes scale: the impulse to maximize market opportunity often traps startups in complexity. Narrowing the problem space enables pattern recognition and repeatable processes. This is the essence of navigating complexity toward groove-in: finding the habitat where capabilities can become distinctive and defensible.

Second, core competency must be articulable: if you cannot state your core competency as a verb in a context, you likely haven't identified it yet. Prahalad and Hamel (1990) use the tree metaphor: visible products grow from less visible but more fundamental capabilities, 'the root system that provides nourishment, sustenance, and stability' (p. 82).

Third, probe-sense-respond in complex domains: safe-to-fail experiments allow learning without existential risk. The PoC phase, though painful, generated crucial knowledge. Fourth, switching costs emerge from workflow integration: true groove-in occurs when innovation becomes embedded in daily practice, not merely adopted as a tool. Users make investments, financial, temporal, cognitive, and social, that create natural barriers to switching. Figure 2 visualises this progression through the domains toward groove-in.

## 3. Groove-In Dynamics in State Digitalization

## 3.1. *Estonia: When Everything Aligns*

Estonia represents perhaps the most celebrated case of successful digital transformation in governance. Following independence from the Soviet Union in 1991, Estonia embraced digital-first governance with remarkable consistency. Today, approximately 99% of public services are available online, with over 99% of citizens possessing digital IDs enabling secure authentication (e-Estonia, 2023; European Commission, 2023). The Estonian Information System Authority reports that X-Road, operational since 2001, processes over 2 billion queries annually across 2,800 organisations (Estonian Information System Authority, 2023). Tax filing takes an average of three minutes for most citizens (OECD, 2023).

Estonia's digital identity now covers over 99% of its 1.3 million citizens, whereas Romania remains last among EU member states in the Digital Economy and Society Index (DESI 2023), with fewer than one-fifth of citizens regularly using e-government portals.

Estonia's groove-in success stems from several reinforcing factors. First, a fresh institutional slate: post-Soviet independence provided an opportunity to design digital infrastructure without legacy system constraints.

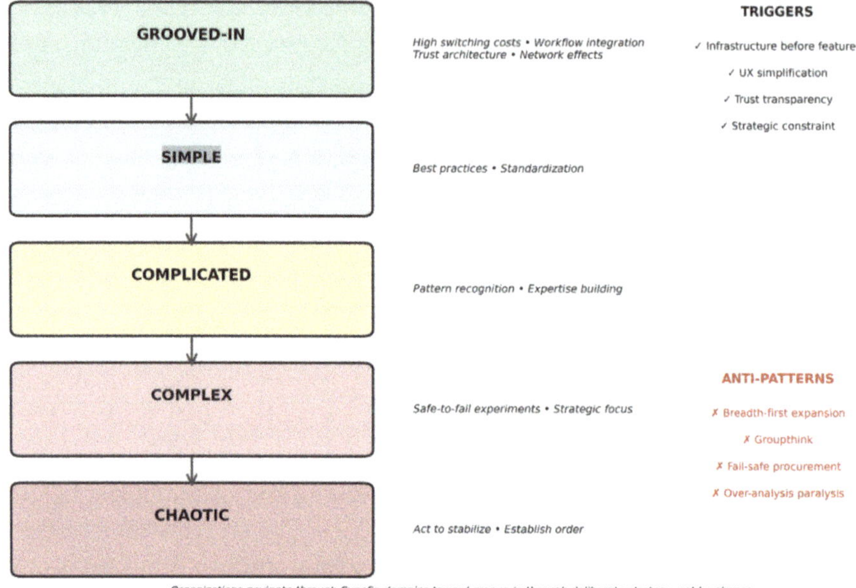


Figure 2. The Groove-In Ladder–organizations navigate through Cynefin domains toward groove-in through deliberate strategy, not by chance.

When Estonia regained independence, it had to build new state institutions from scratch. This meant digital systems could be designed as primary infrastructure rather than retrofitted onto existing processes.

Second, a small population scale: with 1.3 million citizens, Estonia could achieve faster iteration and tighter feedback loops. The entire country functions somewhat like a large-scale pilot, where policy experiments can be conducted, evaluated, and adjusted based on comprehensive data. This scale advantage enabled coordination and consensus that would be dramatically harder in larger nations.

Third, technical foundation (X-Road): X-Road (operational since 2001) is the secure data-exchange backbone that enables cross-agency interoperability under distributed control; it's the foundation before features that later services build on.

Fourth, trust architecture: transparent data access logs allow citizens to see who accessed their information and challenge improper access. This transparency mechanism proved critical for building citizen confidence. The government invested heavily in trust-building through strong encryption, clear communication, education campaigns, and continuous iteration based on user feedback. This transforms the trust dynamic from 'trust us to protect your data' to 'you can verify how your data is used.'

Fifth, user experience simplification: services designed for completion in under five steps, with assisted-digital support for less tech-savvy citizens. Estonia didn't just digitise existing processes; it redesigned services around user needs. The government recognized that navigating technological disruption required making technology's complex aspects invisible to end users. Tax filing exemplifies this: reviewing pre-filled information and clicking submit, a three-minute process.

Crucially, the Ministry of Digitalization observed a powerful social proof mechanism: when grandparents were seen successfully using digital services, the success rate for elderly citizens increased dramatically. This intergenerational demonstration effect created a cascade of groove-in across age cohorts. Sixth, political consistency: sustained cross-party commitment to digital governance over decades allowed long-term planning and prevented disruption from new administrations abandoning predecessor initiatives.

Perhaps most critically, Estonia's approach demonstrates what Beer (1979) calls requisite variety, matching system complexity to environmental complexity. Rather than attempting to control all outcomes centrally, Estonia created enabling infrastructure and allowed specific services to evolve contextually. This is complexity navigation, not complexity elimination. The system co-evolved with citizen expectations and behaviours rather than being imposed top-down.

## 3.2. *Romania: The Complexity of Catching Up*

Romania presents a contrasting picture. Despite geographic proximity to Estonia and shared EU membership since 2007, Romania's digital transformation efforts face persistent obstacles. According to the European Commission's Digital Economy and Society Index (DESI), Romania ranks near the bottom of EU member states in digital public services, with only 26% of internet users interacting with public authorities online compared to the EU average of 65% (European Commission, 2023). The median age of Romanian civil servants is estimated between 50–55 years, with many having entered service during or shortly after the communist period (Romanian Court of Accounts, 2022).

Several structural factors contribute to Romania's digitalization challenges. First, legacy institutional weight: Romania's transition from communism involved gradual institutional evolution rather than clean breaks, leaving deep path dependencies. Communist-era governance patterns emphasizing control and compliance over service delivery remain embedded. Government IT systems often reflect decades of incremental patches rather than coherent digital architecture.

Second, population scale and diversity: with 19 million citizens spread across varied urban-rural contexts and significant digital literacy gaps, achieving uniform service delivery proves far more complex than in compact Estonia. Substantial regional inequality exists in internet access, digital skills, and institutional trust.

Third, political volatility: frequent government changes disrupt long-term digitalization strategies. Ministers of digitalization have changed frequently, each bringing new priorities and sometimes abandoning predecessor initiatives for political differentiation. This creates a stop-start dynamic preventing accumulation of learning and relationships necessary for groove-in.

Fourth, trust deficit: lower institutional trust, partly reflecting corruption perceptions, creates citizen scepticism toward digital government initiatives (World Bank, 2023). This becomes self-fulfilling, as low adoption reinforces perceptions that digital services are unreliable. Trust is absent at multiple levels: citizens doubt data security; frontline employees doubt systems will ease their work; middle managers fear transparency will expose inefficiencies.

Fifth, siloed competencies: digital capabilities exist in scattered pockets but lack coordination. Individual ministries may develop functional systems that cannot interoperate, creating islands of capability. The absence of something equivalent to X-Road means citizens navigate disconnected systems with separate accounts and credentials.

Sixth, procurement complexity: public procurement processes designed to prevent corruption often become so rigid that they block iterative learning, though EU-funded or externally audited programs show exceptions where oversight enables more adaptive approaches. Multi-year procurement cycles misalign with rapid technological change. By the time systems are deployed, technology may be outdated and user needs shifted.

The demographic challenge compounds these issues. Digital transformation requires not just learning new tools but fundamentally reconceptualising the state-citizen relationship, a cognitive shift many find uncomfortable. Unlike Estonia's intergenerational demonstration effects, Romania faces the inverse dynamic. Older public servants controlling gatekeeping functions often lack both digital literacy and incentive to acquire it.

The overly specified bureaucracy presents a fundamental mismatch with digital service design principles. Romanian administrative procedures accumulate steps over time, each added to prevent past abuse or satisfy political demands, with none ever removed. Digitising these processes without redesigning them simply moves paper-based complexity online, creating digital interfaces to fundamentally analogue logic.

These challenges interact systemically. Low trust reduces adoption, reducing political incentive to invest, perpetuating low trust. Siloed competencies prevent interoperability, limiting service quality, reinforcing citizen preference for in-person transactions. Rigid procurement prevents experimentation, prevents learning, keeps the system stuck in complex or chaotic domains.

To be clear, Romania has made progress in specific areas. Electronic signatures exist, certain tax services operate online, and pilot projects demonstrate viable paths. Individual agencies and municipalities have achieved local successes. The point is not absolute failure, but that systemic groove-in, where digital services become the natural, default mode of citizen-state interaction, remains elusive.

## 3.3. *Applying Cynefin: Why Romania Isn't Estonia*

The Estonia-Romania comparison becomes analytically powerful when viewed through Cynefin. Estonia successfully moved digitalisation challenges from complex to complicated to simple/clear domains through deliberate progression. In the complex phase (1990s), Estonia engaged in early experimentation with digital ID, X-Road architecture, and service design through safe-to-fail pilots. They didn't know what would work, so they tried multiple approaches, learned from failures, and built on successes. In the complicated phase (2000s), they analysed what worked, developed expertise, and applied lessons systematically. Patterns emerged, best practices developed, and specialised knowledge accumulated. In the simple phase (2010s-present), they established mature operational models with predictable service delivery that can be replicated.

Romania, by contrast, oscillates between chaotic and complex domains. Political changes create periodic chaos disrupting emerging patterns before they stabilise. Absence of sustained experimentation platforms prevents movement from complex to complicated. When pilots succeed, they often cannot scale because institutional support evaporates. When pilots fail, blame follows rather than learning. In Cynefin terms, there's no shared understanding of which domain various challenges belong to, leading to misapplication of approaches.

Critically, attempts to import Estonian best practices, moving directly to simple domain solutions, fail because they lack contextual adaptation that complexity requires. Romania tries copying X-Road architecture without first building institutional trust and coordination capability that makes such infrastructure viable. The technology may be sound, but the system rejects it.

This is not a failure of will or capability but mismatch between approach and context. Estonia's success depended on specific enabling conditions, small scale, political stability, post-independence malleability, that Romania cannot simply replicate. Romania needs a Romania-specific groove-in strategy acknowledging its distinct habitat characteristics and working with them rather than against them.

## 3.4. *Comparative Analysis: How Groupthink Manifests Differently*

Here we shift from parallel case studies to explicit comparison. Groupthink operates as a universal barrier to adaptation, but its manifestations and remedies differ fundamentally between startups and states. This comparative lens reveals why both domains struggle with similar cognitive traps despite opposite organisational structures, and what each can learn from the other's adaptive strategies.

Both startup and state contexts face a common barrier to groove-in: groupthink. Janis (1972, 1982) identified how cohesive groups, under pressure to maintain unanimity, suppress dissenting views and critical evaluation. His analysis revealed structural conditions promoting conformity: high group cohesiveness, insulation from outside opinions, lack of methodical search procedures, directive leadership, and high stress with low hope of better solutions.

In startups, this manifests as founder teams reinforcing each other's assumptions about market fit, dismissing customer feedback challenging their vision, or persisting with failing strategies because admitting error threatens group cohesion. When surrounded by believers, co-founders, early employees, supportive investors, founders can convince themselves the market will eventually understand their product, even when users repeatedly signal otherwise.

In government digitalisation, groupthink takes different but equally damaging forms. Government organisations tend toward risk aversion, preference for precedent, and suppression of dissent in the name of political unity or administrative hierarchy. Policymakers may convince themselves citizens want services designed for bureaucratic convenience rather than user needs. Political appointees often arrive with predetermined agendas and limited time horizons. Career civil servants learn that raising objections can stall careers.

What Argyris (1977, 1991) calls 'double-loop learning', questioning underlying assumptions rather than merely adjusting tactics, becomes nearly impossible under groupthink conditions. Groupthink traps organisations in single-loop learning, optimizing execution of strategies that may be fundamentally flawed. The result is what Janis termed 'self-censorship,' where individuals suppress doubts to maintain apparent consensus.

The startup's pivot required breaking groupthink: admitting the broad 'enterprise AI' vision wasn't working demanded that co-founders challenge shared assumptions. This proved emotionally difficult because it meant acknowledging time and resources had been invested wrongly. Similarly, Romania's digitalisation progress requires government leaders to acknowledge when imported best practices don't fit Romanian contexts, even when this admission is politically uncomfortable.

## 3.5. *Required Core Competencies for Public Sector Groove-In*

Successfully navigating public sector complexity requires core competencies often either underdeveloped or fragmented across government. Prahalad and Hamel (1990) argue core competencies must be collectively learned across organisations, integrated at the corporate level rather than residing in individual units. For public institutions, this translates to capabilities spanning departmental boundaries and hierarchical levels. However, government structures typically reinforce silos through separate budget lines, distinct career tracks, limited cross-agency mobility, and competing mandates.

Policy entrepreneurship, the ability to recognise innovation opportunities and mobilise support across institutional boundaries, requires individuals understanding both technical substance and political process. Such individuals are valuable but often not recognised by traditional public sector systems prioritising specialised expertise and procedural compliance. Policy entrepreneurs must navigate formal authority structures while building informal networks, balance technical rigour with political savvy, and persist through slow government timelines.

Cross-sectoral collaboration, essential for addressing complex challenges, requires government agencies to work effectively with private firms, nonprofits, and community organisations. This demands capabilities in network governance, collaborative problem-solving, and managing partnerships where hierarchical authority is limited. Traditional public administration training emphasises vertical accountability, leaving public servants ill-equipped for collaborative roles.

Institutional learning, the capacity for organisations to capture, share, and apply knowledge across units and over time, faces particular government challenges. High turnover of political appointees disrupts continuity. Siloed structures prevent knowledge sharing. Budget pressures reduce training investment. Performance metrics focused on efficiency may discourage experimentation necessary for learning. Creating learning architectures overcoming these barriers requires intentional design and sustained commitment.

## 4. Cross-Domain Synthesis: Toward a Startup-State Mindset

### 4.1. *Parallel Dynamics Across Habitats*

Despite radically different operational contexts, startups and states navigating complexity display remarkable parallels (Figure 3). The comparison reveals complexity is not domain-specific; it arises from system and environmental characteristics rather than organisation type. Whether a small, agile startup or large, hierarchical government agency, any organisation facing emergence, nonlinearity, and uncertainty must develop adaptive capabilities.

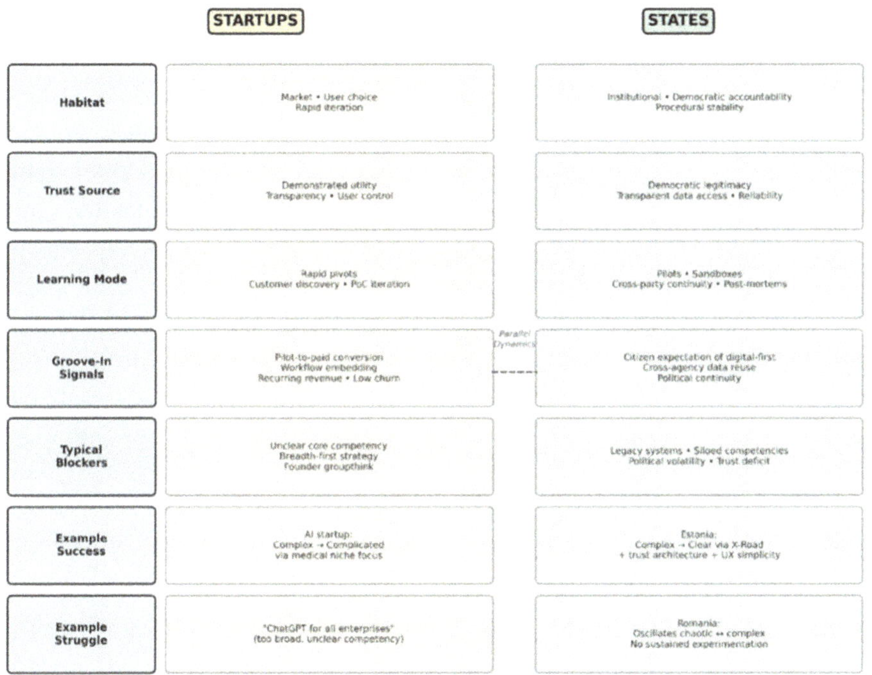


Figure 3. Startup-State Comparison Matrix – despite different operational contexts, startups and states face parallel groove-in dynamics.

Both face the strategic focus paradox: startups want maximum market opportunity while governments want comprehensive coverage, yet premature breadth traps both in complexity. Both require trust architecture that cannot be demanded but must be earned through transparency, reliability, and demonstrable value. Both benefit from safe-to-fail experimentation where complex domains require learning through controlled experiments rather than big-bang implementations. Both struggle with groupthink where cohesive cultures become echo chambers suppressing critical feedback. Both need core competencies clearly articulated.

## 4.2. *Why This Comparison Matters: Beyond Surface Analogies*

The startup-state comparison risks appearing forced, what does a three-person AI venture have to teach a national government, or vice versa? The answer lies not in direct transference but in pattern recognition across complexity domains.

Three reasons justify this cross-domain analysis:

First, complexity is scale-invariant. The Cynefin framework's domains apply equally whether managing three employees or three million citizens. A startup trapped in the complex domain faces the same fundamental challenge as a government ministry: how to learn when cause-effect relationships are only apparent retrospectively.

Second, organisational blind spots correlate inversely with speed. Startups fail quickly through groupthink around product-market fit; states fail slowly through institutional inertia. Both fail by misdiagnosing their domain. Examining both extremes illuminates the full spectrum of complexity navigation challenges.

Third, mutual learning breaks domain-specific orthodoxy. Startup culture fetishises speed; government culture prioritizes stability. Each represents an over-optimisation that the other can correct. States can learn experimental courage from startups; startups can learn trust architecture from digital governance pioneers. Neither should copy the other wholesale, but both benefit from understanding alternative adaptive strategies.

The analysis demonstrates how the same cognitive trap manifests under opposite organisational conditions, and how solutions must be tailored to habitat while respecting universal principles.

## 4.3. *What Each Context Teaches the Other: From Comparison to Translation*

Having established why the comparison matters and how groupthink operates across domains, we now translate insights into actionable principles. The goal is not convergence but informed adaptation, taking patterns that work in one habitat and translating them for another.

Startups can learn from states that infrastructure precedes features. X-Road enabled interoperability before specific services were built. Transparency builds trust as Estonia's data access logs demonstrate. Simplicity drives adoption through five-step maximum service design reflecting user-centred thinking. Long-term consistency matters, reminding startups groove-in requires sustained investment beyond initial enthusiasm.

Conversely, states can learn from startups that strategic pivots aren't failure but demonstrate adaptive capacity. Rapid iteration reveals truth through cheap experiments testing assumptions. User feedback trumps stakeholder consensus. Niche focus enables scaling as startups master narrow-use cases before expanding, whereas governments attempting comprehensive transformation simultaneously often achieve neither breadth nor depth.

## 4.4. *Six Principles for Groove-In*

Synthesizing across both domains, six principles emerge for achieving groove-in in complex habitats:

- **1. Navigate complexity consciously**: Use frameworks like Cynefin (Figure 1) to diagnose which domain you're operating in and match your approach accordingly. Misdiagnosis, treating complex problems as complicated or simple, is more dangerous than problem difficulty itself.
- **2. Embrace strategic constraint**: Narrow problem scope to enable pattern recognition, expertise development, and repeatable processes. Breadth is a consequence of depth, not a substitute for it.
- **3. Build trust architecture explicitly**: Make transparency, reliability, and value delivery visible through system design. Trust emerges from demonstrated behaviour, not stated intentions.
- **4. Create safe-to-fail experimentation spaces**: Complex domains demand learning through controlled experiments. Design pilots where failure generates knowledge without existential consequences.
- **5. Practice double-loop learning**: Question underlying assumptions, not just tactical execution. Combat groupthink through structured dissent and diverse perspectives.
- **6. Articulate and cultivate core competencies**: Identify what you uniquely do well, state it clearly, and align strategy around it. Core competencies are organisational moats protecting value creation from erosion.

**Box 1. Measures That Matter - Groove-In Indicators**

## Startup Context:

- Pilot-to-paid conversion rate $\geq 60\%$
- Percentage of target workflows embedded (not just users signed up)
- Data migration completed (% of customers)
- 90-day retention rate; net negative churn
- Time-to-value (median time to first insight/action)

## State Context:

- Percentage of services end-to-end digital (no office visit required)
- Average steps to completion (target $\leq 5$)
- Assisted-digital uptake and drop-off rates
- Cross-agency data reuse rate (transactions using shared infrastructure)
- Transparency portal usage ('who accessed my data') and dispute resolution SLAs

## 5. Conclusion: Dancing With Complex Systems

This chapter set out to answer a deliberately provocative question: what can a three-person startup and a national government learn from each other about navigating complexity? The answer, as the comparative analysis reveals, is substantial, not because they should imitate each other's methods, but because examining extreme organisational forms under similar complexity pressures illuminates universal principles while highlighting contextual constraints.

Donella Meadows's insight that opens this chapter, 'We can't control systems or figure them out. But we can dance with them!' captures the essence of groove-in dynamics. Neither startups nor states can command their habitats into submission. They must learn the habitat's rhythms, adapt to its constraints, and find spaces where their capabilities align with environmental needs. Perhaps the dance begins when startups and states stop seeing each other as opposites and start learning as partners.

The metaphor of dancing emphasises responsiveness, rhythm, and mutual adaptation. Good dancing requires both structure and improvisation, both individual skill and attunement to one's partner. Similarly, navigating complexity requires organisations to maintain core identity and capabilities while remaining open to continuous learning and adjustment. The startup and state domains offer natural laboratories for observing adaptive dynamics under very different conditions.

Groove-in represents that moment when innovation shifts from peripheral to integral, when switching costs, network effects, and workflow embedding make an innovation part of the habitat's natural functioning. For startups, this manifests in user adoption inertia and recurring revenue. For states, it appears as citizen expectation of digital-first service delivery and institutional muscle memory around digital processes. Groove-in involves more than market penetration or policy rollout, it requires the actor to become contextually embedded, attuned to stakeholders, sensitive to feedback, and responsive to shifting conditions. It is the result of co-evolution between innovation and the environment.

The path to groove-in differs by context. The startup's strategic narrowing looks different from Estonia's infrastructure-first approach, and both look different from what Romania needs. Yet underlying principles transcend domains: conscious complexity navigation, strategic constraint, trust architecture, safe-to-fail experimentation, double-loop learning, and articulated core competencies. The goal is not convergence toward a single model but mutual learning that strengthens both domains.

Perhaps most critically, this chapter argues for epistemic humility. The cases presented illustrate theoretical patterns but do not constitute comprehensive empirical validation. They are observations meant to provoke thought and pattern recognition, not definitive proof. Complex systems resist simple causation; what worked in one habitat under specific conditions may fail elsewhere.

The contribution here is conceptual: extending groove-in from Arthur's increasing returns framework to encompass broader socio-institutional embedding; demonstrating parallel dynamics across startup and state contexts; and providing sense-making tools (particularly Cynefin, Figure 1) for navigating complexity rather than denying it. This shift in perspective, from mechanism to habitat, from adoption to embedding, from individual to systemic, reveals why the same principles of complexity navigation apply across radically different organisational forms.

For practitioners, whether founding startups, leading digital transformations, or crafting policy, the call is toward adaptive capability rather than deterministic planning. We cannot control complex systems, but we can become better dancers. We can sense which domain we're operating in, experiment safely, learn genuinely, build trust deliberately, and groove into our habitats with increasing skill. The challenges facing contemporary societies, such as climate change, technological disruption, social polarisation, and economic inequality, all exhibit complexity characteristics. Addressing them effectively requires both entrepreneurial innovation and governmental coordination.

In the AI-disrupted era, where technical capabilities commoditise rapidly and competitive advantages erode quickly, the organisations that thrive will be those that develop genuine core competencies rooted in their unique habitats. For startups, this means resisting the temptation to be everything to everyone and instead finding the specific context where integrated capabilities become defensible moats. For governments, this means recognizing that digital transformation is not primarily a technical challenge but a challenge of building systemic trust, ensuring inclusion, and maintaining democratic legitimacy while adapting to technological possibility.

Groove-in thus emerges not only as a metaphor but as a lens for examining viability in complex socio-technical systems, where organisational, technological, and institutional adaptation co-evolve toward systemic resilience.

That, ultimately, is what groove-in means: not dominating your environment but becoming sufficiently integrated with it that your innovation becomes indispensable to its functioning. Not control but belonging. Not conquest, but co-evolution. Groove-in is the successful outcome of the adaptive process, when an organisation becomes so well-attuned to its environment that it can both influence and be influenced by its context, creating value while sustaining itself over time. Achieving groove-in requires patience, reflection, capability development, and willingness to question assumptions. It cannot be rushed or imposed but must be cultivated through sustained engagement with complexity.

## References


Argyris, C. (1977). 'Double-loop learning in organizations'. *Harvard Business Review*, 55(5), pp. 115–125.

Argyris, C. (1991). 'Teaching smart people how to learn'. *Harvard Business Review*, 69(3), pp. 99–109.

Arthur, W. B. (1989). 'Competing technologies, increasing returns, and lock-in by historical events'. The Economic Journal, 99(394), pp. 116–131.

Arthur, W. B. (1996). 'Increasing returns and the new world of business'. *Harvard Business Review*, 74(4), pp. 100–109.

Beer, S. (1979). *The heart of enterprise*. New York: John Wiley & Sons.

Blank, S. (2013). 'Why the lean start-up changes everything'. *Harvard Business Review*, 91(5), pp. 63–72.

e-Estonia. (2023). *We have built a digital society and so can you*. https://e-estonia.com/

Estonian Information System Authority. (2023). *X-Road statistics and overview*. https://www.ria.ee/en/state-information-system/x-road.html

European Commission. (2023). *Digital Economy and Society Index (DESI) 2023 – Romania country report*. https://digital-strategy.ec.europa.eu/en/library/digital-economy-and-society-index-desi-2023-romania-country-report

Hock, D. (1999). *Birth of the chaordic age*. San Francisco: Berrett-Koehler.

Holland, J. H. (2006). 'Studying complex adaptive systems'. *Journal of Systems Science and Complexity*, 19(1), pp.1–8.

Holling, C. S. (1973). 'Resilience and stability of ecological systems'. *Annual Review of Ecology and Systematics*, 4(1), pp. 1–23.

Inter-American Development Bank. (2023). *Estonia: The digital republic*. https://blogs.iadb.org/conocimiento-abierto/en/estonia-the-digital-republic/

Janis, I. L. (1972). *Victims of groupthink: A psychological study of foreign-policy decisions and fiascoes*. Boston: Houghton Mifflin.

Janis, I. L. (1982). *Groupthink: Psychological studies of policy decisions and fiascoes* (2nd ed.). Boston: Houghton Mifflin.

Meadows, D. H. (2001). Dancing with systems. *The Academy for Systems Change*. https://donellameadows.org/archives/dancing-with-systems/

OECD. (2022). *Digital government review of Romania: Towards a digitally-enabled state*. https://doi.org/10.1787/3b2b7a70-en

OECD. (2023). *Digital government review of Estonia 2023*. https://www.oecd.org/publications/digital-government-review-of-estonia-2023-2e7b83b3-en.htm

Prahalad, C. K. and Hamel, G. (1990). 'The core competence of the corporation'. *Harvard Business Review*, 68(3), pp. 79–91.

Ries, E. (2011). *The lean startup: How today's entrepreneurs use continuous innovation to create radically successful businesses*. New York: Crown Business.

Romanian Court of Accounts. (2022). *Raportul public pe anul 2022* [Public report for 2022]. https://www.curteadeconturi.ro/Publicatii/Raportul_public_pe_anul_2022.pdf

Snowden, D. J. and Boone, M. E. (2007). A leader's framework for decision making. *Harvard Business Review*, 85(11), pp. 68–76.

World Bank. (2023). *GovTech Maturity Index 2023: Enhancing public sector digital transformation.* https://documents.worldbank.org/en/publication/documents-reports/documentdetail/2c1fca46-1a2e-4635-bf7e-1b20c832cb9a

# CONCLUSION

We are all facing multiple assaults upon our sense of certainty, order and understanding of how our world functions. Whether it be our continued failure to address climate change and environmental impacts, what Radu Orghidan has brilliantly described as the 'epistemological violence' flowing from artificial intelligence and technological change, the impact of hybrid work upon identity and performance, or geopolitical change, is the soup of "unfathomable uncertainty" (Tett 2026) that we all must navigate every day. In addition to helping explain and make sense of what is happening in these different spaces and what is driving surging complexity, this book has provided tools, structures and lenses with which to assist you in navigating the strange new world that we find ourselves in.

Orghidan is clear that we are at a tipping point where the future economy and organisation of work will be designed by default or design, if we want decision-making to be informed by ethics that go beyond pure economic utilitarianism. He provides a 5 step set of principles to guide us through the technological complexity that is AI:

1. Design for continuous reconfiguration
2. Distribute decision-making but resist diffusion of personal responsibility.
3. Eliminate the obsolete for adding new, so that technology is a tool of creating new efficiencies and opportunities and not just a means to add new layers of bureaucracy.
4. Preserve human meaning-making and reserve strategic questioning for humans.
5. Design for justice, not just efficiency, and embed ethics into your technological infrastructure and organisational cultures.

Melhuish notes how introducing AI in a way that empowers staff isn't just an ethical issue, it is also a practical one, since evidence is already emerging of organisational resistance to such technologies. Bochis and Melhuish both sustain Orghidan's point that the challenge of AI is cultural and psychological as much as it is technical. The challenge is what Melhuish calls a sociotechnical one, where executives need to repurpose their organisation's culture away from single-loop learning and embrace far more double-loop learning if they are to be able to adapt and reconfigure at the pace required and avoid becoming victims of creative destruction.

Both Melhuish and Bochis underline the need to develop trust, based upon psychological safety, if organisations are to become the complex adaptive systems that both of them demonstrate as the most effective way of sustainably managing and governing the interplay between people and technology that AI requires. This is, of course, a clear means of developing Taylor's points about the need to create systems that enable local experimentation that use the mattress effect to distribute risk, but overlap, or nest, in such a way that learning can be powerfully amplified across the organisation quickly. Since they are deeply rooted in networks, developing more distributed complex adaptive systems might also be a useful framework with which to consider regulating the algorithms of social media platforms and manage the dependencies and deepfakes that Zehndorfer and Oltean have shown to be plaguing our societies. Bochis provides a clear checklist of tools and processes by which executives can integrate AI to operationalise the development of complex adaptive organisations and create the sort of octopus organisations (Werner and Le-Brun, 2025) that Taylor described.

All of the authors are clear that if, in the words of Orghidan, the role of AI and related technologies is to be by design and not default then executives and decision-makers need to position AI strategically and culturally as what Bochis calls scaffolding for human potential. The challenge is the sociotechnical one, described by Melhuuish. Left as a purely technical decision, AI usage will only exacerbate the existing inequalities and tensions, some of which are described by Zehndorfer and Oltean.

The Innovation Fitness Test, developed by Lewis, is a clear example of a tool that provides a structure for matching your organisation to needs of your operating environment, whilst positioning human staff in the driving seat. In essence the model is a framework for planning and organising the safe-to-fail experimentation that is a key requirement of working with complexity. In a world where the relationships between cause and effect are novel, innovation is the only way forward. As Dragos-Radoi discovered, this is a process of co-evolution between the innovation and its evolving environment that cannot be directed, only facilitated. Lewis notes the cultural challenges involved in such work, but his experience doing this as the basis of global product innovations for leading consumer healthcare businesses underlines just how valuable it can be. Echoing Taylor and Boichis' earlier remarks, Lewis shows that, whilst not every organisation needs to be equally innovative, developing innovation fitness leads to greater resilience, which is key to surviving turbulent times.

Resilience is not only central to the economics of complexity. Gleadle shows how developing organisational cultures and processes that seek to internalise waste as foregone opportunities unlocks enormous economic potential, whilst simultaneously reducing environmental impact. In other words, tools like the Innovation Fitness Test, based upon cultures of double-loop learning, both improve performance and significantly reduce ecological damage. As such the Sphere Economy is really a means of developing complex adaptive systems that work with nature, rather than trying to master it.

Muresanu shows how when using tools of complexity, it is possible to hold onto the essence of what you do and how you create value whilst significantly shifting your focus towards something closer to what Gleadle would think of as sustainable. For her, technology is enabling the development of platforms that can orchestrate, rather than simply control, a process of nesting overlapping communities of practice that sounds very similar to Ostrom's (2015) polycentric clustering. So sharp has her analysis proven that despite its clear challenge to traditional strategy, the board of the bank she works for is thinking about how to work with her proposals.

If Muresanu describes an example of reimagining strategy in a complex world, Vescan shows how to deliver genuine operational change in a turbulent environment. It is clear from her work and the suggestions from previous authors that leaders need to let go of control and best practices and become facilitators of experimentation and adaptation, based upon self-organised structures. As Dragos-Radoi found, the challenge is to learn to dance with complexity and adapt to its rhythm through experimentation, rather than design. Similarly, Gheorghes found that shifting the culture and leadership in this way enables organisations to "learn to redesign themselves through experience". Once again mirroring the arguments of Melhuish, Gheorges found that the challenge is not so much technical as cognitive and emotional. This is the reality of what Bochis calls the scaffolding for human potential and it closely chimes with the ideas of Orghidan and Melhuish, without which Vescan notes we cannot really develop the resilience that she and Taylor argue is essential for thriving in complexity.

What all of the authors show is that, in the words of Gheorghes, "Learning, in this [complex] context, becomes both method and outcome: awareness institutionalised as practice." As the complexity that surrounds us continues to rise, the most powerful thing that we can do is resist the temptation to retreat into simple solutions with people like us and expose ourselves to ideas and experiences that are wider and different from our own. If digital technology is to be a tool and not a master that shapes our behaviour we must learn from the experiences described by Oltean and Zehndorfer, question the inevitably of our submission before technology and develop distributed systemic resilience.

Although it is counter-intuitive, surviving complexity is about imagining how we achieve our objectives in new ways. That requires innovative thought, which several of the authors here have clearly shown rests upon double-loop learning. For whilst technology matters and is driving much of the complexity, in the end it is humans that ascribe meaning to our relationships with technology and the world. If nothing else this book is a clarion call to ensure that we don't let these relationships be framed by our inertia and constructed by default, but rather by design.

## References

Werner and Le Brun (2025), 'Become an Octopus Organization: How Your Company can Adapt to a Complex World'. *Harvard Business Review* (November/ December).

www.ingramcontent.com/pod-product-compliance
Ingram Content Group UK Ltd.
Pitfield, Milton Keynes, MK11 3LW, UK
UKHW060714010726
472620UK00004B/44